Byrne's Dictionary of Irish Local History
from earliest times to c.1900

Joseph Byrne

MERCIER PRESS

FOR SIOBHÁN

 Mercier Press receives financial assistance from
the Arts Council/An Chomhairle Ealaíon

MERCIER PRESS
Douglas Village, Cork
www.mercierpress.ie

Trade enquiries to
COLUMBA MERCIER DISTRIBUTION,
55a Spruce Avenue, Stillorgan
Industrial Park, Blackrock, Co.
Dublin

© Joseph Byrne, 2004

1 85635 423 7

10 9 8 7 6 5 4 3 2 1

Cover: A copy of letters patent to
Thomas Denn, 27 November 1682
(courtesy of Kieran Sheehan)

A CIP record for this book is available
from the British Library

Printed in Ireland by ColourBooks Ltd

Contents

Acknowledgments   6

Foreword   7

A Note on Weights and Measures   9

Abbreviations   11

Dictionary of Irish Local History   13

Bibliography   332

Useful References and Research Guides   348

Web Sources for Local Historians   350

Acknowledgments

A dictionary can never aspire to perfection. Like history itself, there can be no last word. To readers dismayed to discover that I have omitted that which they are most earnestly in search of, I offer a humble *Mea culpa*. No one will be more disappointed than I when next I stumble across a term that should have been included. At the same time, were publication to be withheld until universal satisfaction could be guaranteed the utility of the present text would be deferred forever. I owe an incalculable debt to Raymond Gillespie and James Kelly for their support, advice and direction while this work was in progress. It was in Dr Gillespie's masterly MA classes in local history at NUI Maynooth that the idea for this dictionary was first conceived and Dr Kelly's encyclopaedic knowledge of eighteenth-century Ireland has spared me not a few blushes. Thanks are also due to the countless historians whose work I mined for explanations and definitions. Finally, I would like to thank the unfailingly helpful staff of Dr Cregan Library, St Patrick's College, Drumcondra, where a considerable proportion of this volume was prepared.

Foreword

Traces, tracks, relics, sources, evidence. These are the stuff of history but they are not history. History begins when the human mind engages with the evidence and tries to make sense of its significance for earlier communities. That is no easy task. The evidence may resist interpretation because the context within which it was created has been obscured over time. It may be the product of institutions long fallen into desuetude. It may be infused with complex imagery or language from Ireland's rich multiethnic, multilingual, multicultural and religiously plural past. However we encounter it, our first challenge is to 'read' it and given the incalculable loss of Irish historical records over the years we must learn to do it well. Unfortunately, there is no handy cipher to unlock the secrets of the past and most dictionaries are too generalised to answer the specific concerns of local historians. Excellent though it is, the *Oxford English Dictionary* falls short when dealing with the Irish context. S. J. Connolly's *The Oxford companion to Irish history* should find a place on every local historian's bookshelf but only partially serves as a companion to Irish local history. Some thoughtful Irish historians, recognising the needs of a broader (and growing) non-specialist audience, append glossaries to their work or incorporate explanations in parentheses. Many, however, do not. So what was an 'angel'? Castle chamber? Raskins? A Cunningham acre? Letters patent? And where do you go to find out what a Brunswick club was? Or the meaning of legal terms associated with the courts and land conveyancing? This dictionary attempts to answer such questions for Irish local historians.

Although intended primarily for local historians, readers should not be surprised to encounter entries here that, at first glance, might be considered more relevant to national history. It is axiomatic that all histories gain from a consideration of the big picture and, local societies, however isolated, did not exist in a vacuum. Their personalities were forged out of the interplay between the local and the wider world to such an extent as to diminish local studies that ignore the regional or national dimensions. That interrelationship is acknowledged by the inclusion in this book of numerous entries relating to national and regional institutions such as parliament and the courts, to administrative structures, religion, education, historical records, land law, lay associations, political movements, architecture and archaeology.

In chronological terms the subject-matter of this dictionary ranges from early times to the close of the nineteenth century. The story of local communities, of course, does not end with the nineteenth century. The abundance, variety and accessibility of sources for the twentieth century make that period an exciting new frontier for local historians.

So abundant, in fact, that a dedicated volume of its own would be required to do it justice. Time constraints rendered that impractical and I have elected to focus on earlier, less familiar and less accessible periods.

Structurally the *Dictionary of Irish Local History* is not dissimilar to a traditional dictionary but there are a number of significant differences. Many definitions have been enlarged to explain the history of an institution or process or to document change over time. All entries are fully cross-referenced – bold type indicating a separate entry – and, where appropriate, readers are directed to articles and books which contain an extended treatment of the relevant topic and to the holding archives, libraries or repositories of related primary historical sources. Abbreviated references below each entry can be located in full in the bibliography at the end of the book. All local historians, be they aspiring or experienced, will find something of interest in the research guide section and website directory which close this book.

A Note on Weights and Measures

Although metrological standardisation began in Ireland in the mid-nineteenth century, many traditional units (the Irish mile and acre) persisted in use into the twentieth century and that most antique of land divisions, the townland, is with us yet. Prior to standardisation, a complex range of weights and measures were employed which varied (sometimes radically so) from district to district. In parts of Co. Clare in the 1820s a bushel of potatoes contained six stones six pounds but elsewhere in the county it weighed sixteen, eighteen or twenty stones. To complicate matters, the Clare bushel also evidenced seasonal variability: the stone weighed sixteen pounds in summer but eighteen in winter to take account of encrusted clay. At a broader level metrological variability was influenced by commodity, by quality and even point of sale. At the bottom of the distribution network, for example, a wide range of agreed yet non-standard local measures such as pottles, creels and paniers were employed and small domestic containers were frequently pressed into service. An added local refinement was the sale of dry goods in heaped or level measure. Finally, time itself was a variable as some measures fell into disuse over time and others were introduced by colonists.

Gaelic territorial divisions were arranged hierarchically to a regular plan, size being determined by variables such as soil quality, relief and the size of the lordship to which they were connected. Most were erased in the sixteenth and seventeenth centuries as the social order which regulated them collapsed under the pressure of conquest and colonisation. Ballybetaghs, ballyboes, sessiaghs, gnieves, capell lands and horsemen's beds lost their currency under the new order although many survive as placenames or lie obscured behind baronial, civil parish or townland boundaries. Paradoxically, as deeds and charters were rarely used by the natives, our knowledge of indigenous spatial divisions derives to a considerable degree from the bureaucracy of plantation itself. The names and dimensions of Gaelic spatial units are preserved in manuscript form, sometimes for the first time, in the maps, inquisitions, surveys, land grants and books of distribution which documented the settlement process. Historians and geographers have used these sources with some profit to enhance our understanding of the socio-economic and political structure of Gaelic Ireland but, overall, the spatial picture remains incomplete. Given these uncertainties, a detailed treatment of Irish measures is not possible within the parameters of the present work. A supplementary reading list is appended overleaf to facilitate further reading.

Adams, I. H., *Agrarian landscape terms: a glossary for historical geography* (London, 1976).

Andrews, J. H., *Plantation acres: an historical study of the Irish land surveyor and his maps* (Omagh, 1985).

Bourke, P. M. Austin, 'Notes on some agricultural units of measurement in use in pre-famine Ireland' in *IHS*, xiv (1964–5), pp. 236–245.

Connor, R. D., *The weights and measures of England* (London, 1987).

Duffy, Patrick J., 'Social and spatial order in the MacMahon lordship of Airghialla in the late sixteenth century' in Duffy, Patrick J., Edwards, David and FitzPatrick, Elizabeth (eds), *Gaelic Ireland c.1250–1650: land lordship and settlement* (Dublin, 2001), pp. 115–137.

Erck, John Caillard (ed.), *A repertory of the enrolments of the patent rolls of Chancery in Ireland, James I,* (2 vols, 2 parts, 1846–1852).

Feenan, Dermot and Kennedy, Liam, 'Weights and measures of the major food commodities in early-nineteenth century Ireland: a regional perspective' in *RIA Proc.*, C, cii, (2002), pp. 21–45.

Freeman, Martin (ed.), *The compossicion booke of Conought* (Dublin, 1936).

Hill, George, *An historical account of the plantation of Ulster at the commencement of the seventeenth century* (Belfast, 1877).

Hogan, James, 'The tricha-cét and related land measures' in *RIA Proc.*, C, xxxviii, no. 7 (1928–9), pp. 148–235.

Inquisitionum in officio rotulorum cancellariae Hiberniae asservatorum repertorium (2 vols, Dublin, 1827–9). Chancery inquisitions for Leinster and Ulster.

Larcom, Thomas, 'On the territorial divisions of Ireland' in HC 1847 (764) L. 1.

McErlean, Thomas, 'The Irish townland system of landscape organisation' in T. Reeves-Smyth and F. Hammond (eds), *Landscape archaeology of Ireland* (Oxford, 1983), pp. 315–39.

Morrin, James (ed.), *The patent rolls of Henry VIII, Edward VI, Philip & Mary, Elizabeth I and Charles I* (3 vols, 1861–1863).

Report of the commissioners appointed to inquire into the state of the fairs and markets in Ireland, HC 1852–3 [1674] XLI; *Mins of evidence,* HC 1854–5 [1910] XIX.

Second report of the commissioners appointed by His Majesty to consider the subject of weights and measures, HC 1820 (314) VII.

Wakefield, Edward, *An account of Ireland, statistical and political* (2 vols, London, 1812).

Abbreviations

Anal. Hib.	*Analecta Hibernica*
app.	appendix
Archiv. Hib.	*Archivium Hibernicum*
AS.	Anglo-Saxon
c.	circa (about)
Collect. Hib.	*Collectanea Hibernica*
d.	died
DHR	*Dublin Historical Record*
Econ. Hist.	*Economic History*
ed(s).	editor(s)
EHR	*English Historical Review*
ff.	and the following pages
Fr.	French
Gr.	Greek
HC	House of Commons
HMC	Historical Manuscripts Commission
HMSO	Her Majesty's Stationery Office
IER	*Irish Ecclesiastical Record*
Ir. Econ. & Soc. Hist.	*Irish Economic and Social History*
IHS	*Irish Historical Studies*
IMC	Irish Manuscripts Commission
Ir.	Irish
Ir. Cath. Hist. Comm. Proc.	*Proceedings of the Irish Catholic Historical Committee*
Ir. Jurist	*Irish Jurist*
Ir. Sword	*Irish Sword*
Ir. Texts Soc.	Irish Texts Society
JCHAS	*Journal of the Cork Historical and Archaeological Society*
Jn. Ecc. Hist.	*Journal of Ecclesiastical History*
L.	Latin
Louth Arch. Soc. Jn.	*Journal of the Louth Archaeological and Historical Society*
Med. L.	Medieval Latin
NA	National Archives
NHI	A *New History of Ireland* (9 vols, Oxford, 1976–)
NLI	National Library of Ireland
OE	Old English
OFr	Old French

passim	in various places
PRI rep. DK	Report of the deputy keeper of Public Records in Ireland
PRONI	Public Record Office of Northern Ireland
repr.	reprint
R. Hist. Soc. Trans.	Transactions of the Royal Historical Society
RIA	Royal Irish Academy
RIA Proc.	Proceedings of the Royal Irish Academy
RSAI	Royal Society of Antiquaries of Ireland
RSAI Jn.	*Journal of the Royal Society of Antiquaries of Ireland*
ser.	series
UJA	*Ulster Journal of Archaeology*
W.	Welsh

A

abbroachment. The offence of forestalling or purchasing goods before they reach the market in order to retail them at a higher price. *See* forestall, regrate.

abjuration, oath of. An oath of renunciation. Several acts were passed in the seventeenth and early eighteenth centuries requiring the abjuration (renunciation) of the pope's spiritual and temporal authority, Catholic doctrine and/or the claim of the Stuart pretender to the throne. The first (1657) required the oath-taker to deny the pope's spiritual and temporal authority and repudiate Catholic doctrine. The second, a contravention of the **treaty of Limerick** (which asked only for an oath of allegiance to William III), was passed by the English parliament in 1691 (3 Will. & Mary, c. 2) and required members of parliament to renounce papal authority and the pope's power to depose a monarch. This oath remained effective until the passage of the **Catholic emancipation** act in 1829. The third, passed in 1703 (1 Anne, c. 17), abjured the pretensions of the Stuarts to the throne and was imposed on Irish office-holders and professionals such as teachers, lawyers and, later, Anglican ministers. In 1709 (8 Anne, c. 3) registered Catholic priests were required to take the oath but this they largely refused to do. The oath prescribed for all office-holders by the Irish parliament following the **Act of Supremacy** (1537) was also effectively an oath of abjuration in that it required the oath-taker to acknowledge the monarch as the supreme head of the church in Ireland and England. (Fagan, *Divided loyalties*, pp. 22–48; Wall, *The penal laws*, pp. 17–19.)

abjure the realm. To avoid a criminal prosecution in medieval times a criminal might take shelter in the sanctuary of a church and abjure the realm before a **coroner**. This meant that he must swear to leave the country by the nearest port and never return. During the reign of Henry VIII he was branded so that if he ever chose to return he would be instantly recognisable and hanged.

absence. To safeguard the security of the Anglo-Norman colony in Ireland fines were levied on tenants holding by **knight-service** (chief tenants) who, without royal licence, absented themselves from their estates and went abroad. *See* Absentees, Statute of.

absentee landlord. In the eighteenth and nineteenth centuries, a pejorative term to describe a landlord who resided in England and left the administration of his estate to agents or middlemen. Some landlords, of course, could not help but be absentees as they held land in different parts of the country or in both England and Ireland. (Malcomson, 'Absenteeism', pp. 15–35.)

Absentees, Statute of. Passed at Westminster in 1380, this legislation followed a series of earlier ordinances directed against chief tenants who absented themselves from their estates and thereby neglected the defence of the Anglo-Norman colony. It enacted the king's entitlement to two-thirds of the profits of the estates of long-term absentees and the imposition of fines for casual absences to offset the costs incurred by the state in meeting the defensive shortcomings created by their absence. Between 1483 and 1536 a further five absentee acts were passed by Irish parliaments. (Cosgrove, 'England', pp. 526–7.)

abuttal. A clause in a deed which identifies the location of a property being conveyed by naming the tenants of adjoining lands or physical features such as rivers or the king's highway which bound it.

accates. (Fr. *achater*, to pay) Provisions that were purchased as opposed to those that were produced in the home.

account rolls. Manorial accounting records maintained on the charge (rents, fines, heriots, profits) and discharge (payment of labour, purchase of seed and equipment) system. Few account rolls survive for Ireland. One of the most interesting is the *Account roll of the priory of the Holy Trinity, Dublin, 1337–1346*, edited by James Mills and published by the Royal Society of Antiquaries of Ireland (1890–1). In 1996 it was re-issued with an introduction by James Lydon and Alan Fletcher.

achievement. Anything which a man is entitled to represent of an armorial character including a shield, crest and motto, of which the shield is the most important.

acre. The Irish acre was the spatial measure most widely employed in Ireland from the seventeenth century and certainly the predominant unit by the nineteenth. One Irish (or plantation) acre was equivalent to 1.62 statute (English) acres. The statute acre (in use in parts of Cork, Waterford and some north-eastern counties in the nineteenth century) contains 4,840 square yards compared with the Irish measure of 7,840 square yards. In parts of Ulster, the Cunningham or Scottish acre of 6,250 square yards to the acre was employed. The difference in area between the Irish, the Cunningham and the statute acre derives from the use of a linear perch of varying length, the Irish perch measuring seven yards, the Cunningham six-and-a-quarter and the statute five-and-a-half. Prior to the general acceptance of the Irish measure a range of other measures were used, often with significant regional variations, measures which related more to the productive capacity of the land than to a specific spatial concept. *See* balliboe, ballybetagh, capell lands, cartron, collop, cowlands, gnieve, great acre, horsemen's beds, mile, ploughland, quarter, sessiagh, soum, tathe. (Andrews, *Plantation acres*, pp. 4–18; Bourke, 'Notes on some agricultural', pp. 236–245.)

acta. (L., pl of *actum*, act) Decrees passed by or a record of the transactions of a council, cathedral chapter, ecclesiastical court or Catholic synod.

adminicle. (L. *adminiculum*, a prop) Any supporting or corroborative evidence necessary for the trial of a case.

admiralty court. A court with jurisdiction over shipping and mercantile cases including piracy and prizes at sea, shipboard deaths, sailors' pay, collisions, wreck and salvage. It was established in Ireland in the sixteenth century under the supervision of the English admiralty. Although admirals were appointed in Ireland during the middle ages their appointments appear to have been honorific and maritime issues were usually dealt with in **chancery**. Provincial vice-admirals were appointed in the sixteenth century but such posts were sinecures and the functions were performed by deputies. As was the case with the English admiralty courts, the Irish court engaged in disputes with other courts, with the lord deputy and with town corporations and individuals who claimed to possess the right of jurisdiction over admiralty cases by charter. The Irish admiralty court remained subordinate to the English high court of admiralty until it became an independent court, the high court of admiralty, in 1784 (23 & 24 Geo. III, c. 14) following the passage of **Yelverton's Act.** Appeals from this court lay to the court of appeal in chancery and from thence to the Irish **privy council.** The admiralty court became a division of the high court following the re-modelling of the Irish courts by the **Judicature Act** of 1877. In 1893 it was merged with queen's bench on the death of the existing judge. (Appleby and O'Dowd, 'The Irish admiralty', pp. 299–320.)

adventurer. A person who advanced a sum of money under the 1642 Adventurers' Act (17 Chas. I, c. 34) for the suppression of the 1641 rebellion, the return for which was to be a proportional grant of forfeited land in Ireland. (Bottigheimer, *English money.*)

advowee. One who has the right of presentation or **advowson** of a church **benefice.**

advowry, avowry. In medieval times, a small annual payment made by a native Irishman to his lord to secure his freedom and the right to pursue an action in court which would be undertaken by the lord on his behalf. An action taken by an Irishman on his own behalf would fail on the simple basis that he was an Irishman. (Hand, *English law.*)

advowson. The right of patronage or presentation to a church **benefice**, a right which normally belonged to the person who built the church but in the twelfth and thirteenth centuries was granted to a religious house and with it went the **tithe.** In the sixteenth century when the monasteries were dissolved (*see* dissolution) tithe was frequently alienated to laymen and thus the right of presentation fell into lay hands. *See* dissolution

adze. An axe-like tool with a thin curved blade mounted at right-angles to the shaft used for shaping wood.

aetat, *aetatis*. Abbreviated *aet.*, the Latin for aged, at the age of.

afer. A low-bred workhorse.

afforced council. In medieval and early modern Ireland the **justiciar** occasionally strengthened the **privy council** by requesting the attendance of leading magnates of the Pale who, as tenants-in-chief, were obliged to assist him. Afforced councils were usually associated with the imposition of a general **cess** or important military matters. *See* great council.

agistment letting. A short-term lease of land for grazing purposes, the pastoral equivalent of **conacre**. *See* tithe agistment.

agnate. A kinsman whose descent can be traced exclusively through the male or paternal line. The relationship is described as agnatic. *See* cognate.

Agriculture and Technical Instruction, Department of. In 1895, following his successful introduction of the **co-operative movement** to Ireland, Horace Plunkett began to promote the case for the establishment of a board of agriculture and technical instruction to advance the agricultural economy. His proposal was taken up by a cross-party body of Unionist and Parnellite MPs (the Recess Committee) which persuaded the government to legislate for the creation of the Board of Agriculture and Technical Instruction in 1899. The board rationalised a variety of different functions performed by a number of different bodies and brought 10 institutes, including the Royal College of Science, Albert College and the Forestry centre at Avondale under its wing. It was guided by three advisory bodies whose membership included representatives of local government. The department devised experimental schemes for improving livestock and crop yields, employed itinerant agricultural lecturers, made agricultural loans and encouraged afforestation. It was criticised for the level of bureaucracy that characterised its operation and for some less than effective appointments. Plunkett, too, was criticised. He had been appointed vice-president of the board and assigned responsibility for agriculture and technical instruction, fisheries, statistics, disease prevention in plants and animals, supervision of the **National Library**, the National Museum and later the Geological Survey of Ireland but his appointment was terminated in 1907. (West, *Horace Plunkett*.)

ague, Irish ague. Probably typhus which, along with dysentery, afflicted English armies on the march during the fifteenth and sixteenth centuries. Typhus has been recorded as early as the thirteenth and as late as the twentieth centuries in Ireland. It is a lice-borne disease which flourished in the crowded, unhygienic living conditions of the work-houses in the 1840s and was dispersed by hordes of vagrants on the move in search of sustenance.

aid. (L., *auxilium*) The assistance in cash owed by a tenant to his lord in necessitous times. Such payments were made to enable the lord to be ransomed, on the occasion of the knighting of his eldest son or upon the marriage of his eldest daughter.

aistire. (Ir.) A bell ringer.

alb. A narrow-sleeved, white linen robe worn by a priest.

alderman. A member of a city corporation or town council next in rank in the order of citizens to the mayor. He was appointed for life. In the seventeenth century, Dublin was governed by a mayor, bailiffs (sheriffs), 24 jures (aldermen), 48 demi-jures (sheriff's peers) and 96 numbers (guild representatives). The aldermen played an important role in the appointment of the mayor and the bailiffs. Bailiffs were elected from the 48 or 96 by the votes of mayor and aldermen and the incoming mayor was appointed from amongst themselves by the aldermen and bailiffs. Vacancies among the aldermen were filled by recruitment from the demi-jures. In modern times the councillor elected first in each ward is styled alderman. (Edwards, 'The beginning', pp. 2–10.)

Alen's Register (*Liber niger Alani*). An episcopal or diocesan register compiled by John Alen, archbishop of Dublin (1528–34), which contains documents assembled and annotated by Alen in his efforts to recover rights and properties lost to Christ Church Cathedral by the negligence of earlier prelates. The records date back to the Anglo-Norman conquest and include a wide range of information on the episcopal manors of the see. See **Reportorium Viride**, a companion to the register, and **Crede Mihi**, the surviving portion of the most ancient register of the archbishops of Dublin. (McNeill, *Calendar*.)

ale silver (ale tol). A tribute or rent paid annually to the lord for the right to brew ale within a **liberty**. *See* tolboll.

alias, **writ of**. A second or further writ issued after an earlier writ had proved ineffectual. *See* outlawry.

alienation, right to. The right to transfer the ownership of property to another. As the crown was the supreme owner of land, tenants-in-chief (see *in capite*) were required to seek permission for such alienations to ensure that the crown was not defrauded of the **feudal incidents**. Failure to do so incurred alienation fines. *See* mortmain.

allocate, writ of. A writ issued out of **chancery** to the treasurer and barons of the **exchequer** requiring them to give an allowance to an individual accounting there in respect of money spent by him on the king's behalf. (Connolly, *Medieval record*, p. 16.)

allodial tenure. Absolute ownership of land. Under the feudal doctrine of tenures absolute personal ownership of land did not exist. *Nulle* *terre sans seigneur* (no land without a master) expresses the point that no land was held by a subject and not held of some lord. All land was held of the crown and escheated (reverted) to the crown in cases of **attainder** or felony or where no heir emerged to lay claim to it. In modern times such land reverts to the state in the Republic of Ireland. *See* estate.

alnager. An official examiner and attestor of the measurement and quality of woollen cloth. He attested its value by affixing a seal. The term 'alnage' refers to the inspection and the fee paid for it.

altarages. Originally voluntary offerings made upon the altar but the term came to embrace a whole range of ecclesiastical dues which went to make up a clergyman's income including the small **tithe**, tithe of fish in coastal parishes and **oblations** or offerings for specific church services or feastday dues. They did not, however, include the great tithe. *See* dues.

alum. A compound of aluminum used anciently to bind dyes in cloth.

amanuensis. 1: A secretary 2: A person employed to take dictation or copy manuscripts.

ambry. A recess in a church wall to the side of the altar where the sacramental vessels were stored.

amercement. The equivalent of the modern fine, imposed for breaches of the law or manorial customs. A fine differed from an amercement in that fines were imposed by the courts, amercements were assessed by a jury of the offender's peers.

amice. 1: A piece of white linen, oblong in shape and embroidered with a cross, worn around the neck and over the shoulders by a priest at mass. It was worn under the alb 2: A hood edged with fur with attached cape which was worn anciently by clergymen. Calabar, the fur of a brown squirrel, was often employed as edging.

Anabaptist. A radical sixteenth-century Protestant movement which regarded infant baptism as blasphemous. Infants, they maintained, could not discriminate between good and evil and until this faculty emerged they could not repent and accept baptism. As the first generation of Anabaptists considered their childhood baptisms invalid, they submitted to a 'second' adult baptism following a public confession of sin and faith. This was an offence according to contemporary legal codes and Anabaptists were persecuted and expelled from many towns across Europe. Anabaptists believed in the separation of church and state, opposed oath-taking, denounced the use of the sword, believed they were living at the end of all ages and some adopted a communistic style of living which stressed the community of goods. Most early Anabaptist leaders died in prison or were executed. In Britain and Ireland in the seventeenth century the term was used loosely (and pejoratively) to describe **Baptists** or **dissenters** and to portray them as social revolutionaries.

anchorite. A hermit.

Ancient Order of Hibernians. A Catholic, nationalist association founded in New York in 1836 with origins in the secret agrarian movements of the eighteenth and early nineteenth centuries, the Hibernians' motto 'Faith and Fatherland' reflected its twin goals – to defend the faith and advance the national cause. The order developed largely as a response to Orangeism in the nineteenth century, attracting members by organising parades which comprehended all the paraphernalia of Orange marches. Its masonic-like regalia and activities attracted Catholic businessmen who found in it an alternative to the almost exclusively Protestant masonic order and its role as a benevolent society appealed to workers. Dominated by **Clan na Gael** in the United States in the 1880s, the order was one of the largest and most powerful Irish-American organisations but the fissiparous nature of the American body infected the Irish branch. Between 1884 and 1902 the Irish branch split over the admission of members of Irish descent (as opposed to those of Irish birth) and split again in 1905 over whether the order should register as a friendly society. Nevertheless, membership grew dramatically after 1900, notably in Ulster (where the problem of sectarianism was most acute) and in Dublin, rising to 60,000 by 1909. The order played an important role in Catholic social life, embracing reading rooms, card playing, billiards, choral and religious activities. The Hibernians supported and financed the Irish parliamentary party under John Redmond and encouraged Irish voters in England to vote for the Labour Party. In 1904 Joseph Devlin was elected president of the Board of Erin, the body which represented the majority of Hibernians in Ireland, and the order became part of his nationalist political machine. Along with the northern Nationalist Party, the Ancient Order of Hibernians went into serious decline from 1970 when both were replaced by more aggressively assertive nationalist and republican bodies. No longer politically active, the order now operates principally as a benefit and social society. (Buckley and Anderson, *Brotherhoods*; Pollard, *The Ancient*, pp. 110–132.)

andirons. Fire-dogs.

angel. A new issue noble, a gold coin valued at 6s. 8d., so called because it bore the image of the archangel Michael slaying a dragon. It was in use from the late fifteenth to the mid-seventeenth centuries.

Anglican. A member of the Established church or **Church of Ireland**. Also known as an Episcopalian. The term was first used by Edmund Burke in 1797.

Annales. A term coined from the journal *Annales d'histoires économique et sociale* (1929) to describe a French historiographical movement whose leaders, Lucien Febvre, Mark Bloch and Ferdinand Braudel, rejected the traditional historiographical emphasis on the state, high politics, diplomacy, institutions, events and the culture of elites in favour of an integrated view of history which encapsulates the experiences and lives of whole populations. Bloch's *Feudal Society* (1939–40), for example, approaches feudal society not in terms of formal institutions but rather from an anthropological perspective as a complex network of interpersonal relationships. From its inception interdisciplinary co-operation has been a distinctive feature of *Annales* histories. In addition to traditional documentary sources, *Annales* historians drew heavily on economics, anthropology, linguistics, science, psychology, folklore, the material world and geography. They employed quantitative methods to assess the impact of fluctuations in trade, agriculture and demography. *Annales* innovations were neither unprecedented nor unparalleled but they had never before been assembled so comprehensively. The effect was to broaden the scope of history to embrace social groups and aspects of human behaviour which had been neglected by traditional historians. *Annales* historians also introduced a new concept of historical time. They replaced the traditional idea of a single, linear historical time in favour of a parallel series of co-existing times to account for the differing rates of change not only between but within civilisations. In *The Mediterranean and the Mediterranean world in the age of Philip II* (1949), Braudel discusses three different times: the almost static or immobile time of the geographical Mediterranean (*longue durée*), short or medium term social and economic change (*conjoncture*) and the rapid changes of political events (*événements*). *Annales* historians did not ignore entirely the role of political events and individuals – the third part of Braudel's *Mediterranean* is, in fact, devoted to political events – but the early generation tended to view events as superficial in comparison with deeper long-term changes. As a result they eschewed traditional narrative history in favour of problem-oriented history involving the whole range of human activities and experience. The movement has been criticised for replacing one orthodoxy with another but *Annales* historians have recently begun to look again at the role of events and individuals and, indeed, the use of narrative. (Burke, *The French*; Iggers, *Historiography*, pp. 51–64.)

annals. Native Gaelic sources of Irish history which were originally records kept in monasteries but from the sixteenth century also came to be compiled by learned laymen.

annates. The first fruits of a new clergyman's **benefice** which originally were remitted to the pope. After the Reformation benefice holders were required to pay the income of the first year of appointment to the crown. *See* Board of First Fruits, twentieth parts, *valor ecclesiasticus*.

annuity. 1: A sum of money paid annually to maintain the beneficiary of a will or deed. It was raised by a charge on the rental income of the land (rentcharge) or by loan or mortgage which were also repaid by rentcharges. A widow's annuity was known as **jointure** 2: In the late nineteenth and twentieth centuries, the annual re-payment by a small-holder to the **Irish Land Commission** on the sum advanced by the commission to enable him to purchase his holding.

antiquarian. A collector of antiquities or facts about the past. The term is used currently to describe pseudo-histories which contain lists of facts without interpretation or comment. Antiquarian histories, pre-occupied as they have been with the genealogies and achievements of the gentry and clergy in local communities, contributed consider-ably towards the low status occupied by local history, a situation only recently ameliorated with the emergence of local histories charac-terised by sensitive reconstructions of society and economy and in-vestigations of individual and collective mentalities. Given the de-struction of Irish state records in 1922, however, it must be acknow-ledged that modern Irish historiography would be all the poorer with-out the legacy of transcripts of original records bequeathed us by nine-teenth-century antiquarians as they burrowed in the Public Record Office. (Marshall, *The tyranny*, pp. 46–62.)

apostasy. The renunciation of one's religious faith.

applotment. *See* tithe applotment.

apport. In medieval times, the surplus produced by a priory which was sent to the mother house after expenses incurred in the administra-tion of priory lands had been deducted.

appraiser. A valuer of property such as goods distrained for non-pay-ment of rent or treasure trove. Appraisers also valued the property of a deceased person to compile a probate inventory.

Apprentice Boys. A Protestant Unionist association founded in 1814 as the Apprentice Boys of Derry to commemorate the shutting of the gates of Derry city against the Catholic Jacobite army on 7 December 1688 by thirteen apprentices. The shutting of the gates was promp-ted by the circulation of a forged letter which aroused fears of a Pro-testant massacre. Apprentice clubs commemorate the shutting on 20 December and the lifting of the siege on 12 August. (Haddick-Flynn, *Orangeism*, pp. 368–374.)

appropriate. **Tithe** assigned to an ecclesiastical figure other than the local clergyman is styled 'appropriate'. Where all of the tithe, great and small, was so assigned it was termed 'wholly appropriate'. *See* tithe, im-propriate.

approver. 1: A steward or bailiff who supervised the letting of the king's lands or royal manors to the monarch's best advantage, collected the royal revenue and accounted for his transactions at the **exchequer** 2:

An informer, particularly one who turns king's evidence.

appurtenance. A building or right associated with or pertaining to a particular property, including outbuildings, mills, kilns, commonage, dovecotes or subterranean minerals.

apse. An arched recess at the end of a church.

a.r. Anno regni or **regnal year**. Literally, the year of reign of.

archdeacon. The chief deacon, next in rank to a bishop. In some Anglican dioceses it was the archdeacon's duty to assist the bishop in diocesan affairs but in others the post was merely titular. Archdeacons originally wielded considerable power, sometimes even rivalling that of the bishop, but they were severely curbed by the Council of Trent. In England in the eighteenth century archdeacons exercised considerable authority over diocesan clergy but although there were 34 in Ireland they had no such jurisdiction. They were often simply accessories to the cathedral, some not even having a stall in the chapter. It was only in the nineteenth century that the archdeacon emerged as a fully functioning middle-manager in the Established church structure. The title is honorific in the Catholic church.

ard plough. Probably the earliest form of plough used in Ireland, the ard or light plough consisted of a wooden frame, curved at one end, with a pointed wooden or stone share projecting from the base of the curve. The addition in later times of a **coulter**, a vertical metal blade placed slightly forward of the share, improved the efficiency and speed of the plough by cutting through matted roots. Neither share nor coulter, however, were able to turn the sod and it was not until the **mouldboard** was fitted that the typical ridge and furrow ploughing pattern was achieved. (Mitchell, *The Shell guide*, pp. 143–4.)

Ard Rí. High-king. The question of high-kingship and its effective reality remains disputed. Mostly the phrase appears to denote overlords above the rank of king of a *tuath*. Two other attributions, *Rí Erenn* (king of Ireland) and *Rí Temro* (king of Tara) were also assigned to powerful overlords, notably in the case of the Uí Néill who appear to have fitted the bill as supreme rulers of Ireland.

argent. In heraldry, denotes the colour silver or silvery-white.

Arianism. A heretical fourth-century doctrine which argued that the Son, though divine, had emanated from the Father at a specific time and was therefore not co-eternal with him. The Father created the Son and so the Son was subordinate and of a different substance to Him. Thus, Christ was neither fully human nor possessed of a divinity identical with God. In the nineteenth century Irish Presbyterianism was riven by a controversy over Arianism, leading to the secession of some ministers to form the Remonstrant Synod in 1830. *See* General Assembly of the Presbyterian Church in Ireland, New Light, Presbyterian, Seceders, Synod of Ulster, Southern Association.

Armagh, Book of. The only surviving complete copy of the New Testament from the ninth century, the *Book of Armagh* was written by the scribe Ferdomnach (died c. 845) and his assistants for the Abbot Torbach. Comprising 215 vellum leaves, the manuscript also contains St Patrick's Confession, the lives of Muirchiú and St Martin of Tours and the memoirs of Tirechán. It forms part of the collection of Trinity College, Dublin.

'Armagh Expulsions'. An Orange attempt to cleanse Armagh of Catholics following the defeat of the Catholic **'Defenders'** at Loughgall in 1795. Assassination and intimidation led to the flight of several thousand Catholics to Connacht and other parts, the disgruntled refugees spreading Defenderism wherever they settled. (Miller, 'The Armagh troubles', pp. 155–191.)

Armagh, Register of. A series of eight volumes (seven of which comprise original manuscript records) relating to the affairs of the archbishops of Armagh (1361–1543) which constitutes the largest single corpus of original material for the late medieval period. It contains letters, mandates, examinations of witnesses, *acta*, marital cases, letters **patent**, excommunications, clerical inhibitions, deprivations and appointments, probate matters and cases on appeal. Although the registers are named after individual prelates, they are not always completely co-extensive with their period of episcopal rule. (Armagh Register.)

armiger. (L., an armour bearer) A person entitled to bear heraldic arms. A squire.

Arminianism. A hotly-disputed liberal Calvinist doctrine espoused by the Dutch theologian Jacobus Arminius (1560–1609) which maintained that salvation was possible for all, a belief contrary to strict Calvinist teaching on predestination. To Arminius the idea that the elect were chosen before Adam's fall seemed incompatible with the mercy of God and implied that human will had no role to play in salvation. John Wesley was influenced by Arminianism as was the Methodist church which grew out of the Wesleyan movement. *See* Calvinism.

arquebus (hagbush). A portable firearm that was supported on a rest.

arraign. To indict.

Arroasian. The form of **Augustinian** rule which St Malachy encountered at the abbey of Arrouaise in the diocese of Arras c. 1140. The Arroasians borrowed severe observances from the **Cistercians** including a strict rule of silence, abstinence from meat and fats and the wearing of a white habit with no linen. Between 1140 and 1148 Malachy promoted the spread of Arroasian observance particularly in the northern half of the country and wherever he encountered opposition appears to have established distinct communities alongside many episcopal seats. After his consecration as archbishop of Dublin,

St Lawrence O'Toole adopted Arroasian observance at Christ Church Cathedral, one of the few cathedrals in Ireland to do so. Convents of Arroasian canonesses were also established in Ireland, the first being the senior house at St Mary's Abbey, Clonard (c. 1144). By the fourteenth century the Arroasian observance had begun to wane and there are few recorded Arroasian houses after that time. *See* nuns. (Dunning, 'The Arroasian', pp. 297–315.)

articlemen. The term usually comprehends persons admitted to the articles of surrender of Limerick or Galway at the close of the Williamite War. Relatively generous terms were offered to the Jacobites because William was anxious to close the war in Ireland and transfer his troops to Europe. Under the articles, the estates of the garrisons and citizens of Limerick and Galway were guaranteed provided they submitted to the king and did not opt to leave for France. Almost one-half of the land remaining in Catholic hands by 1703 was held by articlemen. *See* Limerick, Treaty of (1691).

Articles of Religion (1615). A series of 104 articles or doctrinal statements prepared and agreed at the 1613–15 **convocation** of the **Church of Ireland**. Compiled by James Ussher, professor of divinity at Trinity College, they included the bulk of the 1571 convocation of Canterbury's **Thirty-Nine Articles** but controversially omitted the thirty-sixth which refers to the ecclesiastical orders of deacon, priest, bishop and the procedures for episcopal consecrations, an omission which appears to reflect the puritan or Calvinist-leaning nature of the Irish church. The articles confirmed the church's adherence to the doctrine of predestination. A rigid and severe Sabbatarianism was espoused. The pope was condemned as the anti-Christ, royal supremacy was upheld, Catholic ceremonies and traditions were declared contrary to the teaching of the bible and the **Anabaptist** doctrine of the community of property was denounced. Under Lord Deputy Wentworth the articles were suppressed by the 1634 convocation and replaced by the Thirty-Nine Articles in an attempt to make the Church of Ireland correspond more closely to the English church.

assart. Marginal, waste or wooded land that was cleared and drained and brought into cultivation. Also known as extent land.

assay. 1: A proof 2: The assay of metals is the examination of precious metals to test their fineness. Weights and measures are assayed to ensure that they weigh or measure what they claim to do.

assignment. The transfer of a right or entitlement, usually a lease or mortgage.

assistant-barrister. To raise the standard of justice dispensed by the justices of the peace the **lord lieutenant** was authorised from 1796 (36 Geo. III, c. 25) to appoint an assistant-barrister of six years standing in each county to assist the justices at the **quarter-sessions**. The assistant-barrister was also given the power to hear **civil bills** to the sum of £20 in cases of debt, £10 in cases of **assumpsit** and £5 in cases of **trover**, trespass and **detinue**. Later the monetary limits were increased and he was empowered to deal with cases of assault and the recovery of small tenements. From 1851 he became the chairman of quarter-sessions and could act in the absence of the justices. In 1877 the office was abolished and replaced by that of county court judge. *See* justice of the peace.

assize. 1: A court sitting, literally the jury summoned by writ to sit together to try a cause 2: In earlier times the term referred to the writs that operated in assize courts, the assizes of *novel disseisin*, *mort d'ancestor* and *darrien presentment* 3: The twice-yearly assize courts (county courts) trying civil and criminal cases replaced the **eyre** courts of the thirteenth and fourteenth centuries.

assize, commission of. A commission to conduct an assize was issued by the **king's bench** to the judges of assize, empowering them to hear civil and criminal cases on circuit. Commissions of **gaol delivery** were normally given to judges of assize and from the sixteenth century they also heard civil actions of *nisi prius*, cases which had begun in the fixed courts and were brought to the point where the verdict of a local jury was necessary.

assize courts. Civil and criminal cases were heard before the assize courts. They were presided over by the judges of assize who were dispatched to the counties on twice-yearly circuits (spring and summer). They succeeded the itinerant justices in **eyre** but the disturbed nature of the country prevented the establishment of a regular circuit until the close of the seventeenth century. There were five circuits (six between 1796 and 1885) until their abolition in 1924 when they were replaced by the circuit courts in the Irish Free State (and by the crown courts in Northern Ireland from 1978). A winter assize was added from 1876 to deal solely with criminal cases. Dublin city and county did not form part of the assize circuit. A permanent commission, the 'County of the City of Dublin', sat at Green Street to hear criminal cases presided over by a judge of the king's bench. A second commission dealt with cases arising in the county. Increasingly the assizes came to deal solely with criminal cases. From 1796 civil actions were heard by an **assistant-barrister** in each county and by the mid-nineteenth century civil jurisdiction was being exercised by the **quarter-sessions**. The spring and summer assizes were the occasion for the meeting of the **grand jury** which, in addition to determining the validity of indictments before the courts, also performed important local government functions. *See* civil bill.

Association for Discountenancing Vice and Promoting the Knowledge

and Practice of the Christian Religion. A Protestant, proselytising educational society, the Association for Discountenancing Vice was founded by three members of the Established church in 1792 and funded initially by subscription. After it was incorporated in 1800 the association began to receive annual grants of public money which transformed it from a distributor of religious books and pamphlets into a provider of elementary education. Whenever a suitable school site was acquired the association advanced money to pay the cost of construction and contributed towards teachers' salaries. Titles to such schools were vested in the local Anglican minister and church-wardens. Schools in receipt of aid were not allowed to accept grants from other public institutions, the teachers must be Anglicans, all literate pupils were required to read the scriptures and only the Church of England catechism was taught. Children of all faiths were welcomed and non-Anglicans were excused the catechism but all had to read scripture. In 1819 about 50% of the enrolment of 8,800 pupils was Catholic. By 1824, when the association was receiving public funds in excess of £9,000, it controlled 226 schools which provided a very basic education in the 'three Rs'. By this time the association had embraced a more actively proselytising role and began to expose Catholic children to catechetical classes. This prompted a mass exodus from the schools. In 1825 the Commissioners of Irish Education Inquiry slated the association's school system, noting that the education of non-Anglicans was entirely an accidental and secondary object of the association. After the introduction of the national system of education in 1831 the well of public funds dried up and the educational activities of the Association for Discountenancing Vice withered. In a new guise – and shorn of the reference to discountenancing vice – the Association for the Promotion of Christian Knowledge (APCK) developed as the publishing wing of the Church of Ireland. The records of the association are held by the Representative Church Body Library. (Akenson, *Irish education*, pp. 80–83; *Idem, The Church of Ireland*, pp. 139–42.)

assumpsit. (L., he has undertaken) 1: A promise to fulfil a bargain 2: A common law action to recover damages resulting from a breach of contract or promise. Assumpsit first emerged in cases where goods entrusted to the defendant had been damaged through his negligence. Later the emphasis shifted from negligence to failure to keep a promise. Every contract executory (to be executed in the future) incorporates an assumpsit because when a person agrees to pay a sum of money for goods or deliver a product for a certain sum he assumes or promises to pay or deliver. Failure to fulfil the promise means that the other party may have an action of the case on assumpsit.

attachment. The seizure by a creditor of the goods of his debtor wherever he can find them.

attachment, writ of. A writ to enforce the judgement of a court by which a defaulter is committed to prison for contempt by his non-compliance.

attaint. A legal term which signifies a writ of judgement against a jury in a court of record which has returned a false verdict contrary to the evidence or because of an erroneous statement of the law by the judge. Originally jurors producing a false verdict were liable to have their homes torn down, their meadows ploughed and their lands forfeited but this was later replaced by a monetary fine and a new trial ordered.

attainder. 1: From 1539 a formal declaration by parliament and without trial that a person was a traitor. Once a bill of attainder was introduced or passed in parliament the attainted person was effectively outside the law, deprived of all civil rights, disabled from seeking redress in the courts (although he could defend himself) and he forfeited his estate. By 'corruption of blood' the attainted lost his right to inherit or transmit property 2: Attainder was the legal outcome of judgement of death or outlawry in cases of treason or a felony, the results of which were similar to attainder by parliament. By law no person could be tried or attainted of high treason but by the evidence on oath of two witnesses to the same treasonable act. *See* outlawry.

attorney-general. Senior crown law officer who advised the **privy council** on legal questions and conducted state prosecutions. He explained and defended the royal interest in parliament, a role which required him to be in attendance regularly in the house.

attorney, letter of. A deed creating a substitute to act for one of the parties in a conveyance. In medieval times this was usually executed to grant or receive seisin of a property.

Augustinian Canons, Austin Canons. The Augustinian Canons (in full, the Canons Regular of Saint Augustine, abbreviated OSA) appeared in Ireland in the mid-twelfth century through the influence and promotion of the ecclesiastical reformer St Malachy and became the predominant religious order in Ireland. Its constitution was based on the Rule of St Augustine, a series of instructions written by the theologian St Augustine of Hippo (d. 430). Malachy introduced a version of Augustinian rule known as the Arroasian observance after an inspection of the Augustinian house at Arrouaise in Arras (c. 1140). After Malachy's death in 1148 new Augustinian houses were founded, many of which were Arroasian, some for canonesses and some jointly owned by canons and canonesses.

Augustinian Friars, Austin Friars. The Augustinian Friars (in full, the Order of Hermits of St Augustine, abbreviated OESA), a mendicant order, appeared in Ireland, probably from England, c. 1282. By 1300 there were four houses in Ireland, rising to twenty-two by the time of the dissolution of the monasteries. Administratively, Ireland was considered one of the four 'limits' or sub-provinces of the English province and was itself subdivided into four regions (*plagae*) viz., Munster, Connacht, Leinster and Ulster with Meath. Connacht survived the suppression of the mid-sixteenth century and the order experienced a revival from 1613 which continued right through the seventeenth and eighteenth centuries. The closure of the Irish noviciates by the Congregation of Propaganda Fide in 1751 (and of the continental seminaries some decades later) reduced the numbers seeking to join the order and led to a decline which was not arrested until the following century.

Austin friars. *See* Augustinian Friars.

autograph. A manuscript in the hand of the author.

avowry. *See* advowry.

B

'Back Lane parliament'. *See* Catholic Convention.

backside. A yard or plot behind a house.

badging. In the late seventeenth and eighteenth centuries some parishes (including a number in Dublin city and Ulster) introduced a system of badging licensed beggars to ensure that only deserving local beggars were permitted to operate within the parish boundaries and to curb the activities of able-bodied strolling vagrants who infested the streets and were a burden on the parish poor list. Badging was permitted under a 1772 poor relief act (11 & 12 Geo. III, c. 30) which empowered committees in every county and city of a county to badge beggars and construct workhouses (houses of industry) for the restraint and punishment of sturdy idlers. *See* industry, house of.

baile. (Ir.) Homeplace or townland preserved in placenames as Bally. Over 5,000 townland names in Ireland commence with Bally. *See* townland. (Hughes, 'Town and baile', pp. 244– 58.)

bailey. Walled courtyard or forecourt, generally rectangular in shape. *See* motte and bailey.

bailiff. 1: A senior manorial official who supervised the daily operation and functioning of the **manor**, including the keeping of surveys and **account rolls** 2: Bailiffs (Ballivi – always used in the plural form) were borough officials, second in rank to the mayor, who exercised judicial powers as magistrates in the civil courts. The title sheriff was later substituted for bailiff.

Balfour Acts. *See* Purchase of Land (Ireland) Act, 1891.

balister. 1: An archer 2: A crossbow archer.

balk (baulk). A narrow ridge of unploughed grassland dividing cultivated land in the openfield system.

ballastage. A toll paid for the right to remove ship's ballast from the bed of a port.

Ballast Office. Precursor to the Dublin Port and Docks Board, the Ballast Office Committee was established by the Irish parliament (6 Anne, c. 20) in 1707 to effect improvements in Dublin harbour. The irregular taking on and throwing out of ballast had seriously disabled the port and reduced its capacity to receive larger vessels. It was generally acknowledged that a regulatory office was required to oversee the raising, furnishing and discharge of ballast. Several private initiatives were proposed but the corporation of Dublin successfully resisted these encroachments on its civic authority. When the corporation itself proposed a ballast office bill, the admiralty objected on the basis that this was an infringement of the lord high admiral's rights. The bill passed the Irish parliament after the corporation acknowledged the admiralty's authority and agreed an annual payment of 100 yards of best Holland duck (a strong linen cloth). In 1729 (3 Geo. II, c. 21) and again in 1785 (25 Geo. III, c. 64) the Irish parliament legislated for the cleansing of the ports, harbours and rivers of Cork, Galway, Sligo, Drogheda and Belfast and for the erection of ballast offices in each town. From 1786 the Ballast Committee Office was replaced by the Ballast Board which was tasked with cleansing and deepening the port and maintaining the harbour at Dún Laoire. Spoil dredged from ports was retained for use as ships' ballast. In 1807 the Ballast Board was renamed the Dublin Port and Docks Board. (Falkiner, *Illustrations*, pp. 186–190.)

balliboe. Unit of spatial measurement in Tyrone, three of which made a quarter. As a quarter was estimated to contain about 240 acres, the balliboe amounted to about 80 acres and therefore was broadly similar to the tate of Fermanagh and Monaghan.

ballybetagh. (Ir., *baile biataigh*, the steading or farmstead of a *biatach* or **betagh**) A unit of land measurement comprising four quarters. A quarter was generally considered to contain about 240 acres, Irish measure, so that a ballybetagh may have amounted to about 1,000 Irish acres. Thirty ballybetaghs made a *tricha-cét* or **cantred** or **barony**.

Ballymote, Book of. A compilation written at Ballymote, Co. Sligo, largely the work of Solomon O'Droma and Manus Ó Duigenann. Consisting of 251 vellum leaves, it contains **Lebor Gabála Érenn,** chronological, genealogical and historical pieces in prose and verse relating to saints, remarkable Irishmen and important families. It also includes tracts on ogham alphabets, ancient history, the rights, privileges and tributes of the learned and ruling classes together with a Gaelic translation of the history of the Britons by Nennius. (Atkinson, *Ballymote*.)

'the banker'. In the nineteenth century a pig raised for market to pay the rent. Also known as 'the gentleman who pays the rent'.

bankruptcy court. During the eighteenth century cases of bankruptcy were dealt with by the issuing of individual commissions and this continued to be the case until 1836 when a permanent commissioner in bankruptcy (two from 1837) was appointed by the lord lieutenant. The commissioners in bankruptcy were barristers of ten years' standing and removable only by an address to the crown from both houses of parliament. The court for the relief of insolvent debtors, established in 1821 and headed by similarly qualified barristers, was united with the commissioners in bankruptcy in 1857 to form the court of bankruptcy and insolvency. In 1872 this court was re-styled the court of bankruptcy. (McDowell, *The Irish administration*, pp. 109–110.)

Baptist church. The earliest Baptist congregations were established in Irish towns in the mid-seventeenth century by Cromwellian soldiers. The strength of their presence within the army was regarded as a threat to discipline and civil order for Baptists shared a belief in adult baptism with the sixteenth-century radical European **Anabaptists**, and, by extension, were often pejoratively so labelled. Numerically insignificant in the eighteenth century, Baptist numbers rose to over 7,000 by the turn of the twentieth century, aided by the **evangelical revival** of 1859. Today there are about fifty Baptist congregations in Ireland. Baptists believe that faith must precede baptism. Since baptism can only be valid after a profession of faith, they repudiate the practice of infant baptism. Organisationally, Baptists are congregationalists; they believe that the local congregation, under Christ, is the sole authority in matters of faith and worship. Local congregations are voluntarily associated with the Baptist Union of Ireland but remain autonomous. *See* Independents. (Greaves, *God's other children*, pp. 25–7; Gribbon, 'Irish Baptist Church', pp. 183–191.)

Baptist Society. An avowedly proselytising body founded in London in 1814. The society was most active in Connacht where it set up schools and provided financial aid to other schools that agreed to abide by its rules. Preaching and teaching were conducted through the medium of the Irish language, accompanied by the usual distribution of bibles and religious tracts. (Rusling, 'The schools', pp. 429–42.)

baptizandi nomen. In Catholic baptismal registers, the baptismal name of the child.

baptus est/bapta est. He/she was baptised.

bar. In heraldry, two broad horizontal bands across the centre of an **escutcheon**.

barbican. An outer defensive tower or gate.

bardic schools. The early history of bardic schools remains unclear. In pre-Norman times lawyers, poets and historians were educated in church schools but there may also have been secular academies for poets. The picture is much clearer from the fourteenth century with frequent annalistic references to lay schools for poetry, law, medicine, history and music. Each school was presided over by an *ollamh* to whom students were apprenticed by fosterage agreements. Although books were used, the core of each discipline was transmitted by verse or prose and had to be learned by memory. Bardic schools flourished until the tide of patronage ebbed with the collapse of the Gaelic lordships in the sixteenth and seventeenth centuries. (de Blácam, *Gaelic literature*.)

Barebones Parliament. The temporary assembly devised by Oliver Cromwell to draft a constitution after the dissolution of the Rump in 1653.

bargain and sale. A form of conveyance created by the English Statute of Enrolments (1535) as an alternative to the cumbersome **feoffment**. Unlike the feoffment, the bargain and sale was valid without seisin. In other words, the vendor was not required to physically enter on the land to perform the ceremonial livery of seisin. It is recognisable because the action clause in the deed of conveyance reads 'granted, alienated, bargained and sold'. The Irish Statute of Uses (10 Chas. I, c. 1, 1634), however, required the bargain and sale to be indented, sealed and enrolled within six months in one of the king's courts of record. Many landowners disliked the public nature of this form of conveyance. A different form of conveyance, the **lease and release** – which emerged around 1600 – superseded the bargain and sale and provided a legally valid yet discreet instrument for land transactions.

bargain and sale, lease and release combined. Often drafted in a single conveyance, the combined 'bargain and sale, lease and release' was an attempt by conveyancers to circumvent some of the less satisfactory aspects of each individual form. First, the grantor bargained and sold a lease of his property for a **peppercorn** rent. Under the 1634 Statute of Uses the grantee was deemed to be in possession and therefore he did not have to enter the property to take possession. As the estate being conveyed was a lease there was no need to enrol it. Next, by deed of release the grantor conveyed his **reversion** to the grantee. *See* use, feoffment to.

bar haven. A harbour at the entrance to which lies a submerged sandbank.

barmkin. An enclosure about a castle which served as a refuge for people and animals.

baronial police force. A precursor of the Royal Irish Constabulary, baronial policemen or 'Barnies' were introduced in 1773 and operated in rural areas in support of the magistrates, executing warrants, collecting revenues and preserving the peace. The baronial force was diminutive – it never exceeded a national complement of 600 men – and notoriously inefficient. Several attempts were made at reformation. In 1787 a police act (27 Geo. III, c. 42) permitted grand juries in disturbed areas to appoint 16 sub-constables for each barony under the supervision of a government-appointed chief constable. In 1792 a new baronial force was inaugurated but that proved incapable of dealing with the widespread agrarian unrest of the early nineteenth century and was replaced in 1814 by the peace preservation force. *See* Peace Preservation Act (1814), police. (Beames, *Peasants*, p. 157 *passim*; Boyle, 'Police', pp. 90–116; O'Sullivan, *The Irish constabularies*, pp. 11–12, 16; Palmer, *Police*.)

barony. An ancient division comprising a number of townlands which were thought to have been co-terminous with the *tuath* or multiples of the *tricha-cét* (pre-Norman territories occupied by the native Irish). Although some baronies are co-terminous with *tuatha*, the vast majority are not for there were 97 *tuatha* and 273 baronies. This suggests that many baronies were the creation of Anglo-Norman colonists. The barony corresponds roughly to the English hundred and was also known as a cantred. Baronies later became subdivisions of Irish counties when the country was shired and were widely used from the sixteenth century for administrative purposes. Both the **Civil Survey** (1654–6) and the **Down Survey** (1654–9) were conducted along baronial lines and county rates were paid to the **grand jury** on a baronial basis.

Barrack Board. *See* Board of Works.

barrel. In Ireland in the eighteenth and nineteenth centuries the barrel was the predominant unit of measurement for agricultural produce rather than the **bushel** or **quarter**. With some exceptions it was in universal use throughout the country. The precise weight of a barrel differed from commodity to commodity. A barrel of wheat or rye weighed 20 stones, of oats 14 stones, of barley or **bere** 16 stones. The official weight of a barrel of potatoes was 20 stones but witnesses at the **Devon Commission** gave weights ranging from 20 to 24 stones. (Bourke, 'Notes', pp. 236–245.)

barrow. A tumulus or earthen mound raised over one or more prehistoric burials.

base court. Any lesser court, such as a manor court, that is not a court of **record**.

basinet, bascinet, bassenet. A skull-cap or helmet made of metal or some other hard material, sometimes pointed.

batter. A sloping wall, narrower at the top than at the bottom, designed to support a house or other building. Batters also served to protect fortifications from undermining.

battery. A number of artillery pieces assembled in one location for tactical reasons.

battle, trial by. Introduced into England and Ireland by the Normans, trial by battle originated in the belief that divine providence would ensure victory to the party in the right in any dispute. It was used to settle criminal, property and debt cases. Initially it was the litigants who fought, making litigation a risky business if the opposition was a skilful fighter. Later, champions were usually employed to fight on their behalf. Trial by battle was repudiated as a barbarity by the church and became obsolete by the 1300s although a case of trial by battle is recorded in the 1580s under Perrot. It was not finally abolished in England until 1819.

baudricke. A belt or girdle.

bawn. (Ir., *bádhún*, cattle fort) A fortified cattle enclosure, constructed to ward off the attacks of wolves or cattle-raiders.

beadle. A mace bearer, parish officer or constable. In the eighteenth century paid and uniformed beadles were employed by the Dublin house of industry to secure vagrants and sturdy beggars and bring them to the house. This duty was discharged at great peril to their own safety for the public sympathised with the beggars and seizures were frequently marked by riots. (Widdess, *The Richmond*, pp. 12–13.)

beaker folk. Early Bronze Age people (c. 2000 BC) who used a distinct type of flat-base pottery.

Beaufort, Daniel Augustus (1739–1821). A London-born Church of Ireland clergyman and scholar, Beaufort was a founding member and librarian of the **Royal Irish Academy** and was active in the Dublin Society. He was a farmer, an architect and a travel-writer but is remembered primarily for his cartographic work. In all, he produced only three maps: a small map of the country's river systems (1792), a map of the diocese of Meath (1797) and his astonishing 6-inch 'Ireland Civil and Ecclesiastical' which appeared in 1792 and in numerous editions subsequently. (Andrews, *Shapes*, pp. 214–247.)

beehive hut. A beehive-shaped, stone building constructed of overlapping stone courses.

beer, small. A low alcohol beer which was also fed to children where the available water was impure and liable to sicken them.

beetle. 1: A wooden or metal tool used to pound potatoes for animal feed. Beetles were also used to wash clothes and to break flax before it was scutched 2: A beetling engine bearing a line of wooden beetles was used to pound linen to create a smooth, soft surface on the fabric.

bellcote, belcote. A belfry constructed like a small house in which the bells are hung.

Belmore Commission (1897–8). At the request of the commissioners of national education the Belmore Commission was established to investigate the possibility of expanding curricular provision in Irish primary schools which, largely because of the **payment-by-results** system, had become too dull and mechanistic. Belmore recommended a broader curriculum that would include practical work such as elementary science, drawing and physical drill. The revised curriculum of 1900, which granted greater organisational freedom to schools and incorporated more practical subjects, was heavily influenced by the commission. Its greatest achievement, however, was to undermine the payment-by-results system by declaring such a system to be incompatible with the provision of a rounded educational programme. From 1900 teaching performance was rated by observation and not by pupil examination. (Belmore; Akenson, *Irish education*, pp. 372–75; *Idem*, 'Pre-university', pp. 534–5.)

benchers. The senior governing members of an inn of court. In the eighteenth and nineteenth centuries the benchers of the **Society of King's Inns** consisted of the **lord chancellor**, the judges, the master in chancery, the king's counsel and the **prothonotary** of common pleas. *See* inns of court

bend. In heraldry, a broad bend from the dexter chief corner to the sinister base. The reverse is known as a bend sinister.

benefice. An ecclesiastical living. An Anglican clergyman usually held a single parish as his benefice but in many cases two or more parishes were formally united and held by a single individual. Unions were normally effected where the income from a single parish was insufficient to support a clergyman.

benefit of clergy. The exemption enjoyed by clergy from the jurisdiction of the civil courts in cases of capital felony. From the middle ages a clergyman charged with a felony before a secular court was required to plead his clergy whereupon (if successful) the case was transferred to the **ecclesiastical courts**. Proof of entitlement to benefit of clergy was determined by a test of the defendant's ability to read the first verse of the fifty-first psalm. Thus literate laymen could plead their clergy because, being literate, they had the potential to be clergymen. Claims for benefit of clergy were not allowed for misdemeanours and in the eighteenth century were prohibited in cases of murder, larceny and house-breaking. Benefit of clergy was rescinded piecemeal in the eighteenth century and abolished outright in the nineteenth (9 Geo. IV, c. 54, 1828).

bent grass. A shore grass which binds sand and prevents drifting. Bent or Marram grass was formerly employed for a variety of domestic purposes. As thatching material marram was not long-lasting and required regular maintenance. Lengths of braided marram stitched together were used as ceiling material to prevent soot and other small bits of roof debris falling on members of the household as they slept. More commonly marram matting did service as carpeting.

bere (also bare, bear). Coarse barley.

besant. A silver coin used in the middle ages worth between one and two shillings.

Bessborough Commission (1880). A royal commission under the chairmanship of the earl of Bessborough tasked with investigating the working of Gladstone's flawed **Landlord and Tenant (Ireland) Act (1870)**. Gladstone's act had introduced a tenant-purchase scheme, legalised **tenant-right** wherever it existed and provided for compensation for improvements or disturbance. Bessborough's key recommendation, the concession of fair rent, free sale and fixity of tenure – led to the enactment of the **1881 Land Law (Ireland) Act** which gave statutory recognition to the **'Three F's'**. (Bessborough.)

betagh. (L., *betagius*, Ir., *biatach*, provider of food) 1: Serf, servile tenant on a manor, the lowest social group in the economy of Anglo-Norman Ireland. These were the most numerous group within a manor's population. They were **bondsmen**, almost invariably Irish and were similar to the unfree **villeins** of medieval England. They were unable to seek redress in the king's courts except through their lord and usually lived in a nucleated settlement some distance from the manor. *See* advowry 2: The Gaelic law texts describe betaghs as base clients who contracted to provide the lord with food-rent, winter hospitality (**cuddy**), manual labour and military service in return for an advance of livestock or land. The contractual nature of the relationship meant that the betagh could withdraw from the agreement provided he returned the lord's advance with deductions for the services he had already supplied. Thus the liberty of the betagh in the Gaelic system was not as circumscribed as that of the betagh on a Norman manor. (Mac Niocaill, 'Origins', pp. 292–8.)

Betham, Sir William (1779–1853). Sir William Betham, **Ulster king of arms**, supervised the construction of an alphabetical index to wills proved in the **prerogative court**, produced brief genealogical abstracts (over 37,000) of most of the wills that pre-dated 1800 and extracted outline pedigrees from them. Betham's industry assumed enormous importance with the large-scale destruction of original testamentary material in the Public Record Office (now **National Archives**) in 1922. His original notebooks were acquired by the Public Record Office with the exception of volumes of pedigrees which can be seen at the Genealogical Office. (Phair, 'Sir William Betham', pp. 1–99; *Guide to the Genealogical Office*.)

bettimore. (Ir., *beiteáil*) The paring and burning of sods in marginal areas to increase the fertility of the soil. This practice resulted in temporary improvements in yield but the land quickly returned to infertility. *See* paring and burning.

bill. *See* civil bill.

birnie, byrnie. An early version of the chain mail shirt, forerunner to the hauberk.

Birrell's Act (1909). *See* Irish Land Act (1909).

Births, Deaths and Marriages, Registry of. Although non-Catholic marriages were registered by the state from 1845, official registration of all births, deaths and marriages for the entire population began in 1864 with the establishment of the Registry of Births, Deaths and Marriages (26 & 27 Vict., c. 11). Births, deaths and marriages were registered in the dispensary district of the **poor law union** in which they occurred, the registrar usually being the medical officer for the district. A superintendent registrar gathered in the returns for the entire union and these were collated and indexed at the General Register Office in Dublin. Only the master indexes are available for public scrutiny at the General Register Office. A small payment is made for a copy of the full entry. (Kinealy, *Tracing*, pp. 13–16.)

black oath. An oath imposed on all Presbyterians in Ulster in 1639 by Lord Deputy Wentworth requiring them to abjure the **Solemn League and Covenant** and swear allegiance to Charles I.

Black Rod. Chief usher of the **house of lords**, so called after the ebony rod carried as symbol of his office. Black Rod's function was to keep order within the house, a role not dissimilar to that performed by Sergeant-at-Arms in the commons. At the opening of **parliament** he was dispatched (as he is today at Westminster) to summon the members of the commons to the house of lords for the opening address.

blackrent. Rent or tribute illegally extorted most commonly by Gaelic chiefs on English marchers in return for protection or agreement to desist from plunder.

blazon. 1: In heraldry, a shield 2: A verbal description of heraldic arms.

Blood's Conspiracy (1663). The plot conceived by disgruntled Protestants (including at least seven members of parliament) to seize Dublin Castle and ignite an uprising throughout the country. The source of their disaffection lay in the **Act of Settlement** (1662) which provided for the restoration to their former estates of Catholics innocent of complicity in the 1641 rebellion. Alarmed at the numbers being restored by the **court of claims** and fearing the loss of their own newly-acquired estates, the conspirators, led by Thomas Blood, assembled in Dublin in March 1663. The administration appears to have been forewarned of the plan which fizzled out when an innkeeper's wife became suspicious of the gathering in Thomas Street. A small number were executed and the parliamentarians were expelled from the house of commons. Blood's later lack of success as an assassin (the Duke of Ormond, 1670) and as a jewel thief (the crown jewels, 1671) appear not to have damaged him in the eyes of the crown. The pardon and grant of land he received from Charles II fuelled suspicions that he had been a spy for many years.

blimp. An airship. The term derives from its designation as type B-limp dirigible. Blimps were employed along Ireland's east coast from 1918 as anti-submarine escorts for cross-channel shipping.

blue books. The official British **parliamentary papers** which include house of commons sessional papers, select committee reports and royal commissions, so called because so many of them, particularly the larger ones, were bound in dark blue covers. Many, in fact, were bound in buff.

bluesay. A light, delicate woollen or serge cloth. Also known as 'say'.

bó-aire. (Ir., cow nobleman?) 1: A prosperous farmer. 2: The head of a *creaght*.

Board of Works (1831). The Board of Works was constituted out of an eighteenth century institution, 'the Barrack Board and Board of Works', whose military division was responsible for quartering the army in Ireland. It also had a civil division which maintained Dublin Castle, the Viceregal Lodge and the **Four Courts**. In the early years of the nineteenth century public money under the supervision of the **lord lieutenant** was voted for the improvement of inland navigation, fisheries and public works such as roads or bridges and to provide employment during periods of hardship. *See* **Inland Navigation, Directors General of.** From 1831 the new Board of Works, staffed with a national inspectorate of engineers, retained these functions but was also given the remit to oversee relief works, drainage, and to maintain public buildings, ports and harbours. The board supplied the majority of members and influenced the conclusions of many committees and commissions established to consider the state's role in infrastructural development. In turn it was charged with the regulation of land use and granted the power to levy those who benefited from drainage schemes. By 1845 it had spent over £1 million in grants and loans. During the famine the board supervised massive public works schemes, employing in excess of 600,000 people daily on road construction and drainage in the winter of 1846–7. These works were shut down when soup kitchens were opened to relieve the distressed who, in any case, were often too debilitated to work on the roads. Under the 1870 **Landlord and Tenant Act** the Board of Works was mandated a role in Gladstone's tenant-purchase scheme, providing loans of up to two-thirds of the price of the holding conditional upon the payment over 35 years of the sale price plus an annuity of 5%. In 1881 the tenant-purchase scheme was transferred to the **Irish Land Commission.** Late in the nineteenth century the Board of Works loaned money for the construction of farm buildings and labourers' cottages and for land improvement. It arbitrated between landlords and the railway companies over the acquisition of land for tracks, was responsible for the maintenance of national monuments and constructed harbours and piers. The Board of Works was re-styled the Office of Public Works after the establishment of the Irish Free State in 1922. (Griffith, *The Irish board*; Lohan, *Guide to the archives*; McParland, *Public architecture*.)

bobbin. Tightly-bound twists of straw arranged in a decorative row along the ridge of a thatched roof.

bog. Irish bogs are broadly classified as either raised bogs or blanket bogs. Raised bogs developed in lowland areas and are raised above the level of the surrounding countryside. They were formed between 7,000 and 10,000 years ago as a result of fen growth on the periphery of post-glacial lakes, through silting and the accumulated deposition of debris from water-living plants. As the fen expanded the lakes gradually shrank and a layer of peat was built up. Sphagnum moss, which thrives on the small amounts of nutrients in peaty soils and rainwater, colonised the surface of the peat in hummocks thus creating a raised effect. Blanket bogs, which appeared about 5,000 years ago largely in upland areas in the west, are believed to have formed because of a deterioration in climate, the clearance of woods and agricultural activity. The impact of natural forces and human intervention resulted in leaching and the creation of a layer of iron pan just below the soil surface. This impeded drainage and the resultant waterlogging encouraged an invasion by rushes, the creation of peat and, later, colonisation by sphagnum moss. Continued waterlogging triggered the spread of the bog so that, in time, wide areas of land were blanketed in a layer of peat. (Mitchell, *The Shell guide*, pp. 122–29.)

bonaght. *See buannacht.*

bona notabilia. In testamentary matters, the case of a person who died possessing goods to the value of £5 or more in a second diocese. In such cases jurisdiction lay not with the diocesan **consistorial court** but with the **prerogative court** of the archbishop of Armagh.

bondsmen. Unfree tenants such as villeins, serfs or **betaghs**.

bonnyclabber. (Ir., *bainne clabair*) Sour, curdled milk which constituted part of the native Irish diet. It was made by adding rennet from the stomach of a calf to milk, causing it to coagulate.

booley. (Ir., *buaile*, a temporary milking place) An enclosure on the summer pasture lands where cattle were milked. Also known as a shieling or bothy. Booley, bothy or shieling huts were constructed to accommodate the herdsmen and women who accompanied the herds. Booleying (transhumance) was a feature of the **rundale** system.

boon work. Unpaid manorial labour service such as ploughing or harvesting owed to the lord by tenants.

bord alexander. A kind of striped silk fabric used for altar cloths and vestments.

bordure. In heraldry, a border round an **escutcheon**. A bordure is a mark of cadency (descent of a younger or cadet branch from the main family line) or, anciently, a mark of bastardy.

borers. Narrow flint flakes, chipped on one or both edges and brought to a sharp point, probably serving to make stitch-holes in leather.

borough. A town conferred with corporation status by a royal charter which also guaranteed the right to self-government. Prior to 1603 they numbered 55 in Ireland. James I enfranchised a further 46 to further the programme of plantation and to secure a Protestant parliamentary majority. Between them Charles I and Charles II added a further 16. The importance of the boroughs lay not in the civic duties they performed – which beyond providing the senior officials in the quarter-sessions, small debt and misdemeanour courts were negligible – but in their role in the election of members of parliament. From the seventeenth century 117 boroughs sent 234 MPs to an Irish house of commons composed of 300 members, thereby giving rise to the comment that the Irish legislature was a 'borough parliament'.

Many boroughs were tiny insignificant places, with few or no inhabitants. Harristown, Co. Kildare, for example, had no houses. Others were large and heavily populated but, as McCracken observes, size was irrelevant. It was the nature of the franchise that mattered. A large town like Belfast whose parliamentary representation was determined solely by a corporation of about one dozen burgesses was just as rotten as Harristown. The elective procedure by which members were sent to parliament varied considerably. In the eight **county boroughs** the electorate included the members of the corporation, the (often nonresident) freemen and the (largely fictitious) forty-shilling freeholders. In the 12 '**potwalloping**' **boroughs** the franchise was vested in £5 householders (including Catholics from 1793) who had resided in the constituency for six months (one year from 1782). Tightly controlled by their manorial lord, a tiny electorate of Protestant freeholders and resident householders sent 12 members to parliament from six **manor boroughs**. Each of the remaining 91 boroughs, Londonderry excepted, was controlled by a patron or patrons. The 55 corporation boroughs contained no freemen and the electorate comprised 12 or 13 burgesses. In the 36 freeman boroughs the freemen as well as the members of the corporation voted.

Catholics were excluded from borough membership by law from 1691 and the franchise remained exclusively Protestant until 1793. Protestant dissenters retained the franchise and could sit in parliament but were denied membership of the boroughs between 1704 and 1780 by the provisions of the **Test Act**. The **Act of Union** severely curbed the elective power of the boroughs, only 33 of which survived with that right intact. By drastically altering the weighting of Irish representation from the boroughs to the counties, the union also paved the way for the Catholic vote to become effective. Nevertheless, the corporations remained exclusively Anglican until the reforms of 1840. *See* franchise, freeman, Municipal Corporations Reform Act (1840), Newtown Act, rotten borough.

bote. Literally, compensation, bote was the right of a tenant to procure timber from the manorial woods for a variety of purposes. It was often incorporated into leases. *See* cartbote, estovers, haybote, houbote and ploughbote.

bothach. (Ir., *both*, a hut) A **cottier.** The Gaelic equivalent of a **villein** or unfree tenant.

bothy. (Ir., *both*, a hut) A rough dwelling or hut on the summer pasture lands, also known as a booley-hut.

'bottle riot'. Orange resentment at prohibitions on 12 July demonstrations and the October dressing of King William's statue lay behind the hissing and abuse visited on Arthur Wellesley, the viceroy, when he attended a performance of *She Stoops to Conquer* in the New Theatre Royal in Dublin in December 1822. During the performance a number of objects, including a bottle, were thrown at the viceregal box inducing Wellesley to believe that a conspiracy to murder him was afoot. The miscreants were apprehended and arraigned on a conspiracy charge rather than for riotous behaviour but the Orange grand jury of Dublin threw it out. Wellesley clearly overreacted to the 'bottle riot' but the episode effectively ended Williamite demonstrations in Dublin. (O'Ferrall, *Catholic emancipation*, pp. 13–15.)

bouchot. (Fr.) A method of mussel culture consisting of a series of upright poles in the sea on which mussel spat settles and matures.

boulder burial. A burial site consisting of a large boulder supported by a number of smaller stones. A shallow pit containing cremated remains lies beneath.

boundary cross. A map symbol used by early cartographers to denote the junction of three properties.

box bed. A canopied bed with closed sides and sometimes hinged doors.

boycott. The practice of isolating and ostracising any tenant who took over the holding of an evicted tenant, so called after Captain Hugh Cunningham Boycott, agent to the earl of Erne in Co. Mayo from 1873, who clashed with the **Land League** in 1880 and whose name became a synonym for social isolation. The principle of the boycott, the eschewing of all social and economic contact with anyone who transgressed a particular code, had been employed in the 1790s by the **Rightboys** and in the 1820s by supporters of Catholic emancipation.

Boyne Societies. Early eighteenth-century, semi-secret Protestant defence and social clubs, initially composed of Williamite veterans, which operated in areas of strong Protestant settlement and together with the *posse comitatus* functioned as an unofficial local defence network until 1715 when a county **militia** was regularised. Boyne societies with their grades, rituals, passwords and signs were, to all intents and purposes, an Orange freemasonry. Their recognition signals derived from incidents associated with the Williamite War and society ceremonies were heavily influenced by Old Testament stories such as the Exodus, the Red Sea crossing and the wandering in the desert. The Orange Order was formed in imitation of the Boyne Societies. (Haddick-Flynn, *Orangeism*, pp. 100–107.)

brace. A cross-beam supporting the chimney-breast or canopy.

bread and ale, assize of. An ordinance defining the quantity and quality of bread and ale within a **liberty**. Short measures or deficiency in quality rendered the vendor liable to fines.

breakens. (Ir., *breacán*) A plaid.

Brehon law. (Ir., *breith*, a judgement) The complex Gaelic legal system which survived into the seventeenth century. It was rooted in ancient Celtic law and leavened with borrowings from canon law after the island was Christianised. The principal law tracts derive from the seventh century and were produced in Brehon 'law schools'. Although they claimed to express the laws of Ireland, the tribalised nature of Irish society ensured that interpretation varied regionally. Brehon law was characteristically local and private – unlike English common law which was supported and diffused by a centralised administrative authority – but, like all legal systems, it was conservative, protected the status quo and favoured those with high social standing. Gaelic society was divided into the free (*sóer*) and the unfree (*dóer*) which corresponded to nobles, men of learning and craftsmen on the one hand and serfs on the other. Compensation was the chief means of righting a wrong and the level of compensation was determined by social standing and the possession of property. Disputes were arbitrated by brehons on the basis of equity and precedence, pledges having first been taken from both parties to ensure that the arbitration would be accepted. Contract rather than tenure was the basis of Brehon property law and contracts were accompanied by sureties as a guarantee that contractual obligations would be fulfilled. The local administration of Brehon law was a matter for the wider kin group, the *derbfine*, to which certain rights and obligations were attached. The kin group, for example, was liable for the compensation payments of a defaulting family member as it was for exacting compensation if one of its members was slain or unable to prosecute in his own right. Land owned by the kin group was divided partibly among the male heirs or devolved as a life estate to the daughters where the male line failed. Subsequently, however, it reverted to the kin group. *See éiric*, kincogish, *tánaiste*, tanistry. (Kelly, *A guide*.)

bressumer. A brace or horizontal beam spanning a large opening and supporting the upper wall.

bretasche. A temporary wooden gallery (brattice) mounted on the battlements of a castle as an additional defence during a siege. The term is also used to refer to the wooden towerhouse erected atop a motte. *See* motte and bailey.

Breteuil, law of. A set of privileges named after the Norman town of Breteuil where it first emerged as a custom. Its principal features included the granting of **burgage** holdings at a fixed annual rent of one shilling, freedom of **alienation** of burgages, a low fixed fine for all but the gravest offences, the limitation of the period for which the lord might have credit, the right of burgesses to own their own **hundred court** and to enjoy a share in common fields. The lord could exact neither **wardship** nor **marriage** and restrictions were placed on the duration of imprisonment of burgesses. Such privileges were usually offered as enticements to lure settlers to Ireland.

bridewell. Originally the name of a sixteenth-century London prison, the term came to describe a prison, a prison for vagrants or a house of correction.

Bright clauses. Provisions in Gladstone's **Landlord and Tenant Act (1870)** which enabled tenants to purchase their holdings in the **Landed Estates Court** with the assistance of an advance of two-thirds of the purchase price from the **Board of Works**. The loan was to be repaid over 35 years at 5%. The scheme was conceived by John Bright who had prompted similar provisions in the earlier **Irish Church Act** (1869).

British Relief Association. A philanthropic society founded in January 1847 to relieve distress in remote areas of Ireland and Scotland. About £470,000 was raised in England, America and Australia, a considerable portion of which derived from subscribers responding to the issuing of a 'Queen's Letter' in which Queen Victoria appealed for aid for Ireland. Victoria herself contributed £2,000. Unlike the Quakers, the British Relief Association did not establish an administrative structure in Ireland to disburse aid. It chose to channel its funds through the British treasury which loaned and granted money to the most distressed unions. Count Strzelecki, the association's Irish agent, clashed with Charles Trevelyan, the treasury secretary, over the manner in which the money was distributed but succeeded in diverting only a small proportion of the funds towards feeding needy schoolchildren in the west. Trevelyan's control over the destination of aid was unfortunate in that he was able to apply it for purposes that would otherwise have required exchequer funding. By autumn 1848 – when the need for relief was increasing – the association's funds were all but exhausted and it began to wind up its Irish operation. As well as feeding schoolchildren, the British Relief Association aided 22 distressed unions and part-aided a further 25. (Kinealy, *This great calamity*, pp. 161–2 *passim*.)

broadcast. The sowing of seed by hand.

Brotherhood of Arms of St George. A force established by the Irish parliament in 1474 comprising thirteen nobles, 120 archers and forty horse to assist in the defence of the Pale. To finance the force a tax of twelve pence in the pound (**poundage**) was imposed on goods being transported into and out of Ireland. This short-lived force was abolished in the 1490s.

Brunswick constitutional clubs. Rabidly anti-Catholic clubs which appeared following O'Connell's by-election victory in Clare in 1828. They were opposed to the granting of **Catholic emancipation** and committed to the belief that only through solidarity and unity could Protestant interests be safeguarded. The name was taken from the duke of Brunswick who presided at a dinner at which the idea for such clubs was first floated. They were a mirror image of the **Catholic Association** even to the extent of collecting a 'Protestant rent'. About 200 clubs were formed with a largely aristocratic membership. Brunswick clubs replaced the lodges of the **Orange Order** which had been outlawed in 1825 along with the Catholic Association under the Unlawful Societies Act (6 Geo. IV, c. 4). After the granting of Catholic emancipation the clubs gradually declined as the Orange Order (legal again since the expiration in 1828 of the Unlawful Societies Act) became the vehicle through which anti-Catholic feeling was channelled. (Haddick-Flynn, *Orangeism*, pp. 231–3, 235; O'Ferrall, *Catholic emancipation*, pp. 207–209.)

buannacht, bonnacht, bonnaught, bonaght. (Ir.) The free quartering of mercenaries on the country by a Gaelic lord as a cost-free stratagem for retaining a standing force. In the sixteenth century the quartering of troops was replaced by a tax (bonaght beg) which was proportionally levied on every **ploughland**. English commentators often confused the terminology so that the mercenaries themselves became known as bonaghts. *Buannacht* was known and employed as **coyne and livery** within the Pale. *See* coshering.

buckram. Coarse linen cloth stiffened with glue.

budge, buge. Lambskin fur with the wool outwards which was used to trim jackets.

bulk. A ship's cargo.

bulk, to break. To unload or partially unload a ship's cargo.

bulkies. A municipally-controlled police force which operated in Belfast from 1816 until 1865 when it was abolished and its policing duties assumed by the Irish Constabulary. (Griffin, *The bulkies*.)

bullaun. (Ir., *bollán*, a small bowl) A **quern** or stone containing a bowl-shaped depression into which grain was poured and ground with a stone pestle.

bundle. Of linen yarn, 60,000 yards.

bundling. A custom which enabled an engaged couple to sleep together and enjoy the comfort and warmth of the marriage bed but without engaging in sexual intercourse.

bungal. (Ir., *bonn geal*, white groat) A Tudor silver **groat** known in Irish as a *bonn geal* and anglicised as 'bungal'.

burials. After the Reformation Catholics continued to be buried in their local graveyards although by law these were now in the custody of the Established church. Until 1824 it was believed by some Protestants that Catholic and dissenter burial services were prohibited in **Church of Ireland** graveyards and the only service that could be performed was that prescribed by the *Book of Common Prayer*. By 9 Will. III, c. 1 (1697) burials within the precincts of former monasteries, abbeys or convents where divine service was not celebrated were forbidden but in rural areas this was ignored. In the cities Catholics were interred in their local graveyards and had prayers recited over their graves by Catholic priests. Local Protestant ministers raised no objections to this practice because they received burial fees without having to perform a service. In September 1823, at the instigation of the archbishop of Dublin, the sexton of St Kevin's church in Dublin, intervened in the burial of Arthur D' Arcy to forbid the recitation of graveside prayers by a priest. Catholics were outraged and a government attempt to legislate its way out of the embarrassment with the Easement of Burials Act (5 Geo. IV, c. 25, 15 April 1824) actually worsened the situation. The **Catholic Association** attacked as intolerable the provision that non-Anglican clergymen must apply to the Church of Ireland minister for permission to assist at gravesides and embarked on a campaign to purchase distinctly Catholic burial sites. Within a few years both Goldenbridge (1829) and Glasnevin (1832) were operative and Church of Ireland ministers were left to rue the sexton's meddling as the well of burial fees dried up. (FitzPatrick, *History*; O'Brien and Dunne, *Catholic Ireland*, p. 51.)

burgage. The holding of a **burgess**, recognisable by a narrow street frontage and a long narrow garden behind the house.

burgess. A town inhabitant or citizen of a **borough** with full citizenship rights. Statute conferred a considerable array of privileges on burgesses, the most important of which included the granting of burgage holdings at an annual rent of one shilling per annum, the right of burgesses to own their own **hundred court** and the entitlement to a share in common fields. This set of privileges was known as the law of **Breteuil**. The offer of burgess status during periods of colonisation was probably a lure to attract settlers. Members of municipal corporations, usually to the number of 12 or 13, were also known as burgesses and possessed important privileges in relation to the election of parliamentary representatives. *See* borough.

burning and paring. *See* bettimore.

buddachan. (Ir.) A measure of oysters containing 360 oysters. One bushel contained two-and-a-half buddachans and weighed one hundredweight.

bushel. A measure of capacity and weight characterised by great regional diversity. In terms of capacity the bushel is equivalent to four **pecks**, eight gallons or 32.239 litres. The imperial bushel, established in 1826, contains 80 pounds liquid measure or 60 pounds in weight, the Tudor Winchester bushel slightly less at 77.6 pounds. *See* barrel.

butt. A cask for wine or ale, the capacity of which varied according to the commodity. A butt of ale contained 108 to 140 gallons whereas a butt of wine contained 126 gallons. Two hogsheads were equivalent to a butt or pipe and two butts or pipes were equivalent to a **tun**.

butlerage. *See* prisage.

buying. *See* ceannuigheacht.

byre dwelling. A one-roomed house in which animals are stabled at one end and people inhabit the other. Known as a 'long house' in England. (O'Neill, *Life*, pp. 12–13.)

C

c. *See* cap.

cadastral. Of or having to do with the extent, boundaries, value and ownership of real property. Cadastral surveys such as **Griffith's Valuation** were conducted for taxation purposes.

caddow. A coarse, woollen blanket or covering.

cairn. A mound of stones heaped over a prehistoric tomb.

caiseal. A **rath** or ring-fort enclosed by a bank or banks of stone and usually located in areas of stony ground. Also known as a *cathair*.

calabar, calaber. The fur of a red squirrel.

calendar. 1: Roman. There were twelve months in the Roman calendar, each of which was subdivided into calends, ides and nones. Calends was always the first day of the month and nones the ninth day before ides counting both days. As ides fell on either the thirteenth (all months except March, May, July or October) or the fifteenth, nones always fell on the fifth or seventh. Dates were reckoned according to the number of days forward to each one. Thus, IV Non. Jan. was 2 January, nones being the fifth. Calends was reckoned in relation to the next month, III Kal. Jan. being 30 December 2: Gregorian. In 1752 the inaccurate Julian calendar was replaced in Britain and

Ireland by the Gregorian calendar which had been operative in Catholic Europe since 1582. The adoption of the Gregorian calendar was attended by two significant adjustments. The discrepancy between the Julian and Gregorian calendars was resolved by advancing the calendar 11 days and the civil and religious year was reconfigured to commence on 1 January rather than 25 March. This latter change has historiographical implications in terms of dating events prior to 1752. To avoid confusion historians normally cite the year according to new style and the day and month according to the old. Thus a contemporary document dated the 15 February 1641 (old style) is modernised as 15 February 1642 (new style). An alternative is to write 15 February 1641/2. See regnal years 3: A chronologically-arranged catalogue or repertory of abstracts of documents (and sometimes documents in their entirety) which serves as an index or finding aid for documents of a given period.

Calendar of state papers relating to Ireland. A 24 volume series containing abstracts of selected correspondence largely from officials in Ireland to the king and organs of government in England for the period 1509–1670. The originals can be found in the State Papers Ireland collection (SP60–63, SP65) in the Public Record Office, London, and on microfilm in the National Library, Dublin. Correspondence for the period 1671–1704 is included in the 81 volume *Calendar of state papers, domestic*. (*Calendar of state papers; Calendar of state papers preserved*.)

calends. See calendar, Roman.

caliver. A light arquebus-type firearm which, unlike the **arquebus**, was not rested on a support or tripod when in use.

calotype. The name given by Charles Fox Talbot to the photographic process invented by him in 1841. Also known as the Talbotype, the photograph was produced by the action of light upon silver iodide, the latent image being subsequently developed and fixed by hyposulphite of soda. The calotype was ousted by Archer's collodium process, paper giving way to glass and a substratum of collodion. (Chandler, *Photography*.)

Calvinism. The doctrines and practices derived from the religious teaching of John Calvin (1509–1564). These include a belief in the superiority of faith over good works, that salvation is achieved solely by the grace of God, that only the elect will be saved (predestination), that the bible is the sole authority for Christian teaching and that all believers are priests. The Calvinist concept of universal priesthood was realised in a presbyterian ministry rather than an episcopal or hierarchical church organisation. See Independents, Presbyterian, *regium donum*, Synod of Ulster.

Cambrensis Eversus. The work of John Lynch (1599–1673), a Catholic priest and historian, *Cambrensis Eversus* (1662) refutes the biased portrayal of Ireland presented by **Topographia Hiberniae** and **Expugnatio Hibernica**, the works of the twelfth-century Pembrokeshire historian, Giraldus Cambrensis (1146–1223). Cambrensis' writings remained in manuscript form until they were published by **William Camden** in 1602. Their publication fuelled existing anti-Irish sentiment in England and attracted a critical response from Geoffrey Keating (1634) and from Lynch who had fled into exile in France in 1652 following the surrender of Galway. Lynch, whose pseudonym was Gratianus Lucis, also published *Alinithologia*, an apologia for those confederates who sided with Ormond against the Rinuccini faction. *See Foras feasa ar Éirinn.*

Cambrensis, Giraldus. *See* **Expugnatio Hibernica** and **Topographia Hiberniae.**

Camden, William (1551–1623). English antiquarian and the author of *Britannia, a topographical survey of Britain and Ireland* (1586 and enlarged later), and *Annales rerum Anglicarum et Hibernicarum regnante Elizabetha*, a two-volume account of the history of Ireland and England under Elizabeth (completed 1617). Only 35 not very reliable pages were dedicated to Ireland in the first edition of *Britannia* but accuracy improved in later editions when Camden was assisted by James Ussher.

Campion, Edmund (1540–81). Campion, an English Jesuit martyr, wrote the *Histories of Ireland* in Dublin in 1569. It was first used by Stanihurst in **Holinshed's Chronicles** (1577) and was published by Sir James Ware in 1633. The work is heavily pro-Old English as one might expect for Campion was a guest of Old English families for two years from 1570–1.

canebeg. (Ir., *cáin beag*, small tax) A small tributary entitlement of the wife of a Gaelic lord out of certain lands.

canon. 1: A priest who lived like a monk 2: In Ireland, a minor member of the cathedral chapter, such as the **vicars choral** but prebendaries were also canons. The canons were responsible for the conduct of religious services in the cathedral 3: A general ecclesiastical rule or decree governing the conduct of public worship 4: The list of acceptable scripture books.

canonical portion. A kind of death duty levied by the church on a deceased woman. The taking of mortuaries on the death of married women was forbidden in 1621.

canting. The auctioning of leases of land by private bids. In nineteenth-century Ireland this encouraged prospective tenants to bid beyond their means.

cantred. A barony. In Irish, **tricha-cét**.

cap. (usually c.). Chapter, as in 23 Vict., cap. 27 which means the twenty-seventh chapter of the statutes enacted in the twenty-third year of the reign of Queen Victoria. *See* regnal years.

capell lands. Gaelic spatial measure. In Kilkenny, three capell lands were equivalent to a **ploughland** or about 100 acres. In Tipperary, the equivalent of 20 great acres, each acre containing 20 English acres. *See* great acre.

capias. A writ commanding the sheriff to perform an arrest or seizure, so-called because the warrant contains the instruction 'That you take' or 'Thou mayest take'. The four forms of *capias* were:

Capias ad respondendum, employed to compel attendance at court.

Capias ad satisfaciendum, after judgement, a warrant to jail a defendant until the plaintiff's claim had been met.

Capias utlagatum, a warrant to arrest an outlaw.

Capias in withernam, a warrant to seize the chattels of a person who has made an illegal **distraint**. *See* witherman.

capital. The head of a column which is located at the top of the shaft.

capital messuage. The manor house.

capite, in. Land held directly from the crown without an intermediary ownership. The tenant was known as a tenant-in-chief or chief tenant and was liable for the **feudal incidents** of **wardship, marriage, relief** and **escheat**. Together with other ancient tenures, tenure *in capite* was abolished in 1662 (12 Chas. II, c. 24) by Charles II. *See* Tenures Abolition Act.

capstone. The flat stone or cover-slab which was supported by a number of large vertical stones and covered in a mound of smaller stones to form a cairn.

Capuchins. An austere, reforming offshoot of the Franciscans, the Capuchins (in full, the Order of Friars Minor Capuchin, abbreviated OFM Cap.) were founded in 1525 and arrived in Ireland in 1615. They were committed to an even stricter adherence to the rule of poverty than the observants. The name derived from the four-cornered hood they wore, the *cappuccio*. *See* conventualism.

Caravats and Shanavests. Two conflicting groups which flourished in Munster and some Leinster counties between 1806–11. Formerly regarded as a faction-fighting phenomenon, the struggles of Caravats and Shanavests is now interpreted as a physical expression of the tension that existed between landless labourers (Caravats) and small farmers (Shanavests). Economic factors such as the collapse of grain prices, a shift from tillage to livestock and a rise in cost and decline in availability of **conacre** land worsened the plight of labourers whose numbers had increased disproportionately since the beginning of the century. The outrages and feuding associated with the Caravats and Shanavests were perpetuated by other secret societies attempting to control conacre rents and improve labourers' wages. *See* Ribbonism, Whiteboys. (Ó Muireadhaigh, 'Na Carabhait', pp. 4–20; Roberts,

'Caravats', pp. 64–101.)

card. 1: To comb wool 2: Carding was a vicious lacerating of the back perpetrated by members of agrarian secret societies against those regarded as enemies. It was inflicted by raking the back with a wool comb. (Beames, *Peasants*, p. 80.)

Carew Manuscripts. A vast archive of documents assembled by Sir George Carew (1555–1629) during his service in Ireland as master of the ordnance and president of Munster. The originals are preserved in Lambeth Palace and the Bodleian Library but many have been calendared. Carew's sojourn in Ireland in the late sixteenth and early seventeenth centuries embraced the period of the Nine Years War, making his papers an invaluable source for the study of the period. (*Calendar of the Carew manuscripts.*)

carrageen. An edible seaweed also used to make jellies, aspics, blancmanges and beverages.

carrow, carrughes. (Ir., *cearrbhach*, a gamester) An itinerant gambler. According to Edmund Spenser, carrows were 'a kind of people that wander up and down to gentlemen's houses, living only upon cards and dice'. In 1571 Sir John Perrot directed that all carrows, bards and rhymers were to forfeit their goods and chattels and be placed in stocks until they had committed themselves by way of surety to forsake their respective trades.

carruca. (Med. L., a plough) A heavy plough with an iron **share, coulter** and **mouldboard** employed in Ireland in areas of English influence during the middle ages.

cartage. 1: The obligation of a tenant or vassal to provide carts for transporting the lord's goods 2: The levying of carts for the transportation of supplies as, for example, when a general **hosting** for the defence of the Pale was declared. In the fifteenth century carts were levied at a rate of one cart for every four **ploughlands**.

cartboote. The right without payment to procure timber from the manorial woods for the purpose of repairing or making carts.

cartouche. An ornamented tablet, usually elliptical, surrounded by scrolls or vines and bearing an inscription or coat of arms.

cartron. A unit of spatial measurement, equivalent to 30 acres in Connacht and 60 acres in Longford. *See* acre.

carucate. (Med.L., *carruca*, a plough) Nominally, the amount of land a team of eight oxen could plough in a year, usually equivalent to 100–120 acres. In 19 Edward III a carucate was declared to be 100 acres but it varied considerably on account of soil quality and could contain up to 180 acres. Also known as a **villate** or **ploughland.**

cashel. *See caiseal, cathair.*

cassock. The black outer garment or frock worn by a clergymen.

cast. 1: Equivalent to three fish. Forty-two casts were equivalent to a

hundred (126) and five hundreds were equivalent to a **mease** (630) 2: In falconry, refers to a couple of hawks which is the number of hawks released or cast off at a time.

castle chamber, court of (Star Chamber). The court of castle chamber was a **prerogative court** rather than one based on common law procedures. It commenced operations in the sixteenth century, the first clerk of the court being appointed in 1563. It was a juryless, inquisitorial court, formally presided over by the **chief governor** with the assistance of the **lord chancellor** and exercised jurisdiction over serious infringements of the law such as official corruption, treason, riot, perjury, libel, fraud, forgery, refusal to produce **recusants** and conspiracies. Such offences were outside the remit of the regular courts and affected good government and the administration of the law. Castle chamber was a popular and speedy court and less expensive to litigants than the regular courts. As a court associated with the royal prerogative it attracted the wrath of parliament and was abolished in England by the Long Parliament. It was never formally abolished in Ireland but lapsed during the **Commonwealth**. Attempts were made to revive it after the Restoration but the house of commons objected and it simply disappeared. The officers of the court continued to draw their salaries until 1701. (*Report on the manuscripts of the Earl of Egmont*; Crawford 'Origins'; Wood, 'The court'.)

cathair. (Ir.) A stone-built open fortress or *caiseal*.

cathedral. The church of the bishop of a **diocese**. The cathedral and its revenues were administered by a **chapter** which in the provinces of Dublin and Cashel usually comprised a **dean, precentor, chancellor, treasurer, archdeacon** and **prebendaries** but which elsewhere had regressed to a simpler form. The actual work of the cathedral was carried out by the **vicars choral,** usually four in number, wherever they existed. The cathedral and its officials were supervised by the dean who also presided as head of the chapter. Most cathedral offices had their corps, a parish or number of parishes whose revenues went to the cathedral officials. Some benefices were highly lucrative and therefore greatly prized. In return, the cathedral officials preached or acted as parish priests in the relevant parish or parishes. In some cases the spiritual duties were performed by a curate or vicar; in others the benefice had no **cure of souls** and the office was a sinecure. The chapter administered the rents and leases which pertained to the cathedral. Revenue accrued from the corporate lands and the rectorial **tithe** (the great tithe) of certain parishes and was held in the common or economy fund for the maintenance of the fabric of the cathedral. After the Reformation Irish cathedrals came under the control of the Church of Ireland and throughout the seventeenth and eighteenth centuries Catholic bishops were compelled to adopt a cautious attitude towards church-building. Catholic chapters were essentially diocesan advisory councils

Catholic Association. Two bodies bore this name. The first was founded in 1756 and represented Catholic commercial and landed interests. It enjoyed a brief existence before being superseded by the **Catholic Committee** from 1760. The second, a popular political pressure group, was founded on 12 May 1823 by Daniel O'Connell and Richard Lalor Shiel to win political representation for Catholics and gain access for them to government positions. Specifically it aimed to adopt 'all such legal and constitutional measures as may be most useful to obtain Catholic emancipation'. The annual membership fee was one guinea and, inevitably, membership was largely confined to the middle class. The groundwork for a broader and more popular base was laid in January 1824 when O'Connell introduced an associate membership which could be had for as little as one penny per month (**Catholic rent**). The collection of fees required the association to organise on a local basis. Local branches, with the enthusiastic support of Catholic clergymen who publicised the rent scheme, organised meetings and petitions and corresponded with the central committee. Their proceedings were regularly reported upon in the newspapers. The Catholic Association campaigned in elections and on issues such as **tithe**, the tolerance shown towards Orange outrages, patronage, education and the administration of justice. It disbanded briefly in 1825 when **Goulborn's Act** outlawed bodies campaigning for church or state reformation but re-appeared within days with a new set of aims purged of political content. The association proceeded to campaign for a census of the Catholic population, a liberal education system, public peace and charity. The great breakthrough came in the Clare by-election of 1828 when O'Connell successfully defeated William Vesey Fitzgerald by 2,057 votes to 982. By law O'Connell was entitled to seek election but was disbarred from taking his seat by the nature of the oath he was required to swear to do so. O'Connell's stunning victory made the emancipation of Catholics inevitable and relief legislation was duly enacted in April 1829. See Catholic emancipation. (O'Ferrall, *Catholic emancipation*; O'Hagan, 'Catholic Association', pp. 58– 61.)

Catholic Committee. The name borne by an eighteenth- and early nineteenth-century moderate body which attempted to ameliorate the position of Catholics in Ireland. It sprang from the earlier **Catholic Association** and was founded in 1760 by John Curry, Charles O'Conor and Thomas Wyse. The committee sought relief for Catholics by addresses to the crown and played a prominent role in the campaign to break the monopoly of the Protestant trade guilds. Initially the Catholic landed gentry were the driving force behind the movement but these were later edged aside by the more aggressive Catholic business and professional classes. John Keogh, a Catholic tradesman, rose to prominence in the association and with Wolfe Tone as its secretary the committee began to flex some muscle. By 1791–2 it was pressing for Catholic enfranchisement. A delegation was dispatched to London to meet Pitt who promised no obstruction to Catholic enfranchisement if the Irish parliament wished to proceed along those lines. The response of the Irish parliament, however, was a pitiful Catholic relief bill in 1792 which went no distance towards answering the franchise demand. Hobart's Catholic Relief Act of 1793 (*See* relief acts), a response to a delegation dispatched from a representative national convention organised by the Catholic Committee in Dublin, proved more substantial in that Catholics were permitted to vote as forty-shilling freeholders in the counties and free boroughs, to bear arms, to become members of corporations, to serve as grand jurors, to take degrees in Dublin University, to hold minor offices and to take commissions in the army below the rank of general. The concession of participation in urban corporations proved a dead letter since it depended on the willingness of the corporations to enlarge their franchise and almost all refused to do so. Catholics also remained excluded from parliament and from senior offices such as lord lieutenant and lord chancellor. Nevertheless, the Catholic Committee dissolved itself in gratitude. It was revived in 1809 and hoped to avoid the **Convention Act** by claiming that its purpose was to draw up a petition and not to challenge parliament. Under pressure from the government it again dissolved and re-emerged as the Catholic Board (1811), made up of named individuals to avoid all claims to representative status. It dissolved finally in June 1814 when the Convention Act was again invoked. *See* Catholic Convention, guilds, Municipal Corporations Reform Act, quarterage. (Edwards, 'The minute book', pp. 3–170.)

Catholic Confederacy. In October 1642, a year after the outbreak of war, **Old English** and native Irish Catholics combined to form an alliance known as the Catholic Confederacy or Confederate Catholics of Ireland. They insisted they were loyal to the crown but determined to secure religious freedom and a role in the government of Ireland. According to the confederate oath of association they aimed to restore the rights of the church, maintain the royal prerogative and defend the liberties of the nation. The confederates established an independent assembly in Kilkenny to govern those parts of the country that had come under Catholic control. A supreme council was appointed, taxes were raised, a mint was established and a printing press set up. The confederate army, though large, was poorly equipped, badly trained and lacked a unified command. Provincial commanders were unable or unwilling to co-operate in the field and failed to take military advantage of the pitiful state of royalist forces throughout the decade. A history of long-standing distrust made the alliance of Old English and native Irish inherently unstable. The Old English dominated the supreme council and sought a speedy conclusion to the war. They were willing to compromise since they realised a parliamentary victory in England spelt ruin for Catholic landowners. The native Irish, having lost their lands in earlier confiscations, had little to lose and wished to press on. An agreement to cease hostilities in 1643 split the alliance and relations deteriorated further in 1646 over the terms of a treaty proposed by Ormond. The supreme council and Old English nobility agreed to provide the king with an army of 10,000 men in return for the abolition of the court of wards, the substitution of an oath of allegiance for the oath of supremacy, the admission of Catholics to all civil and military offices and the lifting of restrictions on Catholic education. Rinuccini, the papal nuncio, and the native Irish demurred. They rejected the proposal for its failure to restore Catholicism. The success of the clerical faction convinced Ormond that any terms that he would find acceptable would be rejected by Rinuccini and he began to make preparations to transfer Dublin to the parliamentary forces. The military and political situation became chaotic in 1648 with Ormond's departure from Ireland. The army was mauled by parliamentary forces, the confederacy split along ethnic lines and the factions went to war with each other. When the dust settled in January 1649, Rinuccini was sidelined and, with episcopal approval, the confederates had signed up to a treaty with the newly-returned Ormond that differed little from that of 1646. Having lasted for seven years, the confederacy was now formally dissolved and Ormond became the leader of anti-parliamentary forces in Ireland. Although he failed to take Dublin in June 1649, the bulk of the island remained in royalist hands. The arrival of Cromwell in August, however, signalled the beginning of the end for confederate hopes. *See* cessation, *Commentarius Rinuccinianus*. (Cregan, 'The Confederate Catholics', pp. 490–512; Gilbert, *History of the Irish Confederation*; Ohlmeyer (ed.), *Ireland*; Ó Siochrú, *Confederate Ireland*.)

Catholic Convention (1792). In December 1792 the **Catholic Committee** convened a representative national assembly in Dublin to draw up a petition for the removal of disabilities imposed on Catholics by the **penal laws**. Membership of the assembly was determined by an election process conducted on a nationwide basis. One or two delegates from among 'the most respectable persons' were chosen by Catholics in each parish to go forward to county meetings where delegates to the national assembly were selected. Over 200 members assembled in Back Lane (hence the phrase 'Back Lane Parliament') on 3 December and agreed to a generalised petition for Catholic emancipation and a specific request for concessions on the **franchise** and membership of the **grand jury**. Suspicious of the Irish administration, the convention by-passed the **lord lieutenant** and presented the petition to George III directly. Many Protestants, both within and without parliament, reacted angrily to the assembly and its petition yet a substantial Catholic relief bill followed. In early 1793 most of the disabilities were removed although Catholics remained excluded from parliament. See Catholic Committee, relief acts. (O'Flaherty, 'The Catholic Convention', pp. 14–34.)

Catholic Defence Association. Founded in the 1850s as a response to the **Ecclesiastical Titles Act** (14 & 15 Vict. c. 60, 1851) which proposed to infringe the liberty of the Catholic church, the Catholic Defence Association comprised a group of Irish liberal MPs who proceeded to campaign for the repeal of the act. They allied themselves with the **Tenant League** by including the Tenant League campaign for lower rents and **tenant-right** within their programme. Pledged to pursue an independent policy in the house of commons and boosted by clerical support, the association returned 48 members to parliament in 1852 but was riven by the acceptance of posts in the new Whig-Peelite administration by two of its leading members, William Keogh and John Sadleir. The alliance was reduced to 26 members in 1853 and to a dozen two years later. It finally collapsed over an 1859 Conservative parliamentary reform bill. (Larkin, *The making of the Roman Catholic Church*, pp. 99–100 *passim*.)

Catholic Emancipation. The phrase used from the 1790s to express the demand of Irish Catholics for the right to sit in parliament, to be members of the **privy council**, to hold senior governmental positions and to become king's counsels and county sheriffs. Decades of agitation – culminating in Daniel O'Connell's election as MP for Clare in 1828 – finally wrenched an emancipating **relief act** (10 Geo. IV, c. 7) from the British parliament in 1829. This legislation effectively repealed many of the outstanding **penal laws**. Catholics could now sit in parliament without renouncing their religious faith, they could become members of corporations and were eligible for most of the higher civil and military offices from which they had been excluded. The positions of regent, lord lieutenant and lord chancellor, however, remained closed to them. (O'Ferrall, *Catholic emancipation*.)

Catholic petition (1805). Although no clear promise had been made, Catholics were led to expect that the passage of the **Act of Union** would be accompanied by a further relaxation of anti-Catholic measures. In 1804 a proposal to petition parliament for Catholic relief was raised at a number of Catholic meetings in Dublin. Knowing George III's antipathy towards concessions to Catholics, the government advised Catholic leaders against pressing the issue at that time. Never-theless, the proposal was carried and a delegation was dispatched to London in 1805 to request Pitt to present the petition in parliament. He refused for he had promised the king that he would resist all at-tempts to bring forward an emancipation bill and he spoke against the petition when it was presented in parliament by the Whigs Fox and Grenville. It was rejected by large majorities in both houses. Two further petitions were laid before parliament in 1808 and 1810 against the background of the **veto controversy**, both of which were heavily defeated. Their addresses rebuffed, Catholics ratcheted up the cam-paign for emancipation in the 1820s. A new body, the **Catholic Asso-ciation**, galvanised the struggle with the successful raising of **Catho-lic rent**, with rallies and marches and, above all, through the mobil-isation of the Catholic forty-shilling freeholders at election time. Ad-dresses and petitions were the means by which Catholic bodies sought to present their grievances to the king and assure him of their loyalty throughout the eighteenth and early nineteenth centuries. Petition-ing (dubbed the 'annual farce' by O'Connell) yielded little in terms of redress but the business of petition-signing gave focus to and help-ed politicise the Catholic masses.

Catholic rent. The payment of one penny per month by Catholics which broadened the membership of the **Catholic Association**. Initiated by Daniel O'Connell to finance the association's activities, it enabled ordinary Catholics to identify with and buy into the struggle for eman-cipation and to demonstrate the strength of their constituency. The Dublin administration recognised the dangers implicit in the success of the Catholic rent scheme. Writing in 1824, William Gregory, an under-secretary, feared it would open 'a direct communication bet-ween the popish parliament (the Catholic Association) and the whole mass of the popish population'. (Bartlett, *The fall and rise*, pp. 329–333.)

ceannuigheacht. (Ir., literally, buying) Protection money paid to a Gaelic overlord to fend off cattle raids.

censer. A thurible or container in which incense is burned.

census. Decennial censuses were conducted in Ireland from 1821. A cen-sus conducted during 1813–15 by William Shaw Mason proved un-satisfactory because the administration was placed in the hands of county grand juries which did not have the competency nor the will for the task. Only ten counties submitted complete returns so that the accuracy of the final tally of 5,937,856 is questionable. Shaw Mason had greater success in 1821 when he employed tax collectors as enumerators but both his and George Hatchell's 1831 censuses re-main suspect because the enumerators had no maps to guide them and some (remote) areas were not counted. Enumerators may also have over-counted in 1831 in the belief that they were to be paid in proportion to the numbers enumerated. From 1841 police constables were employed as enumerators and provided with the new ordnance survey maps on which administrative boundaries were defined. The census of 1841 differed radically, both in concept and structure, from earlier censuses. The 1841 commissioners believed that a census should serve the purpose of a social survey as well as fulfilling its traditional role as an enumerator of population. Accordingly, they sought data on such areas as housing, education, farmers' resources, emigration and the value of agricultural produce. It broke new ground by including a 74 page analysis of mortality by Sir William Wilde, complete with over 200 tables. The 1851 census was the most comprehensive census ever undertaken in the world to that date. It appeared in ten volumes: a single volume general report, a volume for each province, one each on agriculture, education and the national age profile and three volumes on disease and death. A valuable addition was the inclusion of data from the 1841 census to facilitate comparisons. With few exceptions, the census returns for 1821–1851 perished in the fire in the **Four Courts** in 1922 and later censuses were destroyed by government order. The printed statistical aggregates and reports, however, contain a vast range of localised data and constitute a key source for nineteenth-century local studies. The individual returns for the censuses of 1901 and 1911 remain intact and can be viewed at the National Archives. *See* **pension** for extant 1841–51 census extracts produced after 1908 to validate pension claims. (Crawford, *Counting*.)

Census of Ireland circa 1659. Edited by Seamus Pender and published by the **Irish Manuscripts Commission**, the *Census of Ireland circa 1659* is now accepted to be the **poll tax** parish aggregates for 1660. It records the name and rank of local 'tituladoes' or gentry and the number of persons (English and Irish) above the age of 15 years in each parish. It also lists the principal Irish names and their number in each barony. L. M. Cullen has suggested the application of a multiplier of three to poll tax lists to generate a rough indication of parochial populations. Given the demographical uncertainties of seventeenth-century Ireland, however, computations based on this formula must be treated with caution. The poll tax records for the counties of Cavan, Galway, Mayo, Tyrone and Wicklow, together with all but three baronies of Meath are missing. (Pender, *A census*; Cullen, 'Population'.)

certiorari, writ of. A writ issuing out of **king's bench** or **chancery** wherein the king desires to be certified of any record made by any court of record or by certain officials such as the **sheriff** or **coroner**.

cess. A tax derived from the term 'assess' which originally referred to a range of government impositions, notably **purveyance**, **cartage** and six-day labour. **Coyne and livery** (the quartering of troops on the inhabitants of an area) was also, strictly speaking, a cess and proved highly controversial within the Pale in the sixteenth century. Cesses such as purveyance (the governor's right to purvey supplies to maintain his household and retinue) only became objectionable when the king's price fell significantly below the market value of the goods being purveyed and when its incidence increased. Latterly cess was synonymous with tax or rates as in **parish** or **county cess**.

cessation. In September 1643 a tactical cessation of hostilities was agreed between the marquis of Ormond, commander of royalist forces in Ireland, and the confederate Catholic rebels. The cessation enabled Ormond to transfer troops to the beleaguered Charles I in England and provided the confederates with an opportunity to regroup. Neither side benefited greatly from the ceasefire. In protest, royalist commanders such as Inchiquin and Coote defected to parliament and the confederates, by inadequately supporting Montrose (the Scottish royalist commander), failed to lure Monro's Scottish army out of Ulster and back to Scotland. The confederates also blundered in their choice of overall commander, opting for Castlehaven and overlooking the claims of their better generals. The cessations were renewed periodically but despite two attempts to negotiate a peace (the first in 1646 was frustrated by Rinuccini, the second in 1649 came too late in the day to withstand Cromwell) the confederates and the royalists failed to construct an effective military opposition to the parliamentary forces. *See* Catholic Confederacy

cestui que **trust**. A person who has the trust of an estate committed to him for the use (benefit) of another.

cestui que **use**. The beneficiary of a trust to **use**.

cestui que **vie**. A person for whose life an estate is granted.

cf. (L., *confer*) A footnote convention inviting the reader to compare such-and-such a view with the one expressed in the text.

chaffe house. A term used in the books of the **Civil Survey** (1654–56) to denote a cottage thatched with hay or straw.

chafing dish. A vessel or saucepan used for heating food or water.

chain. A measuring line used in land surveying. Originally chains of varying lengths were employed but Gunter's chain (1624) became the standard. It measures twenty-two yards or four poles (perches) and is divided into 100 links, each link of 7.92 inches. An area of ten chains long and one chain wide equals one statute acre.

chalybeate spring. A spring containing iron.

chamberlain. An official of the royal household who exercised control over admission to the royal chamber and therefore controlled access to the king's person. He also administered the household and supervised the king's private estates.

chamfered. Carved or sculpted, specifically the creation of a diagonal surface by bevelling a square edge.

champion ground. (Fr., *champagne*, open field) 1: Countryside dominated by the openfield system of agriculture and nucleated settlements 2: Level, open country.

chancel. The eastern part of a church which contained the high altar, also known as the choir. It was reserved for the clergy and choir. The tithe-owner, whether institutional, clerical or lay, was responsible for the maintenance of the chancel, the upkeep of the nave being the responsibility of the parishioners.

chancellor. A member of a cathedral **chapter**, usually third in rank behind the **dean** and **precentor**, who acted as secretary. He served as the parish priest in the parish attached to his **dignity** or office, was responsible for the cathedral school and keeper of the cathedral records. In the ecclesiastical province of Tuam the chancellor was styled 'provost'. In England the chancellor and vicar-general was usually the same person but in Ireland this was not so.

chancellor, lord. Originally the monarch's notary or secretary, he was, after the **chief governor**, the senior official in the Irish administration. He was a member of the justiciar's (later the **privy**) council, custodian of the great **seal** and head of **chancery**, the secretariat from which all important documents, writs and grants were issued. He was also responsible for government records (a function later transferred to the deputy-chancellor or **master of the rolls**). By the sixteenth century chancery had developed an equity division to deal with disputes concerning land and debt for which the common law provided no remedy. Until 1801, when the master of the rolls was given judicial power, chancery cases were determined by the chancellor sitting without a jury. The process involved was lengthy, cumbersome and expensive. The plaintiff drew up a bill of complaint to which the defendant filed an answer. The plaintiff responded with a replication which was countered by a rejoinder. This correspondence was examined by the chancellor who could compel either party to produce relevant documents or respond to oral interrogation. His decision issued in the form of a decree. After 1801 the chancellor heard cases on appeal from the master of the rolls but from 1856 he was joined in his appellate jurisdiction by a lord justice of appeal in chancery and in 1867 a second judge or vice-chancellor was appointed to hear cases of **first instance**.

chancery, court of. Chancery emerged in Ireland in the thirteenth century with the appointment of Ralph Neville, the English lord chancellor, to the Irish chancery in 1232. It functioned principally as the secretariat of the English administration, the department where important documents, writs and letters **patent** were prepared, sealed and enrolled but it also developed an equitable jurisdiction in disputes for which no remedy lay at common law. The twofold division of chancery as a court of equity and secretariat was completed by the sixteenth century. Chancery holds the distinction of being the only court for which original records survive, some bundles of sixteenth- and seventeenth-century pleadings and answers and books of recognisances having escaped the fire in the Public Record Office in 1922. These, together with nineteenth-century calendars of chancery bills and decrees, are held in the National Archives. Letters patent, the instrument by which the crown conferred grants of land, leases, privileges and office, were required to pass the great **seal** which was in the custody of the lord chancellor, the chief executive of chancery. While the England chancery maintained a sophisticated system of record-keeping with many sub-divisions, in Ireland there were but two: the patent and **close** rolls. Even that distinction rapidly fell into desuetude and all perished in 1922. However, calendars of the patent rolls prepared for the **Irish Record Commission** by James Morrin and John Erck have been printed. The National Archives also holds John Lodge's transcripts of the patent rolls which contain material not included in the calendars. (Connolly, *Medieval record sources*, pp. 14–18; Erck, *A repertory*; Morrin, *The patent rolls*.)

chanter. A chorister, also known as precentor, the leading singer in a **chantry** and a member of the cathedral **chapter**.

chantry. 1: An endowment for the chanting of masses usually for the soul of the founder of the endowment 2: A chapel with such an endowment. *See* guilds, religious.

chapel of ease. A dependent chapel constructed to meet the needs of an expanding population or to cater for parishioners living some distance from the parish church.

chapelry. The jurisdiction of a chapel.

chapman. A pedlar, especially of chapbooks.

chapbook. A popular and inexpensive book hawked by chapmen. Usually of about four pages and illustrated with woodcuts, chapbooks contained ballads, poems, folklore, nursery rhymes, accounts of criminal sensations, in fact anything that would satisfy the public need for light reading.

chapter. The corporate body which managed the property and revenue of a **cathedral**. There is no evidence to suggest that cathedral chapters after the English model of four dignitaries existed in Ireland before the Anglo-Norman invasion in 1169. It was only in the late twelfth and early thirteenth centuries that Norman and Irish bishops began to adopt the structure of English secular cathedrals. Chapters in the ecclesiastical provinces of Dublin and Cashel comprising a **dean, precentor, chancellor, treasurer, prebendaries** and **canons** were established by about 1225 and in every diocese in Ireland the **archdeacon** was a member. The dioceses of Meath and Connor remained without chapters throughout the medieval period, the functions of the chapter being exercised by the archdeacon and clergy. In the provinces of Tuam and Armagh the four dignitaries model was adopted but later simplified. In Tuam the typical chapter comprised a dean, provost (chancellor), archdeacon, treasurer (or sacrist) and at least six canons or prebendaries although in some dioceses the number of canons was indeterminate. An exception was Kilmacduagh which retained the English model and here, too, the chancellor was styled 'provost'. An even simpler form existed in Armagh province where most chapters consisted of a dean, archdeacon and canons. Armagh also contained a number of chapters (Clogher, Derry and Raphoe) that were completely unendowed although there were sufficient benefices to support a chapter. Downpatrick was unique in possessing a Benedictine monastic chapter. Each cathedral had a parish or number of parishes attached to it, the revenue from which went to maintain the offices of the chapter. Some officials were required to act as parish priests in the parishes tied to their stalls/office but elsewhere the spiritual duties were performed by a vicar or curate. Cathedral duties such as keeping service were also required of some dignitaries. Chapter revenues accrued from the rents and renewal fines on leased cathedral lands and from the rectorial or great **tithe** of certain parishes. (Nicholls, 'Medieval Irish', pp. 102–111; Hand, 'Medieval cathedral', pp. 11–14.)

chapter-house. The place of assembly of a cathedral **chapter**.

charge. In heraldry, a device borne on an **escutcheon**.

charnel-house. A building in a cemetery which received the bones of the disinterred when new graves were dug.

charter. A royal writ conferring rights and privileges such as perpetual grants of lands, liberties or manors.

charter schools. Charter schools originated in the Irish charity school movement of the early eighteenth century, a voluntary system which enrolled children of all denominations but provided instruction in the Protestant faith. A key figure in the movement was Dr Henry Maule who founded the Society in Dublin for Promoting Christian Knowledge in 1717. Charter schools were so called after George II's 1734 charter which established the Incorporated Society for Promoting English Protestant Schools in Ireland. Hugh Boulter, archbishop of Armagh, was instrumental in securing the royal charter which enabled the society to solicit donations and bequests. Its activities were boosted in 1747 when the Irish parliament granted it the licensing duty on street hawkers. An annual parliamentary grant was voted from 1751 to 1831 which amounted to in excess of £1 million in the 80 years of its existence. Blatantly proselytising, the schools accepted only Catholic children between 1775 and 1803. The practice of removing Catholic children from their parents to a distant area so that conversion could more easily be achieved was particularly resented. By the 1820s only 34 charter schools were operating and the society was attracting increasingly hostile attacks from Catholic clergy. In educational terms its results were deemed far from satisfactory and many of the pupils were underfed, poorly-clothed and cruelly treated. The charter school system withered as the Dublin administration lost faith in its ability to provide adequately for the educational needs of the poorer classes. After 1832 charter schools were reserved for Protestants of all classes and the quality of educational provision improved. (*First report of the commissioners of Irish Education inquiry*, HC 1825 (400) XII; Milne, *The Irish charter schools.*)

chartulary. 1: A register of charters and title deeds, as of a monastery 2: The place where records were kept.

chattel. Personalty as opposed to realty.

chasuble. A sleeveless outer vestment worn by a priest at mass.

chevaux de frise. (Fr., Friesland horses) Originally revolving bars studded with stakes or spikes employed as a defence against cavalry, the term is also used retrospectively to describe a projecting wall of rocks forming the defensive outworks of a **hill-fort**.

chevron. In heraldry, a gable-shaped band on an **escutcheon**.

chief. In heraldry, a broad band across the top of an **escutcheon**.

chief clerk of the court of king's bench. A sinecure of the chief justice and nominally the principal officer of the court in all matters relative to civil suits, his duties included the enrolment of pleadings and judgements on the civil side of the court but were usually delegated to attorneys.

chief governor. The senior crown official in Ireland who was known in pre-Tudor times as the **justiciar**, *custos*, king's lieutenant, deputy king's lieutenant, deputy justiciar and later as the **lord lieutenant, lord deputy** or viceroy. *See* county governor. (Ellis, *Reform*, pp. 12– 31; Otway Ruthven, 'The chief governors', pp. 227–36; Wood, 'The office', pp. 206–38.)

chief place. In England, the **king's bench**; in Ireland from the twelfth to the late fourteenth century, the **justiciar's court** (forerunner to the Irish king's bench).

chief rent. 1: Crown rent 2: Rent payable by a freeholder to the manorial lord.

chiefry. A tribute or rent owed to a Gaelic overlord by his vassals.

chief secretary. Although nominally ranking below the **lord lieutenant**, the chief secretary was the most important government official in the Irish administration in the nineteenth century. He was effectively the prime minister of Ireland and responsible for the introduction of a vast range of legislation on a broad range of key issues to the extent that enactments were often subsequently popularised under his name. **Goulborn's Act** and the **Balfour acts** are all named after the chief secretaries who introduced them in the house of commons. His frequent absence from the country meant that the bulk of the work in the chief secretary's office was actually carried out by under-secretaries who supervised the administration of almost every public department in Ireland. The National Archives holds the vast range of correspondence (dating from 1790) which passed through the chief secretary's office, an archive which survives to this day because the records were stored in the **State Paper Office** when fire consumed the Public Record Office in 1922. *See* police. (Flanagan, 'The chief secretary', pp. 197–225; Hughes, 'The chief secretary', pp. 59–72.)

chirograph. A writing in which the text is duplicated and then divided through the letters of the word 'chirograph' (or by indent) into two identical parts so that if a dispute should arise later the joining of the two proves them authentic.

choir. The **chancel** of a church.

Christian Brothers. A lay, Catholic teaching order founded in Waterford in 1802 by Edmund Rice (1762–1844) to provide elementary education to the children of poor families. Within ten years the Brothers had established additional schools in Cork and Dublin and in 1820 they gained papal recognition as the 'Institute of the Brothers of the Christian Schools of Ireland'. Shortly afterwards Rice was elected superior-general of the new order, a post he retained until he retired in 1838. In 1827 brothers in Cork seceded from the order to form a distinct diocesan congregation, the Presentation Brothers. With the exception of a brief period in the 1830s, the order remained aloof from the national school system and its attendant grants and payments because the rules of that system would have had to be profoundly modified to accommodate schools so totally immersed in Catholic doctrine and observance. Thus, Christian Brothers' schools were funded by public subscription and church-door collections and only entered the national system after independence. The order established secondary schools throughout the country and founded communities in Africa, the Americas, Australia and New Zealand. Avowedly nationalist, the Brothers' schools educated many of the future separatist and post-independence leaders of Ireland. (Keogh, *Edmund Rice*.)

Chronicles of Ireland, The. A didactic work written by Sir James Perrot, son of Sir John, lord deputy of Ireland (1584–88), which narrates events in Ireland in the late sixteenth century in the hope that lessons might be learned by posterity. It opens with a treatise on historiography, describes the customs and habits of the native Irish and criticises the central administration. Perrot never finished the chronicles which end in 1608 prior to the plantation of Ulster, a process he intended to cover in the work. From a historical point of view the principal value of Perrot's writing derives from the liberal access he had to contemporary records and to the protagonists in the events he describes. (Wood, *The chronicles*.)

Church Education Society. Founded in 1839, the Church Education Society was the Anglican response to the emergence of the non-denominational national school system. It was established because many Anglican clergymen refused to countenance anything other than Anglican control over any system of education the state might introduce. The national system, with its emphasis on non-denominationalism, interfered with their duty to proselytise and they regarded it 'a conspiracy to keep the light of God's word from ever shining upon a Roman Catholic child'. Rather than connect with the state system, they created their own – the **Church Education Society** – which was organised on a nationwide basis through diocesan education societies. **Kildare Place Society** schools were absorbed by the new system which was open to children of all persuasions. All pupils were required to read scripture but only Anglicans were expected to learn Anglican doctrine. Initially the society was well supported and by 1849 the number of affiliated schools had risen from 825 (43,627 pupils) to 1,848 (111,877 pupils). Catholics accounted for over half of the enrolment in 1848. The society soon realised that education was an expensive business and petitioned in 1845 for public funds to support its work. This request was refused and the financial burdens imposed by the decision to remain outside the national system continued to mount. In 1860 the Anglican archbishop of Dublin recommended the society to come to terms with the commissioners of education and it did so soon after. (Akenson, *The Irish education experiment*, pp. 147–201, 286–94, 364–5, 371–2.)

churching. The religious ceremony of purification and thanksgiving through which women were socially reintegrated after childbirth. Traditionally, women recently delivered of a child were unable to perform normal household duties or visit relatives and friends until churched. The basis for this prohibition lay in the belief that the pains of labour were akin to the pains of hell and the act of churching cleansed them of this stigma and re-admitted them to church and society.

Church of Ireland. The Church of Ireland, also known as the Episcopalian or Anglican church, traces its episcopal succession to preReformation times. It became the established state church in Ireland in 1537 and remained so until 1869 (see Irish Church Act). The Reformation made little headway in Ireland at first and its few successes were confined to the tiny proportion of the country where the king's writ ran. No serious attempt was made to convert the native Gaelic-speaking population and the influence of the Catholic counter-reformation ensured that the conservative Anglo-Irish of the Pale chose recusancy rather than attend Anglican services. In tandem with the plantations and an influx of English and Scottish settlers, the church gradually extended its ministry to every diocese in the country with an episcopacy that was largely English – by 1625 only three out of 23 prelates were Irishmen. Throughout much of its history – apart from the early seventeenth century when its Calvinist leanings enabled it to accommodate Presbyterians and puritans within the ministry and the early nineteenth century when it engaged in a vigorous missionary campaign – the church sought to achieve conformity by exclusion or coercion rather than through missionary zeal. Its influence at government level declined when the **Act of Union**, which created the United Church of England and Ireland, permitted only four prelates to sit in the house of lords at Westminster where their impact was minimal. The growing confidence of the Catholic church, the campaign for **Catholic emancipation**, the controversial evangelical '**second reformation**', the injustice of **tithe**, the disproportionate over-endowment of the church relative to the proportion of the population to which it ministered, Anglican attempts to gain control of the national system of education and an inability to effect reform from within all contributed to a diminution of its status and prepared the way for externally-imposed reform by **Whig** governments. In every century the church attempted to reform administrative and pastoral inadequacies and confront the scandals of absenteeism, plurality of benefices and neglect of duty but genuine reform only came about in the nineteenth century when the **Church Temporalities Act** (1833) and the **Irish Church Act** (1869) disendowed the church, stripped it of its privileged position and streamlined its structure. Following disestablishment the church became an independent voluntary body and was compelled to rely on its own resources. A **general convention** of lay and clerical representatives in 1870 resulted in a restructuring of church administration, the establishment of a supreme governing body consisting of bishops, clergy and lay diocesan representatives (the General Synod) and the creation of the **Representative Church Body** to handle the fiscal affairs of the church. (Akenson, *The Church of Ireland*; Milne, *The Church of Ireland*.)

Church Million Act. During the **tithe** war of the 1830s many people defaulted on their payments. Government expeditions to compel the payment of arrears yielded less than the actual cost of the expeditions and failed to halt the spread of anti-tithe violence. In 1833 the Church Million Act (3 & 4 Will. IV, c. 100) was passed, so called because of the sum of money advanced, and the government assumed responsibility for the payment of tithe arrears for the years 1831–3 inclusive, subject to some scaling down of the actual amounts to be paid. It also ceased to pursue defaulters for arrears.

Church Temporalities Act (1833). Despite being packed with sympathisers, an 1831 royal commission on ecclesiastical revenue and patronage confirmed that the Established church was heavily over-endowed and excessively wealthy relative to the proportion of the population to which it ministered. The advent of a **Whig** government committed to church reform ensured the passage of the Church Temporalities Act (3 & 4 Will. IV, c. 37, amended by 4 & 5 Will. IV, c. 90). The moderate Lord Stanley prepared the bill and eased its passage through parliament by engaging Archbishop Beresford, the primate of all Ireland, step by step in the drafting of the measure. The act provided for major administrative and financial re-structuring of the church. Financial savings from the implementation of the act were to be allocated to a newly established body, the Ecclesiastical Commissioners for Ireland (comprising the archbishops of Dublin and Armagh and four other bishops), who were to apply the money to effect improvements in the church. With the establishment of the ecclesiastical commissioners, the **Board of First Fruits** was abolished. The number of archbishoprics was reduced from four to two (Cashel and Tuam were reduced to bishoprics when those sees became vacant) and ten bishoprics were united with neighbouring **dioceses**. The income of several bishoprics, including Armagh and Derry, was reduced. The act also included the first nineteenth-century land purchase provision for tenants. Tenants holding bishops' leases were allowed purchase their holding in **fee simple** subject to annual perpetual rents. The purchase price was paid to the ecclesiastical commissioners who retained any surplus having paid the respective bishops a sum equivalent to the annual rent and renewal fines for the holding. At parish level provision was made for suppressing benefices with congregations of less than 50 souls when next they fell vacant and for their union with neighbouring parishes, a clause which affected more than one-third of Anglican parishes. **Non-cures** were abolished and the right of **church-wardens** to levy parish cess was revoked, thereby removing the civil functions of the parish. The income of some ministers was reduced in parishes where the income was disproportionate to the level of spiritual duties performed. The revenue and tithe of the suppressed bishoprics, the surplus from the reduction in income of some of the remaining bishoprics, the income and property of the suppressed parishes, the remaining funds of the Board of First Fruits, the proceeds of a graduated tax on clerical earnings over £300, the income from non-cures and the surplus remaining after bishops' rents were paid were then applied by the ecclesiastical commissioners towards improving the physical infrastructure of the church. The commissioners funded the building and reparation of churches, purchased land for the construction of **glebe** houses, supported clergymen on small livings and, since parish cess had been abolished, paid parish clerks. After the passage of the disestablishing **Irish Church Act** in 1869, the Ecclesiastical Commissioners for Ireland were replaced by the **Representative Church Body**. (*Report of His Majesty's commissioners of ecclesiastical inquiry*, HC 1831 (93) IX; Akenson, *The Church of Ireland*.)

Church Temporalities Commission. A commission introduced by the **Irish Church Act** (1869) to receive and administer the temporalities of the Church of Ireland. Under the act the church was deprived of all of its property with the exception of churches in actual use and churchyards, schoolhouses, schoolyards and school lands associated with such churches. Glebehouses and glebelands, however, were not excepted though the church was permitted to acquire the houses on favourable terms and the lands at market value. Later the commissioners transferred ownership of these properties to the **Representative Church Body**. By 1880 the commission had paid over £7 million to the Representative Church Body to maintain the existing clergy and the surplus, amounting to almost £4.5 million was used to recompense the Presbyterian church and Maynooth College for the loss of government grants, to relieve distress and fund educational provision. The act also allowed for a land purchase scheme by empowering the commissioners to sell church lands to tenants. Under the scheme, three-quarters of the purchase price was advanced to prospective buyers who repaid the loan by mortgage over 32 years.

church-warden. An Anglican parish administrator. Two unpaid church-wardens were elected annually by the select **vestry** to administer each parish, to protect the church and to serve as its legal representatives. Sextons and parish clerks were often appointed by the select vestry to assist the church-wardens who were also assisted by volunteers and other appointees such as **overseers** who collected the parish cess and distributed money and assistance to those on the poor list. The records of their administration are contained in the church-wardens' accounts.

cillín, céiliúrach. (Ir., *cillín*, little graveyard) A burial site for unbaptised infants, often contained within a walled enclosure and most common in the south-west of Ireland.

cist. A neolithic burial chamber lined with stone.

Cistercian. (The White Monks) A monastic order founded in 1098 at Cîteaux (*Cistercium*) near Dijon by a group of Benedictines from the abbey of Molesme who were dissatisfied with the lax observance of their abbey and anxious to live according to a strict interpretation of the Rule of St Benedict. The order grew spectacularly, most notably after the founding of Clairvaux by St Bernard in 1115. Cistercian life was characterised by the uniform observance of rules and discipline in all houses. All abbots were required to attend the annual general chapter meeting at Cîteaux and a yearly abbatial visitation of all houses was conducted to ensure discipline was maintained. The first Irish house was established at Mellifont in 1142 as part of St Malachy's attempt to reform the church and by 1228 there were 34. From 1216 until 1274 the order came under the scrutiny of the general chapter for diverging from key Cistercian observances. The failure of Irish abbots to attend the general chapter, indiscipline within the Gaelic houses, ethnic tension between Gaelic and Anglo-Norman monasteries and vigorous opposition to external visitations led to the deposing of the abbots of Jerpoint and Mellifont and the assignation of Mellifont and its affiliated houses to foreign houses. Most Cistercian houses were suppressed after the **dissolution** of the monasteries by Henry VIII and it was not until 1832, with the foundation of Mount Melleray, that the order regained a foothold in Ireland. (Conway, 'Sources for the history', pp. 16–23.)

civil bill. A bill of complaint used to initiate legal proceedings, also known as an 'English bill' because unlike its alternative, the **original writ**, it was written in English. It was a short paper document containing the names of plaintiff and defendant, a brief outline of the plaintiff's claim and the date and place when and where the defendant must appear to answer the complaint. The civil bill was served personally at least six days before the commencement of the **assize courts** where the case was tried summarily and determined by the judge of assize. Speed, cost and simplicity explain the popularity of civil bill process. Actions by writ often extended over several terms, costs were prohibitive and original writs were not always available. By contrast civil bill proceedings were completed in a matter of days, cost little more than a pound and the preparation of claim couldn't have been easier; the plaintiff purchased a blank bill, filled in the details and presented it to the defendant. The volume of civil bill proceedings severely taxed the judges of assize and in 1796 an **assistant-barrister** was appointed to hear civil bills exclusively at the **quarter-sessions**. (Greer, 'The development', pp. 27–59.)

Civil Survey. A nation-wide survey conducted by local inquisition between 1654–56 to establish the amount of land forfeited as a consequence of the rebellion of 1641 that was available to be resettled by **adventurers** and soldiers. Although superseded by the more precise, mapped **Down Survey** – which commenced before the commissioners of the Civil Survey had completed their task – the records of the Civil Survey contain details of a highly localised nature of inestimable value to the historian. Here can be found, barony by barony, parish by parish and townland by townland, the names and estates of each landowner, the nature of their tenure, their religious affiliation, the extent, quality and value of the land, the disposition of the **tithe**, the number, quality and value of houses, and associated appurtenances (mills, kilns, fisheries, dovecotes, etc.), occasional details of mortgages and leases, references to manorial courts and some accounts of landowners' deportment during the rebellion. Baronial entries usually begin with a short descriptive summary of the barony and its boundaries and conclude with a statistical abstract and index. Parish entries are similarly structured but somewhat briefer. Some caution is required in relation to the acreages assigned to the various lands for these were arrived at by estimation and may be considerably wide of the mark. Although 27 counties were surveyed (the earlier **Strafford Inquisition** was available for counties Clare, Mayo, Sligo, Galway and Roscommon) only the records for 11 counties survive together with the barony of Muskerry in Cork and some miscellaneous material. All eleven, plus the additional material, have been published by **Irish Manuscripts Commission** under the editorship of R. C. Simington.

Vol. I County Tipperary, east and south (1931).
Vol. II County Tipperary, west and north (1934).
Vol. III County Donegal, Derry and Tyrone (1938).
Vol. IV County Limerick (1938).
Vol. V County Meath (1940).
Vol. VI County Waterford, Muskerry (Co. Cork) and Kilkenny City (1942).
Vol. VII County Dublin (1945).
Vol. VIII County Kildare (1952).
Vol. IX County Wexford (1953).
Vol. X Miscellanea (1961).
(Simms, 'The Civil Survey', pp. 253–63.)

clachan. 1: A loose cluster of **bondsmen's** huts 2: An informal nucleated settlement consisting of dwellings and outhouses associated with the **rundale** field system. Clachan houses (often with an attached *gort* or small enclosed garden) were usually gathered together in a hollow on a lee slope above the infield or permanently cultivated open field. (Proudfoot, 'Clachans', pp. 110–122; Evans, *Irish heritage*, pp. 47–55; *Idem, The personality*, pp. 60–61.)

claims, court of. Two courts of this name were conducted in the 1660s and a third in 1700. The first was established by the Act of Settlement of 1662 to adjudicate on claims of **innocence** of complicity in the 1641 Confederate Rebellion. Persons awarded a decree of innocence in this court were to be restored to land to which they could claim a valid title and since the decree merely confirmed their innocence they were not required to pass new letters **patent**. It opened in January 1663 and closed in August of that year without having completed its task amidst fears that too many Catholics were being restored to their estates. The second court (1666–1669), procedurally similar to the first, was initiated by the **Act of Explanation** of 1665 to remedy the innumerable deficiencies in the Act of Settlement. Decrees of this court were awarded in the form of a certificate which was used to obtain a **fiant** from the **lord lieutenant** to pass letters patent and thereby establish secure title to an estate. Since the estates processed before this court were considered to have been forfeited, successful claimants became liable to the crown for **quit-rents**. A third court of claims was established in 1700 under the **Act of Resumption** to hear the claims of any person with an interest in an estate forfeited before 13 February 1689 (the date of accession of William and Mary). Over half of the claims were allowed in whole or in part, of which more than half were made by Protestants. The actual amount of land recovered under this court was diminutive. (Arnold, *The Restoration*; *Idem*, 'The Irish court', pp. 417–30; 'Abstracts'; Simms, *Williamite*, pp. 136–147.)

claire. A shallow saltwater basin used for greening oysters, located in marshy regions at high tide level.

Clan na Gael. A militant Irish-American separatist movement founded by Jerome J. Collins in New York in 1867 following the collapse of the Fenian insurrection of that year. Its goal was the 'complete and absolute independence of Ireland from Great Britain and the complete severance of all political connections between the two countries to be effected by the unceasing preparation for armed insurrection in Ireland'. From the 1870s, under the leadership and influence of John Devoy (an IRB man), Clan na Gael developed formal links with the **Irish Republican Brotherhood** and recognised the IRB supreme council as the government-in-waiting of the Irish Republic. The Clan viewed home rule as a jumping-off point for armed revolution and to this end provided financial aid to nationalist and home rule politicians in the 1880s. In that decade, too, a militant group within the organisation conducted a campaign of dynamite outrages in Britain. Clan na Gael assisted actively in the preparations for the 1916 Rising, particularly in relation to eliciting German support for the insurrection. The movement split over the terms of the Anglo-Irish treaty, the anti-treaty faction continuing to support IRA action until the death of its leader, Joseph McGarrity, in 1940.

clerestory. A series of windows inserted in the higher reaches of the **nave**, **chancel** or **transept** of a large church above the aisle arches and clear of the roofs of the aisles to light the central areas of the church.

clerk. Short for clerk in holy orders, the term signifies a clergyman.

clerk of the crown, clerk of the peace. The clerk of the crown was a legal officer responsible for the functioning of the **assize courts** in each county and for keeping the records. His equivalent in the **quarter-sessions** was the clerk of the peace who was additionally responsible for the assistant-barrister's court (*See* assistant-barrister). From 1877 both offices were united as the clerk of the crown and peace and registrars were appointed to each county court for civil business. In 1926 the offices of clerk and registrar were merged and the new office was styled county registrar.

clochán. (Ir., *cloch*, a stone) A corbelled, dry stone hut with rectangular interior, constructed without mortar and used as a residence (**booley hut**) or outhouse. Occasionally constructed over a well or **sweat house**. In post-medieval times *clocháns* were relegated to pigsties, henhouses or booleys. Some clocháns were also constructed of wood and wattles. *See* corbel.

cloigtheach. (Ir., a bell house) A round tower.

Clonmacnoise, Annals of. The annals of Ireland from the creation to 1408 AD, originally written in Irish and known to us through Tadhg O'Daly's late seventeenth-century copies of Conell MaGeoghegan's 1627 translation. The original author is unknown. Although prominence is given to historical details relating to families and districts about Clonmacnoise (with frequent mention of the monastic founder, St Kieran), the scholar Eugene O'Curry claimed there was nothing in the book to explain why it was called the *Annals of Clonmacnoise* and points to the fact that the *Book of Clonmacnoise* used in the preparation of the *Annals of the Four Masters* came down only to 1227 whereas this book contains records down to 1408. There are copies in Trinity College, Dublin, and the British Museum. (Murphy, 'The annals'; O'Curry, *Lectures*, pp. 130–139.)

close borough. A term used to describe the majority of Irish boroughs whose parliamentary representation was determined and controlled by a single patron.

close, letters. Letters close were mandates, letters and writs of a private nature, folded or closed and sealed on the outside with the great **seal** and addressed in the name of the sovereign to individuals. By contrast, letters **patent** were open for all to read and take notice of. In England letters close were enrolled separately on the close rolls which were records of the court of **chancery** but in Ireland they were enrolled along with letters patent on the patent rolls.

coarb. (Ir., *comharba*, successor, heir) In ecclesiastical usage the term refers to the successor or heir of the patron saint of a church, abbey or bishopric. Thus the archbishop of Armagh was known as the coarb of St Patrick. More commonly it was used to denote the chief tenant of **termon** land associated with a particular church. Termon land was land originally granted as an endowment by a local temporal lord in return for prayers and masses and as a contribution to the maintenance and upkeep of the church building. The church, in turn, granted the land to a sept or several septs to descend according to the practice of **tanistry** in return for rents and **refection** (hospitality to the bishop on his visitation). A coarb was the head of a greater family or sept or several septs often having under him several **erenaghs** or heads of smaller septs. Although all erenagh land was termon land, the opposite was not the case. Termon land held by a coarb was regarded as having the privilege of sanctuary and any violation of that sanctuary was considered dishonourable and an insult to the patron saint. It was also theoretically free of exactions by the temporal lords. In some areas of the country the terms coarb and erenagh appear to have been synonymous. (Barry, 'The appointment', pp. 361–5.)

coadjutor. A deputy or assistant Catholic bishop with particular responsibility for temporal matters.

cob wall. A wall constructed of clay and straw. Also known as a mud wall or daub.

cocket. 1: The certificate sealed and delivered by customs officers to merchants certifying that goods had been duly entered and duty paid 2: Customs duty 3: The custom house 4: The custom of every **last** of hides.

coibhche. (Ir.) A brideprice paid to the family of the bride, a practice which died out in the sixteenth century and was replaced by the payment of a dowry by the bride's family to the husband.

coercion acts. Although coercion acts were employed in earlier centuries, the term usually refers to the emergency powers employed by government in the nineteenth century to restrict agitation and maintain law and order. These included restrictions on movement and the possession of arms, the suspension of *habeas corpus*, the proclamation of disturbed districts, the imposition of curfews, the extraction of levies to compensate for outrages and the additional cost of policing and the suppression of assemblies and publications. Coercion acts were usually accompanied by procedural changes in the courts. The Suppression of Disturbances Act (1833) provided for trial by military courts and for three years from 1882 a panel of three judges sat to hear specific cases of disorder. Coercion acts, later known as 'Prevention of Crime Acts', operated concurrently with the ordinary law and remained in place into the early years of the twentieth century. (Leadham, *Coercive*.)

coffin ship. Coffin ships were usually converted cargo vessels employed on the emigrant routes to north America during the Great Famine. Lax regulations coupled with poor shipboard conditions led to considerable mortality during the Atlantic crossing, notoriously so on ships leaving Cork and Liverpool for Canada. In 1847 over one-sixth of 100,000 Quebec-bound passengers died at sea or upon arrival. Shipboard mortality was largely a result of 'ship fever' which multiplied in the stinking holds among emigrants already weakened by the famine. Mortality declined when stricter regulations were introduced to govern the transatlantic trade.

Cogadh Gaedhel re Gallaibh. Compiled in the twelfth century, *Cogadh Gaedhel re Gallaibh* is an account in narrative and verse form of the Norse invasion and the resistance to that invasion offered by the Uí Briain dynasty of Munster. Styled by one commentator as 'the official biography of Brian Boruma', *Cogadh Gaedhel re Gallaibh* is a clever piece of propaganda on behalf of the Uí Briain, concluding as it does with Boruma's rout of the Norse at Clontarf in 1014. It was written for Boruma's grandson, Muircheartach, and deals largely with events that occurred in the southern half of the country. (Todd, *Cogadh Gaedhel.*)

cognate. A person who is related on the maternal side. *See* agnate.

cognomen. In Catholic marriage registers, the surnames of the couple.

collar beam. *See* cruck.

collate. To institute a clergyman to a benefice.

collation. A light meal taken on fast days.

collative. An office which is conferred or bestowed.

collodio-type. A photograph produced on glass by the collodium process.

collop. (Ir., *colpach*) Land subject to grazing rights known as collop rights. A collop was the grazing unit for a mature animal. It was equivalent to one horse or two cows or one cow and two yearling calves, six sheep or 10 goats or 20 geese. The number of cattle included in a collop varied from place to place as the word signifies the number an Irish acre of average quality could support. *See* soum, stinting.

colophon. An inscription placed at the end of a book or manuscript providing some details relevant to its production, usually the name of the writer or scribe, the location and the dates of beginning and completion.

combination. A radical eighteenth- and nineteenth-century body of workers who combined to agitate on wages and conditions of employment.

comitatus. In medieval Latin documents, refers to the **sheriff**.

Commentarius Rinuccinianus. A pro-Old Irish (Gaelic) account of the mission of the papal nuncio, Archbishop Rinuccini, following his accreditation to the Catholic confederate government in Kilkenny in 1645. It was written by the Capuchins Daniel O'Connell and Barnabas O'Ferrall between 1661 and 1666 and was based on contemporary documents including the **nuncio**'s and other letters, memoirs, reports and petitions. *See* Catholic Confederacy, cessation. (O'Connell and O'Ferrall, *Commentarius.*)

Commercial Propositions. In 1785 at the instigation of William Pitt, Thomas Orde, the Irish chief secretary, attempted to bring forward measures to place Ireland and England on practically an equal footing with regard to trade. Trade between the two countries would be free of import duties and restrictions and Ireland would be free to engage in trade throughout the empire. In return Ireland was to contribute support for the navy. By the time the proposals were placed before parliament, however, they had been extended from 11 to 20 resolutions and were hamstrung by so many qualifications and restrictions that Orde withdrew them after a first reading in the Irish house of commons. The question of free trade resurfaced in later years as a lure to seduce members to vote for the **Act of Union**. (Kelly, *Prelude*, pp. 76–187.)

commonfield. An agricultural field system consisting of fragmented or interspersed individual holdings (including intermixed demesne land) in large arable fields which operated throughout Leinster, Tipperary and Limerick prior to the widespread enclosures initiated between the thirteenth and sixteenth centuries. Some of the land, held of the manorial lord for rents and labour services, was left fallow every couple of years and tenants enjoyed the associated rights of common grazing after harvest and during fallow periods. The term is often used interchangeably with 'openfield'. *See* course, rundale.

commonplace book. A book in which memorabilia or striking passages are recorded.

common pleas. Ordinary pleas between commoners.

common pleas, court of. The court assigned to resolve civil disputes or common law actions between individuals as opposed to those which involved the crown. It emerged from the *curia regis* or king's court which peregrinated with the king (in Ireland with the **justiciar**) through the country. In England the differentiation in function followed *Magna Carta* which required civil jurisdiction to be administered at a designated place. Shortly afterwards the court began to maintain separate **rolls** and by the end of the thirteenth century was assigned a chief justice. In Ireland in the thirteenth century when the itinerant justices sat in Dublin to hear common pleas the court was known as the bench or common bench. The title court of common pleas was adopted after the English model. Land disputes were the staple of common pleas and it was here that the fictitious cases of **fine** and **recovery** were enrolled. Under the Supreme Court of **Judicature Act** (1877) and later acts the courts system was rationalised. Initially common pleas, along with **chancery**, queen's bench, exchequer and probate and matrimonial came under the umbrella of the high court but by the close of the century common pleas, **exchequer**, probate and matrimonial were amalgamated with queen's bench, leaving a high court division of just chancery and queen's bench.

Common Prayer, Book of. The liturgical book used by members of the Anglican churches. Primarily the work of Thomas Cranmer, archbishop of Canterbury, *The First Prayer Book* of Edward VI was introduced in 1549. Pressure from reformers forced a radical revision of text and ceremonies in 1552. After a period of suppression during the reign of Queen Mary it was restored by Elizabeth under the 1560 **Act of Uniformity** which made its use mandatory by all clergymen. The first Irish-language version appeared in 1608. English puritans maintained a long struggle to have all traces of Romanist influence excised from the prayer book and succeeded in having some alterations made. The parliamentary victory in the English civil war resulted in the proscription of the *Book of Common Prayer* but at the Restoration it was once again reinstated and revised. This revision was adopted in Ireland with the passage of the 1666 Act of Uniformity. In Ireland additional revisions were made in 1878, 1926, 1933, and a new liturgy, the *Alternative Prayer Book*, was introduced in 1984. *See* revision.

commons. The eating of dinners together by the members of the inns of court.

commons, house of. *See* parliament.

Commonwealth. The era of republican government which dated from the execution of Charles I in 1649 to the restoration of Charles II in 1660.

commutation. The substitution of a fixed money payment for service or dues in kind.

composition (1575–95). Inspired by the views of Edmund Tremayne, clerk of the **privy council**, composition was an attempt to extend civil order under the crown, remove the military power of provincial lords and make local garrisons self-supporting by abolishing **coyne and livery** (the means by which the lords maintained their armies) and **cess** (which paid for government forces within the **Pale**). In Connacht and Munster these exactions were commuted to rents payable to the provincial president who would forego the traditional impositions of purveyance, military service and billeting of troops on the country and maintain a standing army to keep the peace. The idea was to transform the local warlords into landlords and it was hoped, once they compounded, that they in turn would compound with lesser lords and a more civil society would emerge. In 1575 Sidney, the lord deputy, offered to abolish cess within the Pale in return for composition but the Palesmen were already in dispute about the extra-parliamentary nature of cess impositions and rejected it, agreeing only to a single payment of £2,000. Ten years later Perrot tried to enforce a permanent composition but, although two further payments were made in 1584 and 1586, resistance to the proposal led to its demise. In 1577 composition was imposed on Munster and Connacht but was overtaken in Munster by the outbreak of the Desmond rebellion and the subsequent plantation. In Connacht composition collapsed with the death in 1583 of the president, Sir Nicholas Malby, but a revised, more moderate version was successfully re-introduced by Perrot in 1585. By a series of indentures agreed between the lord deputy and the leading lords in Connacht, all government impositions were abolished in return for an annual rent of ten shillings per **quarter** (120 acres) of profitable inhabited land. The lords, in turn, agreed to forego traditional exactions on lesser lords and were compensated by annual rents. Succession was to be determined by **primogeniture** rather than **tanistry**. Under Sir Richard Bingham, the provincial president, composition yielded a profit yet Bingham governed the province harshly. The insistence on primogeniture caused little difficulty in Thomond or Clanrickard where it was already accepted but it led to revolts elsewhere which were brutally crushed. The Nine Years War interrupted the collection of the rents thereby disabling the presidency and reducing its effectiveness. *See* provincial council. (Cunningham, 'The composition', pp. 1–14; Ellis, *Ireland*, pp. 304–309, 322–325; Freeman, *The compossicion*.)

compurgation, trial by. In civil cases in medieval times, trial by oath rather than by an assessment of the evidence. The jury decided for or against the defendant according to the number of men (usually 12) who would swear an oath that the oath the defendant had taken was true or that he was innocent. The oath takers, effectively character witnesses, were known as compurgators. To modern eyes this mode of procedure appears ridiculous but that is to overlook the grave consequences associated with false oath-taking in earlier times and the difficulty of assembling so many willing perjurers.

comyn. (Ir., *comaoin*, recompense) Through military activities a Gaelic lord might acquire a large herd of cattle which he hired out among members of the sept in return for rent and other exactions such as **coshiering, coyne and livery**, cessing of **kerne** and **rising out**. This process implies that a lord and vassal relationship was created. Comyn was analogous to the practice of commendation in Europe whereby a man placed himself under the protection of a powerful lord but without surrendering his status or estate and may point to the inchoate development of feudalism itself. Comyn was outlawed in 1610 to sunder the relationship between Irish lords and their vassals.

conacre. Originally corn acre, conacre ground (ranging in size from one quarter of an acre to two acres) was prepared at the owner's expense and let to labourers or small-holders at high rents on eleven month tenures. Land exhausted by over-cropping was let in conacre at lower rates on condition that the cottier manured it for a potato crop. This was doubly beneficial to the owner in that he received the conacre rent and was spared the expense of making the land fit to yield a corn crop in the next year. The price was subject to change in a competitive market and payment was in the form of cash or labour services.

concealed lands. Lands deemed to be illegally withheld from the crown after the dissolution of the monasteries, after forfeiture by outlawry or after crown leases had lapsed. Concealed lands amounted to a revenue loss for the crown and from the 1580s the administration attempted to search out and resume them. This created widespread unease because it encouraged adventurers to make minute examinations of land titles or discover long-forgotten royal titles in the hope of acquiring cheap leases. Four commissions for **defective titles** were conducted in the seventeenth century to enable landholders to obtain clean titles. (O'Dowd, 'Irish', pp. 69–173.)

Confederation of Kilkenny. *See* Catholic Confederacy.

confession and avoidance. The plea of a defendant wherein he acknowledges the truth of the allegations against him but introduces new facts which would entitle him to succeed.

confraternity. *See* guilds, religious.

congé d'élire. (Fr., leave to elect) A royal warrant issued to the dean and chapter of a diocese obliging them to elect a person nominated by the crown to a vacant see. *See* Praemunire, Statute of.

Congested Districts Board (1891–1923). The Congested Districts Board was established by the **Purchase of Land (Ireland) Act** in 1891 to relieve poverty in the west and south of Ireland where too many people were trying to eke out a subsistence on too little land. The board received initial funding of £1.5 million from the surplus left over after the disestablishment of the Church of Ireland. A congested district was defined as a district where the total rateable value divided by the number of inhabitants was less than 30 shillings. In 1891 this criterion applied to over 3.5 million acres with a population of over half a million people. By 1910 that acreage had doubled. The Congested Districts Board was tasked with the development of agriculture, industry and the provision of assistance towards those who wished to emigrate. It became heavily involved in the promotion of cottage industries, fishing, road- and bridge-building and the dissemination of agricultural techniques. A feature of the board's work was the enlarging of small and uneconomic holdings. Birrell's **Irish Land Act** (1909) provided the board with compulsory purchase powers which enabled it to acquire and sell land in congested districts under the land purchase scheme operated by the **Irish Land Commission**. This led to the acquisition of 600,000 acres and the sale of 50,000 holdings. In all over four million acres were purchased by the Congested Districts Board at a cost of £9 million. Its functions were passed on to the Land Commission in 1923. (Micks, *An account.*)

Congregationalists. *See* Independents.

Connacht, Annals of. Attributed to the Ó Duibhgeannain family, this Connacht collection covers the period stretching from the early thirteenth to the mid-sixteenth centuries and derives from a fifteenth-century work by the Ó Maoilchonaire family. The text is close to the similarly-derived **Annals of Lough Key** and was used as a source for the **Annals of the Four Masters**. (Freeman, *Annála Connacht*.)

Connacht, Composition of. *See* composition.

connywarren. A rabbit warren.

Conradh na Gaeilge. (Ir., Gaelic League) An Irish language revival movement founded in 1893 by Eoin McNeill and Douglas Hyde, *Conradh na Gaeilge* promoted the use of Irish through language classes, social evenings and the publication of literary work. It published an Irish language newspaper, *An Claidheamh Soluis*, and established *An tOireachtais*, an annual cultural festival. Its non-political status attracted an eclectic membership which included Protestants and unionists but campaigns to ensure that Irish was retained as a subject in secondary schools and to make it a compulsory matriculation subject in the National University of Ireland added a political cutting edge to its activities. Hyde, a Protestant Gaelic scholar, resigned when it became apparent to him that heavy infiltration by the **Irish Republican Brotherhood** had turned the movement into a separatist organisation. Many of the 1916 rebels were members as were Sinn Féiners and later, the IRA.

conscience, court of. A small debts court associated with municipal corporations where summary jurisdiction was exercised. Jurisdiction was limited to sums of up to 40 shillings and defaulters were liable to imprisonment. The judge was usually the mayor or the ex-mayor for the year following his term of office. (Hughes, 'The Dublin court', pp. 42–9.)

consistorial court. A diocesan ecclesiastical court of the Established church. Until the passage of the Probate Act of 1857 (20 & 21 Vict., c. 8), wills were proved and letters of administration granted in the consistorial court. Other matters dealt with included **tithe** disputes, matrimonial causes, clerical misconduct and immorality. The judges in the 20 consistorial courts were appointed by the bishop and were known as vicars-general. Although in many dioceses the vicar-general was a lay lawyer, surrogates could be appointed and these were usually clergymen. He was assisted by a registrar who retained custody of the records and entered the decisions of the court. Where a deceased person had an estate worth more than five pounds in another diocese (*bona notabilia*) the issue of probate and administration was referred to the **prerogative** and **faculties court** of the archbishop of Armagh. Four **metropolitan** courts exercised original jurisdiction in the archiepiscopal dioceses and served as courts of appeal from the consistorial courts in their respective provinces. Testamentary jurisdiction was transferred to a secular court of probate in 1857. Eleven district registries replaced the consistorial courts and the jurisdiction previously exercised by the prerogative court was henceforth exercised by the principal registry in Dublin. **The Irish Church Act** abolished the jurisdiction of ecclesiastical courts in 1869. *See* probate.

constable. 1: A manorial or parish official elected annually at the **court leet** and later at the **quarter-sessions** to keep or supervise the watch. This unpaid office was introduced in medieval times by the same legislation which instituted the watch. The petty constable was required to assist in distraints, whip convicts, enforce the Sabbath and extinguish fires. Paid substitution was permitted but the constable himself was unpaid. Catholics were banned from holding the post of constable until 1718 when discriminatory legislation lapsed and thereafter the majority of constables were probably Catholic. Until 1734 a high constable was appointed for each barony at the quarter-sessions, later at the Lent **assizes**. *See* police, watch and ward 2: An officer given command of an important castle and garrison or an army.

Constantine, Donation of. A document of disputed authenticity in which the fourth-century Emperor Constantine is purported to have granted the popes temporal as well as spiritual authority over Rome and Western Europe. Although generally regarded as an eighth-century forgery, the Donation was employed to advance papal claims against the temporal powers. On the basis of Constantine's grant, John of Salisbury, secretary to the archbishop of Canterbury, extracted the bull *Laudabiliter* or the Donation of Ireland from the English pope Adrian IV in 1155. This bull, the authenticity of which has also been disputed, permitted the intervention of Henry II in Ireland for the purpose of reforming the Irish church.

constat. (L., It is certain) 1: A certificate issuing out of the court of **exchequer** stating what appears on record concerning a matter upon which a defendant intends to move for a discharge or upon which he intends to plead 2: A copy or exemplification of the enrolment of letters **patent** under the great **seal**.

constitutional settlement (1782–3). *See* Yelverton's Act, 'patriot' party.

contumacy. Contempt. A refusal to recognise the jurisdiction or obey the summons of an ecclesiastical court or to present oneself before it, the penalty for which could be excommunication.

conventicle. Originally a Sunday afternoon gathering of Lutherans to review the morning's sermon and engage in devotional reading and discussion. In Ireland and England in the seventeenth and eighteenth centuries the term came to refer to a non-conformist assembly during the period when such assemblies were regarded as seditious and heretical. Conventicles were outlawed in 1664 under the Conventicle Act (16 Chas. II, c. 4).

Convention of 1660. A convention of 137 Protestant delegates elected on the basis of the parliamentary constituencies which met in Dublin between March and May 1660 to shepherd the country through the uncertainties attending the collapse of the **Commonwealth**. The convention was promoted by a group of officers who had deposed Edmund Ludlow (the English republican commander-in-chief of the army in Ireland) and the civil administration in a *coup d'état* on 13 December 1659. A range of issues including universities and schools, trade, revenue and expenditure and the maintenance of ministers were considered by the assembled delegates but their key concerns were enshrined in a declaration drawn up to validate the assembly and to state its objectives. The members pledged support for the army, repudiated the tyranny of the **Rump**, asserted the right of Ireland to have its own parliament and to tax itself and claimed that Ireland was not bound by acts emanating from the English parliament. They proposed a learned, preaching ministry organised on a parochial basis and supported by **tithe** but there was to be no room for extremists such as **Quakers**, **Baptists**, Sectaries or **Independents**. Principally, the convention was anxious to have confirmed all grants of forfeited land and leases made since 1653 and to this end agents were dispatched to England to lobby the newly-restored king. Their almost complete success in this regard is recorded in the king's **gracious declaration** of November 1660 which was legislatively enacted in the **Act of Settlement** in 1662. To support the army a **poll tax** ordinance was issued, requiring every person above the age of 15 to pay a levy graduated according to social rank. The army, however, benefited little from this ordinance for the bulk of it was presented as a gift to Charles II. (Clarke, *Prelude*; McGuire, 'The Dublin convention', pp. 121–146.)

Convention Act (1793). Introduced against the background of the French revolution, the Convention Act (33 Geo. III, c. 29) was an attempt to repress agitation in favour of electoral reform and Catholic emancipation and to neutralise the activities of the **United Irishmen** and the **Catholic Committee**, both of which had recently held conventions. It outlawed all gatherings which claimed to be representative and which assembled for the purpose of petitioning the crown or parliament for changes in the law. The Catholic Committee had, in fact, dissolved itself after the passing in the same year of

Hobart's Catholic Relief Act of 1793 (*see* **relief acts**). The act was invoked successfully against a revived Catholic Committee in 1811 and against its successor, the Catholic Board, in 1814. *See* Catholic petition.

conventualism. The position adopted by a faction within the **Franciscans** which opposed the severity of the rule of absolute personal and communal poverty. A massive increase in membership led the conventuals to believe that settled houses must be established and this implied communal possessions. Conventuals thus became associated with a laxity of discipline. They were opposed by the observants, zealots who pressed for a literal interpretation of the rule. Guided by the moderation of St Bonaventure the order managed to plot a safe course through the minefield but on his death the old dissensions reappeared. The outcome was a division in the order between the conventuals and the observants. In Ireland the majority of Franciscan friaries were observant by 1538. Some commentators maintain that one of the attractions of observance for native Irish friars was that it enabled them to detach themselves from their Anglo-Irish conventual superiors. However, although observance achieved greater success among the Gaelic Irish, some friaries under Anglo-Irish control also adhered to the observance. Other orders, including the **Augustinians** and the **Dominicans**, also experienced observant reforms and the **Capuchins**, a Franciscan offshoot founded in 1525, were an even more austere observant group.

convert rolls. Certificates of conformity to the Established church were enrolled on the convert rolls which were records of chancery. When the 'Act to prevent the further growth of popery' (2 Anne, c. 6) was passed in 1703, converts from Catholicism to Protestantism were obliged to give proof of conformity. This involved the acquisition of a certificate from the bishop of the home diocese declaring that the person named had renounced Catholic doctrine and sworn the **oath of abjuration** at a public service. From 1709 (8 Anne, c. 3) conformers were also required to take communion from an Anglican minister within six months of declaring themselves Protestant. Only by conforming could a Catholic evade the disabilities imposed on property and profession by the **penal laws**. The original convert rolls were destroyed by fire in 1922 but two volumes of calendars are preserved in the National Archives. In all, they contain the names of almost 6,000 people who conformed between 1703 and 1838. (O'Byrne, *The convert.*)

conveyance, deed of. Introduced by the **Real Property Act** (1845), it replaced the more cumbersome **lease and release** and **bargain and sale** methods of conveyance and established the modern deed of conveyance.

convocation. The bicameral clerical body of the Established church which dealt with church matters, taxation and crown subsidies. The upper house comprised the archbishops and bishops while representatives of the lower clergy sat in the lower house. Until the creation of the General Synod and the **Representative Church Body** in 1870, it was the assembly of bishops and clergy of the united dioceses of the Established church, the representative body of the church. It met after the restoration in 1661 until 1666 and from 1704 to 1711 but never sat again despite petitions to the crown for permission to do so. No convocation was permitted between 1711 and 1869. The episcopacy petitioned unsuccessfully in 1861 and again in early 1869 for permission to hold a convocation to discuss disestablishment. Gladstone refused permission unless they were prepared to deal solely with the means and mode of disestablishment and not the question of disestablishment itself. The episcopacy rejected this and the issued died. The convocation of Canterbury met only once between 1717 and 1847 and that had been a formality. See Irish Church Act (1869), Church of Ireland.

cony. A rabbit.

conyger. (Ir., *coinicéir*) A rabbit warren or connywarren.

cooper. A cask maker.

co-operative movement. The co-operative movement was founded by the Irish Protestant unionist Sir Horace Plunkett following the success of a small co-operative store on his family estate. Plunkett believed there was too much emphasis on tenure and anti-English agitation in Ireland at the expense of increasing the quality and presentation of Irish produce to compete with cheap food imports. The first co-operative society was founded in Doneraile (Co. Waterford) in 1889 and there were 33 creamery and co-operative societies in existence within five years. Plunkett also founded the Irish Agricultural Organisation Society, an umbrella group which propagated the co-operative message through its organ, *The Irish Homestead*. By 1914 there were about 1,000 affiliated societies operating with an annual turnover of £3.5million, of which the creameries accounted for two-thirds. The co-operative movement operates to this day from the same headquarters in Merrion Square, Dublin, that it occupied in 1908. (West, *Horace Plunkett*, pp. 20–35.)

copia vera. Documents which contain the words *copia vera* are true copies and not originals.

coppice. A wood or grove. Woods were often coppiced or pollarded (cut back) to ensure a steady supply of rods for basket-weaving or thatching. Coppicing was carried out at the base of a tree to produce many shoots rather than one trunk. See pollard.

copyholder. A tenant who held land on terms set out in a copy of the manorial court roll. It is not certain to what extent, if at all, this form of tenure existed in Ireland.

coracle. A Boyne, circular **currach** consisting of a hide-covered framework of woven hazel rods. Coracles were worked by two men, one kneeling in front, the other facing backwards to handle the net. (Shaw-Smith, *Ireland's traditional crafts*, pp. 95–6.)

coram rege. (L., before, in the presence of the king) The perambulatory king's court before it became fixed in one location. In Ireland, the **justiciar's court**, later the **king's bench**.

corbel. A stone or wooden wall projection which supports a roof beam.

corbelled roof. A roof constructed of ascending layers of overlapping stone which converge at the top.

cordwainer. A shoemaker.

cores. Coarse, often slightly chipped, flints which are the waste or discarded material of a flint toolworks.

Corinthian. One of the three Greek orders of architecture, Corinthian columns are characterised by capitals richly ornamented with flowers and leaves. *See* Ionic, Doric.

corn laws. Early in the eighteenth century an outbreak of cattle murrain on the continent encouraged Irish farmers to convert tillage land to pasture. The graziers were aided by the Irish parliament which exempted pasturage from **tithe**. Bounties paid on the export of English wheat coupled with tariffs on Irish corn being carried into England acted as disincentives to Irish arable farmers and the shift to cattle-raising accelerated when the British market was opened to Irish cattle in 1758. The Irish parliament voted bounties several times to corn exporters to aid the movement of grain to Dublin but the premiums were tied to grossly unrealistic price levels and proved ineffectual. The introduction of a bounty on the inland carriage of corn in 1759 provided the impetus for an increase in the area of land under tillage but it was the enactment of Foster's Corn Law in 1784 (23 & 24 Geo. III, c. 19) that transformed the face of Irish agriculture. A combination of export bounties and tariffs on imported grain coupled with the increasing demands of a burgeoning British population and restrictions on imports from continental Europe led to a twelvefold increase in grain exports to Britain between 1780 and 1820. Grain exports remained strong over the following decades but government interference in the markets increasingly attracted the ire of anti-protectionists. When the potato crop – the food that facilitated the export of grain – failed in 1845 and 1846, the government dithered over the question of repealing the corn laws. Irish merchants and traders opposed the introduction of free trade in corn claiming that reports of food shortages in Ireland were exaggerated but the British Anti-Corn Law League proved a more powerful lobbyist and the laws were repealed in July 1846. In theory cheaper imports should have lowered the price of grain locally but it was three years before the measure became fully effective. In the interim the government resolved not to meddle in the market, refused to impose a temporary embargo on the export of corn and agreed with the merchants not to sell corn below market prices. Thus the repeal of the corn laws owed more to ideological principles than to the need to provide food for the starving in Ireland. In the long-term the repeal of the corn laws encouraged a shift away from tillage back to livestock-farming which remains the predominant characteristic of Irish agriculture down to this very day.

cornet. The bearer of regimental colours.

cornice. An ornamental moulding projecting from the higher reaches of a wall.

coroner. The office of coroner emerged in Ireland in the thirteenth century. Then, as now, he was required to investigate sudden or unexplained deaths a function deriving from his duty to secure the pecuniary interest of the crown and remembered in his original title – 'crowner'. **Treasure trove, wreck** and sudden death (the chattels of a suicide or the thing which caused the death were forfeited as were the chattels of a convicted felon) all touched upon the prerogative entitlements of the crown and the inquest conducted by the coroner was the means by which such rights were established. His duties were many. He was required to receive abjurations of the realm made by felons in sanctuary; to hear appeals, confessions of felons and appeals of **approvers**. He had to attend or organise exactions and outlawries in the county court. He was obliged to secure all forfeitures of lands or goods to the crown, secure the appearance of witnesses and keep a record of what had happened. The coroner might be required, either alone or with the sheriff, to perform any other administrative duties and he must have enough land in the county to answer the king. He was elected by the oath of 12 men in the county court. The coroner was also the keeper of the pleas of the crown. He recorded the accusations and preliminary pleadings which took place between one **eyre** and the next so that cases could proceed when the justices arrived. *See* abjure the realm.

corporas cloth. The consecrated linen cloth on which the sacred vessels rested during mass.

corporation. *See* borough, Municipal Corporations Reform Act (1840).

corrody. An old age pension, usually purchasable from a monastery, consisting of lodging, food and incidentals. Corrodies were also granted as a reward for service.

corruption of blood. When a person was attainted of treason or felony his blood was said to be corrupt and his lineal blood were unable to inherit. If he was a nobleman or gentry he and all his posterity were declared base.

corsair. A privateer of the Barbary Coast (North Africa).

corviser (also cordwainer). A shoemaker.

coshering. (Ir., *cóisir*, feast) The right of a Gaelic lord to progress among his tenants with all his retinue and be entertained and fed. The term used to describe the food and drink consumed by the lord and his entourage is **cuddy**. The main period for coshering was from New Year's Day to Shrovetide. *See* coyne and livery. (Simms, 'Guesting', pp. 79–86.)

cottier. A cottager, the poorest inhabitant on a manor who lived in a small house with a garden. In later times the cottier was a labourer who was rewarded for his labour with a small potato plot and grazing for one or two cows. Cottiers were not protected by lease and therefore had no security. Recent studies have pointed to a number of distinct usages of the term in pre-famine Ireland. In Munster it meant a smallholder occupying up to ten acres without any labour services attached. In parts of Leinster, Ulster and most of Connacht it applied primarily to one who paid all or part of his rent by labour service. Finally from Dublin to Louth and inland as far as Armagh and Cavan it referred solely to the occupier of a cabin. In the aftermath of the famine it became synonymous with the term smallholder. (Beames, 'Cottiers', pp. 352–3.)

coulter. A vertical metal blade mounted slightly forward of the **share** on the frame of a plough which cut through plant roots and eased the passage of the share. *See* ard plough, mouldboard. (Mitchell, *The Shell guide*, pp. 143–4.)

Council, the Irish. *See* privy council.

country. A district with a distinct identity or personality. The French term *pays* is synonymous with country. Byrne's country, an area co-terminous with parts of modern Co. Wicklow, is styled after the eponymous clan which controlled that region down to the seventeenth century. Factors which contribute towards establishing the characteristic personality of a region include topographical, geographical and geological features (drumlin country, the Burren), specialised agricultural or industrial activity (Golden Vale, Lagan Valley) and culture and language (Fingal, Forth and Bargy). For local historians the 'country' as a unit of study offers an exciting conceptual framework and an alternative to administrative divisions such as the county, barony or parish, the traditional units of study in Ireland. It opens up the possibility of studying social and economic communities whose geographical distribution transcend administrative borders.

country, to put oneself upon the. To present oneself for trial before a jury summoned from the area in which the alleged offence was committed.

county. The administrative division known as the county or shire was superimposed on Ireland between the thirteenth and seventeenth centuries. Shiring, or the making of counties, was the process by which common law and central government control was gradually extended throughout Ireland. It involved the appointment of a **sheriff** (shire-reeve), a **coroner**, an **escheator**, a clerk of the market and justices of the peace. Two knights of the shire were sent from each county to parliament. Counties were formed by uniting a number of baronies or 'countries'. The earliest shirings were Dublin (pre-1200), Waterford and Cork (1211), Kerry and Louth (1233), Tipperary and Limerick (1254), Roscommon (1292), Kildare and Meath (1297), Antrim and Down (c. 1300) and Carlow (1306). Kilkenny (c. 1200) and Wexford (1247) were **palatinates**. Shiring was renewed in the sixteenth century with Westmeath (1543), King's and Queen's counties (Laois and Offaly, 1557), Longford (1565), Clare, Galway, Mayo and Sligo (1568–78) Longford (1571) and the Ulster counties of Coleraine (later Derry), Tyrone, Fermanagh, Cavan (1579). Monaghan, Armagh and Donegal were shired from 1604. Wicklow, in 1606, was the last shire created. *See* country, justice of the peace. (Falkiner, *Illustrations*, pp. 103–142; Otway-Ruthven, 'Anglo-Irish shire', pp. 1–13.)

county cess. A tax levied on occupiers of land within the jurisdiction of counties and baronies to fund **presentments** of the **grand jury** for the construction of roads, bridges and other public works. It was introduced in 1634 (10 Chas. I, c. 1) when royal justices and justices of the peace in the quarter-sessions were given the power with the assent of the grand jury to levy local charges for the construction and repair of bridges and roads.

county borough. County boroughs were towns or cities with small surrounding areas whose privileges were defined by the medieval charters that brought them into existence. Each of the eight Irish county boroughs (Carrickfergus, Drogheda, Galway, Waterford, Cork, Kilkenny, Limerick and Dublin) sent two members to the Irish parliament on a franchise that included freemen, forty-shilling freeholders and members of the corporation. Relatively speaking, the county borough electorate was large, ranging from 500 to 4,000. Parliamentary elections encouraged the creation of fictitious freeholders and honorary freemen as landed and municipal interests fought to gain control over the parliamentary seats. The county boroughs boasted a number of local courts. Dublin had four – **quarter-sessions**, the lord mayor's court, the mayor and sheriff's court and a **court of conscience**. Quarter-sessions had cognisance of all crimes (bar treason) and the remainder dealt with minor offences and disputes, personal actions and small debts, respectively. Cork, Limerick, Derry, Kilkenny and Waterford possessed all but the lord mayor's court. Carrickfergus, Galway and Waterford conducted quarter-sessions and a tholsel court for civil disputes. Waterford also operated a lord mayor's court. See borough, franchise, freeman, Municipal Corporations Reform Act (1840), Newtown Act.

county court. See assize courts, assistant-barrister.

county governor. Although the office was largely honorific, the county governor was the senior legal and civil officer in the county and performed the same function in Ireland as the English lord lieutenant of county. He was commander of the militia and responsible for public order. Invariably he was a senior nobleman in the county and appointed for life. He was required to provide the names of suitable nominees for the commission of peace (the magistracy) and the post of deputy-governor, report on the conduct of magistrates and communicate information about local feelings and conditions to central government. The post of *custos rotulorum* (keeper of the county records) was usually held in conjunction with the governorship. In theory the county governor should have been an effective link between the localities and central government. In reality many governors were absentees or inactive. Moreover, unlike England where there was a single lord lieutenant per county, Irish counties had more than one governor and the multiplicity of competing voices at nomination time became a nuisance and diminished the importance of the office in the eyes of government ministers. In the 1830s the Whigs sought to shed the largely Tory county governors and replace them with lord lieutenants of their own choosing to end extremism and remove one of the obstacles to the appointment of Catholic or liberal magistrates. After 1831 county governors were styled lords lieutenant and their deputies, deputy-lieutenants. In their respective districts, deputies performed the same duties as regards maintaining public order and transmitting information to their superiors as the lords lieutenant performed for the county at large. (Crossman, *Local government*, pp. 15–23.)

couple. 1: A pair of curved timber blades secured by a horizontal tie or collar-beam which provided the A-shape framework to support a roof 2: Of corn, the equivalent of two **quarters** or 16 bushels.

coupled house. A house whose roof is independently or almost independently supported by trusses rising in couples from the floor or below the wall head. See cruck.

couple-beggar (buckle-beggar). In the eighteenth century, a defrocked, unemployed or suspended clergyman (or indeed a person who had never been in orders) who celebrated marriages without licence for a small fee. Some were former Catholic or Anglican ministers who had been deprived of their posts for indiscipline, others were apostate Catholic priests awaiting a living in the Church of Ireland. Couple-beggars were resorted to by eloping couples anxious to wed secretly in defiance of family wishes but also on account of the lower fee charged and because no advance notice was required.

courant. In heraldry, a creature in the act of running.

course (two-course, three-course system). In a two-course system of agricultural rotation half of the land was left fallow each year. Under a three-course system, which appears to have been the predominant mode in the area of Ireland under Anglo-Norman influence, three divisions roughly equal in size were maintained: winter corn, spring crop and fallow. Soil quality appears to have determined whether a two-course or three-course system was employed. Two-course was used where the soil yielded one crop every two years; three-course if it could sustain a crop on two successive years. A fall in population may have prompted a reversion to two-course farming for the manpower necessary to cultivate according to the more onerous three-course system simply wouldn't have been available.

course, writ of. The writ in standard form initiating a legal action, obtainable by the payment of a fee.

court baron (*curia magna*). Granted by royal prerogative, the court baron was the manorial court which administered the set of regulations known as the **custom of the manor**. It recorded the surrender of and admission to land, enforced the payment of services due to the lord and dealt with debts, trespass and disputes between tenants. Sessions of the court baron were conducted perhaps every two or three weeks or as often as there was some business to be transacted.

court cairn. One of the earliest Neolithic communal tombs to appear in Ireland, the court cairn comprises a long cairn of two or more chambers divided by jamb and sill. The chambers are entered by way of a (roughly) circular roofless court which forms a recess at the end of the cairn and probably served as a ritual area. The ceilings of the galleries are corbelled and the sidewalls are formed by large upright stones. Cremated as well as uncremated remains have been found in court cairns together with implements and vessels. Over 300 have been identified in Ireland, dispersed largely across the northern half of the country, Creevykeel in Co. Sligo being a notable example. *See* portal dolmen.

court leet (*curia parva*). A manorial court which tried petty offences (assault and battery, blood drawing, theft and breaches of sanitary or other manorial regulations) that would otherwise have been dealt with in the royal courts. Through the **assize of bread and ale** it was also responsible for ensuring that bread and ale were produced to a reasonable standard and that short measures were not sold. Manor **constables** were elected at the court leet which was held twice a year at Easter and **Michaelmas**. The court leet was usually accompanied by the **View of Frankpledge** but, although included in royal grants, it is not clear to what extent this form of social control was employed in Ireland. All tenants owing suit to the court were obliged to pay 'leet money' or 'leet silver', usually amounting to a couple of shillings, to the lord. The **court leet** declined in the sixteenth century, yielding to the system of justices of the peace and the **quarter-sessions**.

covenanter. *See* Reformed Presbyterian church.

cowlands. In Byrne's country (Wicklow), the equivalent of 30 **great acres.**

Cowper Commission. A royal commission appointed to investigate landlord-tenant relationships, specifically the workings of the 1881 **Land Law (Ireland) Act** and the 1885 **Purchase of Land (Ireland) Act**. Reporting in February 1887, the commission attributed the collapse in crop and livestock prices during the previous two years to American competition, soil exhaustion and credit restrictions. Many tenants were now unable to pay even the judicial fair rents fixed by the 1881 act and those outside the terms of the act were worse off again. Evictions were increasing. The **Plan of Campaign**, a scheme devised by tenant leaders to compel landlords to lower rents, was hampering the work of the land courts. As the value of land had fallen to 18 years **purchase of current rent**, tenant leaders were advising tenants to hold off for better terms. Although the Purchase of Land Act of 1885 was working well, Ulster tenants were dismayed that those who had engaged in disturbances had achieved better terms from their landlords than those who had accepted the government scheme. In its recommendations the commission stressed the importance of maintaining law and order throughout the country. The interval for rent revision, they felt, should be shortened from 15 to five years and judicial rents be set according to the index of agricultural prices. The commissioners believed that land purchase schemes should be continued because landownership promoted good citizenship and loyalty. In areas where holdings were too small to provide a livelihood, purchase schemes should be discontinued and replaced by assisted immigration or emigration. The commission promoted the idea of central creameries as a means of boosting rural industry and increasing exports to Britain and recommended technical training for the youth of impoverished districts. (Cowper.)

coyne and livery. (Ir., *coin-mheadh*, billeting, Fr. *livrée*, livery) A general term for the various Gaelic exactions of **cutting and spending** which involved the free quartering of the lord's dependents on the country, including soldiers, horseboys and horses. Coyne and livery were also known as man's meat and horse meat because it involved the provisioning of men and horses. It was adopted by Anglo-Norman marchers to quarter troops on local populations in defence of the Pale. Coyne and livery was not welcomed by the inhabitants on whom it was imposed. They were required to billet, feed and sometimes pay the wages of the troops. In 1488 coyne and livery was criminalised within the Pale although march lords were permitted to impose it on their own tenants to maintain a standing force. *See buannacht*, coshering, cutting and spending, cuddy.

crannock. A measure of corn used in Ireland at least until the end of the fifteenth century. The precise amount appears to have ranged between one (8 bushels) and two quarters (16 bushels) depending on the cereal. A crannock of wheat consisted of 8 bushels and of oats, 16.

crannóg. (Ir., a structure of wood) A circular lake-dwelling. *Crannóga* were constructed on natural islands in lakes or were man-made. They were located in lakes for strategic purposes and access to them was gained by boat or causeway. It is estimated that there are the remains of upwards of 1,200 *crannóga* in Ireland.

crastin, crastino. In legal documents, refers to the day after any feast day.

creagh. (Ir.) A prey or cattle raid.

creaght. (Ir., *caoraigheacht*, a herd of animals) A group of nomadic herdsmen and their cattle and sometimes the transportable wicker-work huts the herdsmen lived in. Creaghting was the practice of driving cattle from place to place for pasture. *See* comyn, *bó-aire*. (Prendergast, 'The Ulster creaght', pp. 420–30.)

Crede Mihi. The oldest record of the state of the parishes in the diocese of Dublin, *Crede Mihi* contains a list of the churches and associated chapels, the names of rectors, the value of rectories and the institution or ecclesiastic to which or to whom they were appropriated for the period 1179–1264. Although the original was created in the late thirteenth century, additional observations were appended by Archbishop John Alen in the sixteenth century. (Gilbert, *Crede mihi*.)

creel. A wicker basket.

creepie. A low three-legged stool.

crenelles. The openings in a battlement, alternating with the solid merlons, from which defenders were able to launch missiles. Crenellated means embattled.

Crith Gablach. An eight-century Gaelic tract on the legal status and social stratification of lay freemen. Freemen were divided into two orders, commoners and nobles (including kings) and each order was subdivided into many grades. The text discusses the nature of kingship and the relationship between kings and their subjects. *See* Brehon laws. (Binchy, *Crith Gablach*.)

crocket. An architectural ornamentation, often of leaves or flowers, largely associated with the earliest **Gothic** style known as the pointed style.

croft. A small, enclosed arable field or garden adjacent to a house.

cromleach. *See* dolmen.

crown rent. In feudal times, the rent payable to the crown upon the granting of land, commonly known as the chief rent.

crown solicitor. Prior to the nineteenth century it was unusual for the crown to prosecute at the assizes except in extraordinary cases and there was a single state solicitor for the entire country. From 1801, however, crown solicitors were appointed to each circuit as assize prosecutors. By 1880 there were twenty crown solicitors and a crown and treasury solicitor. Meanwhile, from the 1830s the attorney-general had begun to appoint sessional crown solicitors to conduct state prosecutions at the **quarter-sessions** (prosecutions at **petty sessions** were usually undertaken by the police). The offices of crown solicitor and sessional solicitor were amalgamated in the 1880s. The crown and treasury solicitor acted for public departments and prosecuted only at the direction of the government. The post was re-styled chief crown solicitor in 1888 when the offices of crown and treasury solicitor and crown solicitor for the city and county of Dublin were united. When the holder of the office retired in 1905 the post was split between two officials, the chief crown solicitor and the treasury solicitor.

crosslands. Church lands lying within a **liberty** but subject to the crown and not to the lord of the liberty.

crowstep gable. A stepped gable.

cruck. (Literally, crooked) A naturally-curved, timber blade or truss rising from the floor, from below the wall-head or from the wall-head to the apex of the roof. In pairs or couples they are known as cruck trusses and several pairs form the support framework for the roof. Cruck trusses are differentiated by the type of cross-member used to secure each pair. A tie-beam secures the trusses at wall-head height; a collar-beam (or open cruck) knits the trusses near the apex. A truss is not invariably a single timber for two pieces may be scarfed (overlapped) to form a continuous blade. *See* couple, coupled house.

crusie lamp. A pear-shaped, iron pan filled with oil with a strip of twisted cloth laid along the lip to serve as a wick. Originally the wick would have been of rushes and the oil from fish, lard or even butter. Many crusie lamps had a lower pan to collect oil from the wick.

Crutched Friars. *See Fratres Cruciferi.*

cuddy. (Ir., *cuid oíche*, a night's supper) The food and drink consumed by a Gaelic lord and his retinue as he coshered or progressed through his tenants between New Year's Day and Shrovetide. *See* coshering. (Simms, 'Guesting', pp. 79–86.)

cúige. (Ir., one-fifth) In geographical terms refers to the largest spatial subdivision of Ireland, the province. It was known in Gaelic as 'one-fifth' because anciently there were five provinces in Ireland, Ulaidh (Ulster), Midhe (Meath), Laighin (Leinster), Mumhan (Munster) and Connacht, each of which was dominated by a great dynastic family. Ulaidh and Midhe were controlled by the O'Neills, Laighin by McMurrough-Kavanagh, Mumhan by the O'Briens and Connacht by the O'Connors. Apart from the main churches which have (or claim to have) retained a provincial structure continuously since the Synod of Kells in 1152, little use has been made of the province as an administrative division. *See* **provincial council** and **composition** for early modern experiments.

cuirass. Defensive plate armour which protected the body from neck to waist, comprising breastplate, backplate and metal hoops for the hips. Cuirassiers were mounted soldiers who wore such armour.

culdee. (Ir., *Céile Dé*, servant of God) The culdee monastic movement emerged as a reaction to the apparently relaxed discipline which characterised the older monastic foundations during the seventh and eighth centuries. A minority among the monks of their day, culdees often lived within larger communities but devoted themselves to an austere, ascetic life and adhered to the strict observance of their rule. Married men could become culdees but their wives had to live without the priory. Notable culdee leaders included Maelruain (d. 792), abbot of Tallaght, and Dublitter of Finglas (d. 796). (Gwynn, *The rule of Tallaght*; O'Dwyer, *Céli Dé*.)

culm. Coal slack

culverin. A long, slim-barrelled, sixteenth-century cannon, 5.25 inch bore, which fired an 18- to 20-pound missile. It was the heaviest gun in ordinary use at the time. A demi-culverin had a bore of about four inches.

cumal. 1: A female slave. 2: A unit of value. Under **Brehon law** fines and articles were calculated in units of *cumals*. The *éiric* (compensation) for the murder of a freeman, for example, was seven *cumals*. Originally seven female slaves would have been exchanged by way of recompense but later this translated into an equivalent number of cattle, the basic currency of Ireland down to early modern times. Thus a *cumal* was a notional number of cows.

Cunningham acre. A spatial unit of measurement employed in parts of Ulster, equivalent to 6,250 square yards. *See* acre.

curacy, perpetual. A lifelong appointment to a parish that did not have a vicar and out of which the whole of the **tithe** was paid to someone other than the appointee. Thus the curacy was without endowment. Parishes served by a perpetual curacy were those which, in pre-Reformation times, remitted tithe to a monastic institution which appointed the curate. After the monastic **dissolution** the tithe passed into lay hands giving the lay impropriator the right to present to the parish. He paid the curate a sum for his troubles but retained the surplus. *See* appropriate, impropriate, rector, vicar.

curate. A parish priest's appointed assistant.

cure of souls. A benefice with an attached congregation. Some benefices had no souls to be ministered to (non-cures). In such cases the clergyman received the related emoluments or **tithe** but performed no duties.

curia magna. *See* court baron.

curia parva. *See* court leet.

curia regis. (Med. L., the king's court) The king's court or council but in Ireland – because the king so rarely appeared – the justiciar's council which functioned from the beginning of the Anglo-Norman conquest and from which the criminal jurisdiction of **king's bench** evolved.

currach. A round-bottomed, keelless, west coast skin-boat that is propelled by oars. Formerly consisting of a hazel rod framework with a tanned hide covering, modern builders have replaced hazel with wooden laths and cloth now serves in place of hide.

currier. A tradesman who dressed and coloured leather after it was tanned.

cursitor. A court official who drew up writs.

curtain wall. An exterior plain connecting wall between the towers of a castle.

curtilage. A fenced or walled yard or court beside and containing a house and outbuildings.

curtsey (courtesy of England). A widower's right to his wife's estate for life providing a living child had been born to them, i.e., a child had cried within the walls of their home.

custodium, custodiam. A temporary lease of forfeited land perfected by the crown pending a more permanent grant.

custody. An ecclesiastical province of the **Franciscans** who had five custodies in Ireland centred at Dublin, Drogheda, Cashel, Cork and Nenagh.

custom, great and ancient. The great custom, or *magna custuma*, was a medieval levy on the export of wool, **wool-fells** and hides from all ports in Ireland.

custom of the manor. The rules and obligations which governed the relations of tenants to each other and to the lord. These differed from manor to manor.

customary tenure. A manorial tenure held not by deed or lease but according to the custom of the manor.

custos. In medieval Ireland the custos filled the office and exercised all the powers of **justiciar** when the justiciarship was vacant or when the justiciar was in England, a task later fulfilled by the lords justice.

custos pacis. *See* keeper of the peace.

custos rotulorum. Keeper of the county records until the passage of the county courts act in 1877, the *custos rotulorum* was the chief civil officer in the county with responsibility for the appointment of the clerk of the peace. He also administered the oath of office to the sub-sheriff. Normally the post was held in conjunction with the county governorship. *See* county governor.

custumal. An early manorial survey or inventory detailing all the revenue entitlements of the manorial lord. It usually included the names of the tenants, particulars of their lands and rents, services owed, their rights and occasionally the **custom of the manor**. It was superseded by the **extent** which, in addition to the foregoing, included details about the **demesne** land (the land held by the lord himself) and was compiled to establish the annual value of the manor so that the lord could decide whether it was more lucrative to let the land or to work it.

cutting and spending. A term used to describe the various impositions of Gaelic lords on their clients or vassals. Cuttings were levies such as tributes or the obligation to muster a specified number of horse or foot-soldiers during a **rising out**. Spending refers to any exaction which involved the spending or consumption of the client's goods as was the case, for example, with **coshering** and coyne and livery. In return, the lord protected the client from external hostile incursions and hence the phrase, 'spend me and defend me'. (Simms, 'Guesting and feasting', pp. 79–86.)

D

d. (L., *denarius*, pl, *denarii*) The abbreviation used to denote a penny.

daguerreotype. Invented by Louis Daguerre in Paris in 1839, the daguerreotype was the product of an early photographic process in which an impression was taken upon an iodine-sensitised silver plate and then developed by exposure to the vapour of mercury. (Chandler, *Photography*, pp. 4–20, 22–26.)

damask. A shiny, woven fabric of linen, silk or cotton. Damask linen was introduced into Ireland in the seventeenth century by Huguenot refugees who settled in Co. Armagh.

darrien presentment, assize of. An assize conducted to determine who was the last person seised of the right to present to a vacant ecclesiastical living.

daub. 1: Clay, mud, plaster or mortar mixed with straw and stiffened with wattles to form the walls of a cabin 2: A wall so constructed.

deacon. The lowest degree of holy orders.

dean. The head of the clergy in a deanery or division of a diocese. In eighteenth-century Ireland Anglican deans did not exercise a supervisory jurisdiction over the clergy as in England and the office of rural dean was almost extinct. The absence of an efficient middle management layer led to a lack of communication between the clergy and the episcopate. William Bedell, bishop of Kilmore, created new deans in the seventeenth century and they began to re-appear in numbers from the mid-eighteenth century. By 1820 16 of the 22 dioceses had adopted the system of rural dean. Deans were often cathedral dignitaries or outstanding members of the parish clergy. Their duty was to co-ordinate religious policy and ensure that parochial performance was satisfactory. In a cathedral the dean was head of the **chapter** and therefore had considerable temporal duties in managing the revenue and property of the cathedral. He convened and presided over the chapter meetings, gave possession of stalls and benefices to the members of the chapter and ensured that they fulfilled their duties. The dean preached in the cathedral and in the churches of the parishes from which he drew an income. He was responsible for the spiritual welfare of the parishes which comprised his deanery and at least once triennially he was required to visit every church within his jurisdiction. Some deaneries had no **cure of souls** attached and so the office was a pure sinecure. Formerly the crown had patronage of the decanal offices except those of Kildare and St Patrick's cathedral (where the deans were elected by the chapter) and Clonmacnoise (which was **collative** by the bishop of Meath). Nowadays the dean is chosen by the bishop with the exception of St Patrick's cathedral, Dublin, where the dean is elected by the chapter.

deanery. A dean's appointment, the intermediate jurisdiction between a **parish** and a **diocese**.

Deasy's Act. *See* Landlord and Tenant Law Land Act (1860).

de bene esse. A phrase which signifies to allow anything to stand as well done for the present until it comes to be fully examined or tried. Grants of land made conditionally by commissioners at Loughrea to Connacht transplantees in the 1650s to maintain themselves while they awaited a final decree were termed *de bene esse*. Such grants were preliminary to the adjudication of a second set of commissioners sitting at Athlone who were to examine the qualifications of the transplanted according to the terms of the **Act for the Settling of Ireland** (1652) to determine whether they were entitled to permanent grants.

debenture. 1: A bond backed by a financial consideration rather than secured by particular assets such as land 2: During the Cromwellian period, a certificate detailing the amount of money owed for military service in Ireland which was to be redeemed in confiscated land. Debentures were frequently sold on as soldiers decided to return to England rather than settle in Ireland.

debt, writ of. An instruction to the sheriff to order a debtor to return money owing to a creditor or be summoned to appear before the justices of **assize**.

Declaratory Act (1720). The British Declaratory Act (6 Geo. I, c. 5) resolved any uncertainty regarding the British parliament's power to legislate for Ireland and the role of the Irish house of lords in exercising appellate jurisdiction over decisions of the Irish courts. It asserted the right of the imperial parliament to legislate for Ireland and declared the British house of lords to be the final court of appeal in these islands. The act added to the disabilities imposed on the Irish parliament by **Poynings' Law** (1494) and confirmed the subordination of the Irish parliament to Westminster. In June 1782, in response to agitation conducted by the **'patriot' party** and the **Volunteers**, the act was repealed at Westminster (22 Geo. III, c. 51) and the Irish peers were restored to their final judicature. In July (21 & 22 Geo. III, c. 47) Poynings' Law was amended in Dublin and the legislative independence of the Irish parliament was established. *See* Yelverton's Act.

decorated style. The intermediate **Gothic** style of architecture which evolved from the **pointed style** and is characterised by the use of decorative heads, fan vaults, smaller wall areas and greater ornamentation on the stone, notably in the geometrical tracery on the windows. (Stalley, 'Irish gothic', pp. 65–86.)

decree *nisi*. Every divorce decree is initially a decree *nisi*, granted on condition that it does not take effect until made absolute which follows in due course provided no circumstances or reasons emerge in the interim to render it void.

De Donis Conditionalibus (1285). (L., concerning conditional gifts) *De Donis Conditionalibus* (13 Edw. I, c. 1) was enacted to ensure that family estates remained within the family by restraining the alienation of land and the barring of entails. This antagonised many landowners who believed that land should be freely alienable and considered such restraints as contrary to common law. To circumvent (but not contravene) the act and facilitate alienation, the courts accepted two forms of fictitious action, the common recovery and the fine, both of which barred an entail. Thus, despite *De Donis*, the courts ensured the continuation of the principle of the alienability of land. The Fines and Recoveries (Ireland) Act of 1834 abolished fines and recoveries and henceforth a tenant in tail could bar the entail by executing a simple deed of conveyance known as a 'disentailing assurance'. *See* fine, recovery. (Wylie, *Irish land law*, pp. 218–224.)

Deeds, Registry of. Established in 1708 (6 Anne, c. 2) to restrict the possibility of land passing into the hands of Catholics, the Registry of Deeds is a repository of records of land transactions such as leases, conveyances and mortgages together with wills and marriage settlements where they pertained to land. To register a deed, a copy or 'memorial' was made of the original which was then signed by two witnesses, one of whom witnessed the execution of the original deed. This witness then swore before a justice of the peace that the memorial was a true copy of the original and this sworn memorial was presented at the registry. The memorial was transcribed into a large ledger and the memorial was filed away in the vaults. It is the ledger of transcribed memorials that researchers see. (Phair, 'Guide to the Registry', pp. 257–276; Roebuck, 'The Irish registry', pp. 61–73.)

defalcations, defalks. Deductions.

defeasance. A condition in a deed or contract, the performance of which defeats or voids the deed.

defective titles, commission for. A commission for defective titles was the means by which landowners with uncertain titles under English law or possessed of **concealed lands** acquired clean title in return for rents and services. Such commissions were designed to end the depredations of discoverers who were prying into land titles in the hope of ferreting out unsound titles and concealed lands. Four commissions for defective titles were issued in the seventeenth century. The first was established in 1606 by James I to provide an opportunity for the Ulster Irish to secure valid title to their lands. The commission was empowered to compound with those whose titles were unsound and issue new **patents**. When a patent was issued the patentee came within the compass of the feudal tenures system and was liable for **crown rent**, alienation fees and the **feudal incidents**. This was highly advantageous to the crown. With the support of government officials, however, New English adventurers exploited this commission to challenge titles – often of dubious standing under English law anyway – and sought to have them revoked in the hope of securing cheap leases and ultimately freehold possession. Successful adventurers also managed to acquire estates under civil (**socage**) as opposed to the more onerous military tenure (**knight-service**). A second commission in 1615 failed to curb the activities of adventurers and the intention to secure the Irish in their titles remained unrealised. A third, promoted by Wentworth in 1634, emerged during the '**Graces**' controversy when, amongst other things, the Old English were seeking to establish on a statutory basis the security of land held for the previous 60 years. Ostensibly this commission was intended to assuage the concerns of landowners but Wentworth was preparing to increase royal revenue through a thoroughgoing revision of the terms on which land was held from the crown and to increase that revenue by granting new patents which incorporated a change from socage tenure to the more lucrative knight-service. *See* 'thorough'. Discoverers prowling in the wake of the Restoration land settlement left many proprietors uneasy about the safety of their titles and prompted Charles II to issue a fourth commission for defective titles, the **Commission of Grace**, in 1684. The commission was renewed by his son James II a year later and about 500 titles were confirmed. Some Protestant proprietors, conscious of the influence of the Catholic earl of Tyrconnell over the king, feared this commission would be used to undermine their substantial gains under the settlements. Tyrconnell, however, intended far more than that. In 1689, with a Catholic majority in each house of parliament, he had the entire settlement voided. *See* 'patriot parliament'.

Defenders. A Catholic network of secret societies that emerged in Armagh in the early 1780s to resist the disarming raids by the Protestant **Peep O'Day Boys** and whose activities were largely concentrated in south Ulster, north Leinster and north Connacht. The Defenders were associated with the **United Irishmen** and participated in the 1798 rebellion. Very little is known about the structure of the society although it appears to have had a regional and national dimension which other secret agrarian movements lacked. Ideologically, the Defenders appear to have combined a mixture of agrarian, religious, **tithe** and **county cess** grievances with broader concerns and were influenced by the French Revolution and the activities of organised Catholic groups like the **Catholic Committee**. *See* Ribbonism. (Bartlett, 'Defenders', pp. 373–94; Garvin, *The evolution*, pp. 27–9, 37–9.)

deforcement. The forcible dispossession or withholding of property or goods from the rightful owner.

delegates, court of. A post-Reformation innovation comprising a commission of delegates appointed by the **lord chancellor** to hear and determine ecclesiastical appeals formerly made to Rome. It was inaugurated in 1537 by the Act of Appeals (28 Hen. VIII, c. 6) which outlawed appeals to Rome and survived as a court of appeals in matrimonial and ecclesiastical causes until the disestablishment of the Church of Ireland in 1869. The court of delegates lost its appellate role in testamentary cases in 1856 when the civil court of **probate** was established with appeals to the court of appeals in chancery. *See* prerogative and faculties, court of.

demesne. Land held by the manorial lord and not set out to tenants. It was farmed by tenants owing labour services and by hired labour. Leasehold was first used on demesne land and became a lucrative source of income for the lord because it was not circumscribed by the **custom of the manor**. It could be leased at its true market value and was subject to reviews. In leasing demesne land the lord no longer required labour services. Rather than forego this right, labour services were commuted to a cash payment known as **quit-rent**.

demi-jures. Sheriff's peers, 48 of whom sat in the lower house or commons of Dublin corporation together with 96 councillors elected by the **guilds** of the city.

demise. 1: To lease 2: The lease itself.

demurrer. A defendant's assertion during trial that does not deny the veracity of the allegation against him but that the allegation in itself is not sufficient to justify the legal action.

denisation, grant of. A grant of naturalisation under letters **patent**.

deodand. (L., *Deo dandum*, a thing to be given to God) In medieval law a horse, cart or any personal chattel that caused the death of a person. It was forfeited to the crown and used for pious or charitable purposes to appease the deity.

deposition. A sworn statement.

depositions of 1641. Thirty-two volumes of depositions taken from (largely Protestant) eyewitnesses to events dating from the outbreak of rebellion in Ulster in 1641 until the pacification of the country in 1652. Some of the material is clearly hearsay and fanciful but many deponents provide detailed and highly localised accounts of the events they had witnessed or endured. The collection is held in Trinity College, Dublin.

deprivation. The revocation of a benefice by an **ecclesiastical court** for offences committed against clerical discipline.

deputy-lieutenant. The chief governor of Ireland was styled deputy-lieutenant when the nominated lieutenant was in a minority. If the lieutenant was a member of the royal family he usually remained in England and nominated a deputy in his stead.

derbfine. (Ir., true kin) The kin group, all of whose members have descended through the male line. It was from this group that the *tánaiste* or heir to the lord was chosen. *See* Brehon law.

Derricke, John. An English engraver whose *Image of Ireland* (1581) contains 12 heavily-prejudiced representations of life in Ireland in the later sixteenth century. Each image is accompanied by a verse composition which denigrates the Irish or extols Lord Deputy Sidney. The images include representations of a native Irish cattle-raid, a Gaelic lord feasting on the fruits of the raid, Sidney leaving Dublin Castle, a Sidney victory over the Irish and Gaelic lords on their knees before him.

destrier. A war-horse or charger.

detinue. 1: An action at common law for the recovery of a personal chattel (or its value) which had been wrongfully detained. The action could be taken for the recovery of the actual property (**replevin**) or for its market value (**trover**) 2: The illegal detention of a personal chattel from another.

de Tocqueville, Alexis (1805–59). French nobleman, scholar and author of *Democracy in America*, de Tocqueville spent six weeks in Ireland in July and August 1835 with his friend Gustave de Beaumont. During his brief stay his travels took him south to Carlow, Kilkenny, Waterford and Cork and then along the west coast from Killarney to Galway from whence he returned to Dublin. The Frenchmen attended assizes, interviewed Catholic and Protestant clergymen and visited Newport Pratt, Co. Mayo, where they encountered a whole population dying from starvation. De Tocqueville's writing on Ireland is dominated by three themes: poverty, the hatred of the poor for the gentry and the deep bond between the poor and the Catholic church. (Larkin, *Alexis de Tocqueville*.)

Devon Commission (1843). A royal commission of inquiry into the state of law and practice in relation to land in Ireland. It was prompted by William Sharman Crawford's unsuccessful bid in 1835 to introduce legislation to compensate evicted tenants for improvements they had made. Robert Peel established the commission to inquire into the occupation of land in Ireland. As the commissioners consisted of Irish landlords they were unlikely to advance a radical programmes of change in the system of tenure but they did confirm the benefits of **tenant-right** in those areas where it prevailed. They recommended the introduction of a bill to give tenants compensation for improvements but it was defeated in parliament when introduced by Stanley in 1845. The establishment of the Devon Commission represented the first time in which the Irish landed system as a whole was placed in the area of reform. Its report is extremely valuable to local historians for it contains detailed interrogations of landlords and farmers on conditions in the localities. (Devon.)

dexter. In heraldry, the right hand of a shield from the point of view of the person bearing it.

dicker. A pack of ten hides.

dignity. A cathedral office such as **dean, chancellor** or **prebendary**. These offices were greatly prized for they were often supported by the income of several parishes and the emoluments could be considerable.

Dignitas Decani. A sixteenth-century **chartulary** which contains a collection of charters, papal bulls, royal letters, patents, acts of parliament, episcopal correspondence and deeds pertaining to the dean and chapter of St Patrick's Cathedral. (White, *The 'Dignitas Decani'*.)

dillisk. Dulse, an edible seaweed.

dinnshenchas. Placelore.

diocesan schools. Diocesan schools were introduced by 12 Eliz., c. 1 (1570) which enacted that 'there shall be henceforth a free school within every diocese of this realm of Ireland and that the schoolmaster shall be an Englishman or of the English birth of this realm'. Little came of this initiative and by 1791 only 18 of the 34 Protestant dioceses had fulfilled the legislative requirement. Their impact was insignificant for they had in all but 324 pupils enrolled. By 1809 the number of diocesan schools had declined to 17 and by 1831 only 12 were operating. **The Irish Church Act** (1869) protected the life interest of the diocesan schoolmasters but an amending act in 1872 – which permitted them to commute their interest – effectively terminated the diocesan school system. (Diocesan Schools; Akenson, *The*

Irish education experiment, pp. 25–7; Quinn, 'The diocesan schools', pp. 26–31.)

diocese. The district or jurisdiction of a bishop. Irish dioceses derive from three twelfth-century synods, Cashel (1101), Rathbreasail (1111) and Kells (1152), which reshaped the ecclesiastical administration of Ireland along continental lines. Thus the largely monastic basis of administration was replaced by a structure which consisted of four provinces (Armagh, Cashel, Kells and Dublin) each of which was an archbishopric and 22 dioceses. These remained unchanged in the Church of Ireland until the nineteenth century when the **Church Temporalities Act** reduced the number of archbishoprics to two (Dublin and Armagh) and ten bishoprics were united with their neighbours. After the Reformation the Catholic church found it difficult to maintain an episcopal structure within the area controlled by the Dublin administration. Under the direction and supervision of Rome, absent bishops were replaced by regulars and regular clergy performed diocesan tasks that were normally the remit of the seculars. By 1630 nearly every diocese had a resident ecclesiastical authority in the form of a bishop. In the second half of the century many sees fell as a consequence of the Confederate rebellion, the Williamite war and the Banishment Act of 1697 (9 Will. III, c. 1) and it was not until the middle of the eighteenth century that an effective diocesan administration along episcopal lines emerged.

direct-entry house. A house with a front door opening directly into the living space at the opposite end of the room to the hearth. Direct-entry houses were typically features of the western half of the country. *See* hearth-lobby house, jamb.

directory. A listing of names and addresses. The first small-scale Irish trade and commercial directories appeared in the eighteenth century. Over time they expanded to incorporate the legal and clerical professions, the gentry, government and municipal officials and a host of other occupations. Specialised ecclesiastical and medical directories appeared in the nineteenth century and street-by-street listings of householders were carried by publications such as Alexander Thom's annual *Irish Almanac and Official Directory* which appeared in 1844. Directories often contain notes on the history, topography, economic development and administrative structure of towns as well as lists of the principal inhabitants and professional and business people. The best collection of Irish directories can be found in the National Library of Ireland. (ffolliott and Begley, 'Guide to Irish directories', pp. 75–106.)

discoverer. An amending act (8 Anne c. 3, 1709) to the 1704 'popery act' (2 Anne, c. 6) introduced the discoverer who was enabled to obtain possession of a Catholic's land where he could show that there had been an evasion of the penal land laws. In practice the majority of discoveries were collusive actions agreed between Catholic land-owners and Protestant intimates to secure an estate from hostile discoverers but families were often riven by the activities of discoverers within. *See* Penal Laws.

discovery. The pre-trial disclosure of facts or documents pertaining to a court action.

Disestablishment. *See* Irish Church Act.

dispensary. Privately funded local health centres first appeared in the eighteenth century to provide health care for the poor, maternity facilities and inoculations. Their numbers grew after 1805 (45 Geo. III, c. 110–111) when provision was made for partial funding by local subscription and matching **grand jury** grants. Subscribers were entitled to issue tickets to the sick to enable them to attend the dispensary where a medical officer was employed to provide free medical attention and medicines. By 1840 there were over 600 in operation, supported by the provision of an infirmary and fever hospital in each county. In 1851 responsibility for the dispensaries was transferred from the grand juries to the **poor law unions** under the Medical Charities Act (14 & 15 Vict., c. 68). The **poor relief** act of the same year laid upon the boards of guardians of each poor law union the duty of dividing their union into dispensary districts, in each of which a local committee comprising poor law guardians and *ex-officio* guardians were to maintain a dispensary and appoint and pay a medical officer. Under the 1898 **Local Government (Ireland) Act** dispensary committees were abolished and their duties placed in the hands of the boards of guardians. In the 1920s the dispensary network came under the control of boards of health and public assistance and from 1942 the county councils assumed responsibility for their maintenance and upkeep.

dissenter. A person who dissented from or opted out of the established church, the Church of Ireland. Dissenters did not conform to Anglicanism or subscribe to its forms of worship and so are also known as nonconformists. Included among the dissenting tradition were **Presbyterians, Baptists, Independents, Quakers, Huguenots, Moravians** and **Methodists**. Although the term dissenter is usually understood to embrace non-Anglican Protestants, Catholics were also technically dissenters and all ultimately became liable to the **penal laws**.

dissolution. Initiated in 1537 as part of Henry VIII's ecclesiastical reforms, the dissolution of the monasteries in Ireland led to the closure and confiscation of about 130 houses by the close of the century. Dissolution was both a means of extending the Henrician reformation – the monastic **regular** orders remained loyal to papal authority and opposed Henry – and an instrument for increasing royal revenue.

The blow was softened by the granting of life pensions to members of religious houses (but not to mendicants) and the passage of relevant legislation was facilitated by sweeteners to the Old English gentry in the form of additional land grants. Major beneficiaries included senior administrators such as the lords deputy, Leonard Grey and Anthony St Leger, and about 20 New English settlers. The suppression was not a cataclysmic event for monastic life was already in decline and the bulk of Irish monasteries remained untouched, located as they were in areas under native Irish control beyond the compass of central administration. Nor did it turn out to be a revenue cash cow for less than £2,000 accrued to the exchequer from the dissolution. (Bradshaw, *The dissolution*; Mac Niocaill, *Crown survey*; White, *Extents of Irish.*)

distaff. In genealogy, the female or maternal side of the family.

distraint. *See* distress.

distress. A distraint. The remedy by which landlords sought to secure the payment of arrears by seizing the goods of a debtor, selling them and retaining what was owed. The procedure fell into disuse because of technicalities which had been introduced for the benefit of the tenant, the non-observance of which voided the whole proceeding and exposed the landlord to heavy damages. A proper demand for rent must be made, only the landlord or his agent could make the distress, entry to a premises could not be made by breaking a door and distresses were prohibited between sunset and sunrise and on Sundays. Certain goods were exempted from distress as were stranger's goods found on the premises. Under Deasy's Act (**Landlord and Tenant Law Land Act**, 1860) distress could not be made for arrears of rent due for more than a year. The net effect was that a legal proceeding by distress for the recovery of arrears of rent was almost always adopted.

district court. The modern successor to the petty sessions.

district electoral division. Formerly a poor law division, a district electoral division comprised a number of townlands grouped together for local electoral purposes.

doffer. A textile worker who removed the full spindles or bobbins of wool or cotton from the carding cylinders to make room for empty ones.

dolmen. *See* portal dolmen.

Dominican Friars. The Dominican or Black Friars were mendicants who settled in Dublin and Drogheda in 1224. By 1300 they had about 24 friaries, rising to 38 by the time of the **dissolution** of the monasteries (1538–42). Founded in 1215 by St Dominic, the order was particularly dedicated to preaching and hence the abbreviation, OP, the Order of Preachers.

domicilium. In Catholic baptismal registers, place of residence.

donjon. The keep or great tower of a castle.

Doric. The earliest and simplest of the three Greek orders of architecture, the Doric style is distinguished by fluted columns that lack bases and stand directly on platforms. The capital is a plain flat square beneath which is a convex moulding and below this again a number of small rings or channels.

dorse. The back of a document, hence the term 'endorse'.

double pile. An eighteenth-century house style comprising an arrangement of six rooms in two ranges (piles), each range of three rooms built one behind the other. The ranges were separated by two middle rooms. The middle room to the front of the house, the entrance hall, opened onto rooms on either side. The main reception room lay to the rear of the entrance hall and it too opened onto a room at either side. The main elevation of a double pile house was three, five, or seven windows wide, arranged symmetrically. The style was introduced to Ireland by Sir Edward Lovett Pearce in 1731 with the construction of Cashel Palace in Co. Tipperary.

doublet. A tight-fitting jacket worn between the fourteenth and sixteenth centuries.

doubling ordinances. Royal ordinances issued in 1643 and 1647 which offered to double the amount of land due to any **adventurer** who contributed an additional quarter of his original subscription to fund the suppression of the Irish rebellion. The generosity of these terms was enhanced by the fact that the allotments were to be made in Irish rather than in English measure. After the Restoration in 1660, however, the doubling allowance was cancelled and adventurers received land equivalent to the actual value of their adventure. Subsequently they also had their land grants retrenched by a third.

dovecote. A pigeonhouse or *columbarium* used to provide meat to the lord's table.

dower. The right of a widow to a **life estate** in one-third of her husband's realty (real estate) where that estate was held in **fee simple** (freehold). It did not apply in cases where the property was a life estate, a joint tenancy or was leased.

dowry. An endowment of property or money brought by the wife to her husband upon marriage.

Down Survey (1654–56). A mapped record of land forfeited as a consequence of the 1641 rebellion, suggested and supervised by William Petty and so called because the forfeited estates were measured and plotted down on maps. The Down Survey lacks the detail provided by the **Civil Survey** inquisitions but provides a more precise measurement of estates. Barony, parish and townland are the divisions employed in the survey. Baronial entries commence with a description of soil quality and a listing of rivers. Then follows a list of the parishes in the barony and related observations. Detailed parish entries note boundaries, soil quality and the number of forfeited townlands contained therein. The most important parts of the survey – the schedules of forfeited lands – are contained in the **terriers** and accompanying numbered parish maps. Lands classified as 'Protestant Lands' were not measured as these were not to be re-distributed. (NLI, MS 714; Larcom, *The history of the survey*; Ó Domhnaill, 'The maps', pp. 381– 392.)

dragoons. Heavy cavalry.

Drapier's Letters. A series of seven letters penned anonymously by Jonathan Swift in 1724–5 which attacked the English government proposal to mint copper halfpence for Ireland and rejected the legitimacy of the **Declaratory Act**, arguing that Ireland, as a kingdom no less than England, had the right to make laws for its own governance. *See* Wood's Halfpence. (Swift, *The Drapier's letters*.)

dripstone. A stone or hood moulding protruding over a window or door, the function of which was to divert rainwater.

drisheen. A sheep's blood pudding traditionally associated with Co. Cork.

drugget. A coarse woollen fabric.

duanaire. A Gaelic poem-book or anthology.

Dublin Bench. The **justiciars' court** and sometimes known as the chief place or county court of Dublin, it was the principal royal court in Ireland in the twelfth and thirteenth centuries. It was presided over by the **justiciar** and from about 1400 was re-styled the **king's bench**.

Dublin Metropolitan Police. The failure of the parish **watch** to deal with public disorder in the city led to the establishment in 1786 of a centralised, permanent and uniformed police force in Dublin. After several reformations this force metamorphosed into the Dublin Metropolitan Police in 1838. Modelled on the London Metropolitan Police, the DMP remained outside the control of the national Irish constabulary until its demise in 1925 when it was incorporated into the garda síochána. (de Blaghd, 'The DMP', pp. 116–126.)

Dublin Philosophical Society (1683–1708). Founded in Dublin by **William Molyneaux** on the model of the Royal Society in London and with a membership drawn largely from the graduates of Trinity College, Dublin, the Philosophical Society was the earliest of the learned societies to appear in Ireland. Though its existence was short-lived and punctuated by periods of inactivity, the society attracted many prominent figures including William Petty (first president), Narcissus Marsh, George Berkeley and William King. The society's transactions revolved to a great extent around the reading of scientific papers at meetings and experimentation of a practical nature. (Hoppen, 'The papers', pp. 151–248; *Idem*, 'The Dublin Philosophical Society', pp.

99–118.)

Dublin Society. *See* Royal Dublin Society.

dues, small. Small dues were fees paid to the local Anglican minister by all parishioners for christenings, churchings, marriages and funerals. Catholics and Protestant dissenters had to pay these fees even though no ceremony was ever performed. They also had to pay dues to their own ministers for the performance of the actual ceremony. Small dues were a vexation which, along with the rate at which **tithe** was fixed, featured amongst the complaints of agrarian combinations such as the **Oakboys**. They also led to the emergence of the **couple-beggar** who offered cut-price rates for marriages. In the mid-eighteenth century small dues amounted to 2*s*. 6*d*. for marriage, 1*s*. 6*d*. for christenings, 1*s*. for funerals and 4*d*. as a composition for offerings at church festivals. *See* burials.

dulse. Dillisk, an edible seaweed.

dún. (Ir.) A drystone defensive enclosure similar to a rath and dating to the Iron Age.

during good behaviour. *See quamdiu se bene gesserint*.

during pleasure (*durante beneplacito nostro*). *See quamdiu se bene gesserint*.

Durrow, Book of. A seventh-century ornamented copy of the four gospels which, according to the *Annals of Clonmacnoise*, had magical qualities. It contains 248 folios and is held in the library of Trinity College, Dublin. (*Evangeliorum*.)

'Dutch Billy'. A gable-fronted, urban dwelling influenced by Dutch building principles.

E

Eadem. (L., same) A footnote convention used to repeat the name of the immediately preceding female author but a different work. *Eaedem* is used where the work is that of a number of female authors. *See Idem*.

easement. A right over a neighbour's land conferred on a landowner by virtue of his ownership, including right of way, light, support and water.

Easter. A term in the legal and university year commencing shortly after Easter. *See* sittings.

Ecclesiastical Commissioners. *See* Church Temporalities Act.

ecclesiastical courts. Ecclesiastical courts dealt largely with marriage and testamentary matters, ecclesiastical administration, cases of clerical misconduct, defamation and suits for the payment of **tithe**. There were 26 in Ireland: the court of prerogative and faculties, 24 consistorial or diocesan courts and the ecclesiastical court of Newry and Mourne. The four metropolitan courts (the diocesan courts of the archbishops) also exercised appellate jurisdiction for the province. Appeals from the metropolitan courts were heard in the court of delegates. Ecclesiastical courts were conducted under the jurisdiction of the bishop but he was not permitted to preside over them. Instead responsibility for their conduct was delegated to a vicar-general, a clergyman or lay person with a secular degree of doctor of law. *See* consistorial court, court of delegates, court of prerogative and faculties.

Ecclesiastical Titles Act (1851). A draconian piece of penal legislation (14 & 15 Vict., c 60) directed against the Catholic hierarchies of Britain and Ireland, triggered by the papal decision to restore a Catholic episcopacy in Britain and by the action of the Irish Catholic bishops at the **Synod of Thurles** in denouncing the **Queen's Colleges** and the treatment of tenants by landlords. Piqued at this demonstration of Catholic insolence, Lord John Russell, the Whig prime minister, proposed to end papal aggression by penalising the assumption of any territorial title in the United Kingdom by any Catholic archbishop, bishop or dean and by declaring all deeds and documents signed by them to be illegal. All bequests for the maintenance of such offices and charitable bequests devised in trust to a bishop by virtue of his office were to be voided and forfeited to the crown. The act, passed in July 1851 against the advice of the law officers, was ineffectual. No one was ever prosecuted and it was repealed in 1871 (34 & 35 Vict., c. 53). The idea of the Whigs introducing penal legislation and Russell's attacks on Irish Catholics in parliament proved damaging only to the party and himself. The Whigs lost influence in Rome and Ireland and within a year Russell was eclipsed by Palmerston. By including Ireland in the legislation he also succeeded in creating an independent Irish party in the house of commons. *See* Catholic Defence Association. (Kerr, '*A nation of beggars*'? pp. 241– 81; Larkin, *The making of the Roman Catholic Church*, pp. 81–5, 92–5, 99–100.)

economy fund. The corporate income of a cathedral. The fund derived largely from the rents on cathedral lands and renewal fines, the principal claim on which was the maintenance of the cathedral building.

Education, Commissioners of. Established in 1806, the inquiry of the Commissioners of Education was a reconstitution of a 1791 Irish parliamentary commission of inquiry whose report was neither published nor presented in parliament. *See* Education, Report on. The commissioners produced 14 reports on contemporary educational provision in Ireland by the close of operations in 1812, the most significant of which – the fourteenth – provided the blueprint for the national system which emerged in 1831. Its key recommendations included the establishment of a permanent body of education commissioners to administer parliamentary grants to schools for the poorer classes and to control textbooks. Under the proposed system no attempt would be made to influence or alter the religious beliefs of the pupils and to this end the report distinguished between literary and moral education (which the commissioners regarded as the realm of the state) and religious education (which they acknowledged was the prerogative of clergy of the respective denominations). The commissioners' reports impacted little on contemporary provision for the state was already funding Protestant education societies such as the Incorporated Society (**charter-schools**) and the **Association for Discountenancing Vice** but they contributed significantly to the growing consensus about the shape of educational provision that would ultimately emerge. (*Fourteenth report from the commissioners of the Board of Education in Ireland*, HC 1812–13 (21) V. 221; Akenson, *The Irish education experiment*, pp. 76–80.)

Education Inquiry (1824–27). The Irish Education Inquiry was established by royal commission in 1824 in response to Catholic disquiet over the activities of state-funded, proselytising educational societies, the paucity of funding for Catholic schools, the administration of the **lord lieutenant's school fund** and the extensive state support for the **Kildare Place Society**. Of the five commissioners all but one, Anthony Blake, were Protestants. In addition, Leslie Foster, MP, was a member of the Kildare Place Society and William Grant supported the **London Hibernian Society**. Nevertheless, the commission's nine reports – based on statistical evidence, oral and written submissions and exploratory interviews with Catholic prelates – condemned the Protestant educational bodies, recommended the reduction and ultimate withdrawal of public money from the Kildare Place Society and proposed the absorption of existing voluntary schools into a state system under a new board of management. This board, the commissioners recommended, would oversee schools of general instruction in which Catholics and Protestants would receive a common literary and moral but separate religious education. To this end two lay teachers should be appointed to each school, one of whom must be a Catholic in a predominantly Catholic area or a Presbyterian in a predominantly Presbyterian area. Although Protestant ministers would have access to the schools for the purpose of religious instruction, the spiritual education of Catholic children would fall within the compass of the lay Catholic teacher. The board would receive title to all schoolhouses and be the sole authority for teacher appointments and dismissals. It would hire inspectors, control all moneys related to schoolhouse maintenance and would exercise jurisdiction over texts for general instruction. Despite numerous attempts to bridge the gulf between the Anglican and Catholic hierarchies concerning gospel extracts to be used during common instruction, the commissioners failed to come up with a formula to satisfy all sides. The commission's failure to achieve consensus resulted in the appointment in 1828 of a **select committee** of 21 members under Thomas Spring-Rice which proposed a system of united education under a salaried board of education that would safeguard the religious beliefs of pupils. Ministers of all denominations would oversee the religious instruction of their respective denominations and, subject to approval, the board would print books recommended by the different episcopal authorities for religious instruction. Four days were to be set aside for combined literary and moral education, the remaining two days being assigned for separate religious instruction. School buildings (subject to local provision of a site), teacher-training and gratuities, school requisites and the appointment of inspectors would be funded or part-funded from public money. The report of the select committee was opposed by the Established church and welcomed by Catholic prelates. Nothing came of it, however, until 1831 when its key recommendations became the founding principles of Stanley's new system of national education for Ireland. The second report of the commission of Irish education inquiry (1826-7) comprises an extensive survey of existing school provision at parish level abstracted from the returns of Protestant and Catholic clergymen. Teachers' names and salaries are given, together with details on attendance, religious composition of the pupils and school location. (Education Inquiry; Akenson, *The Irish education experiment*, pp. 92–102.) *See* Education, National System of.

Education, National System of. The national system of primary education was established in 1831. The regulations for the conduct of the system were founded not on statute but on a series of instructions contained in a letter from Edward Stanley, chief secretary for Ireland, to the duke of Leinster. These regulations derived primarily from an 1828 select committee report on Irish education (see Education Inquiry) that had in turn been informed by earlier commissions and inquiries. Stanley's original letter has not survived but two slightly different versions were published during the early years of the system (see Akenson below for both versions). In his letter, Stanley reviewed developments in Irish education to date. He declared the **Kildare Place Society**, then in receipt of considerable public funds, to be incapable of allaying Catholic fears of proselytisation and therefore not a fit body to be entrusted with responsibility for national education in Ireland. He then proceeded to outline the system that was to be established in Ireland. A superintending board of education, the Commissioners of Education in Ireland, was to be created, com-

posed of men of high personal character including leading ecclesiastics of high rank from the different denominations. This board would
exercise complete control over schools that connected with the
system. The chief purpose of the national system was to educate children of all persuasions in the same school. Accordingly the board would
look with favour on joint applications for aid from Catholics and
Protestants. A local contribution of one-third of school building
costs together with provision for furniture and books and a contribution towards a teacher's salary were required for any school to
receive public funds. Schools would be kept open four or five days
each week for moral and literary instruction and the remaining day
or two was to be set aside for the religious education of pupils by their
respective clergymen. The commissioners would exercise complete
control over the funds voted by parliament and over the textbooks
to be used in the schools. Local managers would have the right to appoint and dismiss teachers but the commissioners also had the power
to dismiss in cases where they were dissatisfied with the conduct of
the school. Teachers were to be hired from model or training schools
to be established by the board. However well-intended, the national
school system very rapidly drifted away from the blueprint outlined
by Stanley. The churches exerted powerful pressure on the weak
supervisory board of education and within decades the system became *de facto* denominational. For many years the Church of Ireland
refused to have any dealings with the national system, many Anglican clergymen believing that the education of children was properly
a matter for the established state church. An Anglican institution,
the **Church Education Society**, was founded to compete with the
national system but by the 1870s the expense of maintaining the
society drove it into the state system. The board of education published annual reports on all aspects of the administration of the system and accumulated a vast amount of detailed information on local
schools through the reports of visiting inspectors, applications for
connection, school registers, correspondence, records of salaries and
grants and the investigation of complaints. Detailed studies of many
local national schools are possible using these sources which are held
in the **National Archives**. *See* Cowper Commission, Belmore Commission, general lesson, model schools, payment-by-results, Powis Commission, Stopford rule, vested schools. (Akenson, *The Irish education
experiment*; Coolahan, *Irish education*, pp. 3–51.)

Education, Report on (1791). In 1788 a committee of the Irish house
of commons was formed to examine contemporary educational provision. The work was concluded in 1791 but the report was neither
presented nor published and no copies of it have survived. However,
the committee's findings were made available to the Commissioners

of Education Inquiry (1806–12) and the Endowed Schools Commission (1856) and it is through their reports that the 1791 report can
be reconstructed. The parliamentarians were severely critical of existing educational provision (*see* diocesan, royal, parish and charter
schools) and developed a set of proposals designed to rid the school
system of contentious sectarian features. They proposed to place the
parish schools under local control (involving lay Catholic representation) and grant access to clergymen of all denominations to mini-
mise the possibility of proselytisation. Overall direction and supervision of the system would be vested in a state central board of control. Although these proposals remained dormant for decades they
set the agenda for the early nineteenth century debate on education
out of which the national system emerged in 1831. (Corcoran, *State
policy*, pp. 149–191; Akenson, *The Irish education experiment*, pp. 69–
74.) *See* Education, Commissioners of.

effigy tomb. A tomb bearing a likeness of the deceased. The sides of the
tomb may be adorned with coats of arms and religious iconography,
all of which help to identify the deceased and illuminate aspects of
contemporary religious devotion. Also known as a table tomb.

éiric, éraic. (Ir.) A body fine (compensation) payable under the **Brehon
law** system for homicide. The payment was in two parts, payment for
the injury (*éiric*) and an honour price (*lóg n-enech*) related to the rank
of the individual killed. The *éiric* comprised a fixed payment of seven
cumals (female slaves but more usually their equivalent value in
livestock) for a freeman and was paid to the **derbfine** or agnatic kin
of the dead man. One-third of the *éiric* was paid to the victim's lord
if he played a part in securing the fine. The honour-price was divided
between the victim's maternal and paternal kin. In the event of a
murderer defaulting, the blood fine devolved to his kin group and if
they failed to provide compensation the victim's kinsmen were obliged
to wage a blood-feud to exact retribution.

ejectment. Eviction, the legal remedy for the non-payment of rent.

ell. A linear measure equivalent to 45 inches, used to measure linen
cloth.

eloign. (Fr., *eloigner*, to remove to a distance) To carry off goods beyond
the jurisdiction of the sheriff. *See* withernam.

embattled. An architectural term to describe a building boasting battlements. These were not always for defensive purposes. The parish
churches of the fifteenth century (and the Gothic revival churches
of the nineteenth) were embattled for decorative purposes.

embracery. The offence of influencing a jury illegally and corruptly.

embrasure. A window or door with internally bevelled or chamfered
sides.

enceinte. An enclosing wall or fortification.

Encumbered Estates Acts. Steep poor law rates and declining rental in-come during the famine drove many landowners into insolvency. The Encumbered Estates Acts (11 & 12 Vict., c. 48, 1848 and 12 & 13 Vict., c. 77, 1849) were intended to resolve the problem of massive indeb-tedness by facilitating the sale of encumbered (indebted) estates, dis-charging the debts and providing purchasers with clean title. Properly this should have been the responsibility of **chancery** but that court proved unable to meet the challenge of large scale indebtedness. The government hoped the new legislation would break the log-jam and transform the face of Irish agriculture with an injection of capital from Britain. The 1849 act superseded and improved the earlier act (which would have clogged up the courts with disputes about title) by providing for the establishment of an encumbered estates court pre-sided over by three commissioners or judges to process the sales. The legislation stated that where any land or lease of land was subject to encumbrances the value of which exceeded half the net annual rent, any encumbrancer (creditor) on such land or lease could apply to the commissioners for the sale of the land or lease and so discharge the encumbrances thereon. All encumbrancers, except the person on whose application the sale had been ordered (and even the latter if the com-missioners allowed), could bid for the encumbered property and the successful bidder was vested with an indefeasible title by the court. The judges were authorised to arrange exchanges and divisions – even if lands were not subject to be sold under the act – if this would facili-tate the sale of the encumbered property. They were also empowered to sell lands included in different applications in the same sale. The act did not provide, as the **Devon Commission** had recommended, that any of the purchase money should go to tenants who had carried out permanent improvements. It simply allowed for the replacement of one landlord by another. By 1859 over 3,000 estates amounting to some five million acres had passed into the hands of new (mostly Irish) landlords, many of whom immediately set about evicting tenants. In 1858 the encumbered estates court was superseded by the **landed estate court** which, in turn, became the land judges court in 1877. The records of sales conducted under the encumbered estates acts can be found in the National Archives. Advertisements for the sale of properties, known as estate rentals, contain much to interest the local historian including maps, extents, contents, valuation, details of title together with tenants' names, their rents and tenure. (Lyons, *Illustrated incumbered estates.*)

endowment. A gift of money or property to an institution or person. In-stitutional endowments may comprise the provision of an income or a contribution towards construction, equipping or furnishing costs. The equivalent in human terms was the dowry a woman brought to her marriage.

enfeoff. To invest with a **fee** or **fief**, to grant.

enfeoffment. 1: A deed giving a person the **fee** of an estate 2: An estate obtained in this way.

English bill. *See* civil bill.

engross. To enclose land with hedges and ditches.

engrosser. A court official who levied arrears of debts owing to the crown.

entail. The succession to an entailed estate is limited to a specific line of heirs so that it cannot be sold or passed to anyone else. The holder's interest is that of a tenant for life (*see* life estate). Entails could be barred or destroyed and land freed for sale by a fictitious lawsuit in the court of **common pleas** known as a **recovery**. After 1834 a new process known as a disentailing deed removed the need for such fictitious and expensive actions by enabling an entail to be barred by a simple deed of conveyance. *See De Donis Conditionalibus.*

Enterprise of Ulster (1571–5). A bloody and destabilising private attempt by Sir Thomas Smith and Walter Devereux (earl of Essex) to colonise east Ulster. Smith and his son (also Thomas) were granted north Down and Ards but failed to make any progress when their diminutive force met with stiff resistance from Sir Brian MacPhelin O'Neill. Penned in at Carrickfergus, the troops went berserk. Essex had been granted Antrim and arrived in Carrickfergus in 1573 with over 1,000 men. He pursued a fruitless war against Sorley Boy Mac-Donnell, ordered the butchering of the O'Neills of Clandeboye in 1574 and the massacre of the MacDonnells of Rathlin Island. The younger Smith was killed in 1573 and Essex died in Ireland in 1576. Both incursions proved costly failures.

entry, writ of. A writ employed in an action to recover property where a defendant had entered with apparent justification but (a) through a tenant of the plaintiff who had not been entitled to sell or (b) by way of a lease that had since expired.

entry fine. A fine paid by an incoming tenant to be admitted to a tenancy. It may have involved a fixed or arbitrary payment depending on the **custom of the manor**. Until the seventeenth century the heir of a deceased tenant-in-chief was required to pay **relief** (a fee or entry fine) set at one year's profits of the land to the crown to obtain possession of his estate which was effected through the legal procedure known as suing out livery. *See* livery, to sue out.

eorum residentia. In Catholic marriage registers, the place of residence of the couple.

Episcopalian. A member of the Anglican church (**Church of Ireland**).

Erastianism. A doctrine named after the Zwinglian Thomas Erastus which declares the state to be supreme in both civil and ecclesiastical affairs. Erastus, himself, did not espouse this doctrine. He believed it lawful for the state to punish religious as well as civil offences wherever the citizenry adhered to a single faith. However, he opposed excommunication and denial of the sacraments on the basis that they were not scriptural. The term achieved popularity in England in the 1640s among **Presbyterians** who used it to attack proponents of state supremacy. The eighteenth-century **Church of Ireland** has been described as a thoroughly erastian body in that career advancement and church policies were in every way determined by the government. (Akenson, *The Church of Ireland*, p. 4.)

erenagh. The hereditary tenant of **termon** (church) lands. He was a lay lord whose family held this office and church property from generation to generation in return for rent and **refection**. *See* coarb. (Jefferies, 'Erenaghs'.)

error, writ of. The modern right to appeal was unknown in earlier times. A sentence could only be challenged if the defendant could establish that there was an error on the record of the case either in the pleadings, the issue or the verdict. The writ of error was the means by which such challenges were mounted, compelling a lower court to produce the records for inspection.

escheat. 1: A **feudal incident** entailing the lapse of a property to the lord in default of an heir (*propter defectum sanguinis*) or upon the conviction of a tenant for a felony (*propter delictum tenentis*) 2: To confiscate.

escheator. A local official, often the county **sheriff**, who conducted an **inquisition** on behalf of the **surveyor-general** to determine the rights to property. The escheator was also responsible for levying alienation fines and for detecting breaches of alienation procedures. Provincial escheators were appointed in 1605. *See* alienation, right to.

escheator of Ireland. Important crown official who held all lands temporarily in the king's hands through forfeiture, **wardship** or episcopal vacancy. He took possession of the land on behalf of the king and conducted an **inquisition** *post-mortem* to establish its value and to identify and discover the age of the heir. The escheator gave **seisin** to the heir if of age or auctioned the wardship if the heir was in minority. He apportioned the widow's **dower** and divided the estate if it passed to co-heiresses.

escheatorship of Munster. Until 1793 it was not possible for members of the Irish parliament to resign their seats. There was no Irish equivalent of the Chiltern Hundreds, a temporary office granted to British MPs who wished to resign their seats. Irish MPs might stay away from the house but only death, expulsion, the taking of holy orders or elevation to the peerage or judiciary could terminate their membership. In 1793 the **Place Act** (33 Geo. III, c. 41) required members of parliament to vacate their seats upon accepting government office and the escheatorships of Munster, Connacht, Ulster and Leinster – sinecures worth 30 shillings annually – provided the nominal office to enable them to do so.

escutcheon. In heraldry, a shield with a coat of arms.

esker. (Ir. *eiscir*) A narrow, winding ridge of sand and gravel, often up to several miles long, thought to be channel deposits left behind as a glacier retreated. In boggy areas, such as the Irish midlands, eskers provided dry, natural causeways for movement.

esnecy. The prerogative of the eldest co-parcener (co-heir) to have first choice after an inheritance was divided.

essoin. 1: To excuse one's attendance at court 2: A payment made by a tenant who owed suit to the **manor court** for absenting himself from the court.

Established church. The **Church of Ireland**, Anglican or Episcopalian church which was the state church in Ireland from 1537 until it was disestablished by the **Irish Church Act** in 1869.

estate. In modern usage is usually taken to refer to the ownership of an area of land or the whole of the property (both real and personal) owned by a deceased person. Under feudal law, however, and technically under modern land law, estate answered the question; 'For how long is the land held?' A life estate exists for as long as the tenant lives, an estate in tail for as long as the tenant in tail or any of his descendants lives, an estate in fee simple for as long as the tenant or any of his heirs (whether descendants or not) lives. Under the doctrine of estates a person owned an estate in land and not the land itself for all land was held directly or indirectly of the crown. *See* allodial tenure.

Estates Commissioners. Operating under the supervision of the **Irish Land Commission**, the Estates Commissioners were established by the **Wyndham Act** (1903) to purchase whole estates (rather than individual holdings) and to sell them to the tenants. In conjunction with the **Congested Districts Board**, the Estates Commissioners became active in relieving rural congestion by improving, enlarging and rearranging newly-purchased estates before vesting them in tenant-purchasers. Under the 1907 Evicted Tenants (Ireland) Act they were also permitted to purchase compulsorily the land of evicted tenants and to reinstate them, the first occasion on which such powers were granted in the area of land purchase.

estop, estoppel. In a legal suit, to bar or preclude an allegation or denial of a fact because of one's own previous actions or words to the contrary.

estovers. (L., *estoverium*) Necessities permitted by law, whether they be an allowance, maintenance or nourishment. Alimony for a separated wife or maintenance for an imprisoned criminal are two examples. Houboote – the right of a tenant to take wood from the manorial woods for the repair of his house – was known as the common of estover.

estreat rolls. 1: Manorial rolls which contained a record of **amercements** (fines) together with details of **heriots** and **entry fines** to be paid on the death of a tenant. The fines themselves were known as estreats 2: Exchequer estreat rolls were compiled from the exchequer estreats (sums owed to the crown following legal actions) returned by the royal courts each term. The estreats were used to prepare and issue summonses to sheriffs instructing them to collect the money due. Only one Irish exchequer estreat roll has survived, that for Co. Meath for the years 1463–7. *See* exchequer, court of. (National Archives, NAI EX 1/3).

et seq. (L., *et sequens*, and following) A footnote convention citing a particular page and the following pages.

evangelical revival. A lay Protestant religious revival of uncertain origin which affected Britain and Ireland in 1859. Its greatest successes were achieved among Protestants (especially **Presbyterians**) in the north of Ireland probably because a strong revivalist tradition existed in that region. Catholics remained largely unaffected. Some commentators regard the revival as a reaction to increasing industrialisation; others claim it to be a copycat response to reports of revivalism in the United States. At its most extreme the revival of 1859 was characterised by fits, swoons, visions, hysteria and prophecies but its normal manifestation was an intensified religious practice. The Established church welcomed an increase in devotion but remained wary of the attendant excesses. (Emerson, *The Church of Ireland*.)

exchequer, court of. The office of government, first noted in Ireland in 1200, which dealt with the receipt and payment of money and the auditing of accounts and whose records were enrolled on the **pipe** and **memoranda** rolls. The senior official in the exchequer was the treasurer. Other important officials included the under-treasurer, the chancellor (who kept the exchequer seal) and the barons. Over time two distinct departments emerged within the exchequer. On the receipt and payment side (the lower or inferior exchequer), moneys were received or disbursed on behalf of the crown by two chamberlains and a clerk. On the account side (the upper or superior exchequer), the barons of the exchequer audited the accounts of sheriffs and other officials. The barons also exercised an important judicial function in hearing pleas concerning the financial affairs of the crown or exchequer. In time this jurisdiction was enlarged at the expense of the court of **common pleas** by the use of a legal fiction known as *quo minus*. Commoners could seek to recover debts in exchequer by claiming that they were less able (*quo minus*) to discharge their debts to the crown by the default of the defendant. Serious financial irregularities in the Irish exchequer led to the practice of the Irish treasurer presenting his accounts at Westminster for auditing purposes. Hence, although the original records of the court perished in 1922, records of the Westminster audits survive among the English exchequer records. By the eighteenth century the two most important officials in the exchequer were the deputy vice-treasurer (who performed the functions of the vice-treasurer, receiver-general and paymaster-general) and the teller of the exchequer (who received the revenue, issued receipts and made payments from the treasury). Both wielded considerable influence through the private use of state funds in their keeping. James Ferguson's extensive transcripts from the records of the exchequer court are held by the National Archives. (Connolly, *Medieval record sources*, pp. 18–23; Lydon, 'A survey', pp. 49–134; Phair, 'Sir William Betham', pp. 1–99; NLI, MSS 760–1.)

exigent, writ of. A writ issued out of the court of **common pleas** to the sheriff commanding him to summons a defendant to appear in court on pain of outlawry.

exigentor. The official in the court of **common pleas** who wrote out the writs of exigent.

Explanation, Act of (1665). The act (17 & 18 Chas. II, c. 2) which attempted to remedy the muddle that was the earlier **Act of Settlement** (1662). The principal deficiency in the Act of Settlement was that there was not enough land available to satisfy the claims of Cromwellian settlers, royal grantees, former royalist soldiers and those Catholics who were to be restored as innocents. The new act proposed to create a compensatory land bank by reducing the holdings of Cromwellian grantees by one-third. A **court of claims**, procedurally similar to that established under the Act of Settlement, opened in 1666. Since the estate being conveyed was a re-grant, claimants who succeeded in recovering forfeited land were required to pay an annual **quit-rent** to the crown

Expugnatio Hibernica (*The Conquest of Ireland*). A treatise on the Norman invasion of Ireland by Giraldus Cambrensis (Gerald Barry). Giraldus was born in Pembroke and was educated to the church at St Peter's Abbey, Gloucester, and at Paris University. His knowledge of Ireland derives from two lengthy journeys through the east and south of the country c. 1183 and again in 1185–6 when he accompanied Prince John. In *Expugnatio Hibernica* (1189) Giraldus attempts to justify the invasion of Ireland, criticises the barbarity, idleness and treachery of the natives and extols the discipline and civility of the newcomers, elevating for bravery beyond all others his kin, the Fitz-Geralds. Criticising the failure to press home the initial military advantage gained over the Irish, he outlines the means by which the conquest might be completed. Biased towards his race and family, the work is lacking in balance and needs to be read alongside other sources such as *The song of Dermot and the Earl*, contemporary annals and the *Book of Howth*. *See Topographia Hiberniae*. (Martin, 'Gerald of Wales', pp. 279–292; Giraldus Cambrensis, *Expugnatio*.)

extent. A manorial survey which outlined and valued the composition of the manor including rents and **services** due. The aggregated valuation was equivalent to the sum of money that would be received for the manor were it to be let for a year. (Mills, 'Notices', pp. 37–4; White, *Extents*.)

extent land. Land newly brought into cultivation. *See* assart.

eyre, justices in. In Ireland in the thirteenth and early fourteenth centuries, the circuit of justices of the **Dublin Bench** itinerating throughout the country to hear all pleas and to inquire into matters of concern to the crown. Justices of the eyre were therefore also inspectors of local administration. The eyre helped unify the administration of law in Ireland for the justices heard pleas before the fixed courts as well as in the localities. It was an omnicompetent court unlike the commissions of *oyer et terminer* which were issued to deal with specific individual crimes or an epidemic of a similar type of crime. Although in England there were a number of eyres, there was but one in Ireland – the General Eyre. The eyre fell into disuse because of the irregularity and slowness of the circuit. The speed and efficiency of the regular fixed courts in Dublin proved more attractive to litigants seeking redress. Its duties were also eroded by the emerging justices of **gaol delivery** and justices of **assizes**. The last eyre was held in 1322 in Co. Meath.

F

face. The front of a parchment roll as opposed to the dorse (the back).

faculty. In church usage, the power to perform priestly duties or occupy some clerical position, both of which are licensed by a superior ecclesiastic. In the Anglican church the granting and deprivation of faculties was a function of the post-Reformation court of faculties. *See* prerogative and faculties, court of the.

falcon, falconet. Sixteenth-century light ordnance which fired shot weighing about one pound.

falding. A coarse woollen or linen cloth.

falling. (Ir., *fallaing*) A mantle or cloak.

fardel. 1: A bundle or pack 2: A fourth part, as in a bread farl.

farl. A quarter-circle cut from a circular cake of thin bread.

farm. 1: Originally farm meant food but from the fifteenth century meant rent in cash or kind. The modern use of the word as a tract of land devoted to pasture or cultivation probably derives from leasehold tenure which required the payment of a fixed yearly amount or farm. Thus the condition of tenure (a payment) became applied to its subject (a piece of land) 2: The privatisation of tax collection. Before the emergence of the modern bureaucratic state, taxes, dues and fees owing to the state or church were farmed or let to authorised persons who collected and retained them in return for the payment of a fixed sum. This was largely a matter of convenience. The state did not have the machinery to collect revenues such as taxes or customs duties and the clergy wished to be spared the burden and agitation of collecting tithe.

farra. A hen loft or roost in a house.

fascicle. (L., *fasciculus*, pl, *fasciculi*) One of the divisions of a book which is issued in instalments.

fassaghe lands. (Ir., *fásach*, a desert) Waste lands. The term was used to denote the land lying between the marches of the Pale and the lands of the native Irish which was frequently despoiled by native incursions. *See* maghery.

fasti. (L., *fasti dies*, the authorised days, from *fastus*, lawful) A list or calendar of religious festivals, days on which the courts sit, anniversaries or historical events. *Fasti* of the churches contain episcopal and clerical succession lists. (Cotton, *Fasti*.)

fealty. The oath sworn by a tenant to be faithful to his lord, to respect his person and property and to perform his feudal obligations. It was not required to be performed in the presence of the lord but could be sworn before the steward upon the entry of a son into the tenancy of his deceased father. *See* homage, investiture.

fee. A **fief** or estate in land. In medieval times land held from a lord conditional upon the rendering of **homage**, military and allied services. Land held 'in fee' means **freehold** land.

fee-farm grant. A **fee simple** (freehold) grant to a tenant for an annual fixed rent without any other services but forever. This was of great advantage to the tenant and was offered by lords to lure tenants during periods when there was an abundant supply of land and a scarcity of people to till the land. Land held by fee farm grant was immune from interference by the lord of the manor in that, once fixed, the rents remained unalterable and over the years, as inflation kicked in, the rents became a mere pittance. Freeholders were entitled to dispose of their estates as they saw fit but changes in ownership had to be processed through the manor court and an appropriate **entry fine** paid.

feoffee. 1: A person who holds land **in fee** directly 2: Feoffees in a conveyance to **use** were family intimates who were granted **seisin** of an estate so that were the lord to die while his heir was a minor the crown would be denied the feudal incidents of **relief**, **wardship** and marriage.

feoffment. An early form of conveyance effected through the ceremonial livery of **seisin**. Seisin (ownership) was passed when the parties and witnesses to the conveyance physically entered upon the land, the vendor symbolically handed a piece of turf or keys to the purchaser, uttered an appropriate verbal transfer and the transaction was confirmed by a written deed. Deeds of feoffment are recognisable because the action clause contains the phrase 'given, granted, alienated, bargained and sold, and enfeoffed'. The feoffment, like the **bargain and sale**, was too public an affair for many landowners. A third form of conveyance, the **lease and release**, a secret yet valid instrument, gradually superseded both.

fee simple, tenure in. Tenure by **freehold**, to all intents and purposes an absolute and unlimited tenure, often requiring the payment of a fixed sum known as a **chief rent** or fee-farm rent. A fee simple estate was held by a person in his own right, free from condition or limitation. The fee simple could pass to any heir unlike the **fee tail** which descended to a single class of heirs (the issue of the donee). *See* allodial tenure, fee-farm grant.

fee tail. (Fr., *taillé*, cut down) An estate restricted to a specified line of succession, i.e., to a person and his lawful heirs. *See* entail.

felony. A grave crime such as murder, burglary and house-breaking which was punishable by death and forfeiture of land and goods.

feme covert. (Fr., literally, a woman covered by her husband) A doctrine of English common law well into the eighteenth century which held that a married woman, being under the protection of her husband, was to all intents and purposes legally non-existent. When acting with her husband it was considered that she had no independent will and all her actions were excused because they were performed by his command.

feme sole. (Fr., literally, a woman alone) A spinster, widow or divorcee. A feme sole trader was a married woman entitled to engage in business in her own right independently of her husband.

fencibles. Soldiers or militiamen intended for service in the country in which they were raised for the duration of hostilities. Between 1793 and 1802 fencible regiments were raised in Britain and Ireland, some of whom, largely Scottish, volunteered for service in Ireland.

fenianism. *See* Irish Republican Brotherhood.

feodary. A vassal or feudal tenant who holds land of a superior, subject to homage and services.

feretory. 1: A shrine for relics 2: A room or chapel reserved as a feretory.

fess. In heraldry, a broad horizontal band crossing the centre of an escutcheon.

feudal incidents. The crown's ancient entitlement to **wardship, mar-**

riage, **relief** and **escheat** which were forgiven by the **Tenures Abolition Act** of 1662.

fever hospitals. Following harvest failures in 1816 and 1817, Ireland was devastated by a typhus epidemic which lasted until 1819. In order to contain the epidemic fever hospitals, financed by grand jury presentments of up to twice any sum raised by local subscription, were constructed to contain the epidemic. After 1818 fever hospitals were constructed in every county and borough. However, although augmented by the construction of temporary hospitals, they were unable to cope with typhoid on the scale generated by the Great Famine. More people, it appears, died from fever than from malnutrition during the 1840s. *See* ague and Health, General Board of.

fianna. An ancient Gaelic military order which supported the chief lord and maintained order and whose history is heavily interlaced with the fabulous. It forms part of the Ossianic Cycle which deals with the adventures of Fionn MacCumhaill, his son Oisín, grandson Oscar and other warrior-heroes. (Dillon, *Early Irish literature*, pp. 32–50.)

fiant. (L., *Fiant litterae patentes*, make open letters) A warrant under the privy **seal** to **chancery** for the issue of letters **patent** under the great seal for commissions, grants of land, office, privileges or pardons. In the case of grants of land the warrant named the individual beneficiary and specified the value of land to be granted. Fiants were authenticated by the signature of either the sovereign, the lord justice or the lord deputy of the time. In terms of historical value the patent rolls (on which letters patent were recorded) should properly be of greater interest to the historian than the fiants. In many cases, however, letters patent were not enrolled. Furthermore, the patent rolls were destroyed in 1922 and so patents not found in the calendars of patent rolls – and never enrolled – may be found by reference to the fiants which brought them into effect. (*PRI rep. DK*, Appendices to 7–9, 11–13, 15–18, 21; *Irish Fiants of the Tudor sovereigns*.)

fiat. (L., Let it be done, let there be made) A decree, an authoritative command or order.

fibula. A brooch, buckle or clasp, often richly ornamented and used to fasten a cloak or other item of dress.

fief. A feudal estate of land held in return for the payment of military and allied services to the overlord. *See* fee.

field. In heraldry, the colour of the ground or surface of the shield, usually of metal, colour or fur. The two metals are *or* (gold) and *argent* (silver) and the colours are *gules* (red), *vert* (green), *azure* (blue), *purpure* (purple) and *sable* (black). The furs are *ermine* (white with black spots) and *vair* (bluish-grey and white cup-shaped design).

fieri facias. Commonly known as 'fi. fa.', a writ lying for a person who has recovered judgement for debt and damages in the courts which commands the sheriff to levy the amount of the judgement on the defendant's goods. The sheriff has the power to take anything of the defendant except the clothes he is wearing but is not permitted to break open the door of his house to exercise the writ. A stranger's goods in the possession of the defendant are not subject to the writ.

filacer. An official who filed writs and issued process thereon.

filius/filia. Son/daughter.

final concord. *See* fine.

fine. 1: A payment 2: In land contracts a payment upfront to secure admission to a tenancy (see entry fine) 3: A collusive legal action in which a tenant-in-tail agreed to a judgement being entered against him. It was a fiction initiated to convey a piece of land and confirm a change of ownership or to cancel a previous deed. Originally the tenant allowed himself to be sued for wrongful possession by the person to whom the land was being conveyed, acknowledged the plaintiff's claim, had it approved and then had the title insured by registering it in court. Later the process became a pure formality conducted by lawyers. A final concord (an indented record of the case) was produced in triplicate, the foot of which (the foot of fine) was entered in **common pleas**. The upper left side was retained by the purchaser (the querent), the upper right hand side by the seller (the deforciant). A fictional sum was entered at the bottom of each part together with the seller's warranty to defend the purchaser's title to the property. Post-medieval fines are often accompanied by either a conveyance or a mortgage. Levying a fine was the only means by which a married woman, with the consent of her husband, could dispose of land until 1834.

Fines were also resorted to to bar an entail although the estate produced was a '**base fee**', a fee simple estate which persisted only as long as the entail would have continued had it not been barred and which terminated when the entail would have ended. Say Mr Green has a life estate, with remainder to Mr Brown in tail, remainder to Mr White in tail. If Mr Brown bars his entail in favour of Mr Black, Mr Black's estate endures only as long as Mr Brown or any of his issue lives whereupon the original entail becomes active again and the estate devolves to Mr White and his issue. Unlike the **recovery**, levying a fine did not require the consent of the tenant in possession but a recovery was far more effective and produced a fee simple estate. English fines acts in 1489 and 1540 and the Irish Fines Act (10 Chas. I, c. 8, 1634) overturned the prohibition on the barring of entails which the statute of **De Donis Conditionalibus** had sought to restrict. The courts, in any case, were anxious to keep alive the principle of the alienability of land. The 1834 Fines and Recoveries Act (4 & 5 Will. IV, c. 92) abolished the need for fictive collusion by providing for the barring of an entail by the execution of a disentailing assurance. Henceforth the tenant in tail perfected a conveyance using words that a **fee simple** owner used to pass the fee simple. (Megarry, *A manual*, pp. 55–61; Wylie, *Irish land law*, pp. 221–224.)

finial. In **Gothic** architecture, the carved ornamental foliage adorning a spire or pinnacle.

fire, ordeal by. In medieval times, the means by which an accused person cleared himself of an accusation either by walking barefooted and blindfolded over red-hot ploughshares or by grasping a red-hot iron in the hand. Feet or hands were then bound and if after three days the wound had healed the accused was declared innocent. If they remained unhealed he was guilty.

fireboot, firebote. A tenant's entitlement to an allowance of fuel from the land he occupies.

firkin. 1: A small cask or barrel 2: A measure of capacity which varied according to commodity but which in England was equivalent to a quarter barrel or one half of a **kilderkin**.

First Fruits, Board of. First fruits represented the first year's revenue of all Anglican ecclesiastical benefices which was payable as royal taxation after the Reformation (25 Hen. VIII, c. 22), replacing payments to the papacy known as **annates**. Clergymen were also liable for the twentieth parts, a tax of 12 pence in the pound annually out of all benefices as they were valued at the Reformation. In 1711 the **twentieth parts** were forgiven and the first fruits were granted to the Board of First Fruits, a body established for the purpose of buying up impropriations (**tithe** in lay hands). Composed chiefly of Anglican prelates, the board was empowered to finance the building and reparation of churches, purchase **glebe** land and construct glebe houses. It was funded from 1778 by an annual parliamentary grant – usually of about £5,000 – and received £46,863 as compensation for the loss of clerical boroughs at the **Act of Union**. The annual grant was increased to £60,000 in 1813 but reduced to £10,000 in 1823. In all, more than £1 million was disbursed between the Union and 1823. Initially the money was used to provide interest-free loans to clergymen to build glebe houses. From 1808 (48 Geo. III, c. 65) the board was given the freedom to apply the funds as it saw fit and it began to make non-repayable grants to clergymen with low incomes. This impacted significantly on church organisation. The number of benefices increased by 25%, there was a 30% increase in the number of churches, the number of glebe houses rose from 354 to 829 and the number of absentee clergymen declined. In 1833 the board's functions and income were transferred to the Ecclesiastical Commissioners for Ireland as part of the reforming **Church Temporalities (Ireland) Act**. *See* impropriate.

first instance, case of. A case other than one on appeal.

flachter. A type of push plough used to remove the **scraw** or sod and prepare the turf for cutting. It consisted of a semi-circular or shovel-shaped blade mounted on a shaft which was topped by a broad cross-bar. The blade of the flachter was driven under the sod by powerful thrusts of the thigh against the cross-bar. (Evans, 'The flachter', p. 82–7.)

fletcher. A person who makes or deals in arrows or bows and arrows.

Flight of the Earls. The departure from Ireland on 14 September 1607 of Hugh O'Neill, earl of Tyrone, and Rory O'Donnell, earl of Tyrconnell, Cuconnacht Maguire and about 100 others, the reasons for which remain unclear. Apologists for the earls claim the flight was precipitated by fears that the government was plotting against them or present it as a tactical retreat to seek aid personally from Philip II. Others have argued that the extension of English law to Ulster, the persecution of Catholics and attempts by the government to drive a wedge between Gaelic overlords and their vassals represented developments to which the earls were unable to adapt. Government apologists claim the earls fled to escape justice following the discovery of a plot by O'Neill to seize Dublin Castle and establish a new government. Their flight without permission created the opening for the plantation of Ulster. (Canny, 'The flight of the earls, pp. 380–99; McCavitt, 'The flight of the earls, 1607', pp. 159–73.)

flotsam. Goods afloat in the sea after a ship has sunk or run aground.

flux, bloody. Highly infectious, bacillary dysentery which was transmitted by contaminated food, fingers and flies and characterised by bowel colic, painful and exhausting straining and a bloody discharge from the bowels. It was recorded in Ireland as early as 763 AD and was known as *ruith fola*. According to Gerard Boate, a seventeenth-century Dutch physician, dysentery was so common in Ireland that the English inhabitants called it the 'country disease'.

folio. 1: A leaf of a manuscript 2: A leaf number as in f.8, which means folio 8. The reference f.8r. indicates the front of the leaf (*recto*), the side to be read first, f.8v. is a reference to the back of the leaf (*verso*).

Foras feasa ar Éirinn (A basis for knowledge about Ireland). Written by Geoffrey Keating (1580–1644?), an **Old English** Catholic priest, *Foras feasa ar Éirinn* is a narrative history of Ireland down to the twelfth century. A mixture of history, myth and religion, Keating's history tells the story of the Catholic community in Ireland with particular emphasis on the shared heritage of both native Irish (*Gaeil*) and Old English (*Sean Ghaill*) Catholics. Probably completed in 1634 and not printed for nearly a hundred years, it was the most popular book ever written in Irish and circulated widely in manuscript form. Keating collected a vast amount of material including stories, historical tracts and poems and gained access to manuscripts such as the **Book of Leinster**. He used succession lists of Irish kings as the framework to hold together his narrative. Keating was well versed in the writings of Welsh, English and Old English commentators on Ireland as is evident in the preface to the book where he savages, what he claims were, the false accounts of Ireland produced by **Giraldus Cambrensis, Edmund Spenser, William Camden, Richard Stanihurst, Meredith Hanmer** and **Fynes Moryson**. He was born in Tipperary, a descendant of early English settlers, and was educated to the church at Bordeaux and (probably) Rheims before returning to serve in Ireland in the early seventeenth century. (Keating, *Foras feasa ar Éirinn*; Cunningham, *The world of Geoffrey Keating*.)

forestall. 1: To waylay 2: The offence of impeding normal trading by preventing, purchasing or diverting goods before they reach the market in order to raise prices. Also known as regrating.

forma pauperis. Permission granted by the courts to a pauper to sue without cost. It was introduced by 10 Chas. I, c. 17 (1635) and was allowed where a pauper swore that he was not worth five pounds and acquired a certificate from a lawyer stating that he had good cause to sue.

form of the beads. Introduced in 1538 by the Protestant archbishop of Dublin, George Browne, the 'form of the beads' was a statement of faith to be read during divine service. It repudiated papal authority, pronounced papal bulls and excommunications worthless, affirmed the supremacy of the monarch and outlined church teaching (which, at that time, differed little from Catholic teaching). (Maxwell, *Irish history*, pp. 123–4.)

'49 officers. Officers and soldiers who had served in Ireland before 5 June 1649 and who were entitled to arrears of service pay ('49 arrears') which were to be discharged out of forfeited land in Ireland.

forty-shilling freeholder. *See* franchise.

fosse. A defensive ditch around a farmstead such as a ringfort.

fosterage. The Gaelic practice of fostering out children with the intention of developing or reinforcing political and military connections between the lesser and greater lords. Lesser septs paid to foster the child of a noble family and to have their own children fostered in the homes of nobles. Thus the whole business of fosterage was usually accompanied by the transfer of cattle. Fosterage facilitated the assimilation of the fostering sept into the lord's protection and affinity. Together with **gossipred**, it was banned by the English administration in 1366. *See* Kilkenny, Statutes of. (Fitzsimons 'Fosterage', pp. 138–49.)

foundling hospital. A hospital founded principally to remove abandoned and destitute children from the streets. Two were established in Ireland in the eighteenth century, one each in Dublin (1707) and Cork (c. 1750), both in association with **houses of industry**. Attention to the well-being of inmates was notoriously slipshod and for the majority of children admission to a foundling hospital amounted to a death sentence. Between 1737 and 1743, 2,700 children out of almost 4,000 foundling admissions perished in the Dublin hospital. Conditions appear to have worsened over the years. Reporting in 1827, the commissioners of Irish education inquiry claimed a survival rate of one child in five. Children were accepted from the age of one year, received schooling from age eight to twelve and then progressed to apprenticeships if they managed to survive that long. The Irish Miscellaneous Estimates committee recommended that admissions should cease in Dublin in 1830 but there remained a large number of children such as children at nurse, sick children and newly-apprenticed children who needed support beyond that date. The Cork institution was shut down in 1856. (Foundling Hospital.)

Four Courts. 1: The four central royal courts of justice were **king's bench**, **chancery**, the **exchequer**, and **common pleas**. All evolved from the undifferentiated *curia regis* or king's council, the assembly of advisers and officials which attended the king. The individual courts appear to have developed from specialised smaller committees operating within the *curia regis* which gradually became formalised as separate institutions replete with their own staffs. One of the earliest to develop was the exchequer, the administrative department presided over by the treasurer which controlled income and expenditure. On its judicial side the barons of the exchequer resolved disputes concerning the royal revenues. Chancery, the royal secretariat through which all important state and legal documents passed and where records of the rolls were preserved, was headed by the king's secretary and chief adviser, the **lord chancellor**. The chancellor's role as adviser or conscience to the king in the resolution of cases for which common law provided no remedy led to the delegation of equitable jurisdiction to that court. The sheer volume of work coming before the *curia regis* and the inconvenience to litigants of having to trail around the country after the king prompted the creation of a permanent court at Westminster which heard civil disputes between commoners. This practice was replicated in Ireland in the thirteenth century when the itinerant judges sat in Dublin to hear common pleas. The *curia regis* retained its judicial role and continued to hear criminal cases as well as civil pleas. When a chief justice and **puisne** judges were appointed, this side of the *curia regis* became a separate court too, the court of king's bench. Common law was introduced to Ireland after the English model but because the king's writ ran only within the Pale it was not until the seventeenth century that the Gaelic **Brehon law** was finally supplanted by the royal and local courts 2: The complex of buildings on the bank of the Liffey designed by Thomas Cooley and constructed (with some modifications) by James Gandon. The site was originally intended as a location for a records repository but in 1785 it was decided to relocate the superior courts there from their unsatisfactory accommodation at St Michael's Hill near Christ Church. Comprising a central domed pile and wings which form two quadrangles, the four courts were housed in different corners of the complex. A new building was added to accommodate the rolls court and a *nisi prius* court was later erected. (Culliton, 'The Four Courts, Dublin', pp. 116–131.)

Four Masters, Annals of the. The popular name for *Annála Ríoghachta Éireann*, the *Four Masters* is a synthesis of earlier annals, recording events in Ireland from earliest times down to the beginning of the seventeenth century. The work was compiled by Micheál Ó Cléirigh, Fear Feasa Ó Maoil Chonaire, Cú Choigcríche Ó Cléirigh and Cú Choigcríche Ó Duibhgeannain in Donegal during the years 1632–6. Ó Cléirigh, a Franciscan, travelled throughout Ireland assembling materials for research on history, historiography and other subjects. The *Annals* include detailed descriptions of events of local significance, items of national interest and a small number of references to international events together with references to social and material culture. They are particularly useful for family relationships and references to men of learning. *See* John O'Donovan. (O'Donovan, *Annals*.)

franchise, elective. Until the twentieth century the qualifications which enabled citizens to exercise the elective franchise in Ireland were complex, discriminatory and exclusive. Catholics were disfranchised entirely from 1728 until 1793 and were debarred from parliament from 1691 until 1829 because they would not take the **oath of abjuration** and declare against Catholic doctrine. Between 1704 and 1780 Protestant dissenters, although disbarred from municipal corporations, remained eligible to vote and sit in parliament. Irish women became eligible to vote in local government elections from 1898 but were denied the parliamentary franchise until 1918 when those aged over 30 were enfranchised. In 1923 the Irish Free State reduced the age qualification for women to 21 and the government of Northern Ireland followed suit in 1928. Before the **Act of Union** the 300 seats in the Irish house of commons were filled by the votes of a tiny minority of the population. Trinity College, for example, with an electorate of 92 fellows and scholars, sent two MPs to parliament while 55 corporations, each comprising 12 or 13 burgesses, sent 110. Knocktopher had a single qualified voter in 1783. In all, 97 boroughs (55 corporation, 36 freeman and 6 manor boroughs) were controlled by an individual patron or patrons. Hence, although some boroughs were hotly disputed, contested elections were largely confined to the 32 county constituencies, the eight county boroughs, Londonderry and Swords. Apart from membership of a corporation, **freeman** status or, in the case of the 12 'potwalloping' boroughs, residency of six months (one year from 1782), eligibility to vote was restricted to the forty-shilling freeholders (owners or lessees for lives of land worth forty-shillings above rent). The forty-shilling freehold was the qualification under which Catholics obtained the right to vote following Hobart's 1793 relief act. It was a short-lived concession. The emancipation act of 1829 – which permitted Catholics to sit in parliament – abolished the forty-shilling franchise by raising the threshold to ten pounds and at a stroke reduced the county electorate from over 200,000 to 37,000. The Representation of the People (Ireland) Act (2 & 3 Will. IV, c. 88, 1832) increased the county electorate to 60,000 by admitting more leaseholders and the borough franchise to 30,000 by introducing a single qualification, occupation of property valued at £10 or more. Compared with England and Scotland the Irish elective franchise was hopelessly inequitable. In England one person in five was entitled to vote, in Scotland one in eight yet only one in 20 held the franchise in Ireland. The 1850 Irish Franchise Act (13 & 14 Vict., c. 69) transformed the electoral process dramatically. The county threshold was raised to £12 but the franchise was now extended to embrace occupiers (and not only owners or leaseholders) of holdings valued at £12 or more. As a result, the electorate more than doubled, rising from 60,597 in 1832 to 135,245 by 1851–2. Under the Franchise Act the borough occupier franchise was lowered to £8, a threshold that was subsequently halved from 1868 by the Representation of the People (Ireland) Act (31 & 32 Vict., c. 49). Proportional inequities in the franchise were removed throughout the United Kingdom when a single qualification of £10 was admitted by the 1884 Representation of the People Act. A year later new constituencies were created with the abolition of all but nine of the boroughs and the subdivision of the counties and the boroughs of Belfast and Dublin. Almost 750,000 people were now entitled to vote in parliamentary elections, a figure which climbed to over two million by 1918 when males over the age of 21 and females aged 30 or over were enfranchised (7 & 8 Geo. V, cc 64, 65). Until the introduction of the secret ballot in 1872 (35 &36 Vict., c. 33), balloting was a public affair with the elector's preference being declared aloud and registered alongside his name. Inevitably this enabled landlords to influence their tenants' votes. By the time the secret ballot was introduced, however, tenants had already begun to exercise their franchise unfettered by such intimidation. *See* borough. (Hoppen, *Elections*.)

franchises, riding the. The act of traversing the boundaries of an area of jurisdiction at regular intervals to prevent the boundaries from being altered or forgotten. In the city of Dublin this was carried out triennially and included the delimitation of the maritime boundary by the casting of a spear as far as possible into the sea.

Franciscans (Friars Minor). Founded by St Francis c. 1207, the Franciscans first appeared in Ireland in Youghal and Cork c. 1224 and spread quickly throughout the country after Richard Ingleworth, head of the custody (province) of Cambridge arrived in 1231–2. In Ireland the order experienced the dissension that existed elsewhere in Europe between reforming observant Franciscans who sought a literal and austere interpretation of the simple rule of poverty of St Francis and conventuals who espoused a more liberal position. By 1538 the majority of friaries were observant. In the fourteenth century racial discord between Gaelic Irish and Anglo-Irish friars created tensions within the order which was governed by Anglo-Irish provincials until William O'Reilly emerged as provincial in 1461. After this Gaelic friars dominated and the Franciscans became powerful opponents of the Reformation and Tudor expansion. Although the order was suppressed and its friaries sequestered, the Franciscans continued to operate in the environs of their former houses. They opened continental seminaries at Louvain and Rome to train priests for service in Ireland. *See* conventualism. (Millett.)

Franciscan Third Order Regular. The Third Order Regular developed from the Third Order Secular, societies of lay men and women who wished to live the Franciscan life but could not profess their vows in the First Order (the Friars Minor) or the Second Order (the nuns) on account of their married status. The rule of the Third Order Secular bound members to fasting and abstinence, prayer, confession and communion, works of charity, assembly for religious instruction and simplicity of dress. The Third Order Regular adopted this rule and added the vows of poverty, chastity and obedience. The first evidence of their presence in Ireland comes from an indult sent by Martin V in 1426 and by the fifteenth century there were over 40 houses. The order appears to have been principally engaged with pastoral work and in educating boys and was largely concentrated in Gaelic areas. It declined significantly after 1600 and was extinct by 1635.

frankalmoign. Literally, free alms, frankalmoign was an ecclesiastical tenure in which no fealty was owed and the service to be rendered was the duty to pray for the lord's soul.

frankhouse. A free hospital operated by the **knights hospitallers**.

Frankpledge, View of. A medieval method of social control by which each member of a **tithing** was responsible in law for the good behaviour of the other members. Described by Holdsworth as 'a system of compulsory collective bail fixed for individuals not after their arrest for crime but as a safeguard in anticipation of it' it is uncertain as to what extent it was actually realised on the ground in Ireland. (Holdsworth, *English law*, i, pp. 13–17).

frater, fratry. A refectory.

***Fratres Cruciferi, Crucigeri,* Canons OSA of the Holy Cross, Crutched Friars**. A congregation of **Augustinian** hospitallers which emerged in the twelfth century in Italy, the *Fratres Cruciferi* (the cross-bearing friars) founded at least 15 monastery-hospitals in Ireland in the late twelfth and early thirteenth centuries to serve the poor and infirm. The hospitals were maintained by endowments, bequests and indulgences. As well as the brethren, some of the houses had sisters who worked in the hospitals and appear to have had some involvement in the management of the institutions. They were not military hospitallers like the **Knights Hospitallers of St John of Jerusalem** or the **Knights Templars**. (Brook, *Register.*)

Frauds, Statue of (1695). This statute (7 Will. III, c. 12) was enacted to prevent fraud in relation to trusts, **wills** and contracts for the sale of land by requiring written evidence of the devise. Henceforth all devises of land, including assignments, grants, trusts and wills must be in written form or risk being declared void.

freehold. Tenure in **fee simple**. Freehold land was, and is, a parcel of land held for an indefinite time, as distinguished from a leasehold which is held for a specified period. It generally required the payment of a fixed sum, the **chief rent** or fee-farm rent, and attendance at the manor court. A **heriot** was payable on the death of a freeholder and the heir owed an **entry fine** to enter the land.

freeman. In medieval times, a citizen possessing personal freedom unlike a serf or **betagh**. Freemen could take actions in the common law courts on their own behalf unlike the unfree who relied on their lord or the **custom of the manor** in the case of manorial courts. *See* advowry. Once admitted to the freedom of a corporate town and entered on the register of freemen, a man was permitted to practise his trade and vote in parliamentary elections. Freedom was attained through the completion of an apprenticeship, through descent from one's father, by marriage into the family of a freeman or by grace of the mayor and corporation. In Dublin freedom was obtained through the **guilds**. After the **Newtown Act** (1747) abolished the requirement that freemen must reside within the corporation boundary, the majority of freemen were absentees who appeared only at election time.

freemasonry. Irish freemasonry originated in the 1720s with the founding of a grand lodge to oversee local lodges. In its early years the order was riven by tensions between Jacobite and Hanoverian masons and grand lodge authority was not fully accepted by local lodges for over a century. Masonic association with Enlightenment scepticism and rational inquiry encouraged its growth and, despite papal condemnation, Catholics comprised the majority of Irish freemasons in the late eighteenth century. Daniel O'Connell was initiated in 1799 but subsequently distanced himself from the order. Membership crossed class boundaries to include tradesmen, farmers as well as the gentry and nobility. Masonic groups like The Order of Ancient, Free and Accepted Masons of Ireland copied their structure from the craft guilds, the new freemason passing successively by initiation through the three craft degrees of entered apprentice, fellow craft and master mason. There were also many side and higher orders and degrees. The rituals of initiation and the form of meetings were complex and suffused with images drawn from the building trade. Masonic processions on the feast of St John the Baptist persisted into the early 1800s and were attended by displays of lodge regalia and flags. The use of secret rituals, passwords, signs and handshakes together with its exclusively Protestant composition in the nineteenth century encouraged lurid speculation about the true purpose of the order but such practices and symbolism were copied by many other brotherhoods including the Orange Order and the Ancient Order of Hibernians. Like Orangeism and Hibernianism, freemasonry provided a social and mutual aid network to members. (Buckley and Anderson, *Brotherhoods*; Crossle, *Irish masonic records*; de Vere White, 'The Freemasons', pp. 46–57.)

friendly society. With their guild-like structure and, in some instances, quasi-masonic rituals and regalia, friendly societies emerged in the eighteenth and nineteenth centuries as mutual-aid associations to protect members against expenses incurred through sickness and death. Many employed doctors to provide free medical attention to members and their families, covered funeral expenses and paid death benefit to the bereaved. Members contributed their dues at weekly meetings which were also important social occasions. In 1831 there were over 280 registered friendly societies in Ireland, 119 of which were located in Dublin. The popularity of the friendly society was boosted by the introduction of the National Insurance Act (1911) which legislated for sick benefit and old age pensions for workers who paid an insurance stamp. The act permitted registered friendly societies to collect national insurance payments and to use them to enhance society benefits. After the First World War the increasing involvement of the state in welfare issues and the growth of insurance companies reduced the importance of friendly societies but the support they provided to members continues to be offered by trade and credit unions and in-house company medical aid schemes. (Buckley and Anderson, *Brotherhoods*.)

frist. To grant a delay or respite to a debtor in order that he might pay off what he owes.

fuidhir. (Ir.) In Gaelic society, a 'stranger-tenant', often an outlaw or 'broken man' who came from another tribe and sought the protection of the chief. Although he might be granted cattle and land, his was a tenancy-at-will and could be dispensed with summarily. Within Gaelic society he occupied the lowest strata and was despised by other tribesmen.

fulacht fia. (Ir., roasted deer) Recognisable by mounds of burnt stones in marshy locations, *fulachtaí fia* are ancient cooking spots at the sites where summer hunting parties bivouacked. They usually contain dug-out trunks or plank-lined pits where water was heated by hot stones.

full. To cleanse, thicken and soften woollen cloth by washing, shrinking and beating it with wooden mallets or hazel rods, working with the hands or trampling to leave a short pile across the surface.

fuller's earth. A hydrous silicate of alumina employed in the cleansing of cloth.

fulling mill. A riverine mill where cloth was thickened and cleansed, examples of which are recorded in Ireland as early as the thirteenth century.

funeral entries. The records of funerals of deceased members of families who were entitled to bear heraldic arms. They form part of the heraldic archives of the **Ulster King of Arms** (since 1943 the Genealogical Office) and contain a record of the name and issue of deceased persons, illustrations of their arms and details of the order of funeral processions for the period 1588 to 1691. The genealogical material contained in the funeral entries was important for arms were hereditary and such records were invaluable in cases of dispute. The funeral entries are held by the Genealogical Office and are available on microfilm in the National Library. *See* herald.

furlong. (Literally, furrow long) Originally the length of a commonfield furrow which varied regionally according to the area of the acre in use. The usual length of a furrow is 40 perches which is equivalent to 220 yards, imperial measure. It probably derived from the distance a plough team could plough before resting.

furze. Furze was cultivated for cattle fodder and for firewood in locations where fuel was scarce. (Lucas, *Furze*.)

fustians. Blankets or clothes which went under and over the bedsheets.

G

gabbard. A barge.

Gaelic League. *See Conradh na Gaeilge*.

gaffer. An agent who organised a group of his relations and neighbours to travel to England to reap in the nineteenth century.

gale day. A gale was a periodic payment of rent which in the nineteenth century was payable twice yearly on 1 March and 1 September, the gale days. A 'hanging gale' was permission to be six months in arrears in the payment of rent, a concession granted to enable a tenant to establish himself.

gallicanism. Originally the policy and doctrine of a group within the French Catholic church which sought to limit papal authority in secular affairs, considered the pope to be subject to ecumenical councils, believed papal infallibility on doctrinal matters to be subject to the affirmation of the whole church and favoured the right of secular rulers to make episcopal appointments and receive the revenue of vacant sees. Gallicanism appeared in Ireland in the seventeenth century amongst **Old English** Catholics who expressed a willingness to repudiate the authority of the pope over temporal affairs as a bartering tool to lessen penal impositions on Catholics. In the **remonstrances** of 1661 and 1666 prominent Old English Catholics strove to demonstrate their loyalty (and secure themselves under the Restoration land settlement) by acknowledging that all subjects were bound by the supreme authority of the king in civil and temporal affairs and by repudiating the right of any foreign power to discharge them from their allegiance. The Catholic clergy, however, overwhelmingly opposed this view. Gallicanism re-appeared in the late eighteenth and early nineteenth centuries when a minority of bishops and lay Catholics favoured a British government veto over the appointment of bishops to assuage Protestant fears and accelerate the granting of **Catholic emancipation**. Gallicanism was suspected of **Maynooth College** because the early teaching staff came from France and because the college was beholden to the administration for grants. *See* ultramontanism. (Bowen, *Paul Cardinal Cullen*, pp. 30–84.)

gallon. A Gaelic unit of spatial measurement employed in Co. Cavan, equivalent to 25 acres.

gaol delivery, commission of. A commission issuing from **king's bench** to have those detained in jail delivered up to the justices of **assize** for the determination of their cases.

garderobe. A toilet, usually overhanging a castle wall.

Gardiner's Relief Act. *See* relief acts.

garron. A small, hardy draught horse.

galleting. A decorative feature on house walls created by the insertion of contrasting stones into the mortar.

gallowglass. (Ir., *gall óglach*, foreign soldier) Gaelic mercenary foot-soldier of Scottish descent who fought with a distinctive long-handled battle-axe or sparre.

gauger. An excise official whose duty it was to gauge the capacity of casks or other vessels or containers and assess the customs duty on any dutiable imported goods. The duty of gauger was usually united with that of **searcher**. For the collection of inland duties on beer, ale and spirits the revenue districts of Ireland were divided into 'walks' and a gauger was appointed for each walk. Twice weekly the gauger traversed his walk to examine the accounts of brewers and distillers and record the quantity of liquor brewed. A surveyor examined and attested the gauger's returns and submitted them to the district head (the collector) who charged and collected the duty. (Ní Mhurchadha, *The customs*.)

gauntlet. A leather glove fortified with metal which protected the hands in combat.

gavelkind. Partible inheritance, a system of joint and equal inheritance among males. Typically, under **Brehon law**, the lord divided the land owned by a deceased member of the sept equally between his sons, subject to periodic re-distribution. The 'gavelkind act' (2 Anne, c. 6, 1704) required the estate of a deceased Catholic to be gavelled or partibly divided among his sons. If the eldest son conformed to the **Church of Ireland,** however, the entire estate devolved to him. This act was not repealed until 1778. *See* penal laws, relief acts.

gavellor, gaviller. (OE, *gafol*, rent, tax or tribute) In medieval Ireland, a **tenant-at-will**. He was a **freeman**, largely of English origin, who paid rent and owed suit of court and labour services to the manor. The tenancy-at-will appears to have been nominal in that gavellors holdings were heritable.

Genealogical Office. *See* Ulster king of arms

genealogies. Collections of pedigrees of native Irish overlords which are now considered spurious, certainly for the pre-Patrician era, and propagandist in the sense that they were compiled to validate the accession to lordship of the contemporary lord.

General Assembly of the Presbyterian Church in Ireland. The annual meeting of **Presbyterian** ministers, officers and representative elders from the presbyteries. It exercises overall control in matters of faith, education, property, discipline and the missionary work in the church. It elects its own officers and committees and appoints a moderator whose term of office is of one year's duration. It is the supreme court of appeal for cases taken from the **session, presbytery** or **synod**. The General Assembly was formed in 1840 with the merger of the **Synod**

of **Ulster** and the **Seceders**. In 1854 it was joined by the southern congregations, formerly known as the Southern Association or Synod of Munster.

General Convention. A convention of bishops, clergy and lay representatives that met in February 1870 to guide the Church of Ireland through the vicissitudes of disestablishment and to devise plans for the future administration of the church. It agreed on a constitution and structure for the newly independent body. The General Synod, an assembly of the bishops, clergy and lay representatives, became the supreme governing council of the church (with diocesan synods to supervise local affairs). Bishops were to be elected by an electoral college drawn from all the dioceses within the province in which the vacant see lay. *See* Representative Church Body. (Acheson, *A history*, pp. 200–205.)

general lesson. In accordance with the requirement that schools connected with the national system be conducted on a non-denominational basis, the commissioners of education in Ireland directed that a general lesson on religious tolerance be taught in all schools and that a printed version be displayed in every school. The theme of the lesson was tolerance as Christ exemplified it in his life. Pupils were exhorted to live peaceably with all men, to love and pray for their enemies, to treat kindly those who held erroneous doctrines and to turn the cheek when confronted with unkindly behaviour, violence, quarrelling and abuse. *See* Education, National System of. (*Fiftieth report of the commissioners of education in Ireland* (1883), p. 31.)

german. A relationship in the fullest sense. Fully akin.

gibbet. An upright post with a projecting arm from which an executed felon was suspended.

gleave, glieve. A lance.

glebe land. Land belonging to a parish and forming part of a clergyman's benefice. This freehold land was usually granted to a parish at the time of its foundation (from the eighteenth century) or was purchased by the **Board of First Fruits** to supplement the living. Glebes varied considerably in extent from parish to parish. They were leased out or farmed by the minister. The glebe was a feature of Anglo-Norman Ireland, the Gaelic equivalent being **termon** land (church endowments that were farmed for rent and **refection** by hereditary tenants known as **coarbs** or **erenaghs**). *See* terrier.

glib. Gaelic hairstyle characterised by a long fringe overhanging the forehead and sometimes drawn over the eyes.

Glorious Revolution. The phrase used to describe the events between 1688 and 1689 from the deposing of James II and the accession of William of Orange and James' daughter, Mary, to the acceptance by the new monarchs of constitutional arrangements which severely curbed the prerogative powers of the crown. *See* Rights, Declaration of.

gnieve, gneeve. Gaelic spatial unit, equivalent to ten acres. Two gnieves were equal to one **sessiagh**.

gorget. 1: Neck and throat armour constructed of plate metal 2: A crescent-shaped, beaten-gold neck collar with attached discs at either end. Dating from the Bronze Age and unique to Ireland, almost all gorget discoveries (including that found at Gleninsheen, Co. Clare) have been made in the environs of the Shannon estuary.

gort. (L., *hortus*, a small field) 1: A small parcel of land or close of five or six acres given over to some particular use 2: A small enclosed garden attached to a **clachan** house.

gossipred (compaternity). A relationship cemented through baptismal sponsorship. Like **fosterage** and inter-marriage, gossipred was used in Gaelic Ireland to foster kinship ties between the lord and his extended family and clients. As there was a finite number of children who could be fostered and married off, **gossipred** facilitated the development of additional affinities by enabling a child to be fostered by one family and sponsored by another. What gossipred actually entailed, however, remains unclear. When a man sponsored a child at baptism he became the child's godfather and 'gossip' to the parents. The relationship was then firmed up in any one of a number of ways. At the baptismal font the parties might publicly bind themselves to mutual assistance. There might be a symbolic breaking of bread and a pledge of service or a specific arrangement agreed by voluntary oath-taking. The most solemn arrangement involved all parties receiving the eucharist together and pledging adherence to each other. The whole affair was usually accompanied by gifts. (Fitzsimons, 'Fosterage', pp. 138–49.)

Gothic. There were three identifiable evolutions in Gothic construction during the middle ages: the Early English or **pointed style**, the **decorated style** and the **perpendicular style**. These styles were not rigidly adhered to and there was considerable overlap. The perpendicular style did not occur in Ireland in the middle ages but when Gothicism was revived during the nineteenth century many churches were constructed in that style.

Gothick. A loosely-Gothic architectural style, heavily romanticised and incorporating mock antique features such as towers, turrets, machicolations and follies. It was fashionable in the late eighteenth and early nineteenth centuries. Gothick novels echoed such improbabilities in their settings (ruined abbeys and houses) and plots.

Gothic revival. Heavily influenced by trends in contemporary English architecture, the Gothic revival or neo-Gothic style became the most important architectural movement in Ireland in the nineteenth century. The Church of Ireland set the pace. Funded by the **Board of**

First Fruits, it began to erect small churches in Gothic perpendicular style in the early nineteenth century. Typically these were simple, rectangular structures, often battlemented. A square tower at the western end was topped with a spire and flanking pinnacles. Pointed windows contained simple intersecting tracery. This deliberate invocation of a pre-Reformation style was intended to emphasise the historical continuity of the church. Until the 1820s the Catholic church favoured neo-classicism (as did the Presbyterian and Unitarian churches), a style which was awe-inspiring and evoked an established order. St Mary's pro-cathedral in Dublin (1815, enlarged with a Greek **Doric** portico in 1840) is a notable example. Gradually, however, Gothic came to predominate, initially in perpendicular (Carlow, 1820) or Tudor Gothic style (St Malachy's, Belfast, 1844). The greatest and most influential exponent of Gothic revivalism in Ireland was the English architect, A. W. Pugin (Killarney, 1842, Enniscorthy, 1843). Pugin, who considered classical architecture paganistic and lionised Gothic as truly Christian, encouraged architects to look at earlier Gothic styles such as Early English or the **decorated style**. He despised ornament other than that which enhanced the structure of the church and designed churches that were sympathetic to the ceremonies they were intended to accommodate. There was a clear distinction between nave and chancel, aisles were laid out to facilitate processions and a proper baptistery was provided. His designs incorporated the rich symbolism of earlier Gothic churches with their cruciform plan and triply-divided windows echoing the Trinity. As was the case with all medieval churches, Pugin's internal arrangement was immediately obvious when viewed from without. Both Patrick Byrne (St Patrick's, Blackrock, 1842) and J. J. McCarthy (Dominic Street, Dublin, 1860) were heavily influenced by Pugin's writing and work. Towards the close of the century ornate Gothic church styles yielded to the simpler **Hiberno-Romanesque**, an unpretentious form which incorporated round-headed windows and doorways that were modelled on earlier monastic churches. (Richardson, *Gothic revival*; Harbison, Potterton and Sheehy, *Irish art*.)

Goulborn's Act (1825). Goulborn, the Irish chief secretary, introduced the repressive Unlawful Societies Act (6 Geo. IV, c. 4) in 1825 to curb the **Catholic Association** whose rapid growth had alarmed the English administration. The bill declared unlawful any body (including Orange lodges) that remained in existence for more than 14 days to seek a redress of grievances against church or state. The Catholic Association adroitly disbanded only to reform within days with a modified programme purged of overtly political goals. *See* Brunswick clubs.

Grace, Commission of (1684–8). A sequel to the Acts of **Settlement** and

Explanation, the Commission of Grace was prompted by an unsettling scramble by discoverers to ferret out **concealed land** or land held under dubious title. To quieten the uncertainty, Charles II issued a commission to the **lord lieutenant** in 1684 to appoint commissioners to issue clean title to those troubled that their titles were defective. The commissioners were authorised to compound with the occupiers and grant new tenures direct from the crown for such rents and fines and under such tenures as they thought fit. Protestants suspected the commission to be a 'snare' to open their titles to minute inspection to the advantage of Catholics and a means of increasing royal revenue. Grants under the commission, of which there were approximately 500, were recorded in the *Books of Survey and Distribution* and have been printed in *Third volume of reports to the commissioners on public records in Ireland, 1820–25* (Dublin, 1829). *See* defective titles. (Hatchell, *Abstract*.)

Graces (1625–1641). The 'graces' were a series of royal concessions on land and religious issues to be offered to Ireland in exchange for a number of annual subventions to the crown. The bargaining process was initiated by the **Old English** who wished to demonstrate that Catholicism and royalism were not mutually exclusive. They also sought to capitalise on the threat of a Spanish invasion and the inadequate defences of the country to leverage significant concessions from the crown. In 1628 the Old English Catholics were joined by the New English Protestants (who would have to share the burden of the subsidies) in a parliamentary delegation to England. Most of their 51 demands for reforms of a general nature useful to all sections of the community were readily conceded. These included the reduction of official fees, the easing of licensing controls on exports, the revoking of commercial and industrial monopolies and the introduction of regulations to reduce the depredations of the army on local communities. Many demands which touched on land and religious issues were also conceded such as amendments to the **court of wards and liveries**, the appointment of Old English commanders to new army companies, the right of heirs to succeed and lawyers to qualify by taking the oath of allegiance as opposed to the **oath of supremacy**, the curtailment of the jurisdiction of the **ecclesiastical courts** over Catholics and crown recognition of all land titles of 60 or more years standing. The Old English, however, failed to secure the rights of Catholics to hold office and Catholics remained legally liable for recusancy fines. The New English secured confirmation of the titles of Ulster **undertakers** irrespective of whether they had observed the plantation conditions. In return for these concessions Ireland was to tender three annual subsidies of £40,000, payable quarterly. The money was paid over but the implementation of the graces proceeded slowly. The pledge regarding the appointment of Old English commanders was broken, land titles remained unconfirmed and only the threat of cutting off the subsidies advanced the reform of the court of wards. As the military position improved the government stalled and the most important graces were postponed. In 1632 the government felt secure enough to meet a deficit of £20,000 by more regular exaction of the recusancy fines. Under Wentworth's lord lieutenancy the Old English renewed their demands for the graces but, although further subsidies were voted, their grievances were not met and the security of land titles remained a concern. After Wentworth's execution, and faced with a hostile Westminster parliament, Charles attempted to gain support in Ireland by confirming the graces. Lords Justice Borlase and Parsons, puritans and pro-parliament, who were exercising power in place of the absentee Leicester, prorogued parliament in August 1641 before statutory effect could be given to the concessions. Within months the country was engulfed in war and the graces issue died. (Clarke, *The graces, 1625–41.*)

gracious declaration, the king's. A declaration (14 & 15 Chas. II, c. 2, s. 26) by Charles II in November 1660 of his intentions regarding the settlement of Ireland. Conscious of the fact that his restoration was a result of Protestant endeavours, he confirmed the majority of soldiers and adventurers in their estates. Catholics who could prove that they were innocent of complicity in the Confederate rebellion were to be restored but immediate reprisals (compensation in land) were to be made to those dislodged to accommodate them. As the declaration was construed in Ireland to lack statutory authority, however, no serious attempt was made to execute its provisions. The key elements in the declaration were later enshrined in the **Act of Settlement** (1662). *See* court of claims, innocence.

graddon. (Ir., *greadán*) Meal.

graffane. (Ir., *grifán*) A type of hoe used to cut turf.

grand jury. The forerunner of the modern county council, the grand jury originally comprised 23 large landowners who were nominated by the county **sheriff** and summoned to the **assizes** (and in Dublin to the **quarter-sessions** for the county of the city) to determine whether a *prima facie* case existed for a prosecution to proceed. *See* justice of the peace. The grand jury later assumed responsibility for bridge-building, road maintenance and construction, the partial funding of dispensaries and the construction of fever hospitals and lunatic asylums, all of which were funded by **presentments** (or appropriations). Under an eighteenth-century act (30 Geo. III, c. 25) a person wishing to repair or construct a road was required to cause a survey to be conducted by two engineers and have the details sworn before a magistrate. At the following assizes the grand jury made a presentment to the court of an approved sum of money for the work which was afterwards allowed by the magistrate. The work itself was paid for by the individual promoting it but he recouped his outlay from the grand jury by swearing an affidavit that the project had been completed. The grand jury refunded the money from the **county cess**, the local revenue it was empowered to fix and which was payable by the occupier and not the owner of land. Grand juries were partially circumscribed in fixing the cess by the fact that the assize judges had to approve the presentments (usually a formality) and because the grand jurors themselves were assessed for whatever rate they set. Two full-time officers were employed by each grand jury. The treasurer received the county cess from the collectors and made payments under the direction of the jury foreman and a clerk of the crown kept the county records, drafted grand jury orders and received presentments. Part-time officials were also employed. High constables were appointed to collect the county cess, measurers conducted preliminary surveys and costed projects and overseers ensured that the work was carried out satisfactorily. After 1840 most of the functions of the grand jury were passed to the **poor law unions** and any remaining fiscal and administrative functions were transferred to the county councils after the passage of the **Local Government Act** in 1898. The grand jury continued to examine indictments until the enactment in 1924 of the Courts of Justice Act which provided for direct trial before a jury. The grand jury remained a bastion of Protestantism long after 1793 when Catholics were permitted to become grand jurors. Possessed of liberal powers of taxation, grand juries raised £18 million between 1800 and 1830 but the absence of a system of checks and accounting meant that this massive sum was not prudently applied and the work was often slipshod and unsatisfactory. Many public works were carried out not by qualified engineers but by farmers in the patronage of a grand juror. This phenomenon was not solely the hallmark of the grand juries for the **Board of Inland Navigation** and the **Board of Works** were equally profligate in their management of public works which often appeared to serve the purpose of political favour and patronage rather than utility. (Crossman, *Local government*, pp. 25–42.)

grand sergeanty. One of two chivalric tenures (the other was **knight-service**), grand sergeanty bound the tenant to perform some service for the king such as bearing his banner or performing some deed at the coronation. Only a chief tenant could hold land in grand sergeanty.

grange. The outlying farm of a monastic institution that was worked by lay brothers. Granges were extra-parochial and therefore not subject to **tithe**. At the time of the **dissolution** it had become practice to lease granges to laymen.

great acre. A Gaelic spatial measure which in Tipperary was equivalent to twenty English acres.

great council. A late medieval assembly of the **privy council**, temporal and spiritual peers and Pale magnates, often indistinguishable from (and sometimes functioning as) parliament. After the passage of **Poynings' Law** in 1494 the great council ceased to exercise legislative functions although it retained a consultative role with regard to proposed legislation before it was sent to London for approval. During the Tudor period great councils were summoned to declare a general **hosting**.

greave. Shin armour.

Gregory Clause. *See* 'quarter acre clause'.

grenadier. Originally a grenade-bearing soldier, grenadiers were elite troops usually selected for their height and excellent physical condition.

griddle. A circular metal plate on which bread and cakes were baked.

Griffith's Valuation. Griffith's Valuation is the term commonly used to describe the manuscript and printed documentation produced between 1848 and 1865 in the course of a nation-wide valuation of land and houses. It was undertaken to establish a uniform and equitable basis for the levying of **county cess** and the poor law rate. Local taxation was a contentious issue in the early decades of the nineteenth century. **Tithe** levied for the benefit of the minority Established church was overwhelmingly and unwillingly borne by the Catholic majority. County cess, levied by the county **grand jury** on land occupiers for the purpose of road construction, bridge-building and for the construction and upkeep of public buildings such as courthouses, was prone to manipulation and assessed disproportionately because of inefficient and partisan valuations. From 1838 a third tax, the poor law rate, was introduced to provide relief for the destitute under the Poor Law Act of that year. Completed in 1842, the poor law valuation was criticised because it was conducted by persons unskilled in valuation and it was claimed that the holdings of large landlords had been undervalued.

The first step towards the establishmment of a uniform national system of land measurement and valuation was the creation in 1825 of the Boundary Department of Ireland under the supervision of Richard Griffith (1784–1878). This body was tasked with identifying and sketching the boundaries of every **townland, parish** and **barony** in the country. The registers and sketches produced by the survey, known as 'boundary sketches' or 'boundary records' are retained in the National Archives and the Public Record Office of Northern Ireland. Within a year legislation (7 Geo. IV, c. 2) was passed to make provision for a uniform and equitable system of land and tenement valuation for the purpose of grand jury (county) cess charges. Griffith was appointed commissioner of valuation and work commenced in 1830. As it was the smallest land division, the townland was selected as the basic unit for valuation purposes and hence this valuation became known as the Townland Valuation. It was largely concerned with the taxable fertility value of land and the taxable value of buildings. Towns were not included. The value of land was assessed at the rent that one could reasonably and fairly expect to receive for it in a year based upon its fertility. Each townland was examined independently in lots by three valuators who surveyed the soil and determined an agreed valuation through consensus. This valuation was then entered in a 'land field book', was numbered and then plotted on the six-inch ordnance survey map. Houses to a value in excess of three pounds were valued at the rent they might reasonably be let for in a year with one-third of the valuation deducted. Details were entered in a 'house field book', again after an agreed valuation was established. The townland valuation was completed and printed for 25 counties by 1848. The manuscript books can be found in the National Archives and the Public Record Office of Northern Ireland. Printed versions are available in the National Library, the Valuation Office and the Public Record Office of Northern Ireland.

The introduction of the **poor rate** tax in 1838 and the criticism which accompanied it prompted parliament to re-consider the Townland Valuation. A parliamentary select-committee felt that the tenement (land, house, mill, bog, fishery) was a more appropriate unit for valuation purposes than the lot system employed in the Townland Valuation and recommended that both cess and poor law rate be separately assessed on a tenement basis. Thus, even before the Townland Valuation for county cess had been completed, further legislation (9 & 10 Vict., c. 110, 1846) required Griffith to undertake separate valuations of the entire country on a tenement basis for both cess and poor law purposes. The Tenement Valuation, also known as the Primary Valuation of Tenements, commenced in 1846 moving from south to north and lasted until 1852. For the local historian, three of the manuscript books prepared by the valuators are particularly useful. The 'field' or 'perambulation books' name and number every occupier so that his holding can be located on the valuation map, name the immediate lessor and provide a description and valuation of the holding. The 'house books' name the occupier and describe the function, quality, dimensions and valuation of buildings. The 'tenure books' indicate the mode of tenure, the annual rent and the commencement date and term of leases. The tenement valuation for each union was published and subsequently reprinted to take account of adjudications by a board of appeals on the claims of some occupiers that the valuation was incorrect. The records produced by the Tenement Valuation are in the National Archives and the Public Record Office of Northern Ireland while the Valuation Office retains the numbered ordnance survey maps. The final act in the saga of land and tenement valuation occurred as a consequence of the Tenement Valuation Act of 1852 (15 & 16 Vict., c. 63) which legislated for the creation of a single valuation of lands and tenements for the purpose of all tax assessments. This final valuation, conducted between 1853 and 1865, remained in effect in the Republic of Ireland until 1982.

The loss of the individual census returns for the early decades of the nineteenth century in the Four Courts fire in 1922 together with the official destruction of censuses in the latter half of the century have given Griffith's Valuation a status among genealogists that it might not otherwise have attained. For the local historian, the enormous detail it provides in terms of the extent, quality, valuation and tenure of holdings together with details regarding building use makes it an invaluable resource for re-constructing nineteenth-century communities. Of particular importance is the series known as the 'cancelled books' which are retained in the Valuation Office and regularly updated to document changes of ownership, improvements, alterations to boundaries or the construction of new buildings, all of which affected the accuracy of the valuation. The 'cancelled books' provide a continuous profile of alterations to the fabric of the local environment down almost to the present day.

Completion Dates of the Tenement Valuation (15 & 16 Vict., c. 63, 1852)

Antrim	10 July 1862	Kildare	18 July 1854
Armagh	1 June 1865	Kilkenny	8 July 1853
Carlow	28 June 1853	King's	2 July 1855
Cavan	25 June 1857	Leitrim	6 July 1857
Clare	3 July 1856	Limerick	29 Jun 1853
Cork (City)	9 July 1853	Londonderry	16 July 1859
Cork	20 July 1853	Longford	6 July 1855
Donegal	6 July 1858	Louth	5 July 1855
Down	12 July 1864	Mayo	13 July 1857
Dublin (City)	31 Oct 1854	Meath	10 July 1855
Dublin	5 May 1853	Monaghan	1 July 1861
Fermanagh	4 July 1863	Queen's	28 June 1853
Galway (City)	14 July 1856	Roscommon	1 July 1858
Galway	29 Jun 1857	Sligo	7 July 1858
Kerry	19 July 1853	Tipperary	29 June 1853

Tyrone	13 July 1860	Wexford	7 July 1854
Waterford	5 July 1853	Wicklow	4 July 1854
Westmeath	5 July 1855		

(O'Brien, *The Irish land question*, pp. 85–119; Reilly, 'Richard Griffith', pp. 106–113; Vaughan, 'Richard Griffith', pp. 103–22.)

grist mill. A corn mill.

groat. A coin worth four pence.

grogram. A coarse silk fabric.

groined roof. A roof whose edge is made by the intersection of two vaults.

Gross Survey. Little is known about the Gross Survey (1653–54), an unmapped, civil inquisition into landownership conducted as a preliminary to the sequestration of land forfeited as a result of the 1641 rebellion. Completed by December 1653, the first phase of the survey embraced the ten counties (Antrim, Armagh, Down, Meath, Westmeath, Laois, Offaly, Limerick, Tipperary and Waterford) that were to be allocated to soldiers and **adventurers**. Thereafter the remaining counties were surveyed with the exception of those counties in Connacht for which the **Strafford Inquisition** was available. The records of the Gross Survey were destroyed by fire in the **Four Courts**, Dublin in 1922. (Lyne, 'Three certified Gross Survey extracts', pp. 157–186.)

guardians, board of. The administrative body of a **poor law union** comprising elected guardians and ex-officio guardians such as local magistrates. The boards were usually dominated by middle-class Catholics as opposed to the magistracy and grand juries which were bastions of Protestantism. The electoral process associated with membership of the boards is credited with acculturating Catholics to the mechanics of electioneering. The administrative experience acquired in running the poor law unions from 1840 – when all new local government functions (including public health, sanitation, vagrancy, veterinarian and responsibility for workhouses and orphans) were mandated to the union boards – prepared them for the task of administering the county councils when they emerged in 1898. *See* Poor Law Commission. (Crossman, *Local government*, pp. 43–63.)

guilds, trade and craft. Mutual aid and regulatory associations of merchants or craftsmen in towns and cities. Guilds monopolised trade and industry in their areas, controlled entry into the trades and crafts through apprenticeships and insisted on common standards of workmanship. Each guild had a patron saint and its own chapel with a chantry (endowment) for masses to be said for deceased members. Before the Reformation the Dublin guilds played an important role in the Corpus Christi pageant, each portraying a trade or craft-related biblical scene. Their greatest impact, however, was at the level of municipal politics, their significant presence on urban corporations enabling them to exercise control over many aspects of city life. The 25 trade guilds of Dublin, for example, dominated the municipal government of that city from the fourteenth until the nineteenth centuries, returning 96 members (the Commons) to the council, all of whom became eligible for election as sheriff, alderman and lord mayor. Guild membership, the key to a successful career in city politics, was originally obtained through completion of an apprenticeship or by birth (sons of guild members). Non-tradesmen, however, were admitted in the eighteenth and nineteenth centuries for political reasons. The exclusiveness of the guilds extended beyond control of the trades and crafts. Catholics and Quakers were denied membership except as 'quarter brothers'. *See* quarterage. The Catholic Relief Acts of 1792 and 1793 cleared the way for Catholics to obtain full membership but, with the exception of the tailors, the guilds refused to yield. The weavers, in fact, set a prohibitive membership fee and other guilds claimed that Catholic membership contravened their charters. In the eighteenth century the restrictive practices of the trade and craft guilds clashed with a growing demand for deregulation. Guilds were ideal for small scale undertakings but better communication, expanding markets and large-scale production rendered them superfluous. Combinations of journeymen (the precursors of trade unions) began to challenge the guilds and urban corporations and exclusion from full membership appears to have impacted minimally on a growing and thriving Catholic middle-class. Political power was wrested from the guilds in the nineteenth century. After the passage of the Catholic Emancipation act in 1829 the guild monopoly of civic power was no longer sustainable. The **Municipal Corporations Reform Act** (1840) stripped them of their civic role and all but one, the guild of goldsmiths, were rapidly disbanded. (Clark and Refaussé, *Directory*; Clune, *The medieval gild system*; Webb, *The guilds*.)

guilds, religious. Organisations of lay men and women established by royal charter in the middle ages to promote the spiritual welfare of their members. Also known as sodalities or confraternities, the guilds were governed by a master and two wardens and structured like trade guilds. The chief function of a religious guild was to maintain a **chantry** (or endowment) for the celebration of mass for deceased members. The chantry was supported by bequests, endowments and the income accruing from land investments. Unlike their English counterparts which were abolished in 1547, Irish religious guilds survived the Reformation, remained almost completely within the Catholic fold and continued to support their chantry chapels in Anglican parish churches into the eighteenth century. Catholic confraternities or sodalities began to appear again from the middle of the nineteenth century following the establishment of the Archconfraternity of the Holy Family in Limerick in 1844 by the Dutchman Henry Belletable and the preaching Redemptorists. Within decades there were confraternities throughout the island. Individual confraternities or 'divisions' were divided into sections of up to 20 men. They were led by a secretary and advised by a chaplain. On the feast of Corpus Christi they paraded through towns behind banners dedicated to their patron saint. (Buckley and Anderson, *Brotherhoods*; Clark and Refaussé, *Directory*; Ronan, 'Religious customs', pp. 225–247, 364–385.)

gules. In heraldry, denotes the colour red.

gunmoney. Money coined from melted-down cannon, ordnance, bells and copper and brass objects by order of James II to ameliorate the desperate scarcity of specie during the Williamite War.

H

habeas corpus, **writ of**. Originally a writ by which a court summoned before it a person or persons whose presence was essential for the conduct of its affairs. Later it was used to secure the release of a person improperly incarcerated or the production in court of a detained person. Essentially it acted as a constraint upon the exercise of a capricious arbitrary power. Although *habeas corpus* was legislated for in England no such legislation was enacted for Ireland and this was an issue on which the eighteenth-century **'patriot' party** campaigned. In 1782 they achieved their goal with the passing of Sir Samuel Bradstreet's Liberty of the Subject Act (22 Geo. III, c. 11). However, the chief governor and privy council retained the power to suspend the act by proclamation during an invasion or rebellion and in times of crisis the right of *habeas corpus* was regularly suspended and detention without trial or internment permitted.

hagbush. An arquebus or a portable firearm that rested on a support or tripod when in use.

ha-ha. An eighteenth-century landscape feature, a ha-ha was a sunken ditch which kept livestock from the environs of the big house and, unlike a wall, fence or hedge, ensured an uninterrupted view of the demesne.

halfendale. A half part.

halbert. A weapon that is both a spear and an axe. A pike.

Hanmer, Meredith (1543–1604). An English clergyman, historian and author who came to Ireland in 1591 and served successively as archdeacon of Ross, treasurer of Waterford cathedral, vicar choral at Christ Church and chancellor of St Canice's, Kilkenny. During his twelve-year stint in Ireland Hanmer researched Irish history and consulted contemporary and earlier writers and chronicles, the fruit of which was his *Chronicle of Ireland*. This annalistic compilation commences with the arrival of the Partholonians and includes an Irish-English vocabulary. It was published by Sir James Ware in 1633. (*Ancient Irish histories*, i, pp. 1–410.)

hanaper, clerk of the. In full, the clerk of the crown and the hanaper, he was an official in **chancery** who received the payments for sealing writs and issued patents and commissions. The hanaper itself was originally a hamper into which writs were thrown by the clerk of the hanaper.

hank. Of linen yarn, 3,600 yards.

harp. Officially known as 'coin of the harp', a coinage struck for Ireland in 1534 in less than sterling silver, so called because it bore on the reverse a crowned harp, the arms of the kingdom of Ireland. (Dolley, 'Irish coinage', pp. 408–410.)

hastiuell. Probably a fast-growing variety of barley.

hauberk. A chain-mail tunic.

Hawarden kite. A kite-flying exercise initiated in December 1885 in a letter to the press by Gladstone's son, Herbert, suggesting that Gladstone was in favour of the introduction of home rule in Ireland.

hayboote, hedgeboote. The right without payment to procure wood from the manorial woods for the purpose of fence-making or enclosing a plot of land.

hayward. Manorial official who oversaw the making of hay and harvesting.

headland. Land left unploughed at the end of a field to enable the plough to be turned.

heads of bills. *See* statute.

Health, General (or Central) Board of. An unsalaried body established by the lord lieutenant in 1820 to advise on the institution of local boards of health and to supervise and examine their expenditure. During periods of distress in the 1820s the board confined its reporting to government on areas in the neighbourhood of Dublin. It metamorphosed into the Cholera Board in 1832 (2 & 3 Will. IV, c. 9) in response to the cholera epidemic of that year and played a significant role in shaping government action. The board co-ordinated the collection and distribution of information concerning precautionary and preventive measures and kept in touch with conditions on the ground by insisting on detailed reports from the localities. It instituted local boards of health and appointed health officers, set up dispensaries and small hospitals, provided grants and employed additional doctors where necessary. The fact that the board had no rate-levying capacity and the inordinate demands for medical relief precipitated by the Great Famine led to the piecemeal transfer of its responsibilities to the **poor law unions** and (from 1872) to the Local Government Board. *See* Poor Law Commission.

hearth-lobby house. A house whose entrance lies directly adjacent to the hearth which is separated from the entrance (lobby) by a jamb, screen wall or partition. Hearth-lobby houses have centrally-located hearths and are typically found in eastern areas. *See* jamb, direct-entry house. (Danaher, 'Hearth and chimney, pp. 91–104; O'Neill, *Life*, p. 13.)

hearth tax. A tax of two shillings on every hearth, fireplace or chimney imposed at the Restoration to defray the loss to the crown incurred by the extinction of the **feudal incidents**. Schedules of householders liable for the tax were compiled. Known as hearth money rolls, they do not constitute a complete listing of householders in any given area for the Hearth Tax Act of 1662 (14 & 15 Chas. II, c. 17) exempted persons living on alms or unable to work or those whose houses were too wretched to be assessed. The tax was abolished by the Irish parliament in 1793 at the prompting of Henry Grattan. The hearth money rolls contain a parish by parish record of those who paid the tax and how much they paid. Only a few have survived. John Grenham's *Tracing your Irish Ancestors* (Dublin, 1992) provides a county by county listing of repositories and journals which contain details of the hearth money rolls. (Carleton, *Heads.*)

Hearts of Steel. *See* Steelboys

hedgeboote. *See* hayboote.

hedge school. Fee-paying Catholic schools operating in hedgerows, ditches, sod cabins, barns and church sacristies which emerged (though prohibited) during the penal years of the eighteenth century and persisted in great numbers into the 1820s when they were providing a rudimentary education in the 'three Rs' to an estimated 300,000 to 400,000 children. With the establishment of the national system of education in 1831 their number diminished dramatically. The appendix to the second report of the royal commission on Irish education contains highly-localised detail on a vast number of hedge schools throughout the country. (*Second report of the commissioners of Irish education inquiry*, HC 1826–7 (12) XII. 1.)

helier. A tiler.

herald. A royal messenger and proclaimer. To the herald was entrusted the duties of arranging and ordering precedence in the matter of processions, funerals and state ceremonies. He also regulated the use of arms and recorded the pedigrees of those entitled to bear them. Commissions were issued to the heralds to ascertain, inspect and record the arms in use in a particular county and the records of these visitations contain important genealogical and heraldic detail. Heraldic visitations were undertaken in several eastern counties in sixteenth- and seventeenth-century Ireland to control the use of heraldic arms along the lines established by the English College of Arms. Under the supervision of **Ulster king of arms** (created in 1552) the visitations were intended to establish what arms were in use and by what right they were borne. The visitation records are preserved in the Genealogical Office (since 1943 the successor to Ulster) and on microfilm in the National Library. *See* funeral entries.

hereditament. Inheritance. Corporeal hereditaments consist of the material or physical inheritance such as land, buildings or minerals. Incorporeal hereditaments comprise certain rights or **easements** such as light, right of way, support or water.

heriot. A payment owed to the lord upon the death of a freehold tenant, usually the best living animal of the deceased or a cash payment. *See* mortuary, relief.

Hiberno-Romanesque. A late nineteenth-century architectural style which emerged in reaction to neo-gothicism, the predominant ecclesiastical style of that century. Characterised by round-headed windows and doorways modelled on earlier monastic churches, Hiberno-Romanesque was a simpler and less pretentious form than the ornate Gothic and was felt to be a more appropriate style for Ireland. It was a fashion that gave expression to the upsurge in national feeling and, from an ecclesiastical perspective, emphasised continuity from the early Celtic church.

high commission, court of. An ecclesiastical court comprising clerical and lay members and equipped with special powers to compel adherence to the Reformation, the court of high commission was established in October 1564 at the behest of Elizabeth who made religious conformity a key objective of the Irish administration. Its introduction followed the issuing of a number of regional ecclesiastical commissions to the midlands, the south, the west and Armagh to enforce the religious settlement. The commissioners discovered that the settlement was being ignored throughout the Pale. Catholic priests were receiving support and shelter from the gentry. Political unrest, the heavy involvement of Anglican bishops in central and local administration, the hostility of the increasingly recusant Catholic Old English and the reluctance of Elizabeth to sanction draconian measures to ensure conformity rendered the work of the commission largely ineffective. Fines were rarely paid and where external conformity was achieved, there were not enough preachers to effect a thorough conversion. In all, five commissions were issued between 1561 and 1635 but only the last was in any way effective. Conducted by Wentworth, the 1635 court established uniformity within the Church of Ireland by expelling Presbyterian ministers and successfully recovered alienated church property.

high court of justice. (1652). The court established to try those suspected of complicity in atrocities committed during the 1641 Confederate Rebellion. Evidence gathered to build a case against suspects is contained in the detailed and highly-localised collection of documents known as the **depositions of 1641**.

high cross. A free-standing ringed cross mounted on a steeped base that first appeared in the eight century. Early examples were richly ornamented with abstract designs such as spirals, geometric motifs and interlacing. Larger, structurally complex crosses began to appear in the ninth and tenth centuries with biblical scenes depicted in panels along divided shafts. A cluster of about 30 of these scriptural crosses are located near the Barrow river at Moone. The patrons of later crosses, such as that at Dysart O'Dea in Co. Clare, eschewed the ring and all but abandoned carved embellishments save simple, prominently-positioned depictions of Christ or bishops. High crosses were associated with monastic sites and had an obvious didactic function. They may also have served to delimit boundaries or to enhance the status of the associated institution. (Harbison, *The high crosses*; Henry, *Irish high crosses*.)

High-King. *See Ard Rí*

Hilary. A court session and university term commencing about the feast of St Hilary (January 13) and concluding on 31 March. *See* sittings.

hill-fort. A hill-top enclosure fortified by defensive earthworks of one or more banks. *See* promontory fort.

hip roof. A roof with sloping gable ends. On a half-hip roof the gables terminate short of the eaves.

hiring fair. Farmers sourced servants and labourers at hiring fairs, the largest of which were held in west Ulster in the late nineteenth century. Farmer and labourer or servant negotiated conditions of employment and wages before agreeing a contract of six months duration, the interval between one hiring fair and the next.

hobby, hobin. The light horse of a **hobelar**.

hobelar. A medieval, light cavalryman who rode a **hobby** (or hobin) and was armed with a spear as distinct from the heavily-armoured and less mobile mounted men-at-arms who rode massive **destriers** or war-horses. (Hayes McCoy, 'The hobelar', pp. 12–16.)

Holinshed's Chronicles. Raphael Holinshed's *Chronicles of England, Scotlande, and Irelande* (1577) originated in a plan by the printer Reginald Wolfe to publish 'an universall Cosmographie of the whole worlde' which was to have included the history of every known nation. Holinshed (died *c*. 1580) was to compile the histories but after Wolfe died in 1573 the project was abridged and only the *Chronicles* made it to the press. A considerable portion of the history of Ireland came from the pen of **Richard Stanihurst** (1547–1618), a member of a prominent Dublin family. Stanihurst's favourable treatment of the Kildare rebellion landed him in trouble with the English privy council and he was compelled to revise the text. His treatment of the native Irish was not objective and his re-hashing of some of the fabulous tales of **Giraldus Cambrensis** attracted the ire of both Geoffrey Keating and Philip O'Sullivan Beare. In the second edition of the *Chronicles* (1587), John Hooker supplemented Stanihurst's history with material he compiled from contemporary Irish administrative records. *See Foras feasa ar Éirinn*, Zoilomastix. (Lennon, *Richard Stanihurst*; Miller and Power, *Holinshed.*)

holy water clerk. (L., *aquabajulus*) A clerk who carried the holy water in church services and processions, read the epistle at mass, acted as bell-ringer and performed the duties of sacristan. After the Reformation the office became that of parish clerk.

homage. A symbolic act in which the tenant surrendered to the lord by kneeling and placing his hands within the lord's clasped hands and swore to be his man. The act was an acknowledgement of the reciprocal bond of loyalty and protection that existed between tenant and lord. *See* fealty, investiture.

Home Rule Association. Founded in May 1870, largely as a result of the efforts of Isaac Butt, the Home Rule Association or Home Government Association sought to develop popular support for an Irish parliament with full control over domestic affairs. Functioning more as a pressure group than a political party, the association eschewed involvement in land issues and denominational education and concentrated on pushing a federal solution to the national question. Butt's federalist vision – which saw Westminster retaining authority over defence, war, foreign policy and taxation and continuated Irish representation at the imperial parliament – did not meet with the approval of nationalists who wanted complete legislative independence. The membership comprised a heterogeneous mix of constitutional nationalists, Protestant conservatives, liberals and fenians. It was renamed the Home Rule League in 1873. MPs elected on a home rule platform were required to agree to concentrate their efforts on achieving home rule but they rejected this as it circumscribed their independence. (Thornley, *Isaac Butt.*)

Home Rule Bill (1886). Gladstone's home rule bill offered a modest degree of home rule to Ireland. It conceived of an Irish parliament of two orders that would vote separately and have a suspensory veto over any proposals introduced by the other. There would be an Irish executive responsible to this legislature but important areas such as peace and war, foreign and colonial policy, customs and excise, trade and navigation, the post office, coinage and legal tender would remain the responsibility of the imperial parliament where there would be no Irish representation. One-fifth of the charges of the UK budget for imperial purposes would be met by Ireland and any remaining surplus would be at the disposal of the Irish parliament. The Irish judiciary would be appointed and paid by the Irish government and hold office on the same terms as their English counterparts. The right of appeal to the judicial committee of the **privy council** would remain. A land law act to accompany the bill would contain provisions for the application of the principle of land purchase on a massive scale. **Unionist** fears that the bill represented a stepping-stone towards complete independence were amplified and exploited by Randolph Churchill. The bill also trawled up prejudices regarding the fitness of the Irish to govern themselves. On its second reading in the house of commons the bill was lost by 30 votes to an alliance of Tories and Liberal Unionists.

hooker. A half-decked, single-masted, gaff-rigged vessel with a bowsprit carrying a large mainsail and jib. Hookers were formerly used for transporting turf and livestock off the Galway coast. A smaller version of the hooker, the *gleoiteog*, is used for fishing.

horsemen's beds. A Gaelic spatial measure equivalent to 20 or 30 acres in Kilkenny and Waterford. Known as **cowlands** in Wicklow or **capell lands** elsewhere.

hosting. A military expedition by a royal army and contingents of unpaid militia organised for the defence of **Pale** but also for the benefit of other shires where leading magnates such as the Butlers in Kilkenny and Tipperary took the lead. Generally there were no more than one or two hostings in a year for a maximum of 40 days. Within the Pale the hosting was organised by the lord deputy who agreed with the **privy council** on the commencement date and duration together with the amount of carts that would be required. Instructions for the same were issued in the form of **chancery** writs which were declared throughout the Pale. Cartage – the requirement to provide carts for the transportation of supplies – was usually fixed at a rate of one cart for very four ploughlands. Hostings applied to all free tenants. In areas dominated by the native Irish the equivalent service was called a *slogad* or **rising out** which was declared for the purpose of defending the *tuath* from attack or attacking another *tuath*.

houbote (houseboot). A tenant's right to procure a reasonable amount of timber from the manorial woods for the purpose of housebuilding or house-repair without payment. He was not entitled to cut timber in excess of his immediate needs for future repairs.

houghing. The mutilation of animals, often carried out as part of agrarian campaigns. It involved the hamstringing or cutting of the leg tendons of cattle, thereby crippling them. It is thought to have emerged in the eighteenth century as a result of the widespread conversion of arable land to pasture which reduced the amount of land available for letting to peasants and encouraged landlords to evict. An outbreak of cattle houghing in Connacht in 1711–12, for example, has been attributed to the resentment generated by landlords who upped the rents, evicted defaulters and converted the land to pasture. By 9 Anne, c. 11 (1710) cattle-maiming was made a felony and liability for damages was imposed on the baronies. The practice of houghing, however, pre-dated the eighteenth century. In Antrim in 1585 a small English force under Captain Edward Barkley, frustrated at their failure to locate Sorley Boye MacDonald, carried off most of his cattle but 'houghed' those they could not carry away. (Connolly, 'Law', pp. 51–68; *Idem*, 'The houghers', pp. 139–62.)

hue and cry. 1: The legal obligation on all able-bodied persons within earshot of a crime to pursue miscreants. A fine was imposed on anyone failing to respond to the raising of a hue and cry 2: *Hue and Cry* was the twice-weekly gazette published by police headquarters at Dublin Castle and issued to the constabulary and metropolitan police forces. It contained police regulations, details of stolen animals and property, apprehensions sought by police forces, lists of apprehensions and names and particulars of deserters.

Huguenots. French Protestants who fled into exile to escape religious persecution in their native land. They arrived in Ireland, usually from England, in four waves between the late sixteenth and eighteenth centuries, the largest wave occurring after the revocation of the Edict of Nantes in 1689. They settled in numbers in urban areas, often at the request of local notables who invited them to set up woollen, linen or silk manufactories. Some Huguenots conformed to and were assisted by the Established church. Others chose to adhere to their own non-conformist beliefs. Large Huguenot colonies were established in Dublin, Cork, Lisburn and Portarlington, while smaller clusters of families settled in at least 27 other towns. (Caldicott, Gough and Pittion, *The Huguenots*; Ryan, *Irish Church*, pp. 171–181.)

huke. A Dutch, hooded mantle shaped like a tabard.

hundred. 1: A civil, military and judicial division of an English county, apparently derived from the 'hundred hides', a hide being equivalent to about 120 acres. It was roughly equivalent to an Irish barony 2: The equivalent of 126 fish. A hundred contained 42 casts, each cast comprising three fish.

hundred court. A Saxon institution that was retained as an instrument of civil government following the Norman conquest, the hundred court was a court of burgesses to which every hundreder or **burgess**

was liable for jury service. Every chartered town was granted the right to hold its own weekly hundred court which was distinct from the common law courts.

hungry months. In nineteenth-century Ireland, the months of June, July and August when the old crop of potatoes had been exhausted and the new crop was not yet ready for picking.

husbandman. A fairly prosperous peasant who held 20 or 30 acres by long lease.

I

ice house. An outbuilding, partially underground, where ice gathered during winter was stored to preserve food during the summer months. The ice was usually sourced from an adjacent ice pond. Belvedere House, Mullingar, and Ardgillan Castle in Co. Dublin each possess ice houses. Ice houses or ice stores associated with commercial salmon fisheries, such as those at Ballina and Lismore, were used to preserve fish for export.

Ibid. (L., *ibidem*, in the same place) An abbreviation used in references to cite the same book or passage as has been cited immediately previous.

Idem. (L., same) A footnote convention repeating the immediately preceding male author(s) but a different work. *Eadem* (pl, *eaedem*) is used where the author is female.

imparking. In late medieval documents, refers to the engrossing or enclosure of open field strips.

impropriate. **Tithe** assigned to a lay person. Where all of the tithe of a parish, both great and small, was in lay hands it was termed 'wholly impropriate'. Impropriation of tithe – which was intended to support clergymen in the conduct of their duties – was a consequence of the granting of the lands of the dissolved monasteries to laymen after the Reformation. In receiving a grant of the land they also received the attendant tithe. With the tithe came the **advowson** or right to present and maintain an Anglican clergyman but in many cases, and especially where the lay impropriator was a Catholic, clergymen were poorly paid in proportion to the value of the tithe. In any case many parishes had few or no Anglicans and so the lay impropriator no doubt considered the clergyman privileged to receive anything at all considering the few duties he would be called on to perform. A clergyman's appointment in instances where the tithe was wholly impropriate was known as a **perpetual curacy**. *See* appropriate.

improved land. Land that has been drained and brought into production.

income tax. Introduced in Ireland in 1853 (16 & 17 Vict., c. 34) but earlier in England, income tax affected only a small minority and was introduced as a *quid pro quo* for the extinction by the government of famine debts incurred by the Irish **poor law unions**, the repayment of which imposed a crippling burden on ratepayers.

Incorporated Society for Promoting English Protestant Schools in Ireland. *See* charter schools.

incumbent. A clergymen such as a rector or vicar who possessed an ecclesiastical benefice but not a curate who was merely an assistant to the incumbent.

indenture. (Med. L., *indentare*, to give a serrated edge) 1: An indented document used to record a contract or lease between at least two parties. The contract was written out in duplicate form on a sheet of vellum and cut in two so that in disputes the fitting of the two halves proved them authentic. In a lease the landlord's portion was known as the part, that of the tenant, the counter-part. A tripartite indenture involved at least three parties. Indentures were used to record transactions of some importance. A short-term lease was not worth the bother and was recorded on a straight edged **poll** 2: A sealed agreement binding an apprentice to a master.

Independents. Independents (later known as Congregationalists) formed a minor puritan non-conformist sect which became influential during the Commonwealth (1649–1660) under the Independent Oliver Cromwell. They insisted on the autonomy of each congregation and repudiated a nationally-organised church in favour of loose affiliation. They first appeared in Ireland in the 1640s and included **adventurers** as well as Cromwellian soldiers among their number. About 30 Independent congregations were formed but this number dwindled to a mere handful by the close of the seventeenth century. The Independents enjoyed a revival during the nineteenth century – by 1836 there were 28 functioning congregations – but very few could trace their lineage back to the seventeenth century and the survival of the sect owed much to the missionary efforts of English communities. (Kilroy, *Protestant*, pp. 60–81; Greaves, *God's other children*, pp. 22–25.)

indult. A dispensation, usually of a temporary nature, granted in the Catholic church.

industrial schools. The concept of schools that would educate impoverished, abandoned or delinquent children in the habits of industry, regularity, self-denial and self-reliance was borrowed from an English model and introduced to Ireland in 1869. Industrial schools received convicted children under the age of 12 while convicts aged between 12–16 were dispatched to reformatories. By 1900 there were 70 such schools with a capacity for over 8,000 children operating in Ireland, entirely under religious control yet financed by the state. A degree of supervisory responsibility was accepted by the state in 1908 when the schools became subject to the annual visits of an inspector of reformatories and industrial schools. Industrial schools were abolished in England in 1933 but retained in Ireland until the 1970s when they were slated as 'Dickensian' by the Kennedy Report (Reformatory and Industrial Schools System Report, 1970) which also recommended their closure. (Barnes, *Irish industrial schools*.)

industry, house of. The earliest workhouse in Ireland opened in Dublin in 1706 to receive vagrants. It was funded by a local house tax, a transport levy and voluntary contributions but it was not a success and a parliamentary committee censured the institution for mismanagement and neglect. Closure, however, was ruled out lest the public be inconvenienced by the sudden release of the most miserable and helpless. Financed by a coal tax, the Cork workhouse opened in 1748. In 1772 (11 & 12 Geo. III, c. 30) parliament legislated for the establishment of a poor relief committee in every county and city of a county empowered to badge beggars and construct workhouses or houses of industry. The act proposed a nationwide system of workhouses but, in the event, funding (by subscription and church collections) proved inadequate and only about six (including Cork, Limerick and Waterford) were actually erected. Houses of industry were intended to provide accommodation and work for beggars, vagrants and the needy. Admission was not necessarily voluntary for most inmates were committed there by the courts. Funded by parliamentary grant, the Dublin house of industry was by far the largest, housing up to 5,000 at one point. Here able-bodied men prepared **oakum** for caulking wooden ships, chipped and rasped logwood for dye production and beat hemp for the rope-making industry. Women spun, combed and carded textiles. Some houses of industry received **grand jury** subventions but the Belfast poorhouse (founded 1774) was funded entirely from local subscriptions. Belfast inmates engaged in weaving, cotton-spinning and horticulture. Houses of Industry that survived until the passing of the 1838 Poor Law Act were absorbed into the **poor law** system. *See* badging. (Strain, *Belfast*, pp. 169–180; Widdess, *The Richmond*, pp. 7–30.)

infangenetheof. (OE, *fang*, to lay hold of, seize) The right to seize and prosecute a thief within the jurisdiction of a manor and to confiscate the chattels of a felon or to share in the profits arising from the forfeiture after hanging. *See* outfangtheof.

infield. *See* rundale.

infirmary. By 5 Geo. III, c. 20 (1765), amended 7 Geo. III, c. 8 (1767), parliament legislated for the erection of county infirmaries to be funded by public moneys and private subscriptions. By 1800 there were 26 small and poorly-run infirmaries in the country.

information. A formal accusation of a crime made by a prosecuting offi-cer as distinct from an indictment presented by a grand jury.

Inland Navigation, Directors General of. In 1730 the Irish parliament appointed commissioners of navigation to encourage the develop-ment of canals and improve river navigation with the particular in-tention of increasing tillage and ensuring a cheap and dependable supply of food and fuel for the capital city. Funding for canal-building was secured largely from private subscribers and was supplemented by grants of public money. Enthusiasm for improving the navigability of rivers or building canals outstripped the available capital and many projects were under-financed and remained incomplete. Few justified the expense incurred. The commercial success of the Newry Canal (1731–42) – constructed to facilitate the transport of coal from Ty-rone to Carlingford and onwards to Dublin – derived from the growth of the linen trade. In 1751 the commissioners of navigation were sub-sumed into the Corporation for Promoting and Carrying out an In-land Navigation or the Board of Inland Navigation and granted £7,000 per annum. Between 1778 and 1812 almost £2 million was spent on the Grand and Royal canal systems which linked the east, west and south of the country but neither was a commercial success. At the last session of the Irish parliament before the passage of the Act of Union, £500,000 was earmarked for the promotion of canal building. Salaried commissioners known as the Directors General of Inland Navigation were appointed by the lord lieutenant to assess all applications for grants and to supervise the progress of grant-aided work. Later they were given control of the Shannon navigation and the Tyrone, Newry and Royal Canals. The directors served as a board to develop and regulate fisheries and during the famine of 1822 they maintained roads constructed under the public works relief scheme in the west of Ireland. Subsequently this body was absorbed into the **Board of Works**.

Innisfallen, Annals of. One of the earliest surviving Irish annals and the most significant collection pertaining to Munster, the *Annals of Innisfallen* detail events down to 1326. Almost 40 scribes worked on the manuscript which is associated with monasteries at Emly, Toom-graney, Lismore, Killaloe and Innisfallen. The original is held in the Bodleian Library, Oxford (MS Rawlinson 503). (Best and McNeill, *The annals*; MacAirt, *The annals*.)

innocence, decree of. A decree issued to those who proved in the first **court of claims** (1663) that they were innocent of complicity in the 1641 rebellion. As innocents they were entitled to resume their former estates without having to pass new letters **patent**.

inns of court. Inns of court provided a convenient meeting-place for barristers to dine, discuss legal affairs and exchange gossip. Members could also lease chambers or offices there. In England they function-ed as hostels where apprentice lawyers were accommodated and fed. In time the inns assumed a role in the education of apprentices through lecture sessions known as 'readings' which were presented by able bar-risters. The inns regulated admission to practise and until the late nineteenth century residence at an English inn of court was required for admission to practise in Ireland. *See* King's Inns.

inquisition. Despite its forbidding resonance, an inquisition was simply an inquiry, the means by which **chancery** and the **exchequer** ac-quired knowledge about landownership. It was a local inquiry initi-ated by a request from the **surveyor-general** to the **escheator** to sum-mon a jury of those most likely to be in a position to testify to the ownership of a particular parcel of land and motivated by the need to ensure that the crown was not defrauded of revenue associated with the **feudal incidents**. The inquisition was also an instrument used to establish the extent and valuation of crown lands that were available to be granted as a reward to a loyal or favoured subject. The most extensive inquisition conducted in Ireland was the **Civil Sur-vey** (1654–56) which sought to ascertain the amount of land avail-able to reward **adventurers** and soldiers for their role in the suppres-sion of the 1641 rebellion.

inquisition ad quod damnum. 1: An inquisition conducted by the **es-cheator** to determine whether the crown's interest was prejudiced by the grant of a particular piece of land to a religious house (alienation to mortmain) 2: A writ sued out as a precursor to the granting of liberties by the crown to ascertain whether such a grant might be dis-advantageous or injurious to others.

inquisition on attainder. An inquisition which compiled an inventory of the property and chattels of an attainted individual so they could be taken into crown hands. (Griffith, *Calendar*.)

inquisition *post-mortem*. An inquisition *post-mortem* was activated by a writ of *diem clausit extremitum* to the **escheator** on the death of a tenant-in-chief (one who held land directly from the crown) to en-sure that the crown was not defrauded of the feudal incidents of **ward-ship**, **relief, escheat** and **marriage**. The escheator summoned a local jury to inquire of what lands the deceased was seised, by what **tenure** they were held and to ascertain the name and age of the heir. If the heir was a minor he became the king's ward and the rents of his estate were received by the crown. Usually the wardship was auctioned to the highest bidder subject to some restrictions such as the require-ment that Catholic minors be educated to Protestantism at Trinity College. Inquisitions *post-mortem* contain a brief description of the land, its appurtenances and its value. They are an excellent source for determining descent, property and tenure for in many instances they contain transcripts of deeds, wills and other legal instruments. The format of the inquisition *post-mortem* was later adopted for the compilation of the **manorial survey** which recorded the rents and services owed to the manor. The original medieval Irish inquisitions have not survived but inquisitions concerning landowners who also held land in England may be found in *Calendar of inquisitions post-mortem, Henry III – Richard II* (16 vols, London, 1904–74). *Inquisitionum in officio rotulorum cancellariae Hiberniae asservatorum repertorium* (2 vols, Dublin, 1827–9) contains printed repertories of later chancery inquisitions for Leinster and Ulster. (Griffith, *Calendar.*)

inspeximus. (L., we have inspected) An *inspeximus* or exemplification is a certified copy in charter form that confirms that an earlier document or charter has been inspected and delivers a recital of the original.

inst. An abbreviation for instant, the term refers to the current month as in the twenty-fourth *inst.*, the twenty-fourth of this month.

inter Anglicos. Because of a dispute over primacy in the fourteenth and fifteenth centuries, part of the diocese of Armagh – largely Co. Louth – was presided over by an **archdeacon** and the English half of the cathedral chapter and was served by Anglo-Norman clergy. It was therefore known as the *ecclesia inter Anglicos*. (Watt, 'Ecclesia', pp. 46–64.)

inter Hibernicos. That part of the diocese of Armagh – largely Co. Armagh – administered by the **dean** of Armagh cathedral and half of the cathedral chapter and served by native Irish clergy.

interregnum. The period between the death of Charles I in 1649 and the restoration of the monarchy in 1660.

investiture. The act of creating tenure by investing the tenant in his **fief.** It followed the rituals of **fealty** and **homage.** The lord invested the tenant by handing him an object such as a rod which symbolised his fief. Once invested the tenant had now acquired tenure.

inventory, probate. A list of a deceased person's possessions (but not realty) which accompanies a will. It was compiled by an **appraiser.** Probate inventories are highly valued by local and family historians for what they reveal about the social and economic life of the testator. (Berry, *Register.*)

Invincibles. A splinter group of the IRB with close **Land League** and Fenian connections, the secret revolutionary Irish National Invincibles was formed in 1881 to attack high-ranking government officials. Early targets included the chief secretary, William Edward Forster, and Superintendent John Mahon of the **Dublin Metropolitan Police.** In an action almost universally condemned, members of the Invincibles assassinated the new chief secretary for Ireland, Lord Frederick

Cavendish, and his under-secretary, T. H. Burke, in Phoenix Park on 6 May 1882, the day they arrived in Ireland to take up office. In January 1883, 17 Invincibles were arrested, five of whom (Brady, Curley, Kelly, Fagan and Caffrey) were subsequently executed. Following the executions the organisation collapsed in Ireland. (O'Broin, 'The Invincibles', pp. 113–125.)

Ionic. An architectural style and one of the three Grecian orders, Ionic columns are distinguished by a capital ornamented with four spirals and a fluted shaft. *See* Corinthian, Doric.

Irish Architectural Archive. Founded in 1976 to collect and preserve records of Ireland's architectural heritage, the Irish Architectural Archive now holds the largest collection of historic architectural records in Ireland. In addition to 80,000 drawings, 300,000 photographs and 11,000 printed items, the archive holds related business records, account- and letter-books and architectural models at its premises in 73 Merrion Square, Dublin.

Irish Church Act. The Irish Church Act (32 & 33 Vict., c. 42, 1869) was the legislative instrument which disestablished and disendowed the Church of Ireland and sundered the union of the Anglican churches in Ireland and England. From 1 January 1871 the Church of Ireland ceased to be the state church and became a voluntary body. In recognition of the fact that the people of Ireland had contributed to the grossly over-endowed Irish church, most of its temporalities were seized and vested in commissioners of church temporalities who were to liquidate the assets and re-distribute the funds as specified in the legislation. A corporate body, the **Representative Church Body**, was established to receive ownership of church buildings, glebes and schoolhouses subject to purchase clauses. Existing ministers were protected by compensatory lifetime annuities. Those who elected to retire – and about 1,000 did so choose – were given lump sum payments. The vast majority of clergymen opted to commute their life interest into a lump sum and had it paid to the Representative Church Body which became their new paymaster. In tandem with the disendowment of the Church of Ireland, the *regium donum* to the **Presbyterian** church and the annual state subvention to **Maynooth College** were discontinued. The Presbyterians and Maynooth College, however, were compensated for their losses by final payments of £750,000 and £372,000, respectively, from the former assets of the church. When the foregoing sums were deducted, Gladstone calculated that between £7–8 million would be available to relieve distress in Ireland. The Irish Church Act included one of the earliest land purchase schemes. The Church Temporalities Commissioners were empowered to sell land to church tenants who were aided by the advance of three-quarters of the purchase price subject to a mortgage repayable over 32 years. The idea came from John Bright who advocated a similar scheme in the 1870 **Landlord and Tenant Act**. *See* Bright clauses, Church Temporalities Commission, General Convention. (Nowlan, 'Disestablishment', pp. 1–22; Connell, *Finances*.)

Irish Folklore Commission (*Coimisiún Béaloideas Éireann*). A government commission established in 1935 for the collection, preservation, classification, study and exposition of all aspects of Irish folk traditions. The commission replaced the earlier Irish Folklore Institute (founded 1930) which evolved and recruited from the voluntary Folklore Society of Ireland. A further mutation in 1971 saw the Irish Folklore Commission re-styled the Department of Irish Folklore and its incorporation into University College Dublin. The core of the commission's collection comprises almost 2,000 volumes together with sound recordings, photographs, sketches and plans which were donated or collected by full-time and part-time collectors working in different parts of the country. A schools' collection conducted in 1937–8 in practically every national school in the 26 counties amassed over 1,100 manuscript volumes. The bulk of material printed in *Béaloideas*, the journal of the Folklore Society of Ireland, is drawn from the commission's collection. (Almqvist, ' The Irish Folklore Commission', pp. 6–26.)

Irish Land Act (1909). Popularly known as 'Birrell's Act' (after the then chief secretary for Ireland), this act (19 Edw. VII, c. 42) extended the category of congested districts and authorised the compulsory purchase of lands in congested areas. Payments to landlords were to be made in government stock plus a graduated bonus for bringing their lands to sale. The rate of interest on tenants' repayments was $3^{1}/_{2}$% over 65 years which proved attractive to tenants as some 50,000 holdings were sold under the scheme.

Irish Land Commission. A legal tribunal established by Gladstone to carry into effect the fair rent provisions of the **Land Law Act** (1881). As the Commission's adjudications were legally binding, at least one of the presiding commissioners was a high court judge. Sub-commissions were established to hear applications for fair rents from landlords or tenants throughout the country. The bulk of cases were dealt with by the Land Commission but the county court also played a role in fair rent adjudication. Within a couple of years a majority of tenants had obtained judicial rents that were binding for 15 years and which formed the basis of purchase annuities in the land acts after 1881. Local agreements between landlords and tenants became binding when they were registered in the county court. Between 1881 and 1923 – when its role in fair rent adjudication was abolished – the Commission oversaw in excess of 500,000 fair rent agreements and orders. In addition to acting as a court of arbitration the Land Commission was tasked with facilitating the transfer of land ownership from land-lords to tenants by advancing loans to tenants to purchase their hold-ings. Take-up was slow at first and it required a series of ever more at-tractive legislative acts to entice landlords and tenants into the mar-ket in numbers. The floodgates opened with the **Wyndham Act** of 1903 which remodelled the Land Commission so that its main em-phasis came to be on land purchase and re-distribution. Wyndham established the **Estates Commissioners**, a new body within the com-mission, to administer the provisions of the act. It simplified the land purchase procedure and offered landowners a bonus of twelve per cent to sell entire estates rather than individual holdings. In con-junction with the **Congested Districts Board**, the Estates Commis-sioners became active in relieving rural congestion by improving, en-larging and rearranging newly-purchased estates before vesting them in tenant-purchasers. From 1907 they were empowered to purchase land specifically for the purpose of settling evicted tenants. In 1909 the Land Commission was granted the power to purchase land compul-sorily in congested districts and from 1923 – when it assumed the functions of the Congested Districts Board – this power was greatly enlarged and extended to embrace any untenanted land in the count-ry that was required for the relief of congestion. Thereafter the focus of the Land Commission became the purchase and re-distribution of land, a process which included the radical scheme of transplanting farmers from the west of Ireland to farms in Meath and Kildare. The commission was dissolved by Dáil Éireann in 1992 and its records, in-cluding schedules of areas (land surveys and maps), inspectors' reports and schedules (value for money certification), documents of title, deeds, wills, mortgages and documents of purchase, were transferred to the National Archives building. Containing over six million docu-ments, this vast repository of landed estates records remains, to all in-tents and purposes, inaccessible to researchers. By writing to the Keep-er of Records, Land Commission, Bishop Street, Dublin 8, you may be allowed examine the schedules of areas and accompanying maps but without special permission you cannot access the remaining material. A survey of Land Commission records relating to 9,343 estates was undertaken by Edward Keane for the National Library of Ireland in the 1970s. Keane's bound volumes of reports on individual estates are available for consultation in the catalogue room of the library, toget-her with topographical and names card indexes. *See* Purchase of Land (Ireland) Act, 1885, Land Law (Ireland) Act, 1887, Purchase of Land (Ireland) Act, 1891, Irish Land Act (1909). (Buckley, 'The Irish Land Commission', pp. 28–36; Dooley, *Sources*, pp. 38–41; Kolbert and O'Brien, *Land reform*, pp. 34–45.)

Irish Manuscripts Commission. The Irish Manuscripts Commission

(1928–) was established to survey and report on collections of manu-scripts and papers of literary, historical and genealogical interest re-lating to Ireland. From time to time the commission publishes a volume or volumes relating to specific collections or records. The *Calendar of Ormond deeds*, for example, was published in six volumes while the *Civil Survey* (1654–56) comprises ten volumes relating to the counties of Cork, Limerick, Waterford, Tipperary, Kilkenny, Wexford, Kildare, Dublin, Meath, Donegal, Derry, and Tyrone. *Analecta Hibernica*, the commission's journal, publishes material not extensive enough to be issued in stand-alone publications.

Irish National Foresters Benefit Society. A nationalist **friendly society** founded in the 1870s by seceders from the British-based Ancient Order of Foresters. Borrowing from the craft of forestry, the foresters styled their chairman chief ranger and their welfare officers wood-wards. Weekly dues enabled the society to employ a doctor and pro-vide for the burial of deceased members. With over 9,000 members organised in 128 branches, the Foresters was the largest friendly soci-ety in operation in Ireland. However, it made little impact in the cities where many smaller societies were firmly entrenched and it remained a feature of rural and small town life. (Buckley and Anderson, *Brother-hoods*.)

Irish Record Commission. The Irish Record Commission (1810–1830) was established by royal commission in 1810 for the better regulation of administrative records which were then in a deplorable condition. The commissioners were directed to methodise, regulate and digest the records, rolls, books and papers in the public offices or repositories and to bind and secure those that were decaying. They were to com-pile and print calendars and indices and publish original records of general interest. Sub-commissioners were appointed to carry out these tasks and they set about examining the material stored in the Berming-ham Tower, the parliamentary record office, the rolls office, the chief remembrancer's office and the auditor general's office. Another group was assigned the task of preparing an authentic edition of the Irish statutes for publication. Considerable difficulties were encountered on account of 'the deranged state of the records'. In 1815 they pub-lished the first volume of reports (containing the first to the fifth annual reports) and a second (the sixth to the tenth annual reports) followed in 1820. Both contain the returns with supplements from the above offices (as well as the state paper office in the Record Tower, the office of the **surveyor-general**, the **quit-rent office** and the prerogative office), together with catalogues and inventories. In 1825 the commission published three volumes containing an abstract and reference to the principal records and public documents relating to the Acts of **Settlement and Explanation** then preserved in the rolls and the chief remembrancer's office. In 1812 they decided to publish John Lodge's incomplete work, *Liber Munerum Publicorum Hiberniae or the Establishment of Ireland*. Although the project was abandoned in 1830 *Liber Munerum* finally made it to the printers in 1852. In 1827 the commissioners published *Inquisitionum in officio rotulorum cancellariae asservatorum repertorium* and in 1829 a second volume. The first contained a repertory to the **inquisitions** *post-mortem* for Leinster and the second related to those conducted in Ulster. Unfortunately they were printed in an abbreviated Latin form and unless one is familiar with Latin they are pretty much worthless. Finally in 1828 the commission published the first part of the first volume of *Rotulorum patentium et clausorum cancellariae Hiberniae calendarium* which contains the **patent** and **close** rolls from the reign of Henry II to the reign of Henry VII. The Irish Record Commission was shut down in 1830 for financial reasons. It had been heavily criticised for the disorganised manner in which it went about its business and some of the transcription work of the clerks was lamentable. But for the destruction of original records in the Four Courts in 1922 the collection of the commission's papers in the National Archives would be of little interest to historians today. Now, however, they constitute a key historical source for the history of medieval and early modern Ireland. (Griffith, 'The Irish Record Commission', pp. 29–38.)

Irish Republican Brotherhood. Founded on 17 March 1858 by James Stephens, the IRB was a secret, oath-bound society dedicated to the achievement of an Irish republic by physical force. Although a minority movement, the IRB flourished in the 1860s but the conditions required for a successful rising – a major imperial military engagement elsewhere and a coherently structured, well-armed revolutionary force prepared to take advantage of 'England's difficulty' – were never realised. Forewarned by leaks, the government thwarted an attempted rising in March 1867 and an alternative approach – to attack Britain through Canada – failed on three occasions. Stephens' leadership style was a source of continuing controversy within the movement and his reputation was damaged by his abandonment of the rising promised for 1866. Riven by splits, both at home and in the United States, and with little opportunity for revolutionary action, many IRB members became involved in agitation during the **Land War** (1879–82). Apart from a bombing campaign in England, the IRB was largely overshadowed by the Parnellite push for home rule in the 1880s. The movement was resuscitated in the early years of the next century with the emergence of Sinn Féin, the return to Ireland of the convicted republican bomber Thomas Clarke and the establishment of the militant *Irish Freedom* newspaper. The outbreak of the First World War in 1914 provided an opportunity to strike while the British army was heavily committed in France. The 1916 rising was conceived largely by the supreme council of the IRB and every member of its military council was executed in the aftermath. With Michael Collins as its president, the IRB continued to work for an Irish republic after 1916 through the Irish Volunteers and Sinn Féin but separatism was now a popular issue and there was little necessity for secret societies. In 1921 the supreme council voted eleven to four to accept the Anglo-Irish treaty thereby splitting the movement along pro- and anti- lines during the subsequent civil war. The IRB was dissolved in 1924. (Williams, 'The Irish Republican Brotherhood', pp. 138–149.

Irish Society. Formed in 1609 by 12 shareholding companies of the city of London, the Society of the Governors and Assistants, London, of the New Plantation in Ulster within the Realm of Ireland (or Irish Society) was granted the city and county of Derry to plant in return for fulfilling certain conditions. Solid defences were to be constructed about Derry city and Coleraine and the native Irish were to be expelled and replaced by imported British settlers. Slow progress in meeting these stipulations resulted in fines, sequestration of rents and revenues and the voiding of the society's charter on several occasions. Nevertheless, the companies were reluctant to dispense with native Irish tenants who proved willing to pay high rents. The South Sea Bubble economic collapse in 1720 ended a profitable period for the shareholders forcing several companies to sell out and a few, strapped for cash, proceeded to lease at low rents but with high entry fines. The remaining holdings were disposed of in the late nineteenth century as a result of the Land War and the various land purchase acts. The Foyle fisheries, the last major asset of the society, were sold in 1952. (Moody, *The Londonderry plantation*; PRONI, *Guide to the records of the Irish Society and the London companies.*)

Irish Society for Promoting the Education of the Native Irish through the Medium of their own Language. Founded in 1818, the Irish Society was a proselytising bible group which sought conversions in Ireland through the medium of the Irish language. Teaching missions were established in Cavan, Kerry, Tipperary, Limerick, in all the western counties and on the islands. The society established a system of elementary education involving paid teachers and inspectors and provided a supply of reading material. Its impact as a proselytising body was minimal. *See* Second Reformation.

ironsides. Cromwellian soldiers.

J

j. The Roman numeral for the number 1 which was used at the end of a sequence of numbers probably to deter fraudulent additions. Thus, iijd. = 3d. The practice is still in use in medical prescriptions.

jacks. Leather quilted coats, occasionally plated with iron, worn by native Irish horsemen during the sixteenth century.

jamb. A wall, screen or partition in the lobby of a vernacular cottage. A spy window was usually inserted in the jamb to allow light to penetrate into the living area from the open door and to enable visitors to be viewed. Jamb walls are associated with centrally-located hearths and are typically eastern features. *See* hearth-lobby house, direct-entry house.

jetsam. Goods or any other objects thrown overboard to keep a ship afloat.

jointure. 1: An annuity payable to a landlord's widow charged on the rents and profits of the land for her lifetime 2: An estate settled on a wife to be taken in lieu of dower. *See* widow's dower.

journey. A punitive incursion by crown forces into the territory of the native Irish. Journeys might be of a week's duration and were assembled by writ of the governor's privy seal. Incursions conducted by the sheriff and his *posse comitatus* were known as 'roads'. *See* hosting.

Judicature Act, Supreme Court of (1877). The Irish equivalent of legislation introduced in England in 1873–5, the Irish Judicature Act (40 & 41 Vict., c. 57) radically re-modelled the administration of the courts in Ireland. The existing courts (**chancery**, queen's bench, **common pleas**, **exchequer**, **probate**, matrimonial causes, **admiralty** and **landed estates**) were united into one supreme court which was divided into the high court and the court of appeal in Ireland. The high court comprised five divisions initially: chancery, queen's bench, common pleas, exchequer and probate and matrimonial (admiralty was to abolished and merged with queen's bench upon the death or resignation of the then judge of admiralty). Two further judicature acts (1887, 1897) resulted in the amalgamation of the courts of common pleas, exchequer, probate and matrimonial and admiralty with queen's bench so that by the close of the century the high court had but two divisions, queen's bench and chancery. *See* king's bench. (Newark, *Notes*, pp. 24–5.)

jumper. A term used to disparage those Catholics who converted to Protestantism in return for material benefits during famine times. Also known as 'soupers'. *See* souperism.

jurats, jures. Aldermen, 24 of whom sat with the mayor in the upper house of Dublin corporation. It was from this body that the mayor was elected.

justice of the peace. The local judicial official who conducted the **quar-**

ter-sessions. In the middle ages as the scope of government increased the administration of justice proved beyond the capacity of the *curia regis* alone. In times of emergency local deputies called **keepers of the peace** or *custodes pacis* were appointed to police troubled areas and borders. Initially their function was a military one but this was gradually extended to include the requirement to maintain law and order in the jurisdiction and to prevent disorder by taking **recognisances** for the peace. From the fifteenth century the keepers of the peace were re-styled 'justices of the peace'. They were appointed by a commission of the peace after taking the oaths of supremacy and loyalty. Until the seventeenth century the disturbed nature of the country prevented the establishment of an effective system of quarter-sessions in the localities but thereafter a system similar to the English model emerged. Irish justices exercised a much broader jurisdiction than their English counterparts, empowered as they were to try all cases except treason, murder, felonies punishable by penal servitude for life and felonies of a political or rebellious nature. The justices of the peace also developed an 'out of session' jurisdiction known as the **petty sessions** to deal with offences of a summary nature. The justice of the peace was responsible for the preliminary examination of suspects scheduled to appear before the **assize courts**. On the basis of the evidence before him he decided whether to discharge the suspect or return him to the quarter-sessions or assizes. If he decided that the suspect had a case to answer a bill of indictment was presented to the grand jury which determined whether the bill was true or not. A true bill became an indictment triable before the petty sessions, quarter-sessions or assize courts. The justice of the peace failed to win the confidence of the government or the population at large owing to the incompetence and inactivity of many appointees. Stipendiary magistrates – who exercised the powers of the justices and controlled the constabulary – were appointed in Dublin from 1795 to improve the effectiveness of the administration of justice in the localities and the success of this innovation led to its extension in 1814 to any area proclaimed as disturbed by the lord lieutenant. Permanent and salaried resident magistrates were appointed from 1822 and by the close of the century every district in Ireland had its own resident magistrate. *See* Supremacy, Act of.

justiciar. The chief governor of Ireland in the pre-Tudor period, also known as the *custos*, deputy justiciar, king's lieutenant, deputy king's lieutenant or chief justice. Later he became known as lord deputy, lord lieutenant or lord justice and later again as the viceroy. The justiciar was an omnicompetent official, the senior military, administrative and judicial authority in the land. He was assisted by an advisory council which comprised key government officials (the treasurer, chancellor, escheator and chief baron of the exchequer, judges and the keeper of the rolls of chancery). From time to time the council was afforced (strengthened) by the addition of leading magnates and only rarely would the justiciar act without the assent of his councillors. The justiciar and his council exercised important judicial functions including the hearing of petitions and the resolution of disputes between great magnates, long after the professional courts had become established. See privy council.

justiciar's court. The court, sometimes referred to as 'the chief place', which followed the **justiciar** in his peregrinations throughout the country and the forerunner to **king's bench**. Its official title was *nostrum justiciarum Hiberniae sequentia* or the pleas following our justiciar in Ireland. Few justiciars were trained in jurisprudence and the pleas (both civil and criminal) were heard by an attendant justice. When Richard II came to Ireland in 1394 the justiciar's court, because of the king's presence, became the king's bench in Ireland. After he returned to England the justiciar did not return to the court and thereafter it was presided over by professional judges and retained the name of king's bench. See Dublin Bench.

justiciary rolls. The records of the transactions of the justiciar as he travelled in Ireland, largely comprising pleas heard before the justiciar's court. All but one of the original justiciary rolls perished in 1922 but calendars of late thirteenth- and early fourteenth-century rolls have been published. (Mills, *Calendar of the justiciary rolls*; Wood, Langman and Griffith, *Calendar of the justiciary rolls in Ireland*.)

K

Keating, Geoffrey (Seathrún Ceitinn). *See Foras feasa ar Éirinn*.

keening. A lamentation performed over a corpse by women who were usually hired for the purpose.

keep. The stoutest and most secure part of a medieval castle. Also known as a donjon. Originally it was a free-standing structure without a **curtain wall**.

keeper of the peace. (L., *custos pacis*) From about 1300 an officer appointed by a commission of peace to maintain order in frontier regions. Usually there were a number in each county and they were chosen from the upper strata of local society. The keeper of the peace performed an essentially military role in the localities, holding musters, assessing arms, repressing crime, taking **recognisances** for the peace and conducting parleys with the native Irish. In the fifteenth century keepers of peace began to assume a judicial role and were sometimes referred to as 'justices of the peace' but their primary function was to maintain order. *See* justice of the peace. (Frame, 'Commissions', pp. 3–7; *Idem*, 'The judicial powers', pp. 308–26.)

Kells, Book of. Dating from early in the ninth century, the lavishly-ornamented *Book of Kells* is a Latin gospel book of 340 folios. The original golden cover is missing. As there is no **colophon**, the provenance and craftsmanship is uncertain but it is certainly the work of several hands and may have been begun at Iona and completed in Kells, Co. Meath. Seven legal documents in Irish are included in the text in addition to the religious material. *The Book of Kells* and *The Book of Durrow* were presented to the library of Trinity College, Dublin, by Henry Jones, the seventeenth-century Anglican bishop of Meath. (Henry, *The Book of Kells*.)

kerne. (Ir., *ceitheam*) Native Gaelic footsoldiers who were equipped with swords, bows, darts or javelins. As mercenaries they were often quartered on the country by Gaelic lords (see coyne and livery). Wood-kerne were the sons and relatives of those dispossessed by plantation who took to the woods and used them as a base from which to attack and plunder the settlers.

kerntye, kernety. (Ir., *ceitheam tighe*, household kerne) 1: The lord's personal kerne who performed policing duties such as the capture of wrongdoers and the collection of fines 2: The quartering of the lord's kerne, horses, horseboys and dogs on the local inhabitants. *See* coyne and livery.

keyage. Originally 'quayage', dues paid for tying up at a formal quayside.

Kildare Place Society. Properly, The Society for Promoting the Education of the Poor in Ireland, the Kildare Place Society was founded in 1811 and in its first decade developed one of most advanced systems of elementary education in the world. As the society aimed to provide an education for the lower classes 'divested of sectarian distinctions in Christianity', its schools were religiously neutral. Bible readings were conducted on a daily basis without doctrinal exposition or, to use the contemporary expression, 'without note or comment'. The fact that this approach had already been endorsed by the Commissioners of Education (1806–12) enabled the society to petition successfully for public funds. It received a grant of £6,000 in 1816, rising to £30,000 by 1831. Kildare Place published the first major series of school textbooks in these islands, established model schools for teacher training and provided an efficient school inspectorate. By 1820 26,474 pupils were enrolled in its 381 schools. Some Catholic clergy and laymen were dissatisfied with the composition of the overwhelmingly Protestant board of governors (of which Daniel O'Connell was a member) and with the practice of reading scripture without note or comment but they tolerated the society's educational work until the 1820s. Serious dissension emerged when, against the background of sectarian hostility created by the **Second Reformation** mission to convert Catholics, Kildare Place began to allocate part of its income to a number of Protestant proselytising bodies such as the **London Hibernian Society**, the **Baptist Society** and the **Association for Discountenancing Vice**. O'Connell resigned and Catholic clergymen sought to keep Catholic children away from the schools. Government support was withdrawn from 1831 and public money was diverted into the newly-established national system of education. The remaining Kildare Place schools were later absorbed into the competing Anglican educational system, the **Church Education Society**. *See* Education, National System of, and Education, Commissioners of. (Akenson, *The Irish education experiment*, pp. 85–122, 143–4; Parkes, *Kildare Place*.)

kilderkin. 1: One quarter of a tun, by statute 18 gallons of beer or 16 gallons of ale. A kilderkin of butter weighed 112 pounds 2: A cask.

Kilkenny, Confederation of. *See* Catholic Confederacy.

Kilkenny, Statutes of (1366). Concern about the creeping Gaelicisation of the Anglo-Irish colony led to the enactment of the Statutes of Kilkenny which prohibited the use of **Brehon law** to the Anglo-Normans in Ireland. Settlers were forbidden to use Irish customs such as **fosterage** and **gossipred**, play Irish sports, Gaelicise their names or employ Irish bards. The use of the Irish language was forbidden on pain of attainder and confiscation of estate. (Otway-Ruthven, *A history*, pp. 291–4.)

Kilmainham Treaty. An agreement between Gladstone and Parnell in early 1882 which signalled the end of the **Land War**. Parnell had been jailed for sedition in 1881 and, despite the relatively favourable terms offered by Gladstone's **Land Law Act** (1881), issued a 'No Rent' manifesto from prison to draw attention to the problem of arrears of rent facing thousands of tenants. The 'treaty', negotiated while Parnell was on parole, represented a compromise. Parnell agreed to halt the 'No Rent' manifesto and to wind down agrarian agitation in return for amendments to the 1881 act. These amendments were enacted in the Arrears of Rent Act (1882) which entitled 130,000 tenants to retrospective reductions in their rents. (Lyons, *Charles Stewart Parnell*, pp. 196–204.)

kiln. 1: A structure where corn was dried, common in damp areas 2: An enclosure where a substance is processed by burning. Limekilns were constructed to burn limestone or shells, the remains of which were used to improve the quality of the soil or to provide mortar for building.

kincogish. (Ir., *cin comocuis*, offence of a kinsman) Under **Brehon law**, the liability of the kin group to make restitution for the crimes and debts of its members. Where an offender fled, liability devolved to his sons or father and ultimately to the kin group. *See éiric*.

king's advocate. A senior law officer who appeared for the crown in admiralty cases. In 1886 the treasury proposed to abolish the office and the small salary attached to it but it survived as an unpaid honour until 1924.

king's (queen's) bench. One of the four royal courts and the last to emerge from the undifferentiated *curia regis*. Originally king's bench was the court presided over by the **justiciar** as he attended the itinerant king. However, as the king rarely visited Ireland it was essentially the **justiciar's court** held by the justices as they attended the justiciar. When Richard II came to Ireland in 1394 the justiciar's court naturally became the king's bench in Ireland and when he returned to England the court retained this designation. In the sixteenth century it acquired a fixed location in Dublin where it was presided over by a chief justice and two **puisnes** (three from 1783). King's bench exercised jurisdiction principally over criminal cases, offences against the king's peace falling appropriately into the compass of the court most intimately connected with the monarch. It took cognisance of **common pleas** but the unreliability of juries in civil cases led to the loss of this jurisdiction to **chancery** in the sixteenth century. It was from king's bench that the judges of **assize** were dispatched on circuit to have the gaols delivered up to them, hear civil actions of *nisi prius* and resolve cases referred from the quarter-sessions. Through the issue of the prerogative writs of *mandamus*, *certiorari*, *habeas corpus*, *quo warranto*, and **prohibition** king's bench acquired the latter-day equivalent of the reviewing powers of the modern high court over government and the judicial system. Originally **error** from king's bench in Ireland lay to king's bench in England and ultimately to the English house of lords. From the late seventeenth century a turf war erupted when the Irish house of lords began to assert its right to exclusive power in the case of appeals. The **Declaratory Act** (6 Geo. I, c. 5) pronounced the Irish house incompetent to hear appeals and until 1782 – when the act was repealed – appeals went to the English house of lords. Eighteen years later came the **Act of Union** and the lords brief reign as supreme court of appeal in Ireland ended with the abolition of the Irish parliament. In 1877 the **Judicature Act** (40 & 41 Vict., c. 57) created the supreme court of judicature in Ireland comprising the high court of justice and court of appeal. Subsequently four of the constituent courts of the high court, viz., **common pleas**, **exchequer**, probate and matrimonial and **admiralty** were amalgamated with queen's bench to leave a high court of just two divisions, queen's bench and chancery.

King's Inns, Society of. The regulatory body which governs admission to the profession of barrister-at-law. The oldest institution for the education of lawyers in Ireland, it was founded in 1541 when judges and leading lawyers took a lease of the sequestered property of the

Black Friars north of the Liffey. It was modelled on the English **inns of court** with some significant differences. From the date of its foundation to the late nineteenth century it was not possible to practise as a counsellor in Ireland unless some years had been spent at one of the English inns. No similar requirement applied in England. The self-sufficiency of the English societies is also evident in the fact that they admitted members to practise and called them to the bar. The Irish society could admit them but they must be called by a chief justice. King's Inns was reconstituted in 1607 and its formal record, the 'Black Book', commences in that year. From 1634 voluntary affiliation ceased and membership became a requirement for all barristers who wished to practise in the courts. In 1786 the society was compelled to vacate the Black Friars site to facilitate the construction of the **Four Courts**. A lease was secured on land lying between Henrietta Street and Constitution Hill and the foundation stone was laid in 1795 for its current premises. The library of King's Inns began with the purchase of Mr Justice Robinson's library in 1787 and was enlarged during the first three decades of the nineteenth century when it was designated a copyright library. Catholics were denied membership from 1704 until the close of the century. Their re-admittance was facilitated by the passage of Hobart's 1793 **relief act** which opened the outer bar to them but maintained their exclusion from the office. That was not conceded until 1829. (Keane and Eustace, *The King's Inns*; Cosgrave, 'The King's Inns', pp. 45–52; Duhigg, *History*; Hamilton, *An account of the Honourable Society of King's Inns*; Kenny, *King's Inns*.)

kirk. *See* presbytery.

kistvaen. (W., *cist faen*, stone chest) A prehistoric stone coffin formed of slabs.

kitchen. Any food such as shellfish, fish, meat or eggs consumed with the monotonous potato diet to add relish to the meal.

knight's fee. An estate in land for which the service of one knight (**knight-service**) was required by the crown when a **hosting** was declared. In medieval Ireland there were officially about 425 knight's fees but in reality there were many more for through sub-infeudation the great magnates often exacted cumulative service in excess of what was required to satisfy the crown. Thus, when personal attendance (knight-service) was commuted to a cash payment (**scutage**) the lord made a profit on each hosting.

knight-service. Originally unpaid military service owed in return for tenure of land. Its distinctive feature was the knight's obligation to support his lord with a fixed number of men-at-arms for forty days annually. In Tudor times it denoted the form of tenure itself which was distinguished by heavier feudal dues on the tenant, including

wardship, **relief**, **marriage** and **escheat**. Knight-service was eventually commuted to a cash payment known as **scutage** which was tendered in lieu of personal service. (Otway-Ruthven, 'Knight-service', pp. 1– 15.)

knights hospitallers. The religious and military hospitaller order of St John of Jerusalem was established in the twelfth century to care for the sick and protect pilgrims to Jerusalem. After the fall of Jerusalem in 1187 the hospitallers peregrinated through the islands of the Mediterranean, settling successively at Cyprus, Rhodes and at Malta until 1798 when they were evicted by Napoleon. Hospitallers took the three vows of poverty, chastity and obedience and followed the rule of St Augustine. Like the **knights templars** they were richly endowed with lands throughout Europe. They first appeared in Ireland during the Norman invasion, playing a military role in the subjugation of the native Irish. Here, too, they were endowed with lands and about twenty houses or preceptories were founded, including some which devolved to the hospitallers after the suppression in 1312 of their bitter rivals, the knights templars. The chief house in Ireland was the priory of St John the Baptist at Kilmainham, Dublin. The order also had a number of **frankhouses** or free hospitals in different parts of the country. (Falkiner, 'The Hospital', pp. 275–317; Lennox Barrow, 'The knights hospitallers', pp. 108–112; McNeill, *Registrum*.)

knights templars. The knights templars were members of the Poor Knights of Christ and of the Temple of Solomon, a religious military order established c. 1120 to protect pilgrims to Jerusalem from Muslim attacks. They were known as templars (and each individual branch was styled temple) because their quarters in Jerusalem were located in the area where the temple once stood. In 1128 St Bernard of Clairvaux wrote their rule of life. Although the knights took the three vows of poverty, chastity and obedience, the order acquired vast wealth and property in Europe and the Holy Land through endowments. They appeared in Ireland in the late twelfth century, establishing their chief house at Clontarf. Subsequently they founded about a dozen houses largely in the eastern and southern counties. The knights templars were bitter rivals of that other great military order, the knights hospitallers, and several unsuccessful attempts were made to combine the two orders. Rumours of heresy and immorality, and possibly a desire to seize templar wealth, resulted in the arrest, torture and execution of templars in France and the order was eventually suppressed by papal decree in 1312. In Ireland the templars were imprisoned and interrogated and the bulk of their property was transferred to their enemies, the hospitallers. (Wood, 'The Templars', pp. 327–377; Gwynn and Hadcock, *Medieval religious houses*, pp. 327–331.)

L

l. (L. *libra*, pl, *libri*) The abbreviation used to denote a pound.

ladder farms. Distinctively regular-shaped farms which climb from valley floor into the uplands in parallel lines. They are usually a result of striping, a rationalisation of the field system which followed the extinction of the rundale system in the west. Striping was initiated in the nineteenth century by landlords and later by the **Congested Districts Board** or the **Irish Land Commission**.

Lady Day. The feast of the Annunciation of Our Lady, 25 March, is Lady Day, in ancient times the supposed date of the creation of the world. All Marian feastdays, however, including the Assumption (15 August), the Nativity of Our Lady (7 September) and the feast of the Immaculate Conception (8 December) were known as lady days. Lady Day was also a **gale** day, the date for the payment of half-years rent. Michaelmas Day (29 September) was the other. During the nineteenth century the gale days were 1 March and 1 September. *See* calendar.

Lancaster, Joseph (1778–1838). Lancaster was an educational reformer who promoted the use of the monitorial system in schools, a system widely employed in Ireland in the nineteenth century. Under the Lancasterian method the teacher instructed the more advanced pupils (monitors or prefects) who proceeded to instruct the remainder of the pupils. Designed to meet the basic educational needs of large numbers of pupils with the greatest economy, the procedure was workable but flawed. In effect the teacher became a bystander and pupil learning was characterised by drills, routine and rote memorisation. (Kaestle, *Joseph Lancaster*.)

lancet. 1: A narrow, pointed window 2: A pointed two-edge surgical knife.

land gable. Ground rent for a house site, usually based on the length of the street frontage. (Bolster, 'A landgable', pp. 7–20.)

landed estate courts (1858–1879). The **landed estate courts** were introduced in 1858 (21 & 22 Vict., c. 72) as successor to the post-famine **encumbered estates court** which had been established to facilitate the sale of bankrupt estates. Unencumbered as well as partially encumbered estates could be sold in the landed estate courts. The court rentals – prospectuses issued for the information of prospective buyers – provide details of the estate for sale, the names of occupying tenants, the rents paid and the condition of tenure. The records of the landed estates courts are held in the National Archives.

landjobber. In eighteenth-century Ireland, a lease speculator or rentier, usually a non-farming tenant who took advantage of periods of rapid inflation in land values to invest in leases. *See* middleman.

Land Law (Ireland) Act (1881). Following on the heels of the recommendations of the **Bessborough Commission** (1880), this act (44 & 45 Vict., c. 49) gave statutory recognition to the claim for fair rent, free sale and fixity of tenure. In doing so it recognised the principle of dual ownership of land. The **Irish Land Commission**, a legal tribunal, was established to arbitrate a fair rent between landlord and tenant which became legally binding for a period of 15 years. Tenants were granted a judicial tenancy with provision for rent review and renewal every 15 years and the free sale of their interest in their holding was conceded (subject to the landlord's entitlement to first call on purchase). Initially the act was a success – about three-quarters of qualifying tenants took advantage of its provisions – and rents were reduced on average by about twenty per cent. Excluded from the provisions of the act, however, were a large number of tenants who held an acre or over, 150,000 leaseholders (who had to wait until the 1887 **Land Law (Ireland) Act** to have their rents fixed) and 130,000 tenants in arrears. *See* Kilmainham Treaty. The Land Commission assumed the land purchase functions hitherto carried out by the **Board of Works** under the 1870 **Landlord and Tenant Act** and the proportional advance on the purchase price of a holding was increased to three-quarters, repayable over 35 years at 5%. The commission was also empowered to purchase entire estates and sell off parts to the tenants. Despite these inducements, take-up was limited as the conditions of sale remained too stiff for the majority of tenants.

Land Law (Ireland) Act (1887). Promoted by Arthur Balfour, the 1887 Land Law (Ireland) Act (50 & 51 Vict., c. 33) overhauled the 1881 **Land Law (Ireland) Act**, extended the protection available to tenants and brought leaseholders within the remit of the fair rent jurisdiction of the **Irish Land Commission**. Under this and the Purchase of Land (Ireland) Act of the following year, an additional £5 million was added to the sum provided for land purchase under Ashbourne's **Purchase of Land (Ireland) Act**, 1885. Balfour, a Conservative, believed the wholesale transfer of land from landlords to tenants would resolve unrest in Ireland, the effect of which would be to create a conservative small farmer society with a vested interest in peace and stability. Thus the 1887 and 1888 acts were followed by the 'Balfour Acts', Arthur Balfour's **Purchase of Land (Ireland) Act**, 1891, and his brother Gerald's **Land Law (Ireland) Act**, 1896.

Land Law (Ireland) Act (1896). *See* Purchase of Land (Ireland) Act, 1891.

Land League. Founded in 1879 by Michael Davitt, the Land League aimed to secure rent reductions and the right of tenants to purchase the freehold of their holdings. The boycott and non-payment of rent were the principal weapons employed in the campaign for land reform. Gladstone's **Land Law (Ireland) Act** (1881) and Balfour's **Land Law (Ireland) Act** (1887) and **Purchase of Land (Ireland) Act** (1891) took the steam out of the struggle by initiating the process that was to transform Ireland into a land of peasant proprietors. The Land League lasted until 1881 and was exactly contemporaneous with the **Land War.** (Bew, *Land*; King, *Michael Davitt*; O'Neill, 'The Ladies Land League', pp. 122–133; Palmer, *The Irish Land League*.)

Landlord and Tenant Act (1870). Gladstone's attempt to improve the plight of tenants, this act (33 & 34 Vict., c. 46) legalised Ulster **tenant-right** wherever it existed and provided for compensation for improvements made by the tenant and for disturbance on a tenant's giving up the land. Tenants, however, wanted security of tenure rather than compensation after eviction and unscrupulous landlords circumvented the compensation clause by jacking up rents, forcing tenants into arrears and then claiming the arrears against any improvements. Shortage of land meant that there was a ready supply of prospective tenants willing to venture at the new rent. Tenants who sub-let or let for **conacre** without permission from the landlord or his agent were prohibited from seeking compensation. The scale of any compensation was based not on the rent but on the value of the tenant's interest. If tenants went to court the best they could hope for was monetary compensation but whether they succeeded or failed in the court they were compelled to surrender the land. The act contained what became known as the '**Bright clauses**', named after John Bright, president of the Board of Trade and an ardent advocate of tenant proprietorship. He devised a purchase scheme whereby if a landlord and tenant agreed on a sale price for the tenant's holding, application could be made to the **landed estates court** for the sale of the holding to the tenant. The **Board of Works** would then loan up to two-thirds of the price conditional upon the repayment over 35 years of the sale price plus an annuity of 5%. Bright had suggested a similar scheme a year earlier which was incorporated in the **Irish Church Act**. In the event, neither the compensation measure nor the provision for tenant purchase proved successful. Landlords could still raise rents, tenants evicted for arrears remained helpless and those holding on leases of 31 years had no right to compensation if their lease was not renewed. As regards the Bright clauses, few tenants had the economic muscle to effect purchase and in any case the whole process depended upon the willingness of the landlord to sell. Only 469 loans were made under the purchase scheme, a figure considerably less than the number who purchased under the Irish Church Act. Although generally regarded as irrelevant to the economic and social conditions pertaining in Ireland at the time, Gladstone's first land act was a precursor to his second and more substantial reforming **Land Law (Ireland) Act**, 1881. *See*

Bessborough Commission.

Landlord and Tenant Law Amendment (Ireland) Act (1860). Known popularly as 'Deasy's Act' after Richard Deasy, attorney-general for Ireland (1860–1), the Landlord and Tenant Act (23 & 24 Vict., c. 46) attempted to simplify, consolidate and amend the law regulating the landlord-tenant relationship in Ireland. The act was based on four bills introduced in 1852 by Joseph Napier, attorney-general for Ireland (1852–3). It created a new landlord-tenant relationship by enacting the principle of free trade in land and establishing a contractual relationship rather than one based on **tenure** and **reversion**. Underpinning the legislation was the view that land is the exclusive property of the landlord and the tenant's interest was simply that of an individual who had agreed to pay a sum of money for the use of the land for a limited period. This favoured the landlord at the expense of the tenant in that the tenant had no choice in the matter. The act increased facilities in the matter of proceedings in **ejectment** and tightened the law of ejectment for non-payment of rent and on notice to quit. *See* **Land Law (Ireland) Act** (1881) which revisited the landlord-tenant relationship to the tenants' advantage.

Land War (1879–82). A campaign to secure land reform which began in 1879 with the founding of the **Land League** by Michael Davitt. Using the twin weapons of the boycott and a 'No Rent' campaign, Land Leaguers sought to compel the government to introduce measures to facilitate peasant ownership. An outbreak of famine in the same year, falling prices and an acceleration in the number of evictions gave momentum to the campaign which was accompanied by agrarian outrages and assassinations. Prime Minister Gladstone's response, the **Land Law (Ireland) Act** (1881), was inadequate and failed to end tenant resistance. When Parnell was jailed in October 1881 for sedition he issued a 'No Rent' manifesto. Faced with a slide into anarchy the government compromised and amended the 1881 act to include retrospective rent reductions for 130,000 tenants (Arrears of Rent Act, 1882). Balfour's 1887 **Land Law (Ireland) Act** and **Purchase of Land (Ireland) Act** of 1891 extended the security offered to tenants by Gladstone's land acts and initiated the process of tenant-purchase that was to transform landownership in the country over the next few decades. *See* Kilmainham Treaty.

Larnian folk. A **mesolithic** hunter-gatherer people, largely east-coast dwellers, so called after Larne, Co. Antrim, where Larnian implements have been collected in numbers from raised gravel beaches in the locality. Larnians constituted the second wave of human colonisation when they appeared in Ireland c. 8,000 years ago. Their origin remains obscure. Larnian implements were heavier than those of the **Sandelians** and had carefully re-worked edges. The heavy Larnian axes made forest clearance possible for camp-sites but not, apparently, for agriculture.

last. A measure of weight, capacity or quantity, the precise value of which differed according to the commodity being measured. In terms of ship's cargo a last was equivalent to two tons or 4,000 pounds. A last of wool weighed 4,368 pounds or twelve sacks. A last of gunpowder, however, was equivalent to 2,400 pounds. Twelve barrels of ale, cod or herrings (10,000 fish) and 12 dozen hides equalled a last. A last of grain was formerly equivalent to 12 quarters but latterly 10 (80 bushels).

lastage. (OE, hlaest, a load) 1: A load tax levied on shipping by the **last** 2: Ship's ballast.

La Tène. A Swiss archaeological site at Lake Neuchatel that has given its name to a phase in Celtic culture beginning about 500 BC and ending with the eclipse of the Celts by the Germans and Romans in the century before Christ was born. La Tène handiwork is characteristically abstract, consisting of spirals, round shapes and S-shapes that were applied in symmetrical patterns to ornaments and monuments. In Ireland evidence of La Tène art did not appear before c. 300 BC, the most famous example being the Broighter hoard (Co. Derry) which included a model boat complete with fittings, two torcs, a bowl, a collar and two plaited wire chains, all in beaten gold. (Raftery, *La Tène*.)

latimer. A professional interpreter widely employed in Ireland during the early years of the Anglo-Norman invasion but gradually dispensed with as the settlers became more familiar with the Irish language.

latitat and bill of Middlesex. (L., *latitat*, lurks) A writ issued out of **king's bench** to the **sheriff** of another county stating that the defendant cannot be found in the county of Middlesex and supposes him to have fled into some other county and lies concealed there. The writ commands the sheriff to apprehend the defendant and present him to answer at the king's bench. *Latitat* was a legal fiction employed to attract business to the king's bench which would otherwise have come within the jurisdiction of another court.

latitudinarian. A term used to describe certain seventeenth-century Anglican clerics who argued from reason rather than tradition. Beyond the key tenets of accepted doctrine they allowed for latitude on other teachings. They were the equivalent of the nineteenth-century broad church movement.

latten. A hard, mixed yellow metal resembling brass.

Laudabiliter. A papal bull (also known as the Donation of Ireland) issued in 1155 by Adrian IV which authorised Henry II of England to intervene in Ireland to reform the Irish church. The authenticity of the bull has been the subject of dispute although it is clear that Henry was considering an incursion into Ireland at the time the bull was issued. Whatever else it authorised, the bull did not grant hereditary possession of Ireland to the king of England and it was subsequently refuted. *See* Constantine, Donation of. (Norgate, 'The bull Laudabiliter', pp. 18–52; Sheehy, 'The bull Laudabiliter', pp. 45–70; Watt, 'Laudabiliter', pp. 420–432.)

law adviser. A nineteenth-century appointee and experienced member of the bar who advised the attorney general and the solicitor general on legal issues. He was also retained to offer legal advice whenever the senior law officers were abroad. The office appears to have been discontinued from 1883 when the lord lieutenant instructed magistrates to desist from seeking advice from the legal adviser to the government.

law merchant. A body of principles and customs regulating merchants and their transactions. It originated in the need to safeguard from harassment foreign traders who did not enjoy the protection of local law and to provide some form of security in which traders could negotiate contracts and conduct their commercial dealings. Principally based on Roman law, law merchant was carried wherever traders went and was uniform throughout Europe. It formed the basis of modern commercial law. At local level, fairs and markets were regulated by the **court of piepowder** which was operated by the person who was entitled by letters **patent** to hold the fair.

Law Society of Ireland. The representative body which, by statute, regulates the education, admission and professional standards of Irish solicitors. It evolved from the Society of Attorneys which met in 1774 in response to legislation which aimed to regulate the morals, education and qualifications of solicitors seeking admission as attorneys. The society underwent several name changes in the nineteenth century. It was known as the Law Society in 1831 and as the Society of Attorneys and Solicitors ten years later. Although granted a royal charter of incorporation in 1852, the honour was only formally recognised in 1888 when the society was re-styled Incorporated Law Society of Ireland. Then, as now, it aimed to promote and protect the rights and privileges of attorneys and to ensure respectability to the profession and advantage to the public. In 1994 it adopted its current name.

lazar house, lazaret. A leper hospital of which there were a large number in medieval Ireland. They were maintained through bequests and endowments of land.

lazybed. A raised ridge, two to eight feet wide, thrown up by the spade for the cultivation of potatoes. To some commentators this was indicative of the indolence of Irish peasant farmers. Charles Trevelyan, assistant secretary of the treasury and controller of the purse-strings during the Great Famine, thought the term reflected the ease of the Irish way of growing potatoes but lazybeds were also to be found in

Cornwall and parts of Scotland. It is now regarded as an efficient approach to have adopted where soils were too heavy to be worked and set out as drills. It was well-suited to the small fields and wet and rocky soils where draught animals and heavy ploughs were impractical even if they could have been afforded. The spade, however, was excellent in these conditions. (Evans, *The personality*, pp. 40–1; Trevelyan, *The Irish crisis*, p. 6.)

Leabhar Branach. The poem book or *duanaire* of four generations of the ruling sept of the O'Byrnes of Gabhal Raghnuill, Co. Wicklow, containing poems dating roughly from 1550–1630. The poems were composed by 35 different authors (mostly Leinstermen) and deal largely with military exploits, liberality, quarrels, sickness and death. Fiachaidh Mac Aodha (Fiach McHugh), slain in 1597, is the subject of no less than 28 poems, his father Aodh Mac Seáin, 18, and his son Feilim Mac Fiachaidh, 13. *Leabhar Branach* offers valuable insights into the outlook, policies and culture of a Gaelic lordship during the period in which Tudor and Stuart governments destroyed the power of the Gaelic lords. (Mac Airt, *Leabhar Branach*.)

Leabhar Cloinne Aodha Buidhe. A five-part seventeenth century compilation of poetry, genealogy, rights and annals concerning the O'Neills of Tyrone. It comprises *An Leabhar Eoghanach* (lore of the Tyrone O'Neills), *Ceart Uí Néill* (the rights and renders due the O'Neills), *Geinéalach na gCollach* (genealogy and lore of the McDonnells of Antrim), *Duanaire Cloinne Aodha Buidhe* (the poem book of the O'Neills of Clandeboye) and the annals of the Clandeboye O'Neills. (Ó Donnchadha, *Leabhar Cloinne*.)

Leabhar na gCeart. (Ir., the Book of Rights) An eleventh-century compilation of tributes owed to the seven provincial overlords (Munster, Connacht, Ailech, Airgialla, Ulster, Meath and Leinster) by their tributary vassals. Beginning with the king of Cashel, the tributes of each king are recorded in verse. (Dillon, *Lebor*, p.xlvi.)

Leabhar na hUidhre. (Ir., Book of the Dun Cow) The oldest extant manuscript written entirely in Irish. Comprising 138 folio pages of vellum, it was compiled c. 1100 AD by Maelmuiré Ceilechair (d. 1106 AD) and appears to be closely associated with St Ciaran and Clonmacnoise. The contents are a mixed bag of historical romances and poems from the pre-Christian and Christian eras. It opens with a fragment of Genesis followed by an elegy on the death of St Colmcille, stories from the **Ulster Cycle**, the wanderings of Máel Dún's ship in the Atlantic, imperfect copies of *Táin Bó Cuailnge* and the destruction of Bruighean Da Dearga, a history of the great pagan cemeteries of Ireland, poems by Flann of Monasterboice and tales of the Tuatha Dé Danann. *Leabhar na hUidhre* is held in the library of the **Royal Irish Academy**. (O'Curry, *Lectures*, pp. 182–6.)

leas, leyes, lays. Land rested from tillage by being set out to meadow or pasture.

lease. A grant of property for a fixed period (either for years or the lives of named individuals) in return for rent and conditions or services which are noted in the lease.

lease for lives. A lease perfected for the lifetime of three named persons. It was in the tenant's interest to select names judiciously in order to maximise the duration of the lease. Hence, the names often include those of the sovereign or young children.

lease for three lives renewable forever. A lease which permitted, upon payment of a fine, the insertion of a new name whenever any of the three named persons dropped (died). Effectively it created a perpetuity and approximated the status of **fee simple** or **freehold**. The **Devon Commission,** which estimated that one-seventh of tenanted land in Ireland was held under such leases, heard that the lease for three lives renewable forever originated after the seventeenth-century confiscations and settlements when grantors (often absentees) employed them as a means of asserting their proprietorship periodically while enjoying rents and renewal fines. The 1849 **Renewable Leasehold Conversion Act** (12 & 13 Vict., c. 105) gave legal status to such leases by enabling the lessees to acquire the **fee-farm grant** (freehold) from the lessors subject to a rent that was to be the old leasehold rent plus an estimated sum based on the average annual value of renewal fines.

lease and release. A form of conveyance that emerged around 1600 to supersede the feoffment and the bargain and sale as the most popular instrument of conveyance until its abolition in the nineteenth century when the 1845 Real Property Act (8 & 9 Vict., c. 119) introduced the modern deed of conveyance. There were two stages to this instrument. First the grantor perfected a lease to the grantee for a year at a nominal rent (a peppercorn or bauble) making the grantee a tenant. On the following day the grantor released his rights in the property to the grantee making him full owner. The release effectively meant that the grantor conveyed his fee simple **reversion** to the grantee, placing him in possession of the fee simple. Unlike the **bargain and sale** and **feoffment** the lease and release was a convenient private yet legally valid conveyance.

Lebor Gabála Érenn. (Ir., the Book of Invasion or Settlement) An eleventh-century pseudo-history of the settlement of Ireland. It begins with the creation and traces the settlement of Ireland from Noah's granddaughter, Cesair, through the Fir Bolgs, the Tuatha Dé Danann and down to the Milesians from whom the Gaels were descended. (Macalister, *Lebor.*)

Lecan, Book of. Largely the work of Sligo historian and scribe, Giolla Íosa Mór mac Fir Bhisigh (ancestor of Dubhaltach MacFirbis), the fifteenth-century *Book of Lecan* (or the *Great Book of Lecan*) is a compilation of earlier Gaelic tracts, genealogies and poetry. It is similar to the *Book of Ballymote* in content and arrangement and comprises two copies of **Lebor Gabála Érenn** (the Book of Invasions), copies of historical and genealogical poems and a tract on the families and territorial divisions of Tír Fiachrach in Co. Sligo. *The Book of Lecan* is preserved in the library of the Royal Irish Academy. (Mulchrone, *The Book of Lecan*.)

Lecan, Yellow Book of. (*Leabhar Buidhe Lecan*) Compiled by Donnoch and Giolla Íosa Mór mac Fir Bhisigh, the *Yellow Book* comprises a collection of ancient historical tracts in prose and verse on civil, ecclesiastical and military themes. It contains a collection of family and political poems concerning the O'Kellys and O'Connors of Connacht and the O'Donnells of Donegal, details of kings and battle, an imperfect copy of the *Táin Bó Cuailnge*, a tract on monastic rules in verse, an account of the reign and death of Muirchertach MacErca, king of Ireland, poems on ancient Tara together with a plan and explanation of the Teach Midhchuarta or Banqueting Hall, a biblical account of the Creation and Fall, a copy of Bruighean Da Dearga and it closes with a law tract. The original is in the library of Trinity College, Dublin. (Atkinson, *The Yellow Book*.)

leet money, leet silver, head money, head silver. Associated with the **court leet**, leet money was a small sum payable by all tenants owing suit to the manor court.

Leicester School. Properly, the Department of English Local History, a postgraduate department of Leicester University, the 'Leicester School' is so called because of the contribution of its founder W. G. Hoskins, subsequent heads such as H. P. R. Finberg, Alan Everitt and Charles Phythian-Adams and associated historians such as Joan Thirsk and Margaret Spufford to the professionalisation of local history in Britain. A feature of the published work of the Leicester historians is the use of comparative and contrasting studies, techniques which reflect their belief that the best way to identify what is distinctive or typical about a local society is to consider that society, be it the village, parish, town, county or *pays* (distinctive region), within a broader context. Hoskins' pioneering advocacy of the landscape as a critical source for the reconstruction of past societies, proclaimed most memorably in his work *The Making of the English Landscape*, is echoed in the writing of Everitt, Thirsk and, latterly, Phythian-Adams. Since its foundation in 1948 the 'school' has been continuously exercised by two interrelated issues: what constitutes an appropriate unit of study for the local historian and the relationship between local and national history. A satisfactory resolution to both questions has proved elusive but the debate has alerted historians to the need for greater subtlety in the selection of study units and to the importance of placing that unit within a broader perspective. (Phythian-Adams, *Re-thinking*.)

Leinster, Book of. A twelfth-century compilation collected and transcribed by Finn MacGorman, bishop of Kildare, for Dermot MacMurrough Kavanagh by order of Aodh Mac Crimhthainn, Kavanagh's tutor. It begins with a book of invasions of Ireland followed by a succession of monasteries down to 1169 and the succession and obituaries of provincial and minor kings. The genealogies and pedigrees (*Leinster* contains the oldest surviving collection of pedigrees) of kings and saints relate largely to Leinster. Like the **Yellow Book of Lecan**, the *Book of Leinster* contains poems on Tara and a plan and explanation of the *Teach Midhchuarta* (the Banqueting Hall). There are poems on the wars of the men of Leinster, Munster and Ulster, notably the battle of Ross na Righ between Leinstermen and Ulstermen at the beginning of the Christian period. (Best, Bergin and O'Brien, *The Book of Leinster*.)

less eligibility. *See* workhouse test.

Leth Chuinn. (Ir., Conn's Half) An ancient division of Ireland corresponding to the northern half of the island.

Leth Mugha. (Ir., Mugha's Half) An ancient division of Ireland corresponding to the southern half of the island.

liberal clubs. Liberal or Independent clubs were middle-class organisations established following the general election of 1826 in which Catholic **forty-shilling freeholders** defied their landlords to vote for pro-emancipationists. It was intended that local clubs would be linked through county clubs to a central body in the **Catholic Association** campaign for emancipation. Literacy was a condition of membership which comprised gentry, clergy and literate farmers. (O'Ferrall, *Catholic emancipation*, pp. 145–6, 170–4, 215–27.)

liberate, librate. 1: A chancery writ issued to the exchequer authorising the payment of an allowance or pension 2: A writ to the county sheriff instructing him to take in hand the estate of a person who has forfeited a recognisance 3: A writ issued to a jailer to deliver up a prisoner who has posted bail.

Liber munerum publicorum Hiberniae. A directory of patentee officeholders in Ireland from medieval times down to the nineteenth century. In 1812 the commissioners of the **Irish Record Commission** decided to publish John Lodge's unfinished *Liber munerum publicorum Hiberniae* or the establishment of Ireland. Lodge, deputy-keeper of the rolls and records in the Bermingham Tower, died before 1810. In 1813 Rowley Lascelles was appointed to complete the work but following a disagreement with the commissioners he returned to London. In 1822 he agreed to complete and edit the work but his work was unsatisfactory and in 1830 it was decided not to proceed. At that time the work comprised seven parts and was considered imperfect, incomplete and riddled with irrelevant material. It finally made it to the printers in 1852 in two large folio volumes in the state Lascelles had left it. (Lascelles, *Liber munerum*.)

Liber Niger Alani. *See Alen's Register*.

liberty. A civil jurisdiction, such as a manor, granted by the crown and independent of the county sheriff and the royal courts. The attendant rights and privileges of a liberty were specified in the charter of grant. Some liberties were located in frontier areas and emerged during periods of weak royal authority as a means of exercising control over the borderlands. Others, such as the Earl of Meath's liberty, the archbishop of Dublin's liberty of **St Sepulchre** and the liberty of St Patrick's (which actually lay within the archbishop of Dublin's liberty) were located in areas that had long remained settled. Within a liberty the lord had sovereign power for all but the four reserved crown pleas of arson, rape, **forestalling** and **treasure trove** together with correction of officers and employed an administrative structure rather like royal government writ small. Here could be found a lord, courts, an administration and even an army. The great liberties or franchises were administered by a **seneschal**, a **chancellor** (with his own seal and chancery), a **master of the rolls**, a treasurer and treasury, receivers and collectors, justices, attorneys, an **escheator**, a **coroner**, a chief sergeant and a sergeant-at-arms. *See* palatinate. (Otway-Ruthven, 'Anglo-Irish shire', pp. 1–28; Quinn, 'Anglo-Irish local government', pp. 354–381.)

librate. Of land, as much as is worth one pound per year. *See* liberate.

Lichfield House Compact (1835). A tacit agreement between the **Whigs** and Daniel O'Connell's Irish repeal parliamentarians to work together to keep the Tories from government. O'Connell and his party of about 25 MPs agreed to support a minority Whig government and to desist from pressing for repeal of the union and the disestablishment of the Church of Ireland for the moment in return for a reform package for Ireland. Substantial reforms were never on the cards because the house of lords remained a **Tory** bastion but **tithe** reform (1838), the **Municipal Corporations Reform Act** (1840), an extension of parliamentary suffrage, an increase in the number of Catholics employed by the administration, police reform and a more even-handed application of the law flowed from the compact. (Graham, 'Lichfield House compact, 1835', pp. 209–225.)

life tenancy, life estate. An estate held for the life of the current owner only and not in **fee simple**. It was established by means of a will or marriage settlement. A life estate could not be sold because few would consider purchasing an estate that might terminate suddenly on the death of the vendor. Life tenants could not alter the order of succession which was established by the deed that created the life tenancy. The key legislative impediment to the alienation of family estates was the 1285 statute of *De Donis Conditionalibus* which sought to ensure that family estates passed intact to the next generation by imposing restraints on the alienability of land and forbidding the barring of entails. The courts, however, proved unwilling to accept such limits on alienability and permitted the barring of entails through the fictitious and collusive actions of **fine** and **recovery**. *See* entail.

ligan. Goods thrown overboard in an emergency which sink to the sea bed.

lights. The openings between the **mullions** or piers of a window.

Limerick, Treaty of (1691). The treaty enacted between the Williamites and the remnants of the Jacobite army which allowed the Jacobites free passage to go abroad or, if they wished to remain in Ireland, to be secured against discriminatory laws. Under the civil articles of the treaty Catholics were promised such privileges as were consistent with the laws of Ireland or enjoyed by them under Charles II (which, beyond tolerance, amounted to few) and the property rights of those whose claims were accepted by the **privy council** and a court of nine high court judges were guaranteed. Although William favoured toleration he failed to take account of Protestant anger at the prospect of Catholics apparently getting off the hook. Thus, when the Irish parliament ratified the treaty in 1697 (9 Will. III, c. 2) the military articles and the bulk of claims relating to forfeited estates by persons admitted to articles were legislatively enacted but the religious articles were not. No mention of the right to religious freedom was included in the act and instead repressive **penal laws** were introduced, effectively breaking the spirit if not the letter of the treaty. *See* articlemen, court of claims, Trustees Sale, Williamite confiscation. (Simms, *The treaty of Limerick*; *Idem*, 'The original draft', pp. 37–44.)

Linen Board. A body established and funded by the Irish parliament in 1711 (9 Anne, c. 3) to encourage and regulate the linen industry. Although composed of unpaid commissioners, including Anglican bishops and members of the gentry, the day-to-day business of the board was conducted by full-time officials. An inspectorate was responsible for ensuring that manufacturing standards were maintained and prizes were awarded for superior work by spinners, weavers and bleachers. The domestic industry declined in the early nineteenth century as linen production became mechanised and factory-based. By the 1820s the board was credited with having encouraged experiments which private individuals by themselves would not have risked yet at the same time was criticised for acting as a restraint on private enterprise. The most serious criticism – that public money should not be expended on an industry that was successful in its own right – led to its abolition in 1828 (9 Geo. IV, c. 62). (Crawford, 'The evolution';

Johnston-Liik, *History of the Irish parliament*, pp. 303–311.)

Lismore, Book of. A compilation of religious, military and topographical tracts including a treatise on the lives of Irish saints, a dialogue between St Patrick and two surviving Fianna warriors, extracts from the travels of Marco Polo, an account of Charlemagne's conquests and a description of several hills, mountains, rivers and caverns in Ireland. (Macalister, *The book of Mac Carthaigh*.)

livery. 1: The provision of food, clothing or an allowance to servants 2: A distinctive suit of clothes worn by a servant 3: An allowance of provender for horses. Horses stabled, fed and groomed at a fixed rate are said to be 'at livery'. Hence, livery stable.

livery, to sue out. The act by an heir upon reaching majority of commencing a suit to obtain possession of his estate which was in the custody of the **court of wards** and **liveries**. The heir was required to pay a fine (**relief**) to sue out livery. Failure to observe the legal formalities rendered the defaulter liable to financial penalties. *See* also livery of seisin, majority, ousterlemain, and livery of seisin.

Llanthony *Prima*, Llanthony *Secunda*. Two priories – *Prima* located in Monmouthshire, *Secunda* in Gloucester – that were endowed with lands in Meath, Westmeath, Louth and north county Dublin by Hugh de Lacy and his sub-tenants and held in **frankalmoign** (which liberated them from having to render military service to the crown) or **fee-farm**. The Irish possessions were supervised by a canon known as a proctor. The cartularies of the Llanthony priories contain charters and civil and ecclesiastical documents dating from the twelfth to the fifteenth centuries and are preserved in the Public Record Office, London. (Brook, *The Irish cartularies*.)

Local Government (Ireland) Act (1898). Gerald Balfour's reforming Irish local government act (61 & 62 Vict., c. 37) which provided a system of local government with county councils, district councils and rural district councils, elected bodies chosen on a **franchise** that included women for the first time. Membership of town commissions and district councils now lay open to women but they remained excluded from county and borough councils. The new councils assumed the fiscal and administrative (though not the legal) duties of the grand juries. They were eligible to receive treasury grants and entitled to impose their own local rates and were immediately dominated by Catholic nationalists. Thus control of local government was taken from the landlord ascendancy class and placed in the hands of farmers, shopkeepers and publicans. Local councils did not possess unlimited powers to draw up their own laws, however, for all local enactments had to receive the approval of the supervisory Local Government Board, a body staffed largely by Protestant unionists. *See* grand jury, poor law commission.

Local Government Board. *See* Poor Law Commission.

locative. A surname derived from a placename.

Lough Key, Annals of. *(Annála Loch Cé)* Compiled in Connacht in the sixteenth century with a few additional entries as late as 1636, the *Annals of Lough Key* was apparently the work of the Ó Duibhgeannain's, a learned Gaelic family who had a special association with the Mac Diarmada clan of Loch Cé. They derive from an earlier fifteenth-century text written by the Ó Maoilchonaire family. (Hennessy, *The annals of Loch Cé*.)

loc. cit. (L., *loco citato* or *locus citatus*, in the place cited) A footnote convention, now almost obsolete, referring the reader to a book that has previously been quoted.

lock hospital. A hospital for the treatment of venereal disease. In 1792 the Westmoreland Lock Hospital was opened in Dublin under the direction of the lord lieutenant. Since it proved difficult to attract private subscriptions, it was maintained entirely by public money. Within a short time the hospital was overcrowded and earned a reputation for disorderliness. Two commissions of inquiry and a new board of governors produced significant improvements and by the mid-nineteenth century it was regarded as an efficient and prudently economical institution providing an importance service to a garrison city.

Lodge, John. Lodge's appointment as deputy-keeper of records in the Bermingham Tower represented a turning point in the fortune of Irish administrative records which had suffered serious neglect throughout the eighteenth century. His 26 volumes of transcripts from the rolls were later acquired by the Public Record Office to compensate for the wholesale destruction of the originals in the Four Courts fire in 1922. Lodge edited *Desiderata curiosa Hibernica* (a collection of seventeenth-century documents) in 1772 and his unfinished **Liber munerum publicorum Hiberniae**, a directory of patentee office-holders in Ireland, was taken up by the **Irish Record Commission** in 1812 and partly (and poorly) completed by Rowley Lascelles. Lodge was also the author of *The peerage of Ireland* (later continued and enlarged by Mervyn Archdall).

London Hibernian Society. A proselytsing bible society founded in 1806 and one of the earliest of such groups to use the Irish language as a medium for conversion. Initially Scots Gaelic-speaking missionaries were employed but these were soon dispensed with for they could not be understood and they were replaced by natives. Day, evening and Sunday schools were conducted under the scrutiny of an inspectorate and teachers (who did not have to be Protestants) were paid by results achieved by their pupils under inspection. By 1823 the society claimed to be educating over 60,000 pupils in its schools. It was jointly funded by the **Association for Discountenancing Vice**

and the **lord lieutenant's school fund**. Although the printed regulations governing the schools forbade proselytism and the use of controversial reading matter, pupils were expected to read the bible. As
was the case with the other bible societies, its impact was negligible
and it made few conversions. In the 1820s opposition to Protestant
missionary activities grew in intensity and Catholic children were withdrawn from the society's schools. *See* Second Reformation. (Akenson, *The Irish education experiment*, pp. 82–3.)

long-house, byre dwelling. A common house style in the west consisting of a rectangular stone-built dwelling in which humans and animals lived at opposite ends of a single compartment.

lord deputy. *See* lord lieutenant.

lord justice. In the absence or death of the **lord lieutenant** or lord deputy, three lords justice acted as chief governors of the Irish administration. They were usually crown nominees.

lord lieutenant. The chief governor and senior crown official in Ireland.
In the early modern period the title lord lieutenant was conferred on
members of the royal household, members of important English families
or lord deputies who had distinguished themselves in Ireland. Where
the lord lieutenant chose to remain in England he was represented in
Ireland by a lord deputy or lords justice. In the nineteenth century,
although nominally the head of the administration, the lord lieutenant was eclipsed by the **chief secretary** who was, effectively, the prime
minister. *See* county governor.

lord lieutenant's school fund. The lord lieutenant's school fund was
established in 1819, having been first mooted by Thomas Orde in
1787 as a vehicle to provide funds for the purchase and construction
of schools and for the provision of free education for the poor. Although primarily intended to finance the education of poor Catholics, the money was channelled through Protestant societies. Between 1819 and 1826 the fund commissioners disbursed over £63,000
for educational purposes but little of that sum found its way into Catholic hands. Having been given a free hand to dispose of the money
as they saw fit, the commissioners introduced so many obstacles that
few Catholics succeeded in prising money from their grasp. In the six
years to 1825 all but 12 out of a total of 481 grants had favoured Protestants, largely because Catholics were unable to provide strong
guarantees of local financial aid. The commissioners also demanded
the vesting of title in the local Church of Ireland minister, a requirement that proved obnoxious to Catholics. Slated by the commissioners
of inquiry into Irish education, the fund was extinguished after 1825.
When the national system was established in 1831, public moneys
voted by parliament to the national school system were funnelled to
the board of education through a fund also known as the lord lieute-

nant's education fund. This new fund was administered more equit-
ably and continued to finance the school system until 1848. Thereafter the money was transmitted through the exchequer. (Akenson,
The Irish education experiment, pp. 83–5.)

lord protector. The title assumed by Oliver Cromwell, the principal
puritan military leader, after the forcible dissolution of the **Rump**
(the purged English parliament) in 1653. In 1658 Richard Cromwell
succeeded his father as lord protector but was deposed in April 1659.

lords, house of. The upper house of the Irish **parliament** emerged as a
distinct parliamentary entity in 1536–7 and remained the premier
house until the **Act of Union**. Membership and procedure were regulated by **Ulster king of arms** at least until 1688 after which the house
was self-regulating. It was presided over by the **lord chancellor**. In the
eighteenth century the house comprised 22 spiritual peers (4 archbishops
– all Englishmen – and 18 bishops) and a variable number of temporal
peers. In the first half of the century the lay peers were largely inactive
and the spiritual peers exercised considerable political influence. From
1750, however, the initiative passed to the lay peers as peerages were
offered to loyal politicians for their service in the commons and as
bribes to MPs to stifle parliamentary opposition. Throughout the eighteenth century the house was never full. Many peers were absentees
and although all peers received writs of summons Catholic peers were
unable to attend because of the oath of supremacy. No dissenters sat
in the lords. The influence of the upper house lay chiefly in its control of the composition of the commons with almost half of the seats
in the lower house in the gift of the lay and spiritual peers. The right
of the lords to exercise appellate jurisdiction over decisions of the
Irish courts was voided with the passage of the **British Declaratory
Act** in 1720 but final judicature was restored in 1782. Only fragments
of the early proceedings of the house have survived but the printed
series, the journals, commences in 1634. (*Journals of the house of lords*;
James, *Lords*; McCracken, 'The political structure', pp. 71–72.)

lorimer. A bit and harness maker.

losset. 1: A large, flat wooden disc used as a kneading trough 2: A productive field or good fertile land.

loy. A long, heavy spade used to cut and turn sods to form **lazybeds**.

lucht tighe. (Ir., the members of a household) Mensal lands, the distinct
parcel of land which furnished provisions for a Gaelic lord's table.

lumper. A large, watery potato widely cultivated in Ireland during the
1830s and 1840s. It did not store well but its high yield ensured its
popularity among the poor. Also known as the 'horse potato'.

lunula. A crescent-shaped early Bronze Age ornament worn by women
around the neck.

lynchet. A terrace of soil found on the downward side of a field, a consequence of soil creep from contour ploughing during medieval or earlier times.

M

mace. A club, usually of iron with a wooden handle, designed to smash defensive armour.

machicolation. An opening in the floor of a projecting parapet or in the roof of an entrance through which missiles, stones or hot liquids might be cast upon attackers. A murder-hole.

madder. A climbing plant (*rubia tinctorum*), the root of which was used to make a medium to strong red dye.

maghery. (Ir., *machaire*, a plain) The area controlled by the English administration during the fifteenth century comprising the **Pale** and its **marches** (borders). The 1488 Act of Marches and Maghery defined the Pale boundaries as stretching from Dundalk to Dalkey and as far inland as 20 miles. By a series of parliamentary subsidies the maghery was enclosed piecemeal by ditches and castles as a defence against Irish raids. In 1495 Poynings' parliament obliged the march inhabitants to construct a double rampart and ditch on the boundary of the march with the maghery and additional ditches between the marches and the Irish. For defensive rather than administrative purposes the term 'maghery', the land of peace, was sometimes applied to the Pale to distinguish it from the marches, the land of war. (Ellis, *Reform*, pp. 50–52.)

magistrate. Dissatisfaction with the competence of many justices of the peace led to the emergence in Ireland of the magistrate. Lay part-time magistrates exercised the same judicial powers as a **justice of the peace** at the **quarter-sessions** but like the justices they proved unsuitable despite efforts by successive governments to improve their effectiveness. In 1795 (33 Geo. III c. 36) whole-time stipendiary magistrates exercising control over the city police force were appointed in Dublin. Stipendiary magistrates were introduced to be independent of local (especially Orange and Protestant) influence and control. This initiative proved so successful that from 1814 the lord lieutenant was empowered to appoint 'magistrates of police' and an attendant constabulary force to pacify proclaimed areas. After 1822 resident stipendiary magistrates with no connection to the police could be appointed at the request of the justices of the county. Finally, the 1836 act (6 & 7 Will. IV, c. 13) which legislated for a national constabulary force also provided for the appointment of resident magistrates throughout the country. These, too, were independent of the police and reported to the **chief secretary** on the state of their districts.

By 1912 there were 64 resident magistrates operating outside Dublin. The magistrate presided over **presentment** sessions of the **grand jury** at the **assizes**, acted as an *ex-officio* member of the **board of guardians** of a **poor law union** and in the mid-nineteenth century could appoint police sub-constables. *See* police.

mail. Iron links woven into a metal shirt which was worn to protect the wearer from slashing blows during combat. It was less effective against piercings.

mainprise. The action of procuring the release of a person – who would otherwise be committed to jail – by going surety for his appearance in court on a specific date.

mainpernor. 1: The surety for a released prisoner's appearance in court on a specific date 2: A person who goes surety.

majority, age of. Until 1985 (Age of Majority Act, s.2) the age of majority was 21 years. Prior to the introduction of the **Tenures Abolition Act** in 1662 the wardship and marriage of an heir in minority to the estate of a chief tenant (see *capite, in*) reverted to the crown for the duration of the minority. Customarily wardships were auctioned to the highest bidder who was thereby enabled to take the profits of the estate and demand a marriage price. The guardian was required to maintain the ward and, after the Reformation, ensure that Catholic minors were educated as Protestants at Trinity College. Upon attaining his majority the heir must sue out livery in the **court of wards and liveries** and pay **relief** (a payment usually equivalent to one year's profits of the land) to obtain legal possession of his estate. The crown's pecuniary interest in the business of wardship was increased after the Reformation with the creation of a large number of chief tenancies on lands formerly held by the monasteries and it was the desire to maximise crown revenue from this source that led to the establishment of the court of wards and liveries. The **inquisition** *post-mortem* was the process by which the state detected instances of heirs in minority. *See* ousterlemain.

Malthus, Thomas (1766–1834). The economic and demographic theories of the English economist Thomas Malthus heavily influenced British government thinking on the question of poverty. This is manifest in the ideology which underpinned the 1834 Poor Law Act in England and its Irish equivalent when introduced four years later. Malthus maintained that population expands to the limit of subsistence and only grows when the means of subsistence permit. Population, however, grows exponentially while the food supply increases arithmetically. Thus the food supply will act as a check on population growth unless it is previously checked by self-restraint, vice or starvation, afflictions which can only be avoided by war or disease. Malthusian demographic theory was gloomy and pessimistic. Poverty was an inevitable feature of human existence and state or private charity, by removing the restraint of subsistence, encouraged the poor to pro-create prolifically. Such thinking provided a powerful rationale for blaming the poor for their own misfortunes and absolved the state and the affluent of responsibility. Poor law should be abolished, Malthus maintained, because it limited the mobility of labour and encouraged fecundity. Money spent on relief was wasted. He thought workhouses should be established for severe distress but that conditions within them should be hard. Ireland, with its rapidly growing population, poverty and heavy dependence on a single root crop, appeared to present the English administration with the Malthusian economic model *par excellence*. In fact, however, population growth had begun to decelerate from 1841 and when the Great Famine struck Ireland was producing a surplus of food for export. Malthusian theory also overlooked the safety valve of emigration as a means of reducing demographic pressure on the food supply. The philosophy of Malthus is manifest in the minimalist stance of government during the famine including the stringent administration of poor relief within the workhouses, the ending of **outdoor relief**, an emphasis on local responsibility for distress, the reluctance of government to respond when the crisis became extreme and general during the late 1840s (and, indeed, to reduce what was available as the famine progressed), non-intervention in the markets to halt food leaving the country and agreements with merchants not to sell food below local market prices. (Kinealy, *This great calamity*, pp. 10–18; Ó Gráda, *Malthus*.)

maltster. A maker of malt. In malt-making grain was softened by immersion in water and allowed to germinate after which it was used in the brewing and distilling of alcohol.

manchet. The finest white wheaten bread. *See* paindemaine.

mandamus, order of. (L., we order) A command issuing from the **king's bench** directed to any individual or corporate body or inferior court requiring the performance of some specified duty which pertained to that individual or office.

maniple. An embroidered strip of cloth worn over the left arm at the wrist by a priest at the eucharist.

manor. An estate granted manorial status by crown charter, consisting not merely of land but also certain entitlements, such as the right to hold manorial courts (**court leet**, **court baron** and **court of piepowder**). It was therefore as much a social and legal as a geographical or economic construct. John Norden's 1607 definition of the manor as a 'little commonwealth, whereof the tenants are the members, the land the bulk and the lord the head' neatly encapsulates the three interrelated elements without which a manor could not exist: a lord, tenants and land. In medieval Ireland five classes of tenants have been identified, not all of whom were present on every manor and some – by acquiring additional land under certain conditions – embraced two or more tenures. The highest status belonged to the freeholders, freemen whose estates were heritable and who could dispose of their land as they saw fit. Apart from owing suit of court the freeholders were free of labour services. The *firmarii*, leaseholders owing money rent and labour services, were also freemen as were the **gavellors** (*gavillari*) – rent-paying tenants-at-will who owed services and paid money rent. The **cottiers** (*cotagii*) paid rent for their cottages and **crofts** and worked for the lord and other tenants. At the lowest level were the betaghs (*betagii*), usually the most numerous group on the manor, who occupied the lowest social status and were equivalent to the unfree **bondsmen** and **villeins** of England. Although usually associated with medieval and early modern times, manorial courts persisted in Ireland into the mid-nineteenth century. See bailiff, hayward, infangenetheof, outfangtheof, pinder, seneschal. (*Report from the select committee of manor courts, Ireland*, HC 1837 (494) XV. 69; Gillespie, 'A manor court', pp. 81–87.)

manor borough. A small town absorbed into an adjacent or surrounding **manor** and entitled by royal charter to elect two members to the Irish parliament. There were six in Ireland, the medieval boroughs of Athboy and Ratoath and the four seventeenth-century creations of Mallow (James I), Doneraile, Granard and Mullingar (all Charles II). The lord of the manor exercised complete control over a tiny electorate of Protestant freeholders that ranged in size from 12 in Mullingar to 50 in Granard. Manor boroughs were freely bought and sold throughout the eighteenth century. Only Mallow survived the **Act of Union**.

manor courts. In the eighteenth and nineteenth centuries the manor courts provided a small debt recovery service, exercised common law jurisdiction up to the sum of £200 and retained the ancient jurisdiction of court baron which was held as often as there was business to conduct. Legislation enacted in 1785 and again in 1787 aimed to regulate the courts and their records and ensure that presiding seneschals were suitably qualified. By 1837 there were about 200 manor courts operating in Ireland providing quick and relatively cheap redress to litigants. Critics attacked the seneschals for their incompetence and alleged that some manor courts were conducted in public houses. They were abolished in 1856 (22 Vict., c. 14). For the medieval and early modern manorial courts see **court leet**, **court baron**. (*Report from the select committee of manor courts, Ireland*, HC 1837 (494) XV. 69.)

mansard. A roof with a double slope on either side, the lower slope having a steeper incline than the upper.

manse. Dwelling of a **Presbyterian** or Anglican minister

Mansion House Committee. A nineteenth-century charitable body of concerned citizens which relieved distress during the food shortages of 1831 and which was reconstituted in October 1845 in response to widespread unease generated by the spread of potato blight. Supported by the lord mayor and lord lieutenant, the committee pressed the government to provide relief works, halt the export of corn and shut down distilleries. In 1880, a new body, the Mansion House Fund for Relief of Distress in Ireland was established to provide financial support to local relief committees following the collapse of the potato crop that year. The lord mayor, Edmund Dwyer Grey, presided. By December 1880 the resulting relief fund had attracted subscriptions totalling in excess of £180,000. The minutes of this body were printed and an extensive collection of original records are held in the Dublin Civic Archives in Pearse Street.

mantle. A **falling** or cloak

Manuscript sources for the history of Irish civilisation. Edited by R. J. Hayes, director of the National Library of Ireland, *Manuscript sources for the history of Irish civilisation* is the most comprehensive guide to manuscript sources for Irish history and one of the first ports of call for historians engaged in serious research. It is the most thorough guide to manuscripts held in the National Library and lists most of the collections in public as well as in private hands, both in Ireland and abroad. Microfilm numbers appended to individual entries indicate that the relevant document is available on microfilm. A criticism that Hayes' work mainly drew on the printed catalogues of foreign libraries and overlooked the relevant National Archives has been partly addressed in the supplementary volumes. *See Periodical sources for the history of Irish civilisation*. (Hayes, *The manuscript sources; First supplement, 1965–75*.)

marcate. Of land, as much as is worth one mark per year (13*s*. 4*d*.).

marches. Frontier land of disputed ownership dividing one ethnic group from another.

mark. Money of account, worth 13*s*. 4*d*. or two-thirds of a pound.

market cross. A cross associated with market towns where public announcements were cried.

marksman. An illiterate voter who exercised his franchise by placing his mark on the ballot paper.

marl. A soil consisting of clay and limestone that was spread as a fertiliser or manure. Excessive marling was destructive of land.

marque, letter of. A commission issued by government to private individuals authorising them to capture and plunder enemy merchant shipping. *See* privateer.

marram. *See* bent grass.

marriage. A feudal incident in which the choice of partner of a minor

was of the lord's choosing, inevitably encouraging the lord to demand a price. In the case of estates held *in capite*, the king was entitled to provide wives for his underage wards. Invariably this right
was sold on to others who sought to profit from the marriage, often
without regard to the ward's interest.

marshalsea. A debtors' jail. Until 1872 indebtedness was punishable by
imprisonment. Small debtors were usually lodged in the county prisons
along with other felons but Dublin possessed a number of prisons specifically appointed for debtors, the marshalseas. There debtors were
held until their debts were re-paid, maintained at their own expense
and to a standard of living relative to their means. *See* bankruptcy
court, court of conscience.

mart. 1: A fat cow 2: In the counties of Leinster, a beef that was paid to
the lord 3: In modern usage, a livestock sale.

martello tower. A circular or drum tower constructed during Napole-
onic times as a coastal defence.

martyrology. A medieval register of Christian martyrs containing lists
of saints' (and other) holy days and details of the lives of the saints.
The earliest Irish martyrologies are calendars which name the martyr
and the place of martyrdom under his/her feast day which is often the
date he/she was martyred or died. Later martyrologies provide additional biographical detail. (Kelly, *Calendar of Irish saints*; O'Clery, *The
martyrology*; Stokes, *Félire*; *Idem, Céli Dé*.)

Maynooth College. A Catholic seminary founded in 1795 with the aid
of a government building grant of £8,000 and subvented annually for
a similar amount for many years. Government support for the institution derived from its concern to eradicate the practice of Irish stu-
dent-priests travelling to European seminaries for their education. By
ensuring that Irish priests received their training at home it was hoped
to halt the spread of European ideas and to secure for the government
a toehold measure of influence over the Catholic church in Ireland.
When Gladstone disestablished the **Church of Ireland** in 1869 state
aid to all churches was discontinued and Maynooth received a final subvention of £372,000 which was appropriated from the surplus revenue
of the disendowed church. (*Eighth report of the commissioners of Irish
education inquiry*, HC 1826–27 (509) XIII; Corish, *Maynooth College*.)

meal months. The lean, summer months when stocks of old potatoes
were low, the new potatoes were not ready for eating and grains formed a significantly greater proportion of the native diet.

mearing. A boundary. Intermixed pre-plantation holdings were divided
by mearings and baulks. These were unploughed strips dividing openfield agriculture with, occasionally, slight or temporary fencing.

meather, meadar, meador, meadher. A four-cornered pitcher of uncertain capacity, hollowed out from a single piece of wood and used to

hold butter or oats. In Donegal it had a capacity of two gallons, in Fermanagh six quarts. *See* raskins.

mease, meise, meyse. Equivalent to 630 fish. Five 'hundred', each hundred being 126 fish, was equivalent to a mease.

mechanics' institute. First introduced in Ireland in 1825 with the founding of the Belfast institute, mechanics' institutes were established to provide education to adult workers. Sponsored by middle-class philanthropists, the institutes provided courses of lectures on the Arts and Sciences together with library facilities and reading rooms. Later in the century their work was largely eclipsed by public libraries and other educational institutions. (Cooke, 'The Dublin Mechanics', pp. 15–31; Morton, 'Mechanics', pp. 59–74.)

meere. A Gaelic spatial unit of measurement which in Limerick was equivalent to a quarter or about 240 acres. In Tipperary a quarter meere was equivalent to five **great acres** and four quarter meeres made a **capell land** or 20 great acres.

meitheal. (Ir.) 1: A reaping party 2: The obligation of the base clients or tenants of a Gaelic lord to attend and harvest the lord's corn 3: In modern times the communal harvesting of the corn of each individual in the community.

memoranda rolls. The working records of the upper **exchequer**, the memoranda rolls consisted of copies of documents and notes relating to exchequer affairs. They contained balances, accounts, debts paid to the crown, investigations of financial irregularities, details of the sheriffs' twice-yearly accounts (**proffers**), escheators' accounts, appointments of attorneys, claims for and decisions about allowances, orders for the seizure of property, inquisitions and grants of land. Only two original memoranda rolls survive for Ireland (1309–10, 1319–20) but before its demise in 1830 the **Irish Record Commission** had prepared 43 manuscript volumes of extracts drawn largely from the memoranda rolls for the period 1294–1509. The extant memoranda rolls and the commission's volumes of extracts are in the National Archives. As the accounts of the Irish treasurer (head of the exchequer) were audited at the English exchequer, material relating to exchequer business in Ireland can be found in the English memoranda rolls. *See* pipe rolls. (Connolly, *Medieval record sources*, p. 22; Lydon, 'Survey', pp. 51–134; Phair, 'Sir William Betham', pp. 1–99.)

memorial. 1: A letter of petition 2: A copy of a deed. *See* Deeds, Registry of.

mensal lands. *Lucht tighe* or the lands which traditionally supplied food to the lord's table and hence were free of exactions.

mensal parish. A parish set aside to supply the episcopal table.

mercer. A dealer in cloth, a draper.

merchet. A payment owed to the manorial lord by a tenant for permitting his daughter to marry.

mercy, let him be in. Let him be fined.

mere. (L., *merus*, pure) In a multi-ethnic society – as Ireland was in early modern times – the term *mere Irish* (pure Irish) was used to distinguish the native Gaelic Irish from those Irish-born descendants of Anglo-Norman settlers (the Old English) and the Irish-born descendants of Elizabethan and Jacobean planters (the New English). (Ferguson, 'The "mere English"', p. 508.)

merlon. The solid intervals between the **crenelles** (openings) of a battlement which sheltered defenders from missiles.

meskenningham, meskenningha, miskenninga. A fine imposed for mispleading or for offering a false plea.

mesne lord. An intermediate lord in the feudal chain, one who holds an estate of a superior lord.

mesne process. The intermediate stage in legal proceedings (the first being to select the court appropriate to the alleged offence) by which a court attempted to secure a defendant's appearance and where either plaintiff or defendant might lawfully have the hearing postponed. If the **sheriff** could not locate the alleged criminal to compel his attendance he was exacted or summoned on five successive meetings of the county court and outlawed on the fifth. The final stage in legal proceedings was the action itself.

mesolithic. (Gr., *mesos*, middle + *lithos*, stone) Middle period of the stone age, the hunter-gatherer era, transitional between the **neolithic** and **paleolithic** periods.

messuage. A house with outbuildings and a parcel of land or yard.

metayage. A system of land tenure which required a rental payment by the tenant of a proportion of the produce of his holding, the stock and seed having been provided by the owner.

Methodism. Originally a movement within the Established church, Methodism appeared in Ireland in the mid-eighteenth century and was characterised by an itinerant ministry, lay preaching, an emphasis on disciplined living and evangelicanism. In 1816 there was a division in Methodism between the Primitive Wesleyan Methodists, who favoured a continued presence within the Established church, and the Wesleyan Methodists who wished to secede. The rift was healed in 1878 and the two branches re-united. Methodist numbers grew consistently in the first half of the nineteenth century, peaking at over 44,000 in 1844, but emigration contributed to a decline thereafter. Although its mission to convert Catholics and Presbyterians made little headway, Methodists contributed significantly to the emergence of evangelicalism in Ireland in the nineteenth century. The supreme governing body of Methodism in Ireland is the Methodist Conference which first met in 1744 and was responsible for defining policy, for ordinations and stationing of ministers. The next level in the structure was the district synod which met twice yearly. Further down the hierarchy were the individual circuits which comprised two to four churches served by one minister. Circuit meetings of the minister, officials and lay delegates were held quarterly. Local meetings, known as the monthly class or leader's meetings, were held in a house and concentrated on pastoral affairs. (Cooney, *The Methodists*; Jeffery, *Irish Methodism*; PRONI, *Guide to church records*; Ryan, *Irish church records*.)

metropolitan. The primate of an ecclesiastical province. In Ireland the four metropolitans were the respective archbishops of Armagh, Dublin, Tuam and Cashel. *See* visitation.

Michaelmas. 1: 29 September, the feast of St Michael and All Angels, one of the quarter days when rents were due 2: A term in the legal and university year. *See* sittings.

microlith. A tiny geometrical blade tool from the **mesolithic** age.

midden. 1: A refuse heap or dunghill 2: A coastal site where shellfish were consumed regularly, the evidence of which is preserved in a dense layer of shells.

middleman. Also known as landjobber, rentier or lease speculator, a middleman was a lessee who re-let part or all of the land leased to him. The term appears to have been coined by **Arthur Young** in the eighteenth century. The rise of the middleman is associated with absentee landlords who were anxious to secure a regular income by granting long leases at low rents. The middleman secured a lease on a property and then sublet at a higher rent to maximise his profit, contracting leases which expired before his own in order to treat with the landlord as an occupying tenant. Middlemen employed the tactic of **canting** to secure the maximum possible return on their investment. This involved advertising the expiry of leases in chapels and towns, inviting private bids and leasing to the highest bidder without any consideration being given to the former tenant, a practice not dissimilar to the modern-day sealed tender. David Dickson has challenged the stereotypical view of the middleman as a rapacious parasite by illustrating the complexity of intermediate tenure in terms of origin, scale, function, change over time and regional differentiation. He notes that contemporary critiques of the middleman (some of which were laudatory) differ because the authors were referring to distinct manifestations of the phenomenon. At the close of the eighteenth century the middleman system was in decline caught between the vice of tenant poverty and the determination of landlords to extract a better return from their estates. (Dickson, 'Middlemen', pp. 162–85.)

middle nation. A term used by Anglo-Irish settlers in the middle ages to define their status as neither wholly Irish nor wholly English. (Lydon, 'The middle nation', pp. 1–26.)

Middlesex, bill of. *See latitat*.

mile. A statute mile is equivalent to 1,760 yards, the Irish or plantation mile, 2,240 yards and the Cunningham or Scottish mile, 1,984 yards. The difference derives from the use of a different linear perch, the statute perch measuring five-and-a-half yards, the Irish measuring seven and the Cunningham six-and-a-quarter.

mile line (the 'line'). A belt of land, originally four miles wide, around the coast of Connacht as far as Sligo and south along the west bank of the Shannon which was to be planted by Cromwellians, effectively sealing in the transplanted Irish from the outer world and preventing their escape back to where they had come from. Its breadth was successively reduced to three miles and later to one mile because there was insufficient land to meet the needs of the transplanted.

miles. (L., a soldier) A knight.

militia. Part-time militias or citizen armies were raised in Ireland from the seventeenth century. Until the late eighteenth century – and with the exception of Tyrconnell's Catholic militia – they were exclusively Protestant and brought into being during periods of external threats. In 1715 (2 Geo. I, c. 9) the militia was placed on a statutory basis and all male Protestants between the ages of 16 and 60 were required to muster for four days annually. The force was raised on a county basis by the governors and gentry in each county and organised into county regiments and small independent companies. It was mobilised during the invasion scares of 1739 and 1745 but after 1760 became moribund. After decades of inactivity a full-time infantry force comprising at least 38 regiments was raised in 1793 for service anywhere in the British Isles. This innovation was accompanied by severe anti-militia disturbances as poorer Catholics rioted because they had received nothing from the 1793 Catholic Relief Act (which enfranchised the forty-shilling freeholders) yet now found themselves subject to effective conscription since they could not buy substitutes to perform their militia service. The policy of requiring men to serve outside the home county was designed to inhibit the influence of local affinities. Officered by Protestants but overwhelmingly Catholic in the ranks, the Irish militia was regarded with suspicion by the administration because it was believed to have been heavily infiltrated by **United Irishmen** and **Defenders**. Nevertheless, the force proved adequate during the 1798 rebellion and the anticipated defection of Catholics to the rebels did not take place. The militia continued in active service until 1816. (Bartlett and Jeffrey, *A military history*; Blackstock, *An ascendancy army*, pp. 36–38, 42–3, 50; McAnally, *The Irish militia*.)

millenarianism. A belief in the coming through revolutionary action of a utopian society which took root in Ireland in early decades of the nineteenth century with the dissemination of **Pastorini**'s prophecy that the destruction of Protestant supremacy was imminent. (Donnelly, 'Pastorini', pp. 102–39; O'Farrell, 'Millenialism', pp. 45–68.)

ministers' money. A house tax imposed in lieu of **tithe** in 1665 (17 & 18 Chas. II, c. 7) on householders in Dublin, Cork, Limerick, Waterford, Drogheda, Kilkenny, Clonmel and Kinsale and collected by **church-wardens** for the upkeep of Anglican ministers. The tax was assessed on the yearly value of a house to a maximum of 12 pence in the pound and no house could be rated above a yearly value of £6. It was inequitable in that the burden fell largely on non-Anglicans, on the poorer citizens proportionally greater than the richer and it did not apply to towns in the north. In the nineteenth century about £15,000 was levied annually by this tax. Minister's money managed to escape the tentacles of the **Church Temporalities Act** of 1833 but was reduced by 25% in 1854 and abolished in 1857. A body known as the Ecclesiastical Commissioners for Ireland – which had been established under the temporalities act – was then charged with paying the ministers out of its own funds though it was permitted to recoup the payment from the municipal governments. In the event the municipal governments contributed only a fraction of the payment and after the passage of William Fagan's private member's bill through the commons in 1857 (20 & 21 Vict., c. 8) the ecclesiastical commissioners had to shoulder the entire burden. (Power, 'A minister's money', pp. 183–200.)

misprision. A failure of duty, an omission or misdemeanour committed by a public officer.

mocket. A bib or handkerchief.

model schools. Nineteenth-century district training schools vested in, controlled and funded by the National Board of Education where aspiring primary teachers worked for a six-month period before progressing to the Central Model School in Dublin, a residential training institution conducted on non-denominational principles. The first model school opened in Dublin in 1834 and by mid-century there were 25 in existence. Catholic bishops disapproved of the non-denominational ethos of the training institutions and campaigned against them. In 1862 priests were forbidden to send trainees to the model schools or hire model school graduates and Catholic schoolchildren were withdrawn from 1866. The **Powis Commission** (1870) recommended government subvention for denominational teacher-training and in the 1880s St Patrick's College, Carysfort, Mary Immaculate (Limerick) and the Church Of Ireland Training College were established. Some model schools, shorn of their teacher-training role, continue to operate. (Akenson, *The Irish education experiment*.)

moderator. The president of a **Presbyterian** governing body.

moiety. A half portion.

Molyneaux, William. Author of the *Case of Ireland's being bound by acts of parliament in England stated* (Dublin, 1698), Molyneaux criticised the anomalous legislative relationship between the kingdom of Ireland and the neighbouring island. Ireland was a separate kingdom, had a parliament of its own and was not represented in Westminster. On this basis the English parliament had no right to bind Ireland by legislation passed in Westminster. Molyneux was not preaching separatism for he believed a political union of the two kingdoms with Irish representation in Westminster would be preferable to the arrangement as it was. In the early 1700s there were appeals from Ireland for such a union but they were not heeded in England and the **Declaratory Act** of 1720 copperfastened the subordination of the Irish parliament to Westminster. *See* sole right. (Simms, *William Molyneaux*.)

month's mind. A memorial mass held usually about one month after a person's decease.

monolith. A single upright stone.

Moravian. An evangelical religious sect of Czech origin founded in Saxony by persecuted Hussite emigrants from Moravia, the Moravians appeared in Ireland in the mid-eighteenth century. Their greatest success was achieved in Co. Antrim yet although the missionary work of John Cennick resulted in the formation of over 200 societies, the sect never attained critical numerical mass and by 1836 there were but seven congregations in Ireland. A Moravian model village was laid out at Gracehill, Co. Antrim, in 1746. The records of Moravian congregations in Ireland are retained at Gracehill and are available on microfim in the Public Record Office of Northern Ireland.

mortar. A mixture of water, sand and lime used as cement for construction purposes.

mort d'ancestor, assize of. A possessory action to settle disputes as to who was the immediate heir of a person last seised of a particular estate. It was initiated to recover lawfully inherited land that had been taken by another before the heir was able to take possession. Introduced under Henry II, the writ issued to commence the action demanded of the jury an answer to the question: 'Did X, the ancestor of Y (plaintiff), die seised in his demesne and as of fee of Z (the property) and is Y his nearest heir?' If the jury answered 'yes', the plaintiff was immediately given seisin of the estate. *See novel disseisin*.

mortmain, alienation to. (Fr., dead hand) *Magna Carta* (18 John, c. 39, 1217) forbade the **alienation** of land to corporations or monasteries because, unlike human tenants, corporate bodies cannot die, marry or be in a minority and so the crown was denied its entitlement to the feudal incidents of **escheat**, **wardship**, **marriage** and **relief**. The Statute of Mortmain (1279) increased the penalties for such transactions and periodically between the thirteenth and the sixteenth centuries additional statutes were enacted to forbid alienations to mortmain without licence. Monastic institutions, nevertheless, managed to evade the restrictions imposed by the statute by taking an action for **recovery**, a legal fiction which the courts accepted in order to maintain the principle of alienability of land. *See* use, feeoffment to.

mortuary. Death duty owed to the parish church comprising the second best beast (the best went to the manorial lord as a **heriot** if the deceased were a tenant), a chattel or a payment fixed according to parish custom. Testators often left specific bequests in their wills by way of mortuary. *See* canonical portion.

Moryson, Fynes (1566–1630). Travel-writer, historian and secretary to Lord Deputy Mountjoy from 1600, Fynes Moryson is remembered for his almost universally disparaging views on Ireland and the Irish. In *An Itinerary* (1617), a four volume account of his travels in Europe, Moryson denigrates Irish diet, hygiene, dress, manners, customs and Catholicism, reserving his praise solely for 'usquebagh'. His treatment of the Nine Years War remains valuable, however prejudiced it be, for he was an eyewitness to the later stages of the conflict, was present at Kinsale and the surrender of Hugh O'Neill and continued in Mountjoy's service until the latter's death in 1606. (Moryson, *An itinerary*.)

motte and bailey. A truncated conical mound (motte) of earth, often moated, palisaded and surmounted by a wooden tower together with a lower adjoining palisaded mound or courtyard (bailey). These fortified earthworks, over 300 of which were constructed by the Anglo-Normans in the late twelfth century, were later replaced by stone castles. The greatest density of mottes is to be found in the eastern half of the country representing the extent of penetration of the invaders.

mouldboard plough. A mouldboard plough consisted of a **coulter, share** and **mouldboard**. The coulter (a vertical blade fitted forward of the share) cut through roots, the share opened the ground and the mouldboard, a curved, sloping board or plate fitted above the share, lifted and turned the soil as it was opened to create the typical ridge and furrow pattern. (Mitchell, *The Shell guide*, pp. 143–4, 160.)

mulcture, multure. A fee or payment in kind (usually a portion of flour) owed to the miller for milling cereals or to the manorial lord if he owned the mill. By the nineteenth century the fee had been commuted to a cash payment known as 'mulcture money'.

mullion. An upright bar or pier which divides a window into compartments.

mumping. A begging practice engaged in by noble families of little means to provide a newly-matched daughter with a portion. It usually involved cattle or sheep. Peasants also resorted to mumping, though for items of less worth.

Municipal Corporations Reform Act (1840). A municipal reform bill first introduced in 1835 and enacted five years later after an inquiry into the conduct of municipal corporations revealed considerable defects. In the 1830s there were 68 corporations and boroughs in Ireland, bodies that were only nominally open to Catholics for almost all had chosen not to enlarge the franchise when permitted to do so in 1793. Notoriously corrupt and a bastion of Protestantism, 58 were abolished in 1840 under the Municipal Corporations Reform Act (3 & 4 Vict., c. 108) and their functions passed to the county. The 10 remaining corporations (Belfast, Clonmel, Cork, Drogheda, Dublin, Kilkenny, Limerick, Derry, Sligo and Waterford) were replaced by elected governing bodies with severely limited functions on a municipal franchise restricted to £10 householders. Unlike English corporations, Irish municipal governments were not given control of the police nor the power to elect a sheriff. The power to appoint sheriffs and magistrates lay with the lord lieutenant although from 1876 corporations were permitted to nominate three candidates from whom the viceroy selected one. Catholics were now eligible in their own right for admittance to the corporations of cities and towns and they immediately took control of a number of large councils. Towns with populations of 3,000 people or more could apply for a charter but only Wexford did so. Other boroughs could adopt the measures of an 1828 act (9 Geo. IV, c. 82) which empowered them to elect a body of commissioners with municipal powers limited to such areas as paving and lighting. About 25 towns adopted this course of action and a further 20 (55 by 1878) brought into force the provisions of a revised act of 1854 (17 & 18 Vict., c. 103). *See* borough, guilds, quarterage. (*First report of the commissioners appointed to enquire into the municipal corporations in Ireland*, HC 1835 [323] XXVII; Webb, *Municipal government*.)

muniments. Deeds of title and other such records.

murage. The right granted by charter to citizens to levy customs on persons selling goods in their town to construct or repair defences.

murrain. Any of various cattle diseases such as anthrax, tick fever, plague or pestilence.

muster roll. A list of men and their arms who were available for the defence of an area during a military emergency.

mutiny act. The first English mutiny act was passed in 1689 to suppress indiscipline among regiments that had been ordered into service abroad. Although limited to a year, the mutiny act proved so effective that it was renewed annually. The act reaffirmed the clause in the **Declaration**

of Rights which outlawed the maintenance of a standing army in peacetime without the consent of parliament and asserted that monarch and parliament considered it necessary for the safety of the kingdom to maintain such a force and that good discipline should prevail. Prior to 1779 there was no mutiny act in Ireland. Breaches of discipline were dealt with before a court-martial and punishments dispensed according to the provisions of the English act or by crown prerogative. When the validity of English laws in Ireland was challenged it became apparent that no one could be convicted in Ireland for offences against the English mutiny act. Subsequently the heads of an annual mutiny bill passed the Irish house of commons but were returned from England with no limitation as to time. When the amended bill passed the house (19 & 20 Geo. III, c. 16, 1780), Ireland now operated under a permanent mutiny act which did not require the assent of parliament for the maintenance of a peacetime army, a situation which Edmund Burke condemned as unconstitutional and contrary to the Declaration of Rights. In 1782 (21 & 22 Geo. III, c. 43) the permanent act was repealed and a mutiny act along the lines of the English act was enacted annually until the Act of Union.

N

name books. The letters and notes on placenames and antiquities compiled by John O'Donovan during the course of the Ordnance Survey project to map the entire country from 1824 to 1846. The name books, together with other records of the Ordnance Survey, have been transferred to the National Archives.

naomhóg. At about eight metres long and fitted with a mast and sail, the elegant Kerry naomhóg is the largest of the currachs. It has four seats and consists of a framework of wooden laths covered in tarred cloth.

napping. The act of raising the short hairs or threads (the nap) on homespun frieze or flannel by combing the fabric section by section with a card. Later a few drops of honey were brushed over the fibres and the task repeated. The final stage in raising the nap involved curling the nap with a cork sheet.

National Archives. Until the eighteenth century no serious effort was made to preserve important administrative records in Ireland. The main repository for records of the rolls was the Bermingham Tower in Dublin Castle but other records were considered to be the property of the relevant office-holder. The State Paper Office was established in 1702 to copy official documents from the collections of earlier chief governors but few pre-1690 records were available and the office contributed little towards improving the state of the records. Outbreaks of fire in the Custom House (1711) and the Bermingham Tower (1758) drew attention to the miserable state of the records but little was done to rectify the situation. John Lodge's appointment as deputy keeper of rolls and records in the Bermingham Tower represented a turning point in the fortune of state records. His 26 volumes of transcripts from the rolls were later acquired by the Public Record Office to compensate for the destruction of the originals in the Four Courts fire in 1922. The appointment of the **Irish Record Commission** represented another step forward. The quality of its surveys, indexes, lists and calendars of the records was severely criticised and it was abolished in 1830 but like Lodge's transcripts, the work of the commission attained an unforeseen value after 1922. In 1848 a second commission focused on ordering and publishing **exchequer** material, the most notable legacy of which is James Ferguson's multi-volume transcripts of exchequer records. From 1869 the Public Record Office, established by parliament in 1867 (30 & 31 Vict., c. 70) and housed in a dedicated building in the Four Courts complex, became the central repository for state and local government records. Records previously held in Dublin Castle (except for those retained in the State Paper Office), the Custom House and the courts were transferred there, the bulk of which were subsequently consumed in the 1922 conflagration. Since 1922 the record office has accumulated a large collection of family, estate, business, solicitors' and other records through donations and purchase. It also acquired the chief secretary's massive archive from the State Paper Office. In 1986 the Public Record Office was merged with the State Paper Office to form the National Archives and all government departments were required to lodge official records there on a 30-year rule. The Public Record Office of Northern Ireland was established in 1923 as a central repository for the six counties of Northern Ireland. It holds state, local government, education, ecclesiastical, family and estate records. The reports of the deputy-keeper of public records are the best guides to records held and accessions to the records offices. (Griffith, 'A short guide to the Public Record Office of Ireland', pp. 45–58; Wood, *A guide to the public records*; *Idem*, 'The public records of Ireland'.)

National Association of Ireland. Inspired by William J. O'Neill Daunt who sought to foster co-operation between Irish Catholics and English liberals and founded in Dublin in 1864 by Archbishop Paul Cullen (Dublin) and Archbishop Leahy (Cashel), the National Association was a Catholic middle-class pressure group which sought the disestablishment and disendowment of the Church of Ireland. Members wanted the fund created by disendowment to be used for secular purposes such as social welfare and education and not for the concurrent endowment of the Catholic church as this was liable to be attended by state involvement in the running of the church. Other aims included the re-distribution of land in Ireland and the provision of state aid to denominational schools. The association required parliamentary candidates to pledge not to support parties holding policies on church and land issues contrary to its own. It failed to attract many MPs and only four National Association members were returned to parliament in 1865. Later John Blake Dillon cobbled together a group of 20 or so Irish liberal MPs to provide a coherent bargaining front to deal with the liberal government, a tactic which foreshadowed the 'balance of power' tactic of the later Irish parliamentary party. The association survived into the 1870s largely as a talking shop. (Comerford, 'Gladstone's first Irish enterprise', pp. 432–33; Corish, 'Cardinal Cullen', pp. 13–61.)

National League. See Nationalist Party.

National Library of Ireland. Established in 1877, the National Library inherited both the premises and the library of the Royal Dublin Society in Kildare Street, Dublin. Manuscript acquisition began largely with the appointment of R. I. Best as director in the 1920s. The archives of **Ulster king of arms** were transferred to the library when that office was renamed the Genealogical Office in 1943. Under the directorship of R. J. Hayes, the library developed a collection of family and estate papers including the Ormond MSS and the Boyle papers. A large map and photograph archive was assembled. Over the years the library has compiled a massive microfilm collection of Irish-related documents held in archives worldwide, notably from the state papers in the Public Record Office, London and the manuscript collection of the British Library. Hayes' *Manuscript sources for the history of Irish civilisation* is the best guide to manuscript material in the National Library.

Nationalist Party. Also known as the Irish Parliamentary Party or the National League, the Nationalist Party was a tightly-structured, highly-disciplined political party which developed from Isaac Butt's federalist Home Government Association of the 1870s with the achievement of home rule its overriding goal. Membership increased dramatically following the electoral reforms of 1884–5. Under Parnell's leadership the party achieved unprecedented electoral success in 1885 with the election of 86 Nationalist MPs, all pledged to sit, act and vote, as one. Parnell's earlier obstructionist tactics were abandoned as the party played the 'balance of power' card to force the home rule issue centre stage in the 1880s and again between 1910–14. Although riven by the crisis over the O'Shea divorce case the party survived and regrouped under John Redmond in 1900. Throughout much of its history the Nationalist Party focused on agrarian and Catholic issues and enjoyed the support of a majority of the Catholic clergy. The party's collapse as a parliamentary force from 70 seats in 1910 to six in the 1918 election is usually attributed to the emergence in the wake of the 1916 Rising of the more aggressively nationalist Sinn Féin. Commentators have also cited factors such as the party's adherence to an agrarian campaign in a society that was already undergoing structural diversification, its inability to engage with cultural nationalism, its failure to come to terms with Unionism and its active support for the First World War to account for its demise. It should be noted that electoral reforms in 1918 increased the number of voters to over two million (including women for the first time), almost two-thirds of whom had not voted in the 1910 election. (Connolly, *The Oxford companion*, pp. 381–2; Lyons, *The Irish parliamentary party*.)

National Repeal Association. Founded in 1840 by Daniel O'Connell, the National Repeal Association attempted to repeat the mass agitation technique which delivered **Catholic emancipation** in order to achieve the repeal of the **Act of Union**. *See* Young Ireland.

national school. *See* Education, National System of

nave. The main body of the church. In medieval times the upkeep and maintenance of the nave was the responsibility of the parish, the **chancel** being the responsibility of the tithe-owner.

neolithic. (Gr., *neo*, new + *lithos*, stone) Neolithic farmers reached Ireland about 5,500 years ago equipped with polished axe heads which enabled them to clear forest openings, cultivate cereals and raise domestic animals. Large tombs or megaliths such as the **court tomb**, the **passage grave** and the **dolmen** are relics of neolithic colonisation. *See* Larnian folk, Sandelians.

Ne temere. In 1907 the Sacred Congregation of Propaganda Fide drafted the *Ne temere* decree which was promulgated by Pope Pius X to come into effect in April, 1908. *Ne temere* required that all inter-faith marriages be celebrated by a Catholic priest in order to be valid under Catholic canon law. The non-Catholic partner was required to sign a contract pledging not to interfere with the religion of the Catholic partner. Catholic partners would endeavour to bring their non-Catholic spouses to the true faith and all children of the marriage were to be baptised in the Catholic faith and educated in Catholic schools. Finally, either before or after the Catholic marriage ceremony, the couple were not to present themselves for marriage before a minister of any other religion. In Ireland these stipulations had already become practice following the **Synod of Thurles** in 1850.

New English. *See* Old English.

new interest. The 'new interest' comprised Catholics who had purchased lands from the 1660s, the titles to which were based on the Restoration land settlement. Unlike the majority of their co-religionists, they were lukewarm about attempts to repeal the settlement because they feared the loss of their newly acquired estates.

New Light. A term which refers to the views of a liberal group of **Presbyterian** ministers in the eighteenth and nineteenth centuries which opposed the requirement of the **Synod of Ulster** that all candidates for the ministry subscribe to the **Westminster Confession**, the Presbyterian confession of faith. The non-subscribing New Light group formed a majority within the synod and throughout the eighteenth century subscription was dispensed with, many subscribers leaving to find a home among the **Seceders**. In the nineteenth century the position was reversed. The New Light group, tainted by **Arianism** (the belief that Christ was neither fully human nor possessed of a divinity identical with God), was forced to secede from the Synod in 1830 to form the **Remonstrant Synod**. When subscription was re-imposed the Seceders merged with the Synod of Ulster to form the **General Assembly of the Presbyterian Church in Ireland**.

Newsplan. A census of Irish newspapers listing all newspapers held in the main libraries in Ireland and in the British Library, their publication dates, location and availability in microfim and hard copy. Newspapers are listed by title and the report contains a town and county index. (O'Toole, *Newsplan*.)

Newtown Act (1747). The act (21 Geo. II, c. 10) which removed the necessity for burgesses and freemen to reside in their respective boroughs in order to vote in parliamentary elections. Newtown led to the creation of a large number of honorary and absentee freemen whose sole connection with the borough was to appear at election time and vote as required. In time absenteeism became the rule for freemen. Almost 140 of the 150 freemen of the borough of Dingle, Co. Kerry, did not even reside in the county and the freemen of Kinsale borough resided to a man in Ulster. *See* borough, franchise, freeman.

nil debit. (L.) He owes nothing, the usual plea in an action of debt.

nisi prius, **hearing of.** (L., unless before) Originally a writ commanding a sheriff to empanel a jury at the court of Westminster on a certain day unless the justices of **assize** previously came to his county and tried the case. Justices of assize had the power to conclude cases begun in the fixed courts and which had been brought to the point where the verdict of a local jury was necessary – that is, *nisi prius* – because the cases were adjourned to another meeting of the **king's bench** or **common pleas** *unless before* that meeting the justices of assize should have visited that county. *Nisi prius* was introduced in Ireland in the sixteenth century.

noble. A gold coin worth 6*s*. 8*d*. or half a **mark**, first introduced in 1351. *See* angel.

nocent. Guilty.

nomina parentum. In Catholic baptismal registers, the name of the parents.

nomina patrinorum. In Catholic baptismal registers, the name of the godparents.

nomina sponsorum. In Catholic marriage registers, the Christian names of the couple.

nominy money, nominy penny. A sum of 5% paid to the land agent on the return of goods distrained for non-payment of rent.

nonage. Below the age of 21 years, not of full age. *See* majority.

non assumpsit. (L.) The plea of a defendant in a personal action in which he denies having entered into a promise.

non-conformist. A Protestant, such as a Presbyterian, who did not conform to the Anglican church (also a **dissenter**). Strictly speaking Catholics were also non-conformists.

non-cure. A religious sinecure. An Anglican benefice which did not involve the performance of any religious ceremony since it did not have a congregation. The minister appointed to the non-cure simply collected the emolument pertaining to the benefice. Under the **Church Temporalities Act** (1833) the ecclesiastical commissioners were entitled to void all such appointments when they next became vacant (with the exception of those under lay patronage) and to appropriate the income from the non-cure.

non est culpabilis. (L.) He is not culpable, the plea in an action of trespass.

non est inventus. (L.) He is not to be found, the return of a sheriff following the failure of a felon to answer at five successive county courts.

non-subscribers. Between 1719–26, a dissenting group of Presbyterians who refused to subscribe to the **Westminster Confession**, the statement of Presbyterian doctrine. *See* Presbyterian, Remonstrant Synod, New Light, Seceders, Southern Association.

Non-Subscribing Presbyterian church. *See* Unitarians.

non utlagat. (L.) He is not guilty.

notary, notary public. A legal clerk who took affidavits or depositions and attested the authenticity of deeds and documents.

novel disseisin, **assize of**. The form of action of writ and hearing before a jury began with the assize of *novel disseisin* and was adapted to other cases of civil dispute such as *mort d'ancestor*. *Novel disseisin* (recent deprivation of seisin) determined whether an individual had unjustly disseised (dispossessed) another of his freehold. It was introduced at the Assize of Northampton in 1176 when judges were ordered to hear actions to recover lands of which the plaintiff had been dispossessed arising from May 1175.

nuncupative will. A death-bed testament in which the testator's last wishes were recorded and witnessed.

nuns. The paucity of contemporary records makes it difficult to ascertain the size and state of female religious houses in the centuries prior to dissolution of the monastic institutions. A small number of earlier Celtic female abbeys appear to have continued into the late medieval period to become **Arroasian Augustinian** houses through the influence of St Malachy. Malachy also founded female houses including St Mary's Abbey, the chief Augustinian house, at Clonard in Co. Meath (c. 1144) which had 13 daughter houses. From 1223–4 Kilcreevanty became the leading Augustinian house in Connacht and when Clonard declined c. 1383 it was superseded by Odder. Other female congregations active in Ireland in the middle ages included the **Cistercians**, the Benedictines and the **Franciscans** (represented by six houses of the Order of St Clare in 1316). Female religious were frequently attached to male monasteries where they served in the almonries and hospitals and in the fifteenth and sixteenth centuries female congregations of the **Franciscan Third Order Regular** are recorded in the west and north of Ireland. At the **dissolution** the convents were suppressed and their temporalities confiscated, the superiors receiving small pensions by way of compensation. During the Counter-Reformation attempts were made to revive or establish convents but with little success and according to the Report on the State of Popery there were only nine nunneries operating in Ireland in 1731. The foundation of the Presentation Sisters in 1776 initiated the process that was to result in the great nineteenth-century conventual efflorescence. In 1800 there were only 120 nuns living in 11 houses in Ireland. By 1900 37 female religious orders were active, comprising 8,200 sisters dispersed in 327 communities across the island. The Brigidines (1809), the Sisters of Charity (1815), the Loreto nuns (1821) and the Sisters of Mercy (1828) joined older established orders such as the Dominicans, the Carmelites, the Poor Clares and foreign orders such as the Ursulines and Sisters of St Louis to provide a broad range of welfare, health and educational services. *See* Popery, Report on the State of.(Clear, *Nuns*; Hall, *Women*; Magray, *The transforming power*.)

O

Oakboys, Hearts of Oak. This militant, highly public mid- and south-Ulster combination emerged in 1763 in protest against the passing of the Road Act which required all highways to be repaired by the personal labour of householders along the route. The largely Protestant Oakboys objected to the fact that landed proprietors, in their capacity as grand jurors, often had roads and bridges made for their own convenience with the burden of repairs falling on the poorer ratepayers. Thus it was a protest against the use of public taxes for private roads. They also objected to attempts by the Anglican ministers to exact the strict legal rate of **tithe** and the exaction of small **dues** (fees for christenings, marriages, funerals and **churching**). Wearing oak boughs in their hats, they gathered together to erect gallows and paraded to the clergymen's houses. There they compelled them not to exact more than a specified proportion of the tithe. They also visited the houses of the resident gentlemen and forced them to swear they would not assess the county at more than a specified rate and that they would make no more roads. The sting was taken out of the protest by the passing of a less contentious road act within a few months. (Donnelly, 'Hearts of Oak', pp. 7–73.)

Oates, Titus. *See* Popish Plot.

oakum. Caulking fibre made by picking and unravelling old hemp rope. It was used to stop the cracks in wooden ships.

ob. Contraction of the Latin *obiit* which means he or she died. *See obolus*.

obit. A memorial mass or recitation of prayers performed on the anniversary of the death of a person, usually that of a deceased member of a cathedral or monastic institution, a lay member of a confraternity, a benefactor or well-disposed civic official. Religious institutions such as cathedrals or monasteries maintained a register known as a 'book of obits' in which such dates were entered. (Crosthwaite and Todd, *The book of obits*.)

oblations. Small **dues** and offerings or gifts for religious purposes, usually small monetary payments for specific church services such as weddings, baptisms, churching of women and funerals. Oblations of one penny or halfpenny were also paid at major religious festivals such as Christmas, Easter or on the feast-day of the parish.

obolate. Land worth one halfpenny per year.

obolus. (Abbreviated as *ob*.) A halfpenny or coin of small denomination.

observant. *See* conventualism.

octave. The eighth day after a festival, both days being included so that the eighth day always falls on the same day as the festival itself.

Octennial Act (1768). The octennial act (7 Geo. III, c. 3) introduced the practice of a fixed-term parliament, in this case a period of eight years. Previously parliament was dissolved only on the death or proclamations of the monarch.

O'Curry, Eugene (1796–1862). Self-taught calligrapher, translator and scholar, O'Curry worked for three years in the **Ordnance Survey** where he met **John O'Donovan** and **George Petrie**. He catalogued Irish manuscripts for the **Royal Irish Academy**, Trinity College Dublin and the British Museum. In 1854 he was appointed professor of Irish history and architecture in the Catholic University of Ireland. His lectures (1855–6) on ancient Irish manuscript sources were published in 1861 and a further three volumes of lectures (1857–62) called *The manners and customs of the ancient Irish* appeared posthumously in 1873. (O'Curry, *Lectures*.)

O'Donovan, John (1809–61). Born in Co. Kilkenny, O'Donovan is numbered (along with **Eugene O'Curry** and **George Petrie**) among the outstanding Irish scholars of the nineteenth century. After a three-year stint in the Irish Record Office (1826–9) he transferred to the **Ordnance Survey** where he compiled over 140,000 placenames. His letters which contain notes and observations on the placenames and antiquities of Ireland were published in 50 volumes posthumously between 1924 and 1932 by Michael O'Flanagan. O'Donovan published a grammar of the Irish language in 1845, contributed articles on history and topography to the Dublin *Penny Journal* and to publications of the Irish Archaeological Society (of which he was a co-founder with Eugene O'Curry and James Todd). His translation of *The martyrology of Donegal* was published posthumously by William Reeves and James Todd in 1864. O'Donovan's crowning achievement was his translation of the annals of the kingdom of Ireland by the four masters which issued in seven volumes between 1848 and 1851. *See Four Masters, Annals of*.

oenach. Ancient Gaelic assembly or fair, apparently associated with political or social as well as commercial affairs.

OESA. The Order of Hermits of St Augustine. *See* Augustinian Friars.

office. For devotional purposes the monastic day was divided into seven or eight canonical hours. The night prayers of matins (also known as vigils or nocturns) began at 2am or 3am in the summer and were followed by the singing of lauds at first light in Benedictine monasteries. Thereafter the office was recited at 6am (*prime*), 9am (*terce*), noon (*sext*) and 3pm (*nones*). Vespers (also known as *lucernarium* because candles were lit at its celebration) was recited in the evening and compline, the last of the canonical day-hours, was said before retiring at night.

OFM. The Order of Friars Minor. *See* Franciscans.

ogham. A short-hand writing style based on a 20-letter alphabet derived from Latin. Ogham stones, which were upright and inscribed, were erected as boundary markers as well as gravestones. Over 300 have been identified in Ireland dating from 350 AD to 600 AD.

ogee. An arch or moulding associated with **Gothic** architecture which is described by means of four centres so as to be alternatively convex and concave.

Old English. The Catholic descendants of Anglo-Norman settlers who monopolised government positions until the Reformation, after which they were gradually edged out and replaced by the Protestant New English (Tudor and Jacobean settlers and administrators). In the late medieval period they are also referred to as the 'middle nation' because they represented a middle ground between the Gaelic Irish with whom they shared a common birthplace and the English of England with whom they shared a common ethnic origin. (Canny, *The formation*.)

Old Pretender. James III, the Stuart claimant to the throne of England, who died in 1766.

ollamh. Currently translated as professor, this Gaelic term originally referred to a chief poet, physician, carpenter, goldsmith, metalworker or indeed any person of high status in their profession.

Onomasticon Goidelicum. A dictionary of Irish placenames, their location and the documentary source from which it was extracted. It was compiled by Edmund Hogan between 1900–10 as an aid to scholars working on old Irish manuscripts.

OP. Order of Preachers. *See* Dominican.

op. cit. (L., *opere citato* or *opus citatum*, in the work cited) A footnote convention, now almost obsolete, referring the reader to a work already quoted. In modern usage this is obviated by shortening the original reference. Use *Ibid.* (and the relevant pagination if appropriate) where the work cited is the same as the reference immediately previous.

openfield. *See* commonfield.

oral history. Oral history, the recording and transcription of reminiscences, is a method of gathering evidence rather than a subject area. The evidence acquired supplements and enhances evidence assembled through conventional means. Oral history has grown in popularity over the last 50 years as the boundaries of historical study expanded to embrace groups of people whose lives and experiences heretofore were not considered important enough to be documented. It has opened up new and varied fields of inquiry such as labour history, the social life of families, the socialisation of boys and girls, courtship, urban culture and leisure activities and the experiences of combatants in wartime. The method has limitations. The interviewees may be unrepresentative; they may falsify their accounts; they may have poor recall. These, however, are limitations that historians account for in dealing with all historical evidence. Unrepresentativeness does not make evidence invalid; it only becomes problematic when the experience of a small sample is generalised. Falsification, for whatever reason, is always a possibility but the interviewer should be alert to internal inconsistencies and data provided by the interviewee should be compared with what has been obtained from other sources. (Brewer, *The Royal Irish Constabulary*; Finnegan and Drake, *Sources*; Thompson, 'The voice of the past', pp. 21–28.)

Orange Order. A sectarian association founded in 1795 in Loughgall following an armed confrontation between the Catholic **Defenders** and Protestant **Peep O'Day Boys** in which the Defenders came off worst. The Orange oath required members to pledge themselves to support and defend the monarch as long as he supported the Protestant ascendancy in Ireland. Catholic **relief acts**, competition for land and fear of a French invasion – all of which threatened Protestant dominance in Ireland – heightened sectarian tension and encouraged the rapid spread of the order. Highly confrontational, it almost immediately engaged in pogroms against Catholics who were expelled in large numbers from their homes in Armagh, Down, Tyrone and Fermanagh. By the close of the century the order had attracted almost 170,000 members and the **yeomanry** was heavily infiltrated. Although the order was officially neutral, many Orangemen opposed the **Act of Union** because they believed it was to be accompanied by measures to emancipate Catholics. In the nineteenth century the government made several attempts to curb Orangeism. It was suppressed in 1825, persisted for a number of years in the guise of **Brunswick clubs** but disbanded after 1836 following a critical select-committee report. It emerged renewed under William Johnson to defy the Party Processions Act and became more broadly-based in the 1880s in opposition to the activities of the **Land League** and government proposals for home rule for Ireland. Since 1905 the order has been a constituent element of the **Unionist Party**. (Gray, *The Orange Order*; Haddick-Flynn, *Orangeism*; McClelland, 'The later Orange Order', pp. 126– 137; Senior, 'The early Orange Order', pp. 36–45.)

ordeal, trial by. An early method of legal proof derived from the belief that divine intervention either by sign or miracle could determine an issue between contending parties. If you could clasp red-hot iron, plunge your hand into boiling water or sink when cast into water, God must surely be on your side and therefore you must be right. The role of the court was simply to determine which party should go through the proof and to ensure the forms were observed. As a method of proof it very quickly fell into disuse for the guilty were as like to pass through the ordeal as the innocent and it proved almost impossible to get a conviction. It was condemned by the Lateran Council of 1215 and prohibited by Henry III in 1219. *See* battle, compurgation and fire.

Order of Saint Patrick, The most illustrious. The Order of St Patrick was established in 1783 by George III to reward high officials and peers for their loyalty. Modelled on the Order of the Garter it was the national order for Ireland. It was a one-class order consisting of the sovereign and 15 knights-companions (22 from 1833), none of whom ranked below an earl. The grand master (the sovereign's deputy) was always the current lord lieutenant. Investitures took place in the hall of Dublin Castle and were followed by the installation in St Patrick's cathedral. Six installations were conducted between 1783 and 1868. The prince of Wales, Albert Edward (later Edward VII), got the Patrick at the last installation. The star of the order consisted of the cross of St Patrick on a field argent, surmounted by a trefoil vert charged with three imperial crowns and surrounded by the motto *Quis separabit*. The order's most celebrated insignia – the badge and star worn by the lord lieutenant – were known as the Irish 'crown jewels'. They were stolen in 1907 from a safe in the Bedford Tower and never recovered. The order disappeared after the establishment of the Irish Free State in 1922. (Casey, 'The most illustrious'; Galloway, *The order*.)

ordinary. 1: A prelate, either a bishop or archbishop, who exercises authority over a diocese or province 2: A book listing heraldic descriptions of arms 3: A simple common charge or device on an escutcheon.

Ordnance Survey. The Ordnance Survey was established in 1824 to provide a precise admeasurement of the townlands of Ireland as a precursor to a nationwide valuation of buildings and land. Although the eighteenth-century maps of the British Ordnance Survey (the Board of Ordnance) were produced for military purposes – the threat of a French invasion – the first Irish Ordnance Survey maps were designed to meet civil needs in the area of local taxation. Its military origin, however, was not severed for the nucleus of the new body comprised army officers and soldiers as well as civilians. From 1825 a number of field survey teams, headed up by a lieutenant from the Royal Engineers or the Royal Artillery, commenced the process of mapping the country from north to south using a scale of six inches to the statute mile. The first maps were published in 1833 and by 1846 six-inch maps of the entire country were on sale. The new maps became the basis for the geological survey, the census of population, the creation of new administrative divisions and proved invaluable in the field of valuation. Thomas Frederick Colby, first director of the Ordnance Survey, intended to supplement the maps with a comprehensive biographical memoir of each parish to be compiled from materials accumulated by the field survey teams. The Board of Ordnance, however, took fright at such ambition and cancelled the programme before it had extended beyond the counties of Ulster. The Ulster memoirs have since been published. In addition to maps, the records of the Ordnance Survey contain much to interest the local historian. The field books contain the numerical measurements taken by the surveyors as they progressed, including the dimensions of buildings. A different set of field books, the **name books**, list the various spellings of each townland together with letters and notes on placenames and antiquities. The registers and remark books describe the boundaries of each townland. These records can be found in the National Archives, together with a large volume of correspondence between the surveyors in the field and the central body in the Phoenix Park. (Andrews, *History*; *Idem*, *A paper landscape*; MacNeill, *The Ordnance*; Madden, 'The Ordnance', pp. 155–63.)

original writ. A writ in fixed or certain form which issued from **chancery** to initiate a real (land) action at common law and to summon a defendant in a personal action.

orthostat. (Gr., *orthós*, straight + *statikós*, causing to stand) An upright boulder serving as the wall of a megalithic tomb.

OSA. Order of Saint Augustine. *See* Augustinian.

Ossory, Red Book of. See register, episcopal.

ousterlemain. (Fr., to remove the hand) 1: The taking of land out of the king's hand following a judgement for a plaintiff who claimed that the crown had no title to it. *Ousterlemain* also applied to the extinction of a guardian's control over an estate upon the coming of age of his ward. The action on attaining majority of suing out ousterlemain to obtain possession of an estate is the same as the action of suing out livery. Males came of age at 21 years, females at age 16 2: The writ or judgement associated with such an action. *See* livery, to sue out and majority.

outdoor relief. The provision of relief to paupers through the **poor law** system but without the necessity for them to enter the workhouse. Outdoor relief was specifically prohibited under poor law but the failure of public works schemes to meet the needs of the distressed in 1846–7, the financial strain on the **exchequer** and the realisation that it would be cheaper simply to feed the people prompted the government to re-consider. Under the Temporary Relief of Distressed Persons in Ireland Act (10 & 11 Vict., c. 7), or the Soup Kitchen Act as it was popularly known, public works were phased out by late spring 1847 and replaced by soup kitchens where direct relief in the form of cooked food or soup was to be provided to the distressed. Soup kitchens, run by local relief committees and funded by local contributions and a matching government grant, were to operate until autumn 1847 after which the provisions of the Poor Law Amendment Act (10 Vict., c. 31) – which allowed for outdoor relief under poor law for the first time – would come into play. The aged and infirm, children and widows with two or more dependent children would be entitled to relief either within or without the workhouse. The able-bodied could receive outdoor aid (in the form of cooked food) only in the most desperate circumstances for a period no longer than two months and only if the workhouse was full or infected with fever. In return they were required to work for ten hours at tedious, repetitive and unproductive tasks such as stone-breaking, tasks intentionally designed to discourage applicants from seeking relief instead of productive employment. A requirement that the destitute attend each day at the workhouse to collect the cooked food was intended to restrict the number of applicants for outdoor relief and the delegation of food distribution to shopkeepers or meal contractors meant that there were fewer and less accessible distribution points than had been the case with the soup kitchens. Another factor which inhibited the take-up of outdoor relief was the controversial '**quarter acre clause**' (Gregory Clause) in the Poor Law Amendment Act which deemed that occupiers of more than a quarter acre of land could not be classed as destitute and were therefore ineligible for poor law relief. Thus the starving were required to yield up their means of future subsistence and enter the workhouse if they were to be relieved. Although the quarter acre clause proved a most effective way of restraining applicants from applying for relief, a staggering number of people presented themselves for aid. By February 1848 445,000 people were receiving outdoor relief and by June that figure had risen to 830,000. Soup kitchens, outdoor relief and **rate-in-aid** were the means by which the government progressively heaped responsibility for the economic burden of relief on the poor law unions of Ireland. *See* Malthus. (Kinealy, *This great calamity*.)

outfangtheof.(OE, *fang*, to lay hold of, seize) A medieval manorial franchise which has been interpreted to mean either the right of the lord to seize and prosecute a thief living beyond the manor but captured within or the right of the lord to pursue and seize a thief outside his jurisdiction and to bring him back to try him in his own court. The most likely interpretation is the latter for there already existed a separate franchise, **infangenetheof**, which permitted the lord to prosecute thieves caught within the jurisdiction of the manor.

outlawry. The legal process by which a person was deprived of the protection of the law, forfeited his goods and chattels and the power to seek redress in any court beyond attempting to reverse the outlawry by writ of **error**. Formally, a person was outlawed after writs of *capias*, *alias*, and *pluries* were returned by the sheriff *non est inventus* (he is not to be found). An exigent issued to the sheriff to demand the defendant's appearance at five successive county courts completed the process, failure to show rendering him automatically outlawed. *See* attainder.

outshot. In vernacular architecture, a small rectangular projection in the wall of a cottage designed to contain a bed. It was usually screened by a curtain. The outshot was commonly referred to as a *cuilteach* (back house) in Irish, less usually as *cailleach*. (Lucas, 'Contributions', pp. 81–98.)

overseer. A parish official. Church-wardens bore the responsibility for assisting the poor of their parish but they were assisted by parishioners acting as overseers. The overseer's main function was to assist in the collection of parish cess and distribute relief to the poor. He also aplotted or assessed the parish for the parish cess. In the eighteenth century the overseer became a statutory post.

Owners of land of one acre and upwards in the several counties, counties of cities and counties of towns in Ireland, Return of (1876). Issued by the Local Government Board and modelled on similar publications covering England and Wales, the *Return of owners* lists in alphabetical order the names and addresses of owners of one statute acre and upwards for each county, together with the extent and valuation of their lands. Also included are the numbers of owners of less than one statute acre in each county and the total valuation of such lands together with the grand totals for each county and provincial and national aggregates. (*Return.*)

oyer et terminer, commission of. (Fr., to hear and determine) A commission which developed in the thirteenth century to try and judge criminal cases. Commissions of *oyer et terminer* were issued for the determination of specific individual cases of a serious nature such as treason or murder or an epidemic of a certain type of crime which had broken out over a wide area.

P

pad. An easy-paced horse.

paindemaine. A fine bread.

Pairlement Chloinne Tomáis. An anonymous seventeenth-century verse composition in Gaelic which satirises those Irish natives who rented land from English settlers and helped them develop their estates. The author derides them for their vulgar aping of the new gentry and their fashions while patronage of traditional poetry and music was in serious decline. (Bergin, 'Pairlement', pp. 35–50, 127–31, 137–50, 220–36.)

palatinate. A liberty. A major lordship which exercised jurisdiction exclusive of the royal courts with the exception of the four reserved pleas of rape, arson, **treasure trove** and **forestalling** and correction of officers. Palatine rights were delegated by the crown to the lord so that he was, in effect, a royal official – though a hereditary one – and entitled to the dues and profits that would otherwise accrue to the king. Within the palatinate the lord's writ ran and the lord's peace was kept but it was the king's law that was administered. Royal officials could not enter unless the lord failed to execute a royal writ. Palatinates were administered as small-scale states. The senior official was the omnicompetent **seneschal** who exercised the same functions within the palatinate as the **justiciar** did for the whole country. Other officers included a **chancellor**, treasurer, an **escheator**, **sheriff** and **serjeants**. The palatinate of Tipperary retained its distinct jurisdiction until 1715 when it became defunct with the attainder of the second duke (2 Geo. I, c. 8). (Murnaghan, 'The lordship', pp. 846–59.)

Palatines. Refugee peasant families from the Palatinate of the Rhine who settled in counties Limerick and Kerry (and in smaller groups in Dublin and Wexford) early in the eighteenth century. In all over 800 families arrived in Ireland and a supervisory commission allocated them by lots to a number of landlords. Each family received an annual government allowance of 40 shillings to encourage them to settle. The Palatines conformed to Anglicanism and responded warmly to Methodism but remained culturally and socially aloof from local communities. Although initially successful, the colony was rapidly thinned out by emigration and by 1726 only 126 families remained. (Hick, 'The Palatine', pp. 113–132.)

Pale. The English Pale in Ireland comprised the counties Dublin, Kildare, Louth and Meath, the areas of medieval and early modern Ireland where royal writ ran most completely. *See* maghery.

paleolithic. (Gr., *paleo*, ancient + *lithos*, stone) The earliest stone age period.

paleography. The study of ancient writing and inscriptions. *See* secretary hand.

palimpsest. A manuscript containing an erased yet slightly visible text beneath a new text. Manuscripts were so effaced on account of the scarcity of parchment. The term is used in historical geography to describe a hidden or partially hidden landscape which, if interpreted correctly, can yield evidence about earlier land use.

palisade. A defensive barrier composed of upright stakes driven into the ground.

pall. (L., *pallium*) A robe worn by an archbishop or bishop at his inauguration, the presentation of which indicates his elevation to the episcopacy. The pall is a charge (device) on the heraldic escutcheons of the archiepiscopal sees of Armagh and Dublin.

Palladian. A constantly evolving architectural style which persisted well into the nineteenth century. It was based on the work of Andrea Palladio (1518–1580), a sixteenth-century Italian architect who drew his inspiration from an eclectic range of sources including the classical architecture of ancient Rome, the mannerism of Michaelangelo and Vignola, Bramante and the Byzantine architecture of Venice. Inigo Jones was captivated by Palladio's work when he journeyed through Italy in 1613–14 and used it as a basis for renewing the dated architecture of contemporary England. From 1700 there was a Palladian revival which gained supremacy around 1730. Palladio's *Four books of architecture* were consulted by, among others, Christopher Wren. Bellamont in Co. Cavan, Lord Charlemont's Casino in Marino, Co. Dublin and the provost's house in Trinity College are examples of Palladian architecture in Ireland.

Palles Commission. A **royal commission** appointed to investigate the working of the intermediate education system from its establishment in 1878. Reporting in 1899, The commission heavily criticised the narrow examination programme on offer and acknowledged the heavy burden placed on schools by the **payment-by-results** system. Palles, nevertheless, recommended the retention of public examinations and a modified payments-by-results system whereby grants would be paid in block rather than on the basis of individual examination results. The commissioners proposed a greater emphasis on mathematics and science and to that end suggested a special equipment grant for the teaching of science. *See* secondary schooling. (Palles.)

pannage. The right to graze swine in the woods.

parc. An artificial intertidal growing bed for oysters comprising sections of the foreshore marked off with stones, walls of mud, wattle or cement to retain a couple of inches of water at low tide.

parcener. An heir.

paring and burning. The practice of paring and burning the sod to increase the potato yield in marginal areas by adding phosphates to the acidic soil. The benefits were short-term and the land rapidly reverted to waste within a few years. Also known as bettimore.

parish. An ancient ecclesiastical division denoting the jurisdiction of a priest. The medieval parish became the civil parish of the Established church, the smallest administrative unit of civil government. It was responsible for the upkeep of roads within its boundaries and for the welfare of the aged, sick and abandoned, all of which were overseen by the general **vestry** and financed by the parish **cess**. The civil parish was disestablished by the passing of the **Church Temporalities Act** (3 & 4 Will. IV, c. 37, 1833). This act revoked the right of the **churchwardens** to levy parish cess and thereby ended its civil role. Catholic parishes, a relatively modern creation owing to the difficulties presented by the Reformation, the turmoil of the seventeenth century and the **penal laws**, continue to be formed in the developing suburbs of the larger towns and cities. *See* six-day labour.

parish school. Legislation passed during the reign of Henry VIII (28 Hen. VIII, c. 15, 1537) laid upon the clergy of the Established church the duty to establish a network of English schools throughout Ireland, a duty witnessed more in the breach than in the observance. All beneficed clergymen were required to keep or cause to be kept within their vicarage or rectory an English language school. The statute was poorly implemented and was effective only within the Pale. Additional legislation from 1695 (7 Will. III, c. 4, 8 Geo. I, c. 12 and 5 Geo. II, c. 4) yielded greater results for parish schools began to emerge in numbers throughout the eighteenth century. Heavily oriented towards advancing Protestantism, the schools proved unable to attract Catholic pupils. By 1832 there were only 782 in existence with a total enrolment of 36,498 children. (*Eleventh report of the commissioners of* *the board of education in Ireland*, HC 1810–11 (107) VI; Akenson, *The Irish education experiment*, pp. 21–4.)

park. In medieval documents the term refers to the engrossing of open-field strips. Thus a park is an enclosed field. (Otway-Ruthven, 'Enclosures', pp. 35–6.)

parliament. The word parliament means parley or discussion so any meeting could be called a parliament. In medieval times it referred to a formal meeting of the king in council with attendant judges to consider petitions for redress of grievances. The king could, of course, call upon anyone he chose to assist in council and the need to involve men of consequence in decisions about military matters led to an enlargement of that body. The summoning of magnates and ecclesiastics to the Irish council in 1264 represented the appearance of the first recognisable Irish parliament. Under feudal law freemen could only be taxed by their consent and this principle ensured from 1297 that representatives of the counties and liberties (the commons) became an indispensable part of every parliament. Burgesses (representatives of the towns) and clerical **proctors** (representatives of the lower clergy) appeared later. In the late fourteenth century the lords were detached from the council to become a distinct house but made little impact until the sixteenth century. Notwithstanding these developments, the **justiciar** (the king's representative in Ireland) continued to summon the **great council** – a body which comprised much the same personnel as parliament and performed similar functions – to deal with military affairs. Important medieval legislation included the **Statutes of Kilkenny**, an attempt to halt the creeping Gaelicisation of the colony, and **Poynings' Law**, a Tudor initiative intended to curb overly independent chief governors but which severely limited the ability of the Irish parliament to originate legislation. Poynings' Law and the 1720 British **Declaratory Act** ensured the formal subordination of the Irish parliament to Westminster until both were repealed in 1782–3. In a practical sense, however, the Irish legislature was not toothless. From the seventeenth century Poynings' was partially circumvented by the practice of transmitting heads of bills (see statute) and truculent parliaments could and did refuse to vote subsidies in an effort to force the administration to compromise. Administrative counter-measures included sweeteners such as the grants of sequestered monastic lands which eased the passage of the Henrician church reformation laws. Later, offers of pensions, sinecures and government posts were freely employed. Stiff measures could also be brought to bear to ensure the successful passage of legislation. In the late sixteenth and early seventeenth centuries government majorities were ensured by the creation or elimination of boroughs and the opposition of the clerical proctors to the Henrician reforms resulted in their expulsion from parliament.

Until the eighteenth century parliament met only when there was business to be transacted or when the crown was in need of subsidies or taxes. Long intervals, sometimes of up to 25 years duration, separated successive parliaments. After 1713, however, parliament assembled every second year and from 1785 it met annually. In according parliament an eight-year duration, the 1768 **Octennial Act** abolished the law which allowed for dissolution only upon the death or proclamation of the sovereign. From the seventeenth century it is possible to refer to a parliament of all-Ireland in the geographical sense but it could never be described as a representative assembly. Native Irish representatives hardly ever appeared in it, Catholics were edged out in mid-seventeenth century and eliminated entirely by its close and the Catholic franchise was denied absolutely from 1727. Throughout the eighteenth century it was the exclusive organ of the Protestant landed ascendancy. Over two-thirds of the seats in the commons were filled by the nominees of **borough** patrons and the remainder were elected on a narrow property-based franchise. Until the late 1760s the business of ensuring parliamentary majorities for government bills was managed by **undertakers** (usually the speaker of the house of commons) in return for a share in the disposal of patronage and a say in policy. Thereafter the task of managing parliament was assumed by the now permanently resident lords lieutenant. Patronage and bribery were part and parcel of the way in which accommodations were reached in the eighteenth-century parliament. That reality is reflected (albeit to an unprecedented level) in the promises of office, favour and compensation which seduced many members to vote for the extinction of their national assembly in 1800. A more public-spirited concern for enhancing the role of parliament and improving the social and economic condition of the island is revealed in the '**sole right**' and '**Woods Halfpence**' controversies, opposition to the pension list, the introduction of (modest) Catholic **relief acts** and the campaign of the '**patriot**' **party** to secure better trading conditions and legislative freedom. Party-style politics was a late development, members usually voting as individuals or on the basis of kinship or sectional interests. An embryonic Whig-Tory division emerged in England and Ireland (1704–1714) over the controversies regarding the royal succession, religious toleration and the role of parliament but lapsed after the Tories were excluded from office. Although an Irish Whig party was formed in 1789 the party system developed much slower in Ireland. The enlargement of the franchise and the home rule crisis in the 1880s provided the basis for the emergence of disciplined, highly-organised popular political parties with elected members of the Nationalist and Unionist parties pledged to work and vote along party lines. The transactions of both houses of the Irish parliament from the mid-seventeenth century to the **Act of Union** can be found in *Journals of the house of commons of the kingdom of Ireland* (19 vols, Dublin, 1796–1800) and in *Journals of the house of lords of the kingdom of Ireland* (8 vols, Dublin, 1783–1800). *See* afforced council, cess, franchise, lords, *Parliamentary Register*, privy council, statute, tory, whig. (Johnston-Liik, *History*; Richardson and Sayles, *The Irish parliament.*)

Parliamentary Gazetteer of Ireland (1845–6). A three-volume social, economic, topographical and administrative gazetteer which contains a vast amount of information and statistics relating to pre-famine Ireland. The opening chapter comprises an extensive description of Ireland together with the results of the 1831 and 1841 censuses and innumerable statistical tables on all aspects of contemporary Irish life. Separate articles are given for each province, county, barony, parish, island, town and sizeable village. In 1998 the gazetteer was re-issued in a six-volume edition.

parliamentary papers. Broadly speaking, the parliamentary papers of Great Britain and Ireland embrace everything officially published which concerns parliament and its working. In a narrow and strict sense they are taken to refer to the 7,000-volume bound set or 'blue books' (so called because many were bound in blue) which commenced in 1801 and includes papers (bills, reports and returns) presented to parliament in response to an order, an act or an address. To these were added papers printed by royal command. Using the broader definition, parliamentary papers can be usefully divided into two categories: papers which relate to the agenda, proceedings and debates of the house and papers which give information to the house to inform the legislators. Agenda, proceedings and debates papers include all the papers one would associate with the actual conduct of parliament. They include minutes, agendas, notice papers, votes and amendments. The official account of proceedings can be found in the journals of the house and *verbatim* records of debates are published in *Hansard*. Minutes of standing committees appointed in each session to deal with public bills are also printed and circulated. The second category – information papers – may arise from within the house or from without. Public and private bills, the reports of committees of the whole house, **select committee** reports, returns (papers required by parliament from government departments) and act papers (papers presented to the house by order of an act of parliament and which it has ordered to be printed) are generated from within. The reports of **royal commissions** of inquiry and departmental committees, however, are externally generated.

This vast archive is one of the most important and detailed sources for Irish social, political and economic history in the nineteenth and early twentieth centuries. It has one major deficiency – it is not easy

to extract what you are looking for. There are sessional and consolidated indexes (shelved at the librarian's desk in the National Library) but the method of referencing is complex and confusing. A major
royal commission on poverty in Ireland like the **Poor Inquiry**, for example, will not be found in the indexes because it is listed under its
longer official title. Likewise for the **Devon** and **Bessborough** commissions. Intimidating they may appear but the parliamentary papers
contain so much evidence of a local nature that it is inconceivable
that any historian of the nineteenth century could neglect them. For-
tunately, the unwieldy indexes have given way to a number of more
user-friendly search guides. Although not yet widely available, Chadwyck-Healey's *Index to the house of commons parliamentary papers on
CD-Rom, 1801–1999* is the most advanced research tool available for
locating relevant parliamentary papers. It provides speedy access to the
papers through a multi-search facility which allows readers to search by
key word, title keyword, title, paper type, paper number, session, chairman and year. The fourth volume of Peter Cockton's *Subject catalogue
of the house of commons parliamentary papers, 1801–1900* (Cambridge,
1988) contains a listing (with full referencing) of parliamentary papers
relevant to Ireland. For convenience, papers are organised themati-
cally under five headings: Government and Public Order; Agriculture and the Land; Trade, Industry and Transport; Legal, Social,
Administration, Education; Health and Religious Affairs. Each
heading is subdivided alphabetically into individual topics and is
arranged in the same order as the nineteenth-century bound volumes:
bills, reports of committees, reports of commissions and accounts and
papers. Cockton also cites the filing number of the Chadwyck-Healey
microfiche edition of the parliamentary papers. The Maltbys' thema-
tically-arranged breviate of official publications includes a wide selection of Ireland-related papers, each of which is accompanied by a summary. Susan Parkes has produced a helpful catalogue (with detailed
summaries) of parliamentary papers touching on Irish education. In
an effort to make parliamentary papers more accessible Irish University Press (1968) reproduced almost 5,000 papers in 1,000 volumes
under 36 thematic headings. The IUP series overcame the problem
of related papers scattered over many volumes by bringing them together in single or serial volumes.

Parliamentary papers should be cited accurately to facilitate readers
who wish to examine the original. The form is: session/paper number/
volume number/ volume page number. Example: *Eleventh report of the
commissioners of the board of education in Ireland*, HC 1810–11 (107) VI.
35. Here the session number is 1810–11, the paper is numbered 107
(sessional paper number 107), the volume number in the bound set
is VI and the volume page number on which the report begins is 35.

Paper numbers may be contained within round or square brackets. Round brackets are used for house papers which begin numbering anew at the start of every session. Square brackets are employed to denote papers presented by royal command such as royal commissions of inquiry. Unlike house papers, command papers are numbered continuously over many sessions. There have been five separate series since 1833 when square brackets were first employed and the command numbers themselves were only printed on the papers from 1870 together with the legend C for Command (Cd. from 1900, Cmd. from 1919 and Cmnd from 1956). Example: *Report of Her Majesty's commission of inquiry into the working of the Landlord and Tenant (Ireland) Act, 1870, and the acts amending the same*, HC 1881 [C2779] XVIII. I.

The most accurate means of identifying a paper is by its sessional year and paper number but the sessional year and volume number serves as the call number in the National Library of Ireland which holds the vast bulk of parliamentary papers. (Ford, *A guide*; Idem, *Select list of British parliamentary papers*; Maltby, *Ireland in the nineteenth century*; Parkes, *Irish education*; Shearman, 'The citation', pp. 33–7.)

Parliamentary Register of Ireland. A record of the proceedings and debates of the Irish house of commons during the last two decades of its existence. Words spoken by members in both houses of parliament were privileged and their publication was prohibited. Nevertheless, as in England, the practice developed of memorising the speeches of members, recording them in shorthand or obtaining the speakers' written notes and then publishing them for popular consumption. Inconsistency in recording members' orations was matched by inconsistency in reporting them. Some speeches are given *verbatim*, others reported indirectly and others again are simple summaries. The 17 volumes of the *Register* contain a great deal of biographical as well as political material and therefore are a useful source for examining the relationship between representatives and their borough or county constituencies.

parochial survey. A three-volume survey of 79 parishes published by William Shaw Mason between 1814 and 1819. Mason compiled the survey with the assistance of local Protestant clergymen who provided information about the name, situation, extent, division, climate and topography of their respective parishes. Respondents were also invited to make suggestions for the amelioration of conditions in the locality. Perhaps reflecting the varying degrees of enthusiasm amongst the contributors, the survey is uneven. Some accounts are quite comprehensive, others are brief and not very illuminating. (Mason, *A statistical account,.*)

partible inheritance. A custom similar to **gavelkind** by which land was subdivided equally between the male heirs.

paruchia. By the seventh century Christian Ireland was administered by networks of monasteries (*paruchiae*) supervised by abbots, a structure which superseded, and was later superseded by, an episcopally-dominated diocesan system. *See* diocese.

passage grave. Dating from c. 4500 BC, most passage graves consist of a stone-lined passage leading to a corbelled chamber grave, the whole being covered by a round cairn. Undifferentiated passage-graves are simpler in form, comprising but a passage which also served as a burial chamber. In excess of 300 have been found in Ireland, mostly located in groups on hills in the east but also in counties Sligo and Antrim. Newgrange, Knowth and Dowth, all overlooking the river Boyne, are elaborate passage graves, with side and end chambers creating a cruciform effect. (Herity, *Irish passage graves.*)

passim. (L., *passim*, in various places) Used in footnotes to refer to material that can be found here and there throughout the cited source.

Pastorini. The pseudonym of the English Catholic bishop, Charles Walmsley. His *General History of the Christian Church* contained a millenarian analysis of the *Book of Revelations* which claimed that a violent destruction of the Protestant churches would occur in 1825. Published in 1771, the book achieved a massive circulation through cheap copies and digests from 1817 in Munster and Leinster. Its popularity is thought to relate to the typhus epidemic of 1816–17 and the poor harvests and declining social conditions of the early 1820s. Pastorini millenarianism influenced the Rockite movement. (Donnelly, 'Pastorini', pp. 102–39; O'Farrell, 'Millenialism', pp. 45–68.)

patent, letters patent. A royal writ, the instrument by which land, rights, office and privileges were granted. Patents are so called because the grant begins with the words *Litterae patente* (open letters). They were open grants available for inspection by all, unlike **close** letters which were folded and sealed and to be opened only by those to whom they were directed. They issued from **chancery**, the secretarial office of government which held the authenticating great **seal**, and are recognisable because the great seal hangs from the bottom. Contained within the patent are the grounds on which the monarch was induced to make the grant together with the nature, extent and tenure of the grant and attendant conditions and penalties. The issuing of letters patent was a complex and often lengthy task. It was initiated upon receipt by the lord deputy of a king's letter directing him to make a grant of land to a certain specified value or some office or right to a named individual. In the case of land grants the first requirement was to locate a tract of land in crown hands to the value expressed in the letter. A copy of the king's letter was sent to the **surveyor-general** who examined his records and requested the escheator to conduct an

inquisition. The results of the inquisition were submitted to the auditor general in the **exchequer** as a warranty against fraud and then forwarded to chancery. In the interim the lord deputy sent the king's letter to the **attorney-general** requiring him to draft a fiant (an instruction under the privy seal) to the chancellor to make a grant of land worth so much to the named individual. In chancery fiant and inquisition were put together to form a patent, the great seal was affixed and dispatched to the grantee. The issuing of patents conferring rights, privileges and office was altogether a simpler affair. Although it too could be preceded by an inquisition (see *inquisition ad quod damnum*), the normal procedure involved the delivery of the king's letter to the attorney-general who directed a fiant to chancery to issue a patent under the great seal. Until the seventeenth century letters patent were not required to be enrolled on the patent rolls unless this was specified as a condition of the grant but in any case it was a security to have it enrolled and on record. The original patent rolls, fiants and inquisitions were destroyed in 1922 but nineteenth-century calendars have survived. (Erck, *A repertory*; Griffith, *Calendar of inquisitions*; *Inquisitionum in officio*; *The Irish fiants*; Morrin, *The patent rolls*; *PRI rep. DK*, Appendices to 7–9, 11–13, 15–18, 21.)

'patriot parliament' (1689). The name given by Charles Gavan Duffy to the predominantly Old English Catholic parliament convened by James II in Dublin on 7 May 1689. This short-lived assembly asserted the independence of Ireland and attempted to roll back the mid-century confiscations and land settlements by repealing the Acts of **Settlement** (1662) and **Explanation** (1665). It opened with only six Protestant representatives in attendance in the commons out of a total of 230 members and immediately set about undoing the settlements. An act of attainder was passed attainting almost all Protestant landholders in the country. It was accompanied by an act for liberty of conscience together with legislation for the recovery of waste lands, for the improvement of trade, shipping and navigation and for the establishment of marine schools in the ports. Parliament asserted its independence of the English parliament and forbade appeals from Irish courts to the English house of lords. All came to nought within two years, however, when the Williamite cause triumphed in Ireland. In 1695 the 'patriot parliament' was declared illegal, its acts were annulled and the records of its proceedings were destroyed. (Farrell, 'The patriot parliament'.)

'patriot' party. A loose grouping of eighteenth-century Irish parliamentarians, including Henry Grattan, Henry Flood, Sir William Osborne, Charles Lucas, Gerard Hamilton and the duke of Leinster, which sought to achieve legislative independence for the Irish parliament. They claimed that only the king, lords and commons of Ireland could legally and constitutionally legislate for Ireland and that the power of the privy councils of Ireland and England to amend or reject bills originating in the Irish parliament was unconstitutional. They wanted to establish an independent judiciary, root out corruption and bribery in the administration and parliament, terminate the monopolisation of church and state offices by Englishmen and have a permanent *habeas corpus* act enacted. In the area of commerce they believed that restraints on trade should be lifted and all Irish ports opened to countries not at war with the king. They used the threat of military defeat in the Americas, the strength of the **Volunteer** movement and a refusal to vote supplies beyond six months to prise concessions from the government. In 1779 partial free trade was granted to Ireland when the free export of wool, woollen cloth and manufactured glass as well as free trade with the colonies was permitted. In June 1782 the **Declaratory Act** was abolished and a month later **Yelverton's Act** amended Poyning's law and removed the power of the privy councils to alter Irish bills. A **mutiny act** was enacted annually and the independence of the judiciary was established in the same manner as it existed in England. In 1783 the Renunciation Act confirmed Irish legislative independence by enacting that the people of Ireland were bound only by laws enacted in that kingdom. Henry Flood's attempt in 1784 to reform parliament by abolishing the right of corporations to return members of parliament, by suppressing the **rotten boroughs**, by limiting the duration of parliament to three years and by enfranchising Protestant freeholders was rejected. In 1785 Thomas Orde, the chief secretary, brought forward a measure to grant unrestricted trade between England and Ireland but his proposal was so heavily encumbered that it was withdrawn. In 1789 the 'patriot' party gambled for power by supporting **Whig** attempts to have the prince regent succeed his temporarily insane father with full royal powers. They hoped the prince regent would get rid of Pitt and install Fox, a Whig, as prime minister but the king recovered and the issue died leaving Pitt cautious of Irish independence and awake to the idea of a union of the two parliaments. *See* Commercial Propositions, regency crisis.

patronymic. A name derived from the father or from the paternal line which is usually identifiable by the fact that it has a prefix in Irish such as Mac or Ó. Once surnames became fixed in Ireland, as was the case in England, the patronymic ceased to refer to the father's Christian name and descendants simply inherited the surname.

pattern. (L., *patronus*) A religious festival associated with a holy well involving a procession, a number of circuits of the well and the recitation of prayers. It was held on the feast day of the saint in whose memory the well was named.

pavage. 1: A toll or tax levied towards the paving of highways or streets

2: The right to impose such a levy.

payment-by-results. One of the earliest experiments in tying the salaries of teachers to the results obtained by pupils under examination was conducted by the proselytising London Hibernian Society (1806). Recommended by the **Powis Commission**, the practice became general from 1871 when partial payment of national school teachers' salaries was determined by pupil attainment. School attendance increased considerably but the practice encouraged a narrow, mechanical approach to teaching and learning and was discontinued from 1900 following a critical assessment by the **Belmore Commission**. Payment-by-results was a characteristic feature of second-level education from its inauguration with the passage of the 1878 Intermediate Education Act (41 & 42 Vict., c. 66). Here the government funded schools indirectly through scholarships and results fees to avoid the criticism that it was supporting denominational education. The impact on enrolment and learning paralleled the national school experience. Numbers in attendance rose but teaching methods became mechanistic. Paradoxically, the **Palles Commission** (1899) was endorsing a modified payment-by-results system for intermediate schools at the same time as Belmore was recommending its abolition in primary schools. In 1900 the education commissioners opted for capitation payment and made provision for inspection by school inspectors. *See* second-level schooling. (Coolahan, *Irish education*, pp. 28–30.)

Peace Preservation Act (1814). Chief Secretary Peel introduced the Peace Preservation Act (54 Geo. III, c. 131) in 1814 following an outbreak of agrarian unrest. It provided for the establishment of a uniformed peace preservation force (peelers) to be deployed to any district which had been proclaimed as disturbed by the lord lieutenant. The force possessed a hierarchical military-like structure and operated under a salaried police **magistrate** who was directly responsible to the administration in Dublin Castle. As the cost of maintaining the force was borne by the disturbed district, it was unpopular with ratepayers and local magistrates were reluctant to have their areas proclaimed. Instead they opted to call in the army and invoke the provisions of the Insurrection Act (54 Geo. III, c. 180, 1814). Under this legislation magistrates were permitted to declare a dusk to dawn curfew and suspend trial by jury. In 1817 an amending act (57 Geo. III, c. 50) provided for exchequer subvention of up to two-thirds of the maintenance cost of the force in a proclaimed district. The peace preservation force was poorly paid, badly trained and organised and had a reputation for partisanship. It had served in 16 counties by 1822 when a national constabulary was created and was revived briefly during the tithe war of the 1830s. In 1836 it was amalgamated with the county police force to form the Irish constabulary. *See* police.

peck. A measure of capacity used for dry measures such as corn, normally the fourth part of a **bushel** or two gallons but which varied regionally and according to the goods being measured.

pediment. The triangular space over a Greek portico.

'Peel's brimstone'. Indian corn. In November 1845 Sir Robert Peel arranged for the purchase and importation of Indian corn (yellow meal) as a cheap and nourishing substitute for the blighted potato crop. Poorly-prepared Indian corn caused stomach problems which, together with its yellow colour, resulted in it being called 'Peel's brimstone'.

Peep O'Day Boys. A precursor of the **Orange Order**, the Protestant Peep O'Day Boys was a violent sectarian movement which emerged in Armagh in the 1780s partly in response to the enactment of Catholic **relief acts** and partly because of industrial and land issues related to the linen-weaving industry. They conducted early morning raids on the houses of Catholics, supposedly for the purpose of seizing arms – which Catholics were forbidden to have under the penal laws – and sabotaged linen-weaving equipment. The activities of the Peep O'Day Boys drew a response from the Catholics in the form of the **Defenders**. In 1795 the two groups clashed at the Diamond near Loughgall, after which the victorious Protestants adjourned to Loughgall to form the Orange Order.

peers, trial by. (L., *judicium parium suorum*) A trial not by a jury of one's peers but one in which the judges are the equals of the accused.

peine forte et dure. The practice, which continued as late as the eighteenth century, of pressing to death for refusal to plead to a serious felony. It consisted of placing weights upon the body of a suspect until he agreed to plead or died from the pressure. Sometimes to speed up the process a sharp piece of rock, timber or iron was placed under the back. In 1740 Mathew Ryan was pressed to death in the marketplace of Kilkenny for refusing to plead in a case of highway robbery. To the question why one would choose to submit to such a harrowing death – and few did – rather than plead before a jury, the answer is that in such cases the suspect did not die a convicted felon and consequently suffered no escheat of land or forfeiture of chattels. Standing mute in cases of treason or misdemeanour, however, was regarded as equivalent to a confession. *See prison forte et dure*.

Pelagianism. The doctrine of Pelagius, a British (or possibly Irish) monk of the fourth and fifth centuries, which was vigorously opposed by St Augustine and condemned by Pope Zozimus in 418. Pelagius denied the doctrine of original sin, claiming that Adam's fall did not stain his posterity. He maintained that human nature was essentially good and that we are capable of good without the assistance of divine grace. God had gifted us with a free will and we chose good or evil voluntarily. St Augustine claimed that man was dependent on the grace of

God and could not save himself by his own efforts.

Penal Laws, Popery Laws. The penal laws are usually taken to refer to the series of legislative enactments passed between 1691 (when Catholics were excluded from parliament) and 1727 (when they were completely disfranchised). In reality Catholics had been paying for their adherence to Rome in recusancy fines and gradual exclusion from public office since the mid-sixteenth century. The new impositions were copied from existing laws in England but the Irish laws were not as harsh as those in England. What made them unique in Europe was that here they were imposed by a minority on the majority. The laws were designed to ensure Protestant ascendancy in all spheres of life and to render Catholics incapable of providing support for a Stuart restoration. Punitive laws against Catholic priests and bishops aimed to eradicate Catholicism within a generation by halting the entry of priests from abroad and preventing new ordinations in Ireland. In 1695 Catholic education, both at home and abroad, was forbidden and Catholics were not permitted to bear arms or own a horse worth £5 or more (7 Will. III, c. 4–5). Two years later all bishops and **regular** clergy were banished although parish clergy were permitted to remain (9 Will. III, c. 1) and by early 1698 almost 450 clergymen had been transported. In 1703 (2 Anne, c. 3) every Catholic clergyman entering Ireland after I January 1704 became liable to the same penalties imposed on bishops and regular clergy by the 1697 act. The severest anti-popery legislation was enacted in 1704 (2 Anne, c. 7) when parish clergy were required to register and enter a bond with two sureties of £50 to be of good behaviour on pain of transportation. Catholic clergy were limited to one per parish and the entry of others into the country was prohibited. They were also required to take an **oath of abjuration** renouncing the Stuart claim to the throne. Few clergymen took the oath, encouraged as they were by the pope's recognition of the Pretender as the rightful king of Great Britain and Ireland. Public religious celebrations such as patterns and pilgrimages were declared riotous assemblies and participants liable to be fined or whipped. Catholics were prohibited from buying land, making leases for more than 31 years and leasehold rent was fixed at two-thirds the yearly value of the land. The estates of deceased Catholics were to be partibly (equally) divided among the male heirs but where the eldest conformed the entire was to devolve to him. The status of any Catholic landowner whose heir conformed was immediately reduced to that of a **life tenancy**. Catholics could not act as guardians and Protestant guardians were required to bring up all minors as Protestants. The **Test Act**, a clause appended to the 1704 legislation, disabled Catholics and dissenters from holding office and from practising law, excluded them from serving on grand juries, from municipal corporations and from service in the army or the navy. In the field of commerce, Catholics were excluded from **guild** membership because of the requirement to swear the oath of supremacy but were permitted to hold an associate membership (*See* quarterage). In 1708 the **Registry of Deeds** was established to prevent Catholics from perfecting transactions specifically outlawed by the earlier legislation. A year later a legal procedure (8 Anne, c. 3, 1709) was introduced whereby a Protestant who detected a fraudulent transaction by a Catholic could acquire the Catholic's interest in the transaction. In reality many of the 'discoveries' that flowed from this act were collaborative arrangements concocted between Catholics and their Protestant intimates to ward off the possibility of hostile discoveries. *See* discoverer. In the same year voters were required to take an oath of abjuration denying the pope's authority. A number of Catholics took the oath and continued to vote until the franchise was withdrawn in 1727. The penal laws imposed severe disabilities on Catholics but it is now generally regarded that those which pertained to worship and the clergy were only intermittently enforced and within decades the clergy, including the bishops, were operating freely throughout the country. Catholic landowners were considerably hamstrung by the enactments concerning land and inheritance and those that excluded them from politics and state office. Not surprising, then, that throughout the eighteenth century there was a steady stream of conformism. *See* convert rolls. The first steps in securing the repeal of penal legislation were initiated in 1760 with the founding of the **Catholic Committee**. Piecemeal legislative relief acts began to emerge towards the end of the eighteenth century but penal legislation remained in force until the passing of **Catholic emancipation** bill in 1829. Even then Catholics were not raised to parity with their Anglican countrymen. The offices of viceroy and lord chancellor and membership of the municipal corporations (until 1840) remained closed to them. (Cullen, 'Catholics under the penal laws', pp. 23–36; McGrath, 'Securing the Protestant interest', pp. 25–46; Wall, *The penal laws*.)

pension. The 1908 Old Age Pension Act (8 Edw. VII, c. 40) provided for a pension of five shillings weekly for necessitous people over 70 to be paid through local post offices. The Local Government Board became the central pension authority and claims were investigated by excise officers. As the registration of births was not a legal requirement before 1864 septuagenarians found it difficult to advance proof of age. The census returns for 1841 and 1851, however, were available and for a small fee an official search of the records could be undertaken to ascertain whether the claimant was of age. Although the individual returns for 1841–51 were destroyed in 1922, the pension search records survived and these are available in the National Archives.

pension list. In addition to the civil list, the Irish exchequer funded a pension list which throughout the eighteenth century constituted a part of the patronage system by which government supporters were rewarded for their service. Foreigners, including French residents in England and German royalty – who had performed no service to Ireland – were also given annual pensions charged on moneys voted for public services. In 1756, for example, yearly pensions of £5,000 and £2,000 on the Irish establishment were awarded to the Princess of Hesse-Cassel and Prince Ferdinand of Brunswick respectively. Against the background of an exchequer deficit, restrictions on foreign trade and the burden of a disproportionate military establishment, the pensions list represented a major grievance throughout the century. It more than doubled between 1755 and 1777, rising from £38,000 to £89,000. In 1790 critics of the pension list introduced a pension bill in the Irish house of commons but it was defeated for the very fact that there were 108 members of the house in receipt of salaries or pensions from the government. Three years later a new pension bill (33 Geo. III, c. 34) barred all future pensioners from parliament, excluded from the house all those who held pensions during pleasure or for a term of years and the pension list was slashed from £120,000 to £80,000. Many pensioners, however, were still in place some years later to vote through the **Act of Union**. *See* Place Act.

peppercorn. A nominal rent usually associated with a grant of land in perpetuity, though the lessor remained technically the owner.

perch. Also known as a rod or pole, the imperial perch is equal to five and a half yards. The Irish perch was 21 feet or seven yards which accounts for the difference between the statute acre and the Irish or plantation acre. *See* acre.

Periodical sources for the history of Irish civilisation. Properly, *Sources for the history of Irish civilisation: articles in Irish periodicals*, this series serves as a companion to **Manuscript sources**, both of which were edited by Richard J. Hayes. *Periodical sources* is an index of over 280,000 articles, poems and reviews dealing with the intellectual life and cultural activities of the country which were published in about 120 learned Irish periodicals from 1800 to 1969. Science, philosophy, history and other fields of study are included. Entries are catalogued under the headings: persons, subjects, places and dates. Excluded were articles from trade journals, popular periodicals and journals dealing with current affairs. Articles from Irish language periodicals were not considered because these were already covered in R. I. Best's *Bibliography of Irish philology and of printed Irish literature* and Hayes' own *Clár litrídheacht na nua-Gaedhilge*.

perpendicular style. The third and most prolonged style of Gothic archi-tecture, the perpendicular style is characterised by the employment of vertical lines and features, ornamented flying buttresses, large tra-cery windows and the maximum use of doors and windows. This style did not appear in medieval Ireland but figured prominently in the nineteenth-century Gothic revival. *See* pointed style, decorated style.

peruke-maker. A wig-maker.

pesane, pesante. A gorget of mail attached to a helmet.

Peter's pence. Money paid as a tax or voluntary contribution to the papacy. Formerly, an annual tribute of one penny out of each Catholic house-hold.

petition. The modern right of appeal was unknown in medieval and early modern law. If no fault could be found in the record of the case either in the pleadings, the issue or the verdict, the decision of a court could not be altered. *See* **error, writ of**. However, anyone aggrieved by his treatment before the courts or denied a remedy to his suit could petition the king in his council for justice to be done. The king, as fountain of justice, was regarded as having a residue of judicial power in his hands to grant relief to his subjects, the prerogative. In medi-eval times petitions were usually delegated to the **chancellor**, a prac-tice which led to the emergence of the equitable jurisdiction of the court of **chancery**. In Tudor times a sub-committee of the king's coun-cil hearing petitions for justice metamorphosed into the court of star chamber (**castle chamber** in Ireland) which was barred from hearing cases involving real property. Despite the emergence of a plethora of courts, individuals and bodies continued to present their cases to the sovereign. Catholic associations were particularly active from the middle of the eighteenth century in alerting the crown to the considerable disabilities under which Catholics laboured. *See* Catholic Petition, remonstrance.

Petrie, George (1790–1866). Dublin-born antiquarian, artist and musi-cologist. As a teenager Petrie developed an interest in the antiquities of Ireland and began sketching and documenting field monuments and buildings. He travelled extensively throughout the country study-ing, sketching and describing ruins and collecting traditional airs. Between 1835 and 1846 he was employed by the **Ordnance Survey** where he met **Eugene O'Curry** and **John O'Donovan**. Petrie designed the distinctive Celtic-style type used in O'Donovan's translation of the *Annals of the Four Masters*. In 1845 his *Essay on the origin and uses of the round towers of Ireland* was published as *The ecclesiastical archi-tecture of Ireland*. In 1855 he edited *The Petrie collection of ancient airs of Ireland*. (Stokes, *The life*.)

petronel. A large pistol used by horse-soldiers in the sixteenth and seven-teenth centuries. It was fired with the butt resting against the chest.

petty jury. The trial jury at the assizes as opposed to the the jury of in-dictment, the grand jury. Petty juries, unlike modern juries, were ex-pected to have some knowledge of the defendant's character and of circumstances relating to the case.

petty sergeanty. A tenure in **socage** which required the tenant to supply the king annually with a sword or spurs, or perform some such service of a non-personal nature. *See* grand sergeanty.

petty sessions. Until the passage of the District Justices Act in 1923, petty sessions were the equivalent of the modern district courts, their remit being the trial of lesser offences. *See* justice of the peace.

Philosophical Society (1683–1708). *See* Dublin Philosophical Society.

phytophthora infestans. Potato blight, an airborne fungal disease which attacked the potato crop in the United States, in many European countries and in Ireland (with devastating effect) from 1845. Thought to have been transported from South America to Europe with car-goes of guano (a fertiliser composed of bird droppings), blight propa-gated rapidly in that year's moist, sunless summer. It struck repeatedly throughout the remainder of the century (and remains with us today) but with significantly reduced impact. Demographic pressure had eased, better strains of potato were sown and a preventive copper-based spray was developed.

picard. A large sailing vessel or barge used for coastal or river trade.

piepowder, court of. (Fr., *pieds poudrés*, dusty feet) A market court which regulated weights and measures and resolved disputes, especially those involving travelling traders so they could journey on to the next market to sell their wares. It was operated by the person entitled by right (letters **patent**) to hold the market.

pigeon-house. Dovecote, *columbarium*.

Pigott forgeries. A series of letters fabricated between 1887 and 1889 by Richard Pigott, a Dublin journalist, which purported to show that Charles Parnell was linked to agrarian terrorism. The truth emerged when Pigott cracked under cross-examination in February 1889. Sub-sequently he fled to Madrid where he committed suicide. (Lyons, *Charles Stewart Parnell*, pp. 368–9.)

pile. In heraldry, a triangular wedge with the point near the base of the **escutcheon**.

pillowbeere. A pillowcase.

piment. A wine flavoured with spices.

pinder. The keeper of the manorial pound.

pinfold. The manorial pound where strays were held pending the next session of the manor court.

pinnace. A light sailing ship or tender providing logistical support to war-ships.

pipe. 1: A wine casket 2: A unit of capacity containing half a **tun**, two hogsheads or four barrels.

pipe rolls. Records of the court of **exchequer**, the pipe or treasurer's rolls contained the annual statements of receipts, allowances and arrears of sheriffs, escheators, customs collectors, guardians of royal manors, seneschals and bailiffs. They were known as pipe rolls because they were wrapped around hollow cylinders or pipes. In 1861 there were 184 Irish pipe rolls in existence, comprising the returns of the receipt and expenditure of the royal revenue, the escheators' and sheriffs' accounts which contained many references to land grants, the value of ecclesiastical lands taken into the king's hands by vacancy, exemplifications of the Statute of Westminster against **absentees**, accounts of laymen's lands taken into the king's hands, **prisage** of wine, king's customs and revenues, **quit-rents, wardships** and **escheats**. The pipe rolls were destroyed in 1922 but NLI MSS 760–1 contain Sir William Betham's extracts from the pipe rolls Henry III – Elizabeth I. Some of the material formerly contained in the Irish pipe rolls can be accessed in the English pipe rolls because the Irish treasurer's accounts were audited at Westminster. (Connolly, *Medieval record sources*, pp. 20–22; Davies and Quinn, 'The Irish pipe roll'; *PRI reps DK*, 35–54.)

Place Act. A minor parliamentary reform measure introduced in 1793 (33 Geo. III, c. 41) under pressure from the **'patriot' party** which brought Ireland into line with Britain. The act compelled members to resign their commons' seats and seek re-election upon taking a government post or upon receiving a government pension. It was not retrospective, however, and at the union there were 72 members of the Irish parliament holding government posts (placemen), all perfectly positioned to vote through the legislative union. It was under legislation of this type that William Vesey FitzGerald, on his appointment as president of the Board of Trade, was compelled to resign his seat in Co. Clare in 1828 and fight a by-election. His defeat by Daniel O'Connell was pivotal in the concession of **Catholic emancipation** in 1829.

Plan of Campaign. A continuation of the **Land War** by other means, this scheme was devised by John Dillon, William O'Brien and Timothy Harrington to compel landlords to lower rents through a process of collective bargaining with their tenants. It began in 1886 when a collapse in crop and livestock prices left many tenants unable to pay the rents judicially fixed under the 1881 **Land Law Act**. Tenants who had not benefited from that act were in an even worse position and the number of evictions began to climb dramatically. Under the plan, landlords were requested to lower their rents voluntarily. Those who refused were to be offered a reduced rate by the united body of tenants. If the reduced rent was refused the money was paid into an estate fund which was used to protect and support any tenants who were evicted for supporting the campaign. Landgrabbers were to be deterred by the use of the boycott. Any shortfall was met by subvention from the **National League** which disbursed £250,000 by 1891. Landlords and government responded vigorously to the plan. Some landlords combined in an attempt to defeat the tenants' demands. In 1887 Augustine Birrell, the **chief secretary**, introduced a coercion bill (Criminal Law and Procedure Act, 50 & 51 Vict., c. 20) which gave resident magistrates in proclaimed districts the powers of investigation and summary jurisdiction and authorised the **lord lieutenant** to suppress subversive groups. Both Dillon and O'Brien were jailed under this legislation. Between 1886 and 1890 the plan was initiated on 116 estates and although a majority were resolved peacefully or by agreement after some agitation, 18 estates remained unresolved by 1891. In all about 1,400 families were evicted and some remained displaced as late as 1893 when a special committee was established to consider their predicament. The Plan of Campaign effectively ended in 1890 with the jailing of O'Brien and Dillon and the citing of Parnell as co-respondent in the O'Shea divorce case. (Larkin, *The Roman Catholic Church*.)

plantation acre. Also known as the Irish acre, it was the land measure employed in Ireland during the plantations, equivalent to 7,840 square yards or 1.62 statute acres. *See* acre.

plea rolls. Essentially the journals of all the proceedings in the courts, the plea rolls contained records of decrees, legal suits, actions and inquisitions, enrolments of judicial appointees, enrolments of charters, patents and deeds, legal suits and actions, actions of dower, writs of right of **advowsons**, assizes of *novel disseisin* and *mort d'ancestor*, prosecutions for trespasses in the royal forests and a whole range of miscellaneous material associated with the business of jurisprudence. In 1861 there were 593 rolls in existence dating from 1220 to the reign of Charles I but with the few exceptions all were destroyed in the Four Courts in 1922. A manuscript repertory of 12 volumes of extracts from the plea rolls had been prepared by the **Irish Record Commission** before its demise and these can be found in the National Archives. The third volume of the O'Renehan MSS in Maynooth College Library also contains abstracts from the plea rolls. *See* Philomena Connolly, *Medieval record sources*, pp. 25–6, for all surviving rolls.

plenarty, exception of. The claim advanced by the defence in a hearing of *darrien presentment* that there was no vacancy in the benefice to which the plaintiff claimed the right of presentation, that there was an incumbent and therefore no reason for the assize. (Osbrough, *Studies*, pp. 101–2.)

ploughbote, ploughboot. A tenant's right without payment to procure wood from the manorial woods for the purpose of making ploughs.

ploughland. The amount of land that would provide employment to one plough with a full team of oxen or horses for a year. Although its precise extent varied throughout the country it was normally considered to contain about 120 acres of arable land. Thus it was equivalent to a **carucate** or **villate**.

pluries, **writ of**. A writ issued after two earlier writs had proved ineffectual. *See* outlawry.

Pococke, Richard (1704–1765). An English clergyman who served successively as vicar-general of Waterford and Lismore, archdeacon of Dublin and bishop of Ossory, Elphin and Meath. A compulsive traveller and travel-writer, Pococke published accounts of his tours of Egypt and the Middle East (1743–5) and his accounts of Scotland and England appeared in 1887 and 1888. Between 1747 and 1758 he toured extensively in Ireland, largely in remote areas that had attracted little attention from earlier commentators, but a full edition of his Irish tours only appeared in 1995. Pococke's interests were antiquarian and scientific and on his travels in he carried topographical and other reference works with him to compare his observations with those of earlier commentators. Observations on archaeology, botany, geology, ecclesiastical history and architecture, economic life and agriculture all figure prominently in his writing. Although keen to advance Protestantism in Ireland – he was an enthusiastic supporter of the **charter schools** – Pococke eschewed the moralistic criticisms of native Irish culture and beliefs of earlier visitors in favour of a descriptive, restrained style. (McVeagh, *Richard Pococke*.)

pointed style. The pointed or Early English style was the first stage in the evolution of the Gothic architecture in the middle ages. It derived from the introduction of the pointed arch in the eleventh century. In addition to pointed arches, the style is characterised by plain ribbed vaults, windows without tracery and tall piers with shafts grouped together. *See* decorated style, perpendicular style, both of which represent developments of the pointed style.

police. Following an outbreak of agrarian unrest in 1813, Robert Peel, the **chief secretary**, introduced the **Peace Preservation Act** (54 Geo. III, c. 131, 1814) which created a uniformed, temporary peace preservation force under the direction of a police **magistrate** to restore order in disturbed areas. In 1822 work began on a new police bill to establish a permanent standing force of constables and sub-constables for each county under the supervision of provincial inspectors-general. Magistrates in the counties were authorised to appoint constables and sub-constables but not the higher ranks. This force also operated under a magistrate (Geo. IV, c. 103, 1822). By 1825 Ireland had a professional police force of 4,500 men who were recruited and maintained locally but equipped from central government stores. From 1830 the government nominated the chief Dublin police magistrate and the bulk of police magistrates throughout the country. The inspectors-general, however, were appointees of the **lord lieutenant** and were required to establish uniform discipline and conduct within the force. They were also empowered to move men out of their respective counties as needs dictated. In 1836 Drummond, the chief secretary, amalgamated the peace preservation force with the county police to establish a single, armed and centralised police force, the Irish Constabulary, for the entire country with the exception of the cities of Dublin, Belfast and Derry which had their own police forces. Initially the new force comprised 8,400 men rising to 14,000 by the 1880s. In 1867 it was renamed the Royal Irish Constabulary for its role in suppressing the Fenians. By this time the duties of constables ranged from contentious matters, such as dealing with agrarian violence or assisting with evictions, to the mundane tasks of collecting agricultural statistics, operating as census enumerators and enforcing fishing, food and drugs regulations. From a local historian's perspective the flood of reports dispatched from the localities to the central administration offers a treasure trove of localised detail although caution must always be exercised in employing them. These were the reports of an arm of government that was not naturally well-disposed towards local grievances. The National Archives holds a large collection of records of crime and local disturbances dating from the 1790s. These can be found amongst the Rebellion papers (1790–1807), State of the Country papers (1790–1831), the Outrage papers (1832–1852), the Chief Secretary's Office papers (from 1852), the Fenian papers (1857–1883), the Irish Land League and National League papers (1878–1890), Special Crime Branch papers (1887–1917) and Intelligence (1895–1917). *See* baronial police force, Bulkies, constable, Dublin Metropolitan Police, revenue police, watch and ward. (Herlihy, *The Royal Irish Constabulary*; O'Sullivan, *The Irish constabularies*; Palmer, *Police*.)

poll. 1: A spatial unit of measurement equivalent to 50 to 60 acres 2: A deed (such as a deed poll) involving a single party that was straight edged and not indented for the reason that no other individual required a copy for later authentification.

pollard. To cut a tree back to the trunk to encourage vigorous growth. Pollarding provided an annual crop of flexible rods for basket-weaving and thatching. It was carried out at a height to protect shoots from grazing animals. *See* coppice, scollop.

poll tax. Literally a head tax, the poll tax was imposed on every adult over the age of 15 by the 1660 poll tax ordinance. *See Census of 1659.*

pontage. A maintenance tax levied on the users of a bridge.

Poor Inquiry. The Poor Inquiry was established by royal commission in 1833 to inquire into the condition of the poorer classes in Ireland. It was the largest investigation ever conducted into poverty in these is-lands. Sub-commissioners were appointed to travel throughout the country gathering information about earnings, the nature of employ-ment, cost of living, housing, clothing, food, medical care and local charity. Over 1,500 people were interviewed. The three reports of the inquiry (with appendices and supplements) contain detailed in-formation on pre-Famine conditions in the localities which was submitted by clergymen, justices of the peace and medical officers in response to a set list of interrogatories. Richard Whately, Anglican archbishop of Dublin, was selected by the **Whig** administration as chairman in the hope that the report would be acceptable to Whig economic sensitivities but that hope was dashed with the publication between 1835 and 1837 of the commission's findings. They make bleak reading. The commissioners estimated that over two million people required assistance for 30 weeks of each year and recommend-ed massive state intervention to promote the economic development of the country, most notably in the areas of land reclamation, fishery development and large-scale emigration to the colonies. They re-jected the notion that the English **poor law** system with its emphasis on the provision of relief within a workhouse would go any distance towards ameliorating the impoverishment they had encountered. The commissioners did, however, agree with the government that relief should be discretionary and not an entitlement. For its part, the govern-ment ignored the commission's findings because, they claimed, the commission had exceeded its brief in looking into the causes rather than the symptoms of impoverishment. In any case prevailing econo-mic thought in government circles did not favour massive state inter-vention. Irish poverty, according to this view, was a symptom of back-wardness and could only be addressed by detaching the peasants from the soil and not by a liberal poor law system. Poor law was to be ad-ministered stringently to compel the peasants to give up their small-holdings, to encourage landlords to amalgamate small-holdings and invest in their estates, thereby transforming a country of small-holders, low productivity and **absentee** landlords into a modern capitalist economy. *See* Malthus. (Poor Inquiry.)

Poor Law. Poor law was the means by which the poor and destitute were to be relieved of distress. Extended to Ireland in 1838 (1 & 2 Vict., c. 56) and modelled on the English Poor Law Act of 1834, poor law was financed by local poor rates that were levied on occupiers of land valued at four pounds and over. The intention was to save money by doing away with **outdoor relief** and the provision of public works for the unemployed during periods of hardship. Administra-tively, the country was divided into **poor law unions**, each of which was supervised by a board of **guardians** under the overall direction of a poor law commission. Relief was discretionary and not a right and was to be offered only in the workhouse under the principle of less eligibility (that is, people would only elect to go there as a last resort). Conditions were to be kept so bleak that only the completely destitute would enter. It was utterly inadequate for Ireland where poverty was widespread in rural areas and where admission to a workhouse required families to surrender the holdings on which they depended for subsistence. The poor law system failed to meet the challenge presented by the Great Famine and government was compelled to provide outdoor relief again. In 1847, in an attempt to make responsibility for distress a local rather than a British charge, the **Poor Law Commission** was made autonomous of the Poor Law Board in England, the very weak and the disabled became entitled as of right to relief but tests of destitution were more rigorously enforced. Significantly, outdoor relief was provided for the first time under poor law. Local dispensaries and public health regulations came within the ambit of poor law after the famine and when the supervisory Poor Law Commission was abolished in 1872 its functions were absorbed by the Local Government Board. *See* Malthus, rate-in-aid, relieving officer, workhouse test. (O'Brien, 'The establishment of poor-law unions', pp. 97–120.)

Poor Law Commission. A government-appointed body set up in 1847 (10 & 11 Vict., c. 90) to assume responsibility for the administration of **poor law** in Ireland, a function previously exercised by the English poor law commissioners. The poor law commission exercised a supervisory jurisdiction over local poor law boards. In 1872 (35 & 36 Vict., c. 69) it was merged with the Local Government Board which had been established a year earlier and which, in time, became one of the most important departments in the Irish administration. Both the Poor Law Commission and the Local Government Board comprised the chief-secretary, under-secretary, commissioners, regional inspectors and clerks. In addition to supervising poor law (including a veto over the appointment of and power to dismiss salaried poor law union officials and to summarily dismiss and replace elected boards of guardians), the Local Government Board was responsible for the dispensary system, for organising relief in distressed areas during famine, it arbitrated between rival local authorities and arranged for the transfer of power to the county and rural district councils created by the 1898 **Local Government Act**. After 1898 the board (which was stuffed with unionists and Protestants) was able to limit the freedom of action of the newly-created (largely nationalist and Catholic) councils because its approval was necessary for their acts. The Local Government Board supervised hospitals established under the 1908 Tuberculosis Prevention (Ireland) Act and the distress committees set up under the Unemployed Workmen's Act (1905). Under the 1908 Old Age Pension Act it became the central pension authority.

poor law union. An administrative area in which ratepayers were assessed for the poor law rate, the poor law union was created by the extension to Ireland in 1838 (1 & 2 Vict., c. 56) of the English Poor Law Act of 1834. The area of each union was determined usually by taking the chief market town in an area and attaching to it, without regard to county or baronial boundaries, the surrounding land within a radius of about 10 miles. The only limit imposed was that no townland should be divided. Townlands were then grouped together in electoral divisions for the purpose of electing union officials known as guardians. The poor law union assumed responsibility for tasks previously mandated to the **grand jury** including the maintenance and support of dispensaries, fever hospitals and workhouses but not its judicial function. Each union was administered by a **board of guardians**, partly comprising *ex-officio* members such as magistrates and partly elected officials. In all a total of 163 poor law unions were eventually established, each with its own workhouse. (O'Brien, 'The establishment of poor-law unions', pp. 97–120.)

poor rate. A tax levied on every **tenement** to provide relief to the poor in each of the 130 (163 by 1848) **poor law unions** that had been established by the extension of **poor law** to Ireland in 1838 (1 & 2 Vict., c. 56). Under the 1851 Medical Charities Act poor rate revenue was also used to fund a nationwide dispensary network. The **grand jury** was nominated to carry out a valuation of all tenements within its jurisdiction for the purpose of assessing liability and the **board of guardians** in each union employed valuators to conduct the valuation and to record their findings. The imposition of the poor rate met with opposition in some areas, mainly in the west. In 1843–4 police or military intervention was required in 21 unions to enforce collection. To avoid a repetition, occupiers of property rated at less than £4 per annum were exempted (6 & 7 Vict., c. 92, 1843) and their portion of the rates was assigned to the landlord. This concession boomeranged on tenants during the Great Famine years. Declining rental payments from stricken tenants coupled with increasing poor law taxation stimulated landlords whose properties were heavily subdivided into units valued below £4 to clear their estates, consolidate and convert to pastoral farming. The poor rate valuation, itself, was also a source of friction. Many ratepayers claimed the valuators were unskilled in valuation and had undervalued the holdings of their cronies, the large landowners. This difficulty was overcome by the establishment in 1852 of **Griffith's Valuation**, a single uniform system of land and tenement valuation. From 1898, with the passage of the **Local Government (Ireland) Act**, the responsibility for levying the rate devolved to the county council and in 1946 the poor rate was renamed the country rate. *See* rate-in-aid, 'quarter acre clause'. (Kinealy, *This great calamity*.)

Popery, Report on the State of (1731). In 1731 the Irish house of lords, at the instigation of Archbishop Boulter, appointed a committee to investigate the state of popery in Ireland. Basing its findings on returns submitted by Protestant clergymen, sheriffs and magistrates in the localities, the committee reported that there were 892 regular mass-houses and 54 private chapels served by 1,445 priests, 51 friaries with a total complement of 254 friars, 9 nunneries and about 549 popish schools operating in Ireland. It claimed that 229 mass-houses had been constructed since the death of George I and that papists were openly attending mass. The original returns were destroyed in the Public Record Office in 1922 but the report had already been published in the first four volumes of *Archivium Hibernicum* (1912–15) and in the *Journal of the house of commons of the kingdom of Ireland*, iii (Dublin, 1727–52).

popish plot. *See* Titus Oates.

portal dolmen. A **neolithic**, single-chambered tomb distinguished by tall upright portal or entrance stones, a lower backstone and a large capstone. Some portal dolmens can be found at the end of long cairns and others were elaborated to accommodate small burial chambers in the sides of the cairn. Thus they are are related to court cairns. There are about 150 examples of portal dolmens in Ireland where they occur mostly in Ulster.

portcorn. A rent in kind, usually of corn (wheat, **bere**, malt and oatmeal), owed by tenants to monasteries and abbeys. After the monastic **dissolution** port-corn rents were reserved to the crown and granted to the lord lieutenant, master of the rolls, lord chief justice and the presidents of Munster and Connacht. Tenants were allowed offset the value of these renders against their crown rents. (Simington, *The Civil Survey*, pp. xxviii–xxxi.)

portion. A settlement created for the benefit of the offspring of a deceased landlord that was payable when they attained **majority** or upon their marriage. It was usually raised by a mortgage on the property or **rentcharge**.

portioner. A tenant-farmer who paid a fixed portion of his produce to the landlord in lieu of a money payment.

portionary. Where the income of a medieval cathedral was divided in fixed proportions between a fixed number of dignitaries, the canons were known as portionaries.

portreeve (portrieve). Synonymous with mayor or sovereign, the chief officer of a municipal corporation and enforcer of town regulations.

posse comitatus. (L., the power of the county) The power possessed by the sheriff to summon all men above the age of fifteen to attend and assist in executing the process of the law or perform other acts in maintaining the law.

postea. (L., afterwards) A record of the proceedings and verdict of a trial.

postern. 1: Any gate or door in the wall of a castle or fortification other than the main entrance 2: A sallyport or escape route.

post-house. A house along the post routes where horses were changed.

potato ground. A ready-manured field leased for a one-year term to cottiers to grow potatoes. *See* conacre.

potwalloper. A pejorative term used to describe a person invited to reside in a 'potwalloping' **borough** shortly before a parliamentary election to vote as the resident magnate required. It derived from the requirement that, in addition to a residency of six months (one year from 1782), all electors must have a family and have cooked a meal within the borough precinct to qualify for the franchise. Until 1793, when the franchise was extended to include Catholics, voting rights were restricted to Protestant five-pound householders. There were 12 'potwalloping' boroughs in Ireland (Swords, Knocktopher, Rathcormack, Dungarvan, Lismore, Baltimore, Antrim town, Lisburn, Randalstown, Tallow, Newry and Downpatrick) only four of which (Newry, Downpatrick, Lisburn and Dungarvan) survived the **Act of Union**.

pottle pot. A two-quart pot or tankard.

poundage. 1: Any payment of so much per pound upon the cost of any monetary transaction 2: A duty on imports and exports of so much per pound, usually of the order of 12*d*., originally granted to the crown for defence purposes. In Ireland in the the late fifteenth century, it was the custom of 12 pence in the pound levied on imports and exports to finance a small permanent standing force known as the **Brotherhood of Arms of St George**. *See* tonnage 3: The right to impound wandering cattle. The levy paid to retrieve impounded animals was known as poundaging.

Powis Commission. A royal commission appointed in 1868 to investigate the national system of primary education and to make recommendations for reform. The commission was chaired by the earl of Powis and comprised 14 members, seven Catholics and seven Protestants (including two Presbyterians). Reporting in 1870, the commission felt that the academic progress of schoolchildren had been much less than it ought to have been and recommended the introduction of a system of **payment-by-results** whereby a portion of a teacher's salary would be determined by the performance of each child under examination and a satisfactory level of attendance. They proposed a measure of compulsory attendance for those children in towns who were not actually at work, the abolition of model schools, the ending of the distinction between convent schools and national schools in the matter of state subvention and the ending of the controversial involvement of the Commissioners of National Education in editing schoolbooks. Local areas, according to the commission, should contribute one-third of the state grant to schools or have it rated locally. Finally, it proposed that schools should be permitted to become denominational in areas where two schools, one Protestant, one Catholic, had been in existence for three years and where the average attendance of each was at least 25. These schools were to be free of religious regulation beyond permitting the withdrawal from religious education classes of children of the minority religion. In effect, the commission was proposing to licence denominational schooling in the very areas where conditions were propitious for mixed schooling, thereby destroying the founding principle of the system. In reality this had no bearing on the *de facto* situation as the system had already hardened into a denominational one. The recommendations of the Powis Commission were partially implemented but not with any great success. Payment-by-results increased school attendance but also introduced a mechanical rote-learning approach that was discontinued within a few decades. The National School Teachers (Irl.) Act (1875) introduced a complex mechanism for increasing local contributions but that too was a failure. A partial compulsory education bill was passed in 1892 but it applied only to towns and made allowances for children to help with farming and fishing. The eight-volume Powis report contains the commission's report, minutes and analysis of evidence and special reports on model, training and agricultural schools. The sixth volume contains a national educational census showing the number of pupils actually present in each primary school on 25 June 1868. *See* Belmore Commission and Education, National System of. (Powis; Coolahan, *Irish education*, pp. 24–33.)

Poynings' Law (1495). A law (10 Hen. VII, c. 4) introduced to strengthen royal control and limit the independence of the Irish **chief governor** by requiring him to apply for a licence to hold parliament. He was obliged to submit all bills to the king and his council and have them approved and certified under the great **seal** before parliament could sit. Since parliament could not meet without prior approval of proposed bills and since bills could not be transmitted for approval once parliament was in session, this measure severely restricted the ability of the Irish parliament to originate legislation. In practice this proved inconvenient and by 3 & 4 Philip & Mary, c. 4 (1556) Poynings' was amended to permit additional bills to be transmitted to England after parliament had assembled. This allowed for the seventeenth-century initiative of transmitting 'heads of bills' which enabled either house to originate legislation. Bills transmitted from Ireland remained subject to amendment and veto by the privy councils of Ireland and Britain but parliament determined which bills, in whatever condition they were returned, made it into the statute books. Faced with the threat of war with both France and America, Poynings' Law was amended in 1782 (21 & 22 Geo. III, c. 47) and a degree of legislative independence permitted. Henceforth bills were transmitted 'without addition, diminution or alteration'. The crown retained the power to veto legislation, a power never subsequently exercised. *See* statute, Yelverton's Act. (Edwards and Moody, 'The history of Poynings' law', pp. 415–24; Clarke, 'The history of Poyning's law', pp. 207–22; Kelly, 'Monitoring', pp. 87–106.)

pracas. A type of harrow.

praecipe, **writ of**. *See* right, writ of.

Praemunire, **Statutes of** (1353, 1393). Introduced by Edward III (27 Edw. III, c. 1, 1353) as a sop to popular feeling against foreign clergy, the first statute of *Praemunire* legislated against papal interference in appointments to church positions in England. It forbade appeals to Rome in disputes over patronage and the exercise of legal and financial jurisdiction by the pope in England without royal consent. It was an offence punishable by forfeiture to assert papal supremacy over England as it was for a **dean** and **chapter** who failed to act on royal instructions regarding appointments to vacant sees. The later statute (16 Richard II, c. 5, 1393) forbade on pain of forfeiture the presentation of suits cognisable by English law in a foreign court. It was aimed at those who 'purchased or pursued in the courts of Rome or elsewhere any translations, processes and sentence of execution, bulls, instruments or any other things whatsoever which touch upon the king, against him, his crown, and his regality whereby the king's court was hindered in its jurisdiction over pleas of presentment'. Actions under both statutes were initiated by a writ of *praemunire* to the sheriff to summon the person so accused. In the seventeenth and eighteenth centuries *Praemunire* restrained the ability of Irish Catholic bishops to discipline errant clergymen for the aggrieved cleric could immediately initiate or threaten an action against what was, in effect, the illegal exercise of foreign jurisdiction. *Praemunire* was repealed in Britain in 1967. See *congé d'élire*.

preacher's book. A **Church of Ireland** record of parish worship which includes the date and type of service, the preacher's name, the amount of the offering, the number of people in attendance and the number receiving communion.

prebend. (L. *praebere*, to supply) An endowment from the rents, fees and **tithe** of a parish which provided the living of a **canon** or member of a cathedral **chapter**.

prebendal parish. A parish set aside to support a cathedral **prebendary**.

prebendary. A member of the chapter of a **cathedral** (such as a canon) who held a **prebend**. Prebendaries were called after the parish that provided their living.

precentor. The chapter member responsible for worship in the cathedral. This could involve leading and directing the choir or congregation in the singing of hymns.

predial (praedial). Predial **tithe** was exacted on the profits of the land and accrued from crops such as cereals, vegetables and fruit. Tithe on major crops such as wheat, barley, oats and hay were paid to the **rector** and was known as the great tithe. Small tithe, including the predials vegetables and fruit, the mixed tithe (small animals and animal products) and personal tithe (the fruit of labour and industry) were owed to the **vicar**.

pre-emption. The right of purchasing before another. In other words, the right of first refusal.

Premonstratensian canons. Founded by St Norbert at Prémontré in France, the Premonstratensian canons adhered to the rule of St Augustine with some borrowings, including the wearing of a white habit, from the **Cistercians**. The first Irish Premonstratensian house was founded at Carrickfergus in the late twelfth century. In all about a dozen abbeys, priories and dependent cells were established by the early 1300s in Co. Antrim and the western counties of Sligo, Mayo, Roscommon and Galway. By the seventeenth century all had been suppressed. (Flood, 'The Premonstratensians', pp. 624–31; Gwynn and Hadcock, *Medieval religious houses*, pp. 201–7.)

prepositus. (L., put before) Literally, someone put before others, the term refers to the mayor, **portreeve**, **sovereign** or **seneschal** of a municipal corporation.

prerogative courts. Courts operating alongside the common law courts which arose out of the *curia regis* (king's council) to deal with cases for which no remedy existed at common law or particular areas in which the regular courts would not deal. They were known as prerogative courts because through them the king exercised his discretionary power as sovereign to provide justice to his subjects. They were also a valuable source of royal revenue and, strictly administered, proved effective weapons in enforcing the sovereign's will. **Chancery**, the first and most enduring prerogative court, emerged in the thirteenth century. Other prerogative courts such as the court of **castle chamber** (the Irish star chamber), the court of **wards** and **liveries**, the court of **high commission** and the courts of the presidents of Munster and Connacht appeared in the sixteenth century but were gone by the close of the seventeenth. They disappeared because they came under two-fold attack from the common law courts (which resented the loss of business) and from a parliament which bristled at Charles I's use of the star chamber and high commission to enforce his policies. Only chancery survived into modern times. *See* provincial councils.

prerogative and faculties, court of the. A post-Reformation innovation designed to restructure and police the Church of Ireland, the royally-appointed court of faculties inquired into titles to hold benefices, sanctioned deprivations and licensed pluralities. It granted faculties and dispensations, a jurisdiction previously exercised by the papacy. From 1571 jurisdiction in testamentary matters was added to the commissioners' responsibilities in those cases where a testator held an estate in excess of £5 (*bona notabilia*) in a second diocese. Where a testator also held property in England the will was proved in the prerogative court of the archbishop of Canterbury and a copy proved in Ireland. It became the supreme ecclesiastical court of the Church of Ireland when James I established the court of the prerogative and faculties in 1622 and placed the archbishop of Armagh at its head. This arrangement survived until 1856 when the court lost its testamentary jurisdiction to the newly-established civil court of **probate**. It lapsed entirely with the disestablishment of the Church of Ireland in 1869. *See* consistorial court.

Presbyterian. A member of a distinctively-structured reformed faith which claims scripture to be the final authority in religious matters, that all members of the church are equal under Christ, that the ministry has been given to the entire church and which, in its earlier history, embraced predestination. **Calvinism** provides the key doctrinal basis for Presbyterianism. The Calvinist belief in universal priesthood is manifested in the rejection of episcopal control in favour of equality between lay elders and ministers at all levels of the church from kirk **session** to **presbytery** to **synod** to general assembly. Ministers are chosen by the elders and salaried by the congregation. All officers are elected. After the Reformation the Church of Scotland became Presbyterian and Scottish Presbyterians carried the faith with them into Ireland in the seventeenth century. As the Church of Ireland was a Calvinist-leaning, minority church on the island, Presbyterians were welcomed and their ministers were provided with livings. Presbyterianism experienced a surge in growth following the 1641 rebellion and new presbyteries were established. Moves to enforce religious uniformity, initiated by Wentworth in the 1630s and accelerated after the Restoration, resulted in the expulsion of Presbyterian ministers from the Anglican church (see Uniformity). William III's gratitude for their support against the Jacobites yielded an increased *regium donum* and the religious freedom they enjoyed was secured legislatively by the passing of the Toleration Act in 1719. However, the power and influence of the Church of Ireland ensured that Presbyterians were to suffer, though less severely, the disabilities inflicted on Catholics by the

penal laws. The **Test Act** (1704) led to their exclusion from public office and from membership of the boroughs until it was repealed in 1780. In the eighteenth and nineteenth centuries Presbyterianism was riven by **Arianism** and by the controversy over the issue of subscription to the **Westminster Confession**, the Presbyterian confession of faith. When obligatory subscription was imposed 17 ministers left to form the **Remonstrant Synod** and in 1840 the **Synod of Ulster** merged with the **Seceders** (a pro-subscription body which had seceded earlier over that issue) to form the **General Assembly of the Presbyterian Church in Ireland**. *See* New Light, Southern Association.

presbytery. (L., *presbyter*, an elder) A **Presbyterian** church council formed by all the ministers in a district together with representative elders from each congregational **session**. Although the congregation is responsible for electing the minister, the approval of the presbytery (which also supervises the ordination, installation, transfer and removal of ministers) is required. It exercises religious, financial and legal authority over all the congregations within its district and acts as an appellate court for cases arising in the sessions. *See* General Assembly of the Presbyterian Church in Ireland, synod.

presentment. 1: A formal statement or indictment of finding by a **grand jury** as to whether a *prima facie* case existed for a prosecution to proceed. Grand juries retained this judicial function until their abolition in 1924 when direct trial by jury was introduced 2: The grant of a grand jury towards the construction or repair of a road or building. Such grants were financed by the **county cess** and were considered before a committee of the grand jury at presentment sessions.

presidency. *See* provincial councils, composition.

prest. A loan or advance of money. Irregular and delayed payments to the Irish administration's standing force in the sixteenth century encouraged desertion and indiscipline which the administration tried to forestall through the payment of small prests to enable the troops to feed themselves.

prey, to make a. (Ir., *creagh*) To conduct a cattle-raid. Cattle raids were conducted for the purpose of stealing cattle or to exact a lawful tribute but also to acquire new vassals or clients by impressing the local inhabitants with a demonstration of military prowess.

Pride's purge. On 3 December 1648 Colonel Thomas Pride forcibly prevented the entrance to the English house of commons of about 100 MPs who were considered to be in favour of making concessions to the King. The remaining 200 or so members formed what was known as the **Rump** or the Long Parliament.

primary sources. Historical evidence which emerges at the same time as the event to which it relates is called a primary source. Secondary sources are those which appear after the event they pertain to. This apparently neat distinction requires some qualification. A history of the Great Famine written in the twentieth century is a secondary source for the nineteenth century but a primary source for twentieth-century thinking.

prime serjeant (king's serjeant). A professional law officer of superior rank, the office of king's serjeant at law first emerged in Ireland with the appointment of Roger Owen in the 1260s. From the seventeenth century there were usually two or three serjeants at any one time, known respectively as prime serjeant, second serjeant and third serjeant. They acted as prosecutors and defenders of the king's pleas in Ireland and represented the king's interests in various capacities such as initiating actions to recover rents or lands or enquiring into homicides. As senior law officer of the courts they often replaced judges but were generally occupied in drafting documents or administrative tasks. In Elizabethan times the office of prime serjeant was eclipsed by that of **attorney-general** but it resumed its former precedence under the Stuarts and retained it until the post was discontinued in 1805. (Hart, *A history*).

primogeniture. (L., *primogenitus*, first born) The common law principle of succession to a family estate by the eldest son. The purpose of such preference was to retain estates intact and to prevent excessive subdivision, a practice which, if repeated widely, would dilute the economic and social power of individual families and weaken the whole fabric of landed society. Primogeniture also made it relatively easy to monitor the services and duties owed by chief tenants to the crown. *See Quia Emptores*.

prison forte et dure. A punishment imposed on a suspect to extract a confession or secure evidence, *prison forte et dure* consisted of perpetual imprisonment, starvation and ultimately death. From the time of Henry IV it was replaced by *peine forte et dure* or pressing to death.

privateer. A privately-owned, armed ship, furnished with a letter of marque (government licence) to capture and plunder enemy merchant vessels.

privy council. Originally an advisory body to the **chief governor** comprising a number of selected ministers, the privy council developed into the senior administrative and executive body in Ireland from 1534 until the **Act of Union**. It was distinct from the more general king's council (**curia regis**) which included lesser officials and peers. To curb over-powerful chief governors (such as Garret Mór Fitz-Gerald), the Tudors, as they had done in England from the accession of Henry VIII, reserved the right to appoint those of its choosing to the council together with the six reserved appointments of chief governor, **lord chancellor, treasurer, master of the rolls**, secretary and keeper of the privy seal and chief justice. Moreover, the governor was required not to act against the members' advice. In the absence of the governor the council was presided over by the chancellor and empowered to conduct state business. Although up to 24 members could be nominated to the council usually only about half that number, largely senior officials, attended meetings. Under the Tudors the council began to exercise executive functions, advising, performing routine administrative business and implementing instructions from London. It continued to act in an appellate capacity after its judicial business was transferred to the court of **castle chamber**. Until legislative independence was conceded in 1782 the privy council exercised control over parliament through the powers granted it by **Poynings' Law** to amend, alter or veto bills prepared by parliament. Later it was completely eclipsed by the rise to prominence of the **chief secretary**.

privy seal. *See* seals.

prisage, prizage. Also known as butlerage, prisage was a tax on wine in Ireland and the hereditary perquisite of the Butlers of Ormond through the possession of the title of King's Butler.

probate. The judicial process by which a will purporting to be the last will of a deceased person is declared legally valid. If so adjudged, the will is then admitted to probate and the executor can begin to dispose of the estate. From the twelfth century testamentary jurisdiction lay with the church (the Established church after the Reformation). Wills were proved in the **consistorial court** of the diocese in which the deceased had lived. If, however, the deceased had an estate worth £5 or more in a second diocese, testamentary jurisdiction lay with the **prerogative court** of the archbishop of Armagh. With the passage of the Probate Act in 1857 (20 & 21 Vict., c. 8) jurisdiction in the matter of wills was transferred to a civil court of probate in Dublin, the principal registry, and a nationwide network of eleven district registries. *See* nuncupative will, wills. (ffolliott and O'Byrne, 'Wills', pp. 157–80.

proctor. 1: The Irish **parliament** before the Reformation comprised three houses, the lords, commons and the lower clergy or clerical proctors. The proctors paid a heavy price for their rejection of the Henrician ecclesiastical reforms for Henry directed parliament to legislate for their extinction (28 Hen. VIII, c. 12) 2: Attorneys in the admiralty court were known as proctors 3: For tithe-proctor *see* tithe-farmer.

proffers. Twice yearly, at **Michaelmas** and Easter, sheriffs were required to present themselves at the court of **exchequer** to settle their accounts by paying whatever money they had collected during the preceding months. These payments were known as proffers and they were recorded in the **memoranda rolls** under the heading *proffra*.

prohibition, writ of. A writ issuing out of **king's bench** commanding a judge or any party to a suit to cease from prosecuting a case on the grounds that the case did not belong to that jurisdiction.

promontory fort. A fort located on a coastal headland or mountain spur, the landward approach to which is secured by a **fosse** and bank.

prône. (Fr., *prôner*, to address a congregation) A book of prepared sermons.

protection leasing. A practice in Ulster in the eighteenth century whereby the head landlord guaranteed the leases held by undertenants from a **middleman** were the middleman's lease to be sold on. The undertenants were also relieved of any liability for arrears owed by the middleman.

Protectorate. The title of the government of the British Isles and Ireland for the period 1653–59 when the successive heads of state, Oliver Cromwell (1653–58) and his son Richard (1658–9), were styled Lord Protector of the Commonwealth.

prothonotary. 1: A chief clerk in the courts 2: An official in **common pleas** who reported to the court on matters referred to him by it. He taxed costs, informed the court of its practice and of the state of causes in it, received moneys paid into the court and disbursed them. In medieval times he entered pleas on the rolls, work later done by the master.

province. *See* composition, *cúige*, custody, presidency, provincial councils.

provincial. The superior of all the houses of a religious community within a given province or district.

provincial councils. Provincial councils were established in Munster and Connacht in the late 1560s in an attempt to establish crown authority and extend common law jurisdiction. Headed by a president, the provincial councils included bishops, leading magnates and some lawyers. The president had a small military force and could impose martial law. Although charged with the task of drawing the local magnates closer to the crown and away from Gaelic customs and exactions, local conditions were not amenable to such a programme. Instead the presidents managed to undermine some lords, alienated others and rebellions broke out in the south and west. The expense of restoring order proved too great for Elizabeth and the councils were allowed to lapse. From 1575 Lord Deputy Sidney embarked on a new conciliar programme by which the original goal of extending common law and crown authority to all parts would be achieved by **composition**.

provost. Prison-keeper, **prepositus**, mayor, one in charge, director.

provost-marshall. Officer in charge of the provost guard or military police.

psalter. A book of psalms. The earliest surviving Irish manuscript is the *Cathach Psalter* which dates from c. 560 AD and was written at Iona. It comprises 58 leaves and contains psalms 31 to 106. It is held by the **Royal Irish Academy**.

Public Instruction, Commissioners of (1835). Just four years after a national system of primary education was introduced in Ireland commissioners of public instruction were appointed to investigate 'the state of religious and other instruction and the means of affording the same'. They produced two reports. The first comprises a statistical inquiry into educational provision and the second contains details of existing schools in each benefice, their funding, school attendance and form of instruction. The impact of the introduction of national school system in 1831 on local educational provision can be charted by comparing parish entries in the commissioners' reports with those contained in the second report of the Irish Education Inquiry (1824–7). *See* Education Inquiry (1824–27). (Public Instruction.)

public records. *See* National Archives.

puisne judge. (Pronounced 'puny') A lesser-ranking judge below the lord chancellor, lord chief justice, master of the rolls and the lord chief justice of common pleas.

pur autre vie. An estate held for the life of another person.

purchase of current rents. The strength of the market in landed property can be gauged by calculating the multiples of annual yearly rent required to effect purchase. During the strong market conditions of the 1830s land sold for an average of 25 years purchase of current rents, i.e., the annual rent multiplied by 25. The post-famine collapse in the market value of land is reflected in the fact that land sold for as little as ten to 15 years purchase of annual rents in the 1850s.

Purchase of Land (Ireland) Act (1885). Sponsored by Lord Ashbourne, the Irish lord chancellor, this was the first major statutory provision for land purchase. Under this legislation (48 & 49 Vict., c. 73), the **Irish Land Commission** received £5 million for the purchase of land by agreement. When an agreement to sell was reached the commission advanced the entire purchase price to the tenant, the loan to be repaid over 49 years by an annuity of 4%. The act proved unpopular with landlords because a deposit of one-fifth of the purchase price was retained by the commission until the annuities repaid by the tenant were equivalent to that sum. Only then was the deposit disbursed to the vendor. This defect was not remedied until the **Wyndham Act** was enacted in 1903.

Purchase of Land (Ireland) Act (1891). The Purchase of Land (Ireland) Act (1891) and the Land Law (Ireland) Act (1896) are known as the 'Balfour Acts' because they were introduced successively by the Balfour brothers, Arthur and Gerald, when each held the office of **chief secretary**. The acts proposed the introduction of a new system for underwriting the purchase of holdings by tenants. Under the first act (54 & 55 Vict., c. 48) the landlord was paid from a guaranteed land stock equal in value to the purchase price but repayment of the annuities was to be ensured by varying the amount of interest charged and by providing for additional insurance payments. £33 million was voted to finance the scheme but it proved unpopular with both landlords and tenants, the former because the value of the stock fluctuated and the latter because they found it difficult to calculate precisely their annual commitments. The 1896 amending act (59 & 60 Vict., c. 47) ameliorated these difficulties by increasing the repayment period to 73 years and by reducing the amount of the annuity at the end of each decade of the first 30 years repayment. Despite this, only £13 million was advanced from the fund and applications declined in 1898. Over 46,000 tenants purchased their holdings under the acts, almost double the number who had purchased under the land acts of 1885, 1887 and 1888. A notable feature of the Purchase of Land Act of 1891 was the establishment of the **Congested Districts Board** with the remit to relieve poverty in the west and south of the country. *See* Purchase of Land (Ireland) Act, 1885 and Land Law (Ireland) Act, 1887. (Pomfret, *The struggle*, pp. 263–271.)

puritanism. A Calvinistic Protestant reform movement which flourished in England in the late sixteenth and seventeenth centuries. Puritans were so called because they wished to purge the Church of England of residual Catholic ritual, vestments and iconography. They believed in predestination, that they were God's elect and they sought to extend their vision and morality to embrace the nation. Their attempts to re-shape the Established church (and measures taken by Archbishop Laud to impose conformity) contributed to the outbreak of civil war in England in 1642 and the Puritan Revolution. Presbyterians, a puritan sect, were initially welcomed in Ireland by the Calvinist-leaning Church of Ireland and Presbyterian ministers were given church livings. In the 1630s they came under severe pressure from Wentworth, the lord deputy, who was intent on securing uniformity under the Established church and again after the Restoration when their refusal to give public assent to the revised *Book of Common Prayer* led to their expulsion. Other puritan sects also established themselves in Ireland to form a heterogeneous group known as nonconformists. *See* Uniformity.

purlieu. A deforested tract on the margin of a royal forest.

purlins. Horizontal beams that run the length of a roof. They are supported by the main rafters (trusses) or transverse walls and they, in turn, support the ordinary rafters.

purparty. 1: Land held in purparty is land held jointly with someone else 2: A share of an inheritance.

purpresture, pourpresture. An illegal encroachment upon or enclosure of public or private property.

pursuivant. A junior **herald** and royal messenger. In Ireland there were four pursuivants: Athlone and St Patrick numbers 1, 2 and 3.

purveyance. The crown right to requisition goods at a price below the market rate whether the seller was in agreement or not. Originally the right to pre-empt food and procure transportation, it was extended to Ireland to provision the chief governor's retinue.

putlock hole (puthole, putlog hole). A hole intentionally left in the face of a wall under construction to permit the insertion of a small timber (putlock) as a support for scaffolding and not subsequently filled when the structure was completed.

Pynnar's Survey. In 1619 Nicholas Pynnar, a **servitor** and **undertaker** in Ulster, was directed to survey and make a return of the progress of the Ulster plantation and the performance of the undertakers, servitors and natives in fulfilling their responsibilities under the scheme. An unfavourable report in 1615 by Sir Josias Bodley and a second (in 1616) alerted the planters to the possibility of forfeiture should they fail in their plantation duties and some proceeded to complete unfinished building work and introduce more British settlers. Pynnar acknowledged that progress had been made but considerably less than had been expected given the liberal terms the settlers had received. He found that there remained a great want of buildings and that all but the Scots had refrained from ploughing, the English fearing a native uprising and the Irish being uncertain of their stay on the land. Not only had the natives not been removed from those areas owned by English and Scottish settlers but the City of London had found it more profitable to rent to the Irish than to introduce British tenants. These violations of the plantation agreement enabled Charles II to proceed to confiscate their holdings, a consequence forestalled by the surrender of their letters **patent** and acceptance of others subject to a doubling of the original rents and a fine of thirty pounds per 1,000 acres. See Irish Society. (Hill, An historical account, pp. 445–590.)

Q

quadrans. (L.) A farthing.

Quakers. The Quakers, or Religious Society of Friends, were non-conformists who appeared in Ireland in the mid-seventeenth century. They repudiate the authority of scripture, emphasising instead the 'inward light' or 'inner voice of God speaking to the soul'. They do not outwardly observe the sacraments as other Christian churches because for them baptism and the eucharist are spiritual affairs. Their outspoken rejection of formal church services, the sacraments, church buildings and an ordained ministry together with their opposition to oath-taking, bearing arms and **tithe** elicited repressive measures from both the Cromwellian and Stuart administrations. By the close of the century, however, that position had changed and they were treated with greater leniency. In 1715 Quaker principles were considered when the militia bill was passed and practical toleration was extended to them under the 1719 **Toleration Act**. They practised their faith relatively freely and from 1723 were allowed to participate in the courts without taking oaths. Their reluctance to take oaths, however, ensured that they remained barred from government posts. Favourable treatment was afforded the numerically small but wealthy Quakers as long as they did not impinge upon the privileges of the Established church. Their principled opposition to tithe was a major source of conflict during the eighteenth century and they suffered some financial and property losses but very few were jailed. Quakers are highly regarded in Ireland for their charitable work, notably their energetic philanthropy during the Great Famine. Quaker meeting-houses, where quarterly and monthly meetings are held, are simple structures. The monthly meeting is the principal gathering of Quakers and deals with administrative matters such as property and finance. Membership and individual concerns are dealt with, together with matters referred from the annual meetings. Quakers have kept excellent records from the seventeenth century, including births, marriages and burials. (Goodbody, *Guide*; Grubb, *Quakers*; Wigham, *The Irish Quakers*.)

quamdiu se bene gesserint. (L., during good behaviour) Under their patent of appointment Irish judges held office during the king's pleasure (*durante beneplacito nostro*). In England this form of tenure was fiercely opposed by the English parliamentary opposition in the seventeenth century because it was associated with the royal prerogative and because the Stuarts made liberal use of the powers of summary dismissal to pack the bench with their supporters. In 1701 it was enacted that a judge's commission should continue in force *quamdiu se bene gesserint* (during good behaviour) and he could only be removed by the king if an address was presented to him by both houses of parliament. The position in Ireland, however, remained unchanged until 1782 when agitation by the **'patriot' party** yielded the enactment (21 & 22 Geo. III, c. 50) that secured the independence of Irish judges and placed them on an equal footing with their British counterparts.

***quare impedit,* suit of.** A form of writ issued in cases of dispute regarding the presentation to an ecclesiastical benefice. *Quare impedit* required the defendant to state why he hindered the plaintiff from presenting to the benefice.

quarter (quarterland). 1: A territorial unit with field boundary. 2: A spatial unit of measurement comprising 90–480 acres in Donegal, 120 acres in Connaught (4 cartrons = 1 quarter), 360 acres in Munster (3 **ploughlands** = 1 quarter), 240 acres in Longford, Tyrone Fermanagh and Coleraine and 200–400 acres in the Pale. Four quarters were equivalent to a **ballybetagh**. 3: In terms of volume, a quarter was equivalent to eight bushels.

'**quarter acre clause'**. Introduced during the Famine with the passing of the Poor Law Amendment Act of 1847 (10 & 11 Vict., c. 31, sections 4–18), the penal quarter acre clause or 'Gregory Clause' declared occupiers of more than a quarter of a statute acre ineligible for relief. Thus starving tenants of small-holdings were faced with an invidious choice. They could surrender their sole means of subsistence in return for relief, retain their holding and starve or they could emigrate. Sponsored by William Gregory, a Galway landlord and Co. Dublin MP, the clause was approved by landlords who felt that it militated against unnecessary claims on poor relief (which they would have been required to fund through the **poor rate**). Moreover, landlords were absolved from paying the full poor rate where circumstances forced a destitute family to surrender a holding valued at under £4. Some used the tenants' inability to pay rents to launch a campaign of eviction, thereby sparing themselves the burden of poor rates which lay heaviest on areas where there was a high proportion of holdings valued at under £4. Coupled with a sharp rise in evictions, the quarter acre clause advanced the amalgamation of small-holdings in many areas at the cost of great human misery. *See* outdoor relief, relieving officer. (Kinealy, *This great calamity*, pp. 216–227.)

quarterage. The quarterly payments of guild members to their guilds. The payment of quarterage plus an admission fee known as 'intrusion money' was the means by which Catholics (and other non-freemen), excluded from civic life by the imposition of oaths, were permitted to exercise their trades or crafts in their native cities in the late seventeenth and eighteenth centuries. Quarterage entitled them to an associate membership of the guilds known as the quarter-brother or quarterer. Quarterers had no right to participate in guild elections and were ineligible for office. As quarter-brothers far outnumbered the numbers of brothers, their contributions played an important role in keeping the guilds solvent. Catholics resented the demand for quarterage and challenged the legality of its imposition. From the middle of the eighteenth century they began to default and attempts to enforce payment through the courts were rebuffed by the justices. It now appeared that the privileges and rights claimed by the guilds and corporations of Ireland were contrary to the law. The guilds changed tack and between 1767 and 1775 tried repeatedly and unsuccessfully to have their demands enshrined in legislation. The active opposition of the **Catholic Committee** on behalf of Catholic tradesmen proved too strong for a system that was already in decline throughout Europe and, with the exception of Dublin, had collapsed in Ireland by 1800. (Wall, 'The Catholics', pp. 61–84.)

quarter days. The days on which tenancies began and ended. The four quarter days, **Lady Day** (25 March), Midsummer Day (24 June), Michaelmas Day (29 September) and Christmas Day (25 December), were the days on which rent fell due, although leases usually stipulated 25 March and 29 September for such payments (1 March and 1 September by the nineteenth century). In Gaelic Ireland, the traditional quarter days were Lughnasa (1 August), Samhain (1 November), Imbolg or St Brigid's Day (1 February) and Bealtaine (1 May).

quarter-sessions. The quarterly county court presided over by the **justice of the peace**. It originated in an instruction to the justices of the peace in a county to meet in session four times yearly. Trial was conducted in the same manner as the **assize courts**. The accused was presented by the **grand jury** and tried by the **petty jury**. Serious crimes were usually referred from the quarter-sessions to the judges in the assize courts.

Queen's Colleges. In 1845 Robert Peel proposed for Ireland a state funded non-denominational system of third-level education to be known as the Queen's Colleges, a measure designed to detach moderates, especially Catholic clergymen, from Daniel O'Connell and weaken the push for repeal of the union. Colleges free of religious tests and departments of theology would be established in Belfast, Cork and Galway, staffed by crown-appointed professors. Catholic bishops were divided on the issue. Some favoured acceptance provided they were granted a degree of control at board level, the appointment of Catholic professors to certain departments and public funding for the teaching of Catholic theology. Others rejected the colleges outright. In the end the issue was decided in Rome where papal **rescripts** forbade Catholic clergy to teach or take office in the colleges and discouraged the attendance of Catholic students. Opposition to the Queen's Colleges was re-stated at the **Synod of Thurles** in 1850 and, in a countermove, the Catholic University of Ireland was established in 1854. The scheme went ahead, nevertheless, under the umbrella of the Queen's University of Ireland (from 1879 the Royal University) but it was not a success. Neither, however, was the Catholic University and the debate on how to create a university system to meet the conflicting demands of the different denominations without, from the administration's point of view, public endowment of denominational university-level education continued for decades. The 1908 universities bill (8 Edw. VII, c. 38) represented a compromise between church and state that was broadly acceptable to all. Two new universities were created, the National University of Ireland (which consisted of three colleges at Cork, Galway and the reconstituted Catholic University – now known as University College Dublin) and the Queen's University, Belfast, both of which were to be publicly funded and non-denominational. What made the previously unacceptable acceptable, apart from legal guarantees against proselytism, was the recognition by the churches that the *de jure* non-denominational status of their institutions counted for little when compared with the *de facto* denominational profile of the respective staffs and students. The National University of Ireland, together with the associated **Maynooth College**, became effectively a Catholic university. Queen's became Protestant (largely Presbyterian). (Coolahan, *Irish education*, pp. 105–130; Kerr, '*A nation of beggars*'?, pp. 282–309.)

querela. A complaint, action, suit, accusation or charge.

querent. Plaintiff, complainant.

quern. A bullaun (Ir., *bollán*) or hollowed stone which, with the aid of a stone pestle, was used for grinding corn. A saddle quern was a roughly rectangular piece of stone with a curved upper surface along which another stone or rider was rubbed back and forth over the grain.

questing. The right to gather alms at the altar after mass. Oliver Plunkett disapproved of the practice, conducted by the Dominicans and Franciscans, because he felt it discouraged attendance at mass.

questman. A sidesman or church-warden's assistant.

Quia Emptores (1290). This statute (18 Edw. I, cc 1–3) was an attempt to secure the interests of the crown and greater feudal lords in their feudal entitlements. Excessive sub-infeudation made it difficult to track feudal services and so *Quia emptores* forbade sub-infeudation by chief tenants and alienation to mortmain but permitted free tenants to alienate their land by substitution without the lord's consent provided the services owed to the lord were divided proportionally among the substitutes.

quick. Trees, especially hawthorn, set to form a hedge, so called because the hedge was composed of living or quick-growing trees.

quinzaine. The fourteenth day after a feast.

quitclaim. A deed renouncing all claims to a property.

quit-rent. 1: A rent payable to the crown on forfeited land which had been distributed under the Restoration land settlement acts of 1662 and 1665. In Munster it was levied at a rate of $2^3/_4d$. per acre, in Ulster $2d$., in Connacht,$1^1/_2d$. and in Leinster $3d$. 2: When labour services were commuted to money payments and combined with rent the total money payment owed became known as quit-rent. It was called quit-rent because the tenant was now quit of his obligations to service.

quit-rent office. The agency established after the Restoration to collect quit-rents that were payable by the new owners of all land forfeited after the Confederate War of 1641–52. The quit-rent office also assumed responsibility for little parcels of forfeited land (the 'plus acres') which remained in the king's hands after the **adventurers** and soldiers had received their grants as well as those forfeited lands which had not been distributed by the time of the Restoration in 1660.

quoad ad hoc. (L.) A legal term used to state what the law was as to a matter. It was used in the **court of claims** established under the **Act of Settlement** (1662) to state what the law was with regard to a petitioner's claim.

quiet, to. An instruction to the sheriff to put a person in possession of an estate and protect him from disturbance.

quoin. The external corner of a building. Also the interlocking stones which form the corner.

quo minus, **writ of**. (L., by which the less) 1: A legal device invented by the **exchequer** to attract cases of debt between individuals which properly belonged in **common pleas**. The fiction was based on the claim that default in repaying a debt rendered the creditor *less able* to satisfy the debts he owed to the crown, debts which the crown's revenue court, the exchequer, should have cognisance of 2: A writ to restrain a person from committing waste in a wood having granted **houbote** and **haybote** to another so that the grantee was *less able* to exercise his right.

quo warranto, **writ of**. A writ issued on behalf of the crown to inquire by what right a person or corporate body claimed or usurped a privilege, office or liberty and so determine the issue. It was so named because the defendant was required to show *quo warranto usurpavit* (by what right or authority he lays claim to the matter in dispute). In the 1630s Thomas Wentworth, the lord deputy, used *quo warranto* proceedings to sequester town charters in Ireland, thereby extinguishing 16 **Old English** seats in the Irish **parliament** amongst other tactics to ensure government control of the house of commons. *Quo warranto* proceedings were also used in the late 1680s by Richard Talbot, earl of Tyrconnell, ostensibly to compel corporations to demonstrate that they had exercised their powers according to their charters. In reality he sought to remove the charters and re-model them to accommodate Catholics. In later times matters of this nature were effected by an **information** in the nature of a *quo warranto* filed by the **attorney-general**.

R

rack. An instrument of torture on which an unforthcoming victim was stretched until his limbs were dislocated.

rackrent. To subject to an excessively high rent.

rampant. In heraldry, a creature in profile – usually a lion – standing upright with paws in the air.

rapparee. A tory or bandit. The term derives from the Irish *rapaire*, a half-pike, which some of them bore.

raskins. (Ir., *rusg*, bark) A wooden vessel made by scooping out a hollow in a log to leave an edge of about two inches wide including the bark. It was used as a container for butter and was roughly equivalent to a **firkin**. *See* meather.

rate-in-aid. A temporary tax of sixpence in the pound levied on all rateable property in Ireland to provide additional relief to the most distressed **poor law unions**. It was introduced in 1849 (12 & 13 Vict., c. 24) amidst great controversy because it made relief of distress a charge on the entire country rather than a local one. Thus the more prosperous unions of the north and east were required to subsidise the 22 poorest unions in the west and south. Although Leinster and Munster were taxed more heavily for rate-in-aid, opposition to the proposal was particularly virulent amongst Ulster MPs who saw it as a transfer of taxes from the industrious north to feckless Connacht. Others, including Edward Twistleton, the senior poor law commissioner, objected to the tax on constitutional grounds. As Twistleton saw it, if the Act of Union created a true union then responsibility for distress properly lay with the kingdom as a whole and particularly so in the case of localities that did not have the fiscal capacity to relieve themselves. A second rate-in-aid of two pence in the pound was introduced in 1850. (Kinealy, *This great calamity*, pp. 254–64, 278–9.)

rath (ringfort). A circular or near-circular enclosure protected by a clay bank (*vallum*) and outside trench (*fosse*) or a series of banks and trenches. Within the rath there was a raised mound upon which the farmstead of a lord or wealthy individual stood. Nearly 40,000 have been identified in Ireland and the term figures prominently in placenames. *Raths* are classified as univallate, bivallate or trivallate according to the number of banks which form the enclosure. In areas where stone was plentiful the banks were constructed of stone and the fort was called a *caiseal* or *cathair*. (Stout, *The Irish ringfort*.)

Rathbreasail, Synod of. *See* diocese.

reacaire. (Ir.) A reciter or singer of poems often accompanied by a harper.

Real Property Act (1845). The Real Property Act (8 & 9 Vict., c. 119) simplified the complex process of conveyancing by establishing the ordinary deed of grant as the standard mode of conveyance. It gave to a simple deed of grant the same efficacy in relation to the transfer of all corporeal **hereditaments** and tenements as the conveyance that combined the **bargain and sale** and the **lease and release**.

Recess Committee. *See* Agriculture and Technical Instruction, Department of.

recognisance. 1: A surety entered into before a court or magistrate to refrain from or to carry out a particular act 2: The sum pledged as guarantee.

record. A document on which the proceedings of a court of record were entered including common pleas, pleas of land and criminal proceedings. A court of record was a court entitled to hear pleas as distinct from an inferior court such as a manorial court.

recorder. A magistrate who exercised criminal and civil jurisdiction in a city or borough. The recorder was the sole judge at the **quarter-sessions** held in Dublin, Cork, Belfast, Derry, Cork, Galway and Carrickfergus. Originally he was a person with legal experience appointed by the aldermen and mayor to 'record' the proceedings of the borough courts and to keep in mind the proceedings and the customs of the city or town, his word being authoritative on these matters.

recovery. Alienation by tenants-in-tail was forbidden by the statute *De Donis Conditionalibus* (13 Edw. I, c. 1, 1285) but the courts, believing this to be an unreasonable restriction on landowners, permitted the collusive fiction of recovery by which a tenant-in-tail in possession could bar the **entail** and dispose of his property. In practice the vendor allowed the intending purchaser to bring an action against him for the property. Instead of defending his title the vendor called upon a collaborator (a 'man of straw') who was supposed to have sold him the land previously with good title. Collaborator and intending purchaser then withdrew from the court to parley after which the purchaser returned alone having 'convinced' the collaborator that he had never had title to the land. The court called upon the collaborator three times to return to defend his title but he never did and so judgement was made in favour of the purchaser. As the tenant-in-tail was now deemed never to have been legally possessed of an estate the entail was effectively barred. The 1834 Fines and Recoveries Act (4 & 5 Will. IV, c. 92) removed the need for such chicanery by providing that a tenant-in-tail could bar an entail by the execution of a disentailing assurance, in effect by executing a conveyance using words that a **fee simple** (freehold) owner would have to use to pass the fee simple. Prior to *De Donis* monastic institutions had employed the recovery to evade the provisions of the statute of **mortmain** which outlawed alienations to corporations or monastic institutions. Rather than 'purchase' or receive a grant of land, the institutions 'recovered' land they claimed was theirs as of old title. *See* fine. (Megarry, A *manual*, pp. 57–61: Wylie, *Irish land law*, pp. 219–224.)

recto. Abbreviated in footnotes as *r*, the side of a document which is to be read first. It is the right-hand or front page. The side to be read second is *verso* (*v*). *See* folio.

rector. A rector is the Church of Ireland equivalent of the Catholic parish priest, distinguished from the vicar in that the rector was in full possession of the parish tithe. Where the incumbent received only part of the tithe – if a portion belonged to someone else – he was a vicar. The distinction emerged after the Reformation in the sixteenth century when monastic lands and the accompanying tithe were alienated to lay people and religious institutions such as cathedrals. Where tithe was wholly paid to someone other than himself, the resident minister was known as a **perpetual curate**. *See* appropriate, impropriate.

recusant. In the sixteenth and seventeenth centuries a person, usually a Catholic, who refused to attend Anglican services and denied the ecclesiastical supremacy of the crown. Recusants were liable to fines of 12 pence for every offence committed and office-holders in corporations who refused to take the oath of supremacy were heavily fined and forbidden to hold office. In the early seventeenth century, grand jurors who refused to present recusants were hauled before the court of **castle chamber**, fined and imprisoned. The imposition of recusancy fines was not consistently enforced. During international crises they were often over-looked.

redemption. In a deed the phrase 'subject to redemption' indicates that the transaction is a mortgage.

redshank. A Scottish mercenary footsoldier serving in Ireland.

re-entry. A legal term for eviction and the act of repossession.

reeve. Senior manorial official under the bailiff. *See* **sheriff** (shire-reeve).

refection. Refers to a number of exactions or impositions on local populations obliging them to provide refreshment and lodgings. In its most severe and prolonged form – **coyne and livery** – the inhabitants had to maintain soldiers quartered on the area by the chief lord, together with horses and horseboys. Coshering, another form of refection, involved the provision of refreshment to the chief lord and his retinue as he progressed through his territory. To avoid being eaten out of house and home tenants often substituted cash payments for coshering. The least exacting form of refection was that provided by an **erenagh** to the diocesan bishop on his visitation which usually lasted only a day and, at most, occurred on but four occasions a year.

Reformed Presbyterian church (Covenanters). The Reformed Presbyterian church originated in the seventeenth century with those Presbyterians who sought to adhere strictly to the National Covenant (1638) and the **Solemn League and Covenant** (1642) – hence the name Covenanters. Purists with regard to Presbyterian doctrine, it was not until the mid-eighteenth century that the first Reformed Presbytery was established in Ireland.

regardant. In heraldry, a creature in profile with its head looking backwards.

regency. 1: A period during which a kingdom is administered by a substitute owing to the incapacity or absence of the reigning monarch. In British history the term refers to the period 1810–20 when George III was ill and and the future George IV acted as prince regent 2: A classical style of architecture (c. 1800–30) which borrowed structural and ornamental features from ancient Greece and Rome. Its most noted proponent was the architect John Nash.

regency crisis. In 1789 George III became insane and the Irish parliament voted to request the Whig-associating Prince of Wales to act immediately as regent of Ireland. The Tory government of William Pitt and the Irish administration wanted the regency to be effected by an act of parliament which would have enabled them to limit the regent's powers and delay the appointment. The Irish parliament was emphasising its equality with and independence from the imperial parliament but it was also gambling (unsuccessfully, as it transpired) that the next government would be composed of Whigs. The issue descended into farce when the king recovered his sanity just as the Irish delegation arrived in London to address the Prince of Wales. The independent action of the Irish parliament during the regency crisis raised government concerns about the wisdom of legislative independence and prompted FitzGibbon (the attorney-general) to threaten the Irish house of commons with union should it fail to follow Britain in all regulations of imperial policy. Despite such threats, a strong and coherent opposition, the 'Irish Whigs', emerged to uphold the independence of the Irish parliament. *See* whig clubs.

regicide. A king-killer.

register, episcopal. Episcopal registers are compilations of diocesan documents including papal bulls, royal grants, letters, clerical appointments, resignations and disciplinings, leases and **advowsons**. They may also include stray but interesting material. The fourteenth-century *Red Book of Ossory*, for example, includes a treatise on brandy and the text of 60 songs. *See Alen's Register, Register of Armagh, Crede mihi, Reportorium Viride*. (Lawlor, 'Calendar', pp. 159–208; *Idem*, 'A calendar of the Liber Niger', pp. 1–93; McCaffrey, *The black book*.)

regium donum. Literally, the king's gift or bounty, the *regium donum* was an annual grant of £600 to **Presbyterian** ministers inaugurated by Charles II in 1672. Payments were halted under James II but re-introduced at an increased rate of £1,200 by William III in gratitude for Presbyterian support for the Williamite cause in Ireland. Presbyterian ministers also expected him to legislate for greater toleration but the antipathy of the **Church of Ireland** towards dissenters ensured the rejection of his 1695 toleration bill. The *regium donum* was withdrawn by the **Tory** government in 1710 to prevent the further expansion of Presbyterianism but was restored in 1718 by a **Whig** administration and increased to £2,000. In 1802 the government, seeking to secure the loyalty of Presbyterian ministers – some of whom had been implicated in the 1798 rebellion – increased the grant considerably and paid it directly to the ministers in a graduated scale ranging from £50 to £100 conditional upon continued loyalty. State subvention of Presbyterianism ceased in 1869 when the Church of Ireland was disestablished. In compensation for the loss of the *regium donum*, the sum of £750,000 was given to the Presbyterian Synod of Ulster to be divided equally among its ministers. (Beckett, *Protestant*, pp. 106–115; Pike, 'The origin', pp. 225–269.)

regnal year. Until the seventeenth century deeds were dated by the current year of a monarch's reign which dated from the day, month and year of accession. Thus the regnal year 3 Elizabeth I occurred between 17 November 1560 and 16 November 1561. Acts of parliament were also dated by the regnal year.

William I	14 Oct. 1066 – 9 Sept. 1087
William II	26 Sept. 1087 – 2 Aug. 1100
Henry I	5 Aug. 1100 – 1 Dec. 1135
Stephen	26 Dec. 1135 – 25 Oct. 1154
Henry II	19 Dec. 1154 – 6 July 1189
Richard I	3 Sept. 1189 – 6 April 1199
John	27 May 1199 – 19 Oct. 1216
Henry III	28 Oct. 1216 – 16 Nov. 1272
Edward I	20 Nov. 1272 – 7 July 1307
Edward II	8 July 1307– 20 Jan. 1327
Edward III	25 Jan. 1327 – 21 June 1377
Richard II	22 June 1377 – 29 Sept. 1399
Henry IV	30 Sept. 1399 – 20 March 1413
Henry V	21 March 1413 – 31 Aug. 1422
Henry VI	1 Sept. 1422 – 4 March 1461
	and 9 Oct. 1470 – 14 April 1471
Edward IV	4 March 1461 – 9 April 1483
Edward V	9 April 1483 – 25 June 1483
Richard III	26 June 1483 – 22 Aug. 1485
Henry VII	22 Aug. 1485 – 21 April 1509
Henry VIII	22 April 1509 – 28 Jan. 1547
Edward VI	28 Jan. 1547 – 6 July 1553
Mary	6 July 1553 – 24 July 1554

Philip & Mary	25 July 1554 – 17 Nov. 1558
Elizabeth I	17 Nov. 1558 – 24 March 1603
James I	24 March 1603 – 27 March 1625
Charles I	27 March 1625 – 30 Jan. 1649
Interregnum	30 Jan. 1649 – 29 May 1660
Charles II	29 May 1660 – 6 February 1685
	(Reckoned from 30 Jan. 1649)
James II	6 Feb. 1685 – 11 Dec. 1688
Interregnum	12 Dec. 1688 – 12 Feb. 1689
William & Mary	13 Feb. 1689 – 27 Dec. 1694
William III	28 Dec. 1694 – 8 Mar. 1702
Anne	8 March 1702 – 1 August 1714
George I	1 Aug. 1714 – 11 June 1727
George II	11 June 1727 – 25 Oct. 1760
George III	25 Oct. 1760 – 29 Jan. 1820
George IV	29 Jan. 1820 – 26 June 1830
William IV	26 June 1830 – 20 June 1837
Victoria	20 June 1837 – 22 Jan. 1901
Edward VII	22 Jan. 1901 – 6 May 1910
George V	6 May 1910 – 20 Jan. 1936
Edward VIII	20 Jan. 1936 – 11 Dec. 1936
George VI	11 Dec. 1936 – 6 Feb. 1952
Elizabeth II	6 Feb. 1952 –

regrate. To forestall or abbroach. The offence of acquiring or diverting victuals and goods bound for market to raise prices. It was punishable by imprisonment and loss of the goods.

regular, canons. Members of religious orders living in community usually under **Augustinian** rule as opposed to the **secular** or parish priests.

relief. A **feudal incident** (the others were **wardship**, **escheat** and **marriage**) which required the heir of a deceased chief tenant to make a money payment or fine (usually equivalent to one year's profits of the land) to the crown to take possession of his estate. Relief was paid by an heir of full age. On a manorial estate relief paid by a tenant to the lord was known as an **entry fine**.

relief acts. A series of legislative acts that successively reduced the penal restrictions imposed on Catholics and **dissenters** in the late seventeenth and early eighteenth centuries. Concessions began in 1750 when Catholics were permitted to enter the lower grades of the army. The 'Bogland act' of 1771–2 (11 & 12 Geo. III, c. 21) enabled them to take leases for 61 years of not more than 50 acres of unprofitable land and to be free of taxes on the same for seven years. The relief act of 1778 (17 & 18 Geo. III, c. 40), introduced in the Irish parliament by Luke Gardiner, permitted Catholics to take land at leases of 999 years if they took the oath of allegiance but they could not purchase land in freehold. The 1704 **gavelkind** act (2 Anne, c. 7) was repealed and Catholics could now inherit in the same manner as any other citizen. In 1780 the **Test Act** (19 & 20 Geo. III, c. 6) was repealed, making dissenters eligible for office. Gardiner's second relief act (21 & 22 Geo. III, c. 24, 1782) allowed Catholics who swore the oath of allegiance to purchase, hold and bequeath freeholds and leases on the same terms as Protestants. The performance of priestly duties by Catholic secular clergymen and any regulars then resident in the country was legalised provided such duties were not exercised within a church with a steeple or bell. The assumption of any ecclesiastical title or rank remained forbidden. Catholics could now own a horse valued in excess of £5 and the power vested in the **grand jury** to levy Catholics for the depradations of privateers was revoked. Catholics could open and keep schools if licensed by the local Anglican bishop. In the same year Presbyterian marriages conducted by Presbyterian ministers were legalised (21 & 22 Geo. III, c. 26). Sir Hercules Langrishe's 1792 act (32 Geo. III, c. 21) permitted Catholics to practise law, though they could not become members of the inner bar. Catholic schoolmasters were no longer required to obtain a licence and restrictions were lifted on foreign education, the number of apprentices a Catholic might keep and inter-marriage. Chief Secretary Hobart's 1793 act (33 Geo. III, c. 21) admitted Catholics to a limited franchise, restored their right to vote in parliamentary elections, to become members of municipal corporations and seek civil and military office. The offices of **lord lieutenant, chief secretary**, chancellor of the exchequer, **attorney-general**, solicitor-general, together with membership of the **privy council** remained closed to them, however, and they could not become generals, judges or king's counsels, governors, sheriffs or sub-sheriffs or members of parliament. They could serve in the ranks and hold commissions but only in Ireland and remained excluded from positions in the staff. The remaining disabilities – the right to sit in parliament, to hold senior government and legal offices and military rank above colonel – were largely though not completely removed in 1829 when the relief act which emancipated Catholics was passed.

Relief Commission. A temporary commission established in November 1845 by Robert Peel to advise the government and treasury on distress, to manage food depots nationwide and to oversee and grant-aid the work of local relief committees. It was composed of senior members of the administration including the under-secretary, Edward Lucas, Sir James Dombrain (Inspector General of the coastguard), Edward Twistleton (poor law commissioner), Sir Randolph Routh (Commissariat Department of the army), John Pitt Kennedy (former secretary to the **Devon Commission**), Harry Jones of the **Board of Works** and the scientist, Sir Robert Kane. Lucas' criticism of government policies led to his replacement as chairman by Routh in 1846. The commission was stood down in August 1846 and a second commission was formed in February 1847 under Sir John Burgoyne tasked with supervising the implementation of the Temporary Relief Act (the 'soup kitchen act'), a transitional measure introduced to facilitate the transfer of responsibility from central government to the individual poor law unions in autumn 1847. The records of the Relief Commission (1845–47) are held in the National Archives. (Kinealy, *This great calamity*.)

relief committee. The relief committee provided relief at local level during periods of crop failure and food shortages in the nineteenth century. The pattern began in 1816–17 with the establishment of a central relief committee to allocate funds to local committees during the harvest crisis of those years. It was reactivated in 1822 when the severely wet weather of the previous autumn precipitated the failure of the potato crop. That summer the committee disbursed £175,000 to local committees which distributed food for free or at reduced prices and supported local relief works, supplementing government-organised public works such as road and harbour construction. When blight struck in 1845 the **Relief Commission** was established to organise food depots and co-ordinate the work of temporary local relief committees, to purchase and re-sell at cost price the Indian corn imported by the government. Local committees, if they wished, could instigate small-scale public works to help the impoverished to earn money to purchase food and in extreme cases free food could be distributed. Membership of these voluntary committees usually comprised local gentry, clergymen, merchants and large farmers and they financed their purchases by charitable subscription and a matching grant from the government. By the summer of 1846 almost 700 local relief committees were distributing food to the distressed. These temporary initiatives proved successful in staving off widespread starvation and it was intended to stand down the Relief Commission and the local relief committees from August 1846. The re-emergence of a general blight that month and the failure of the public works scheme to meet the challenge presented by widespread distress led to the establishment in early 1847, under the Temporary Relief of Distressed Persons in Ireland Act (10 & 11 Vict., c. 7), of a new relief commission and the reactivation of local committees to provide direct relief in the form of cooked food or soup in soup kitchens. By July over three million people were being fed daily. In August 1847, however, these temporary measures were ended and the administration of relief was transferred to the **poor law** system in an attempt to make relief a burden on local rather than British coffers.

relieving officer. The Poor Law Amendment Act (10 Vict., c. 31, 1847) which permitted **poor law unions** to give **outdoor relief** under certain conditions, provided for the appointment of relieving officers who were to compile lists of applicants for relief for the poor law guardians. Relieving officers were also empowered to dispense immediate provisional relief in cases of extreme urgency. They frequently found themselves in disputes over relief entitlement arising out of the '**quarter acre clause**' in the same act which forbade the granting of relief to anyone who occupied more than a quarter of an acre of land. Such persons were not considered to be destitute and were eligible for relief only if they surrendered their holding. It was the relieving officer's task to confirm the claims of applicants to occupy a quarter of an acre or less. The government intended this clause to be applied stringently but overlooked the fact that the wives and children of men holding more than one quarter of an acre, however destitute, were thereby deemed undeserving of relief. Legal advice compelled the government to re-consider and poor law guardians were instructed to provide provisional relief in cases of urgent necessity to the families but not the occupier so long as he retained his holding.

remainder. A conveyancing term which refers to the creation of a future interest in an estate, in particular to the possession of an estate by someone other than the grantor at some future time. If Smith conveys the fee simple (freehold) of Ballyduff to Murphy for life and the remainder to O'Brien, upon Murphy's demise the estate will devolve to O'Brien in fee simple. *See* reversion.

remembrancer. A government official whose function it was to collect debts due to the crown. The remembrancer kept a record of income and expenditure in the **memoranda rolls**.

remonstrance. A formal petition in which aggrieved bodies sought the favour of the monarch and the respite of their difficulties. In medieval times, as writs were very expensive, petitioning was the means by which an impoverished and aggrieved party set out the facts of his case and asked for relief of the king. If the petitioner was deemed to have a remedy at law, the petition was denied. After the Restoration in 1660 several remonstrances were submitted on behalf of the Catholics of Ireland. The most contentious, drafted by Richard Bellings in 1661, tried to resolve the difficulties existing between the crown and Catholics regarding the conflicting claims of king and pope to hold supreme temporal and spiritual authority. Ormond, the lord lieutenant, agreed to grant toleration to Catholics in return for an acceptance of the king's sovereignty in temporal affairs and a repudiation of the pope's authority to release subjects from their allegiance. A gathering of Catholic clergy in Dublin in 1666 could agree only to the first of these which Ormond rejected as insufficient. Later Rome expressed its opposition to the remonstrance and the issue died. *See*

Catholic Petition, petition.

Remonstrant Synod. From 1830 the Remonstrant Synod comprised those **Presbyterian** ministers, elders and congregations who had withdrawn from the **Synod of Ulster** rather than conform to the evangelical wing's requirement that all candidates for the ministry subscribe to the **Westminster Confession**, a practice that had ceased in the previous century.

Renewable Leasehold Conversion Act (1849). By this act (12 & 13 Vict., c. 105) leases for lives renewable forever (to all intents and purposes, perpetuities) were converted into **freehold**. *See* lease for lives renewable forever.

rental. A manorial or estate document which records the rents owed to the lord by his tenants. It usually contains the names of the tenants and their rents and is a much briefer manorial record than the **extent** or the **custumal**.

rent roll. Unlike the **rental** – which lists the payments owed by the tenants, – the rent roll is a record of what they actually paid. It contains the names of the tenants and their payments.

rentcharge. A charge placed on the rental income of an estate to repay a mortgage or to provide an **annuity** for a member of the landowner's family.

Renunciation, Act of (1793). *See* Declaratory Act, parliament, statute, Yelverton's Act,

replevin. A legal action dating back to the fourteenth century which was initiated to seek the return of property wrongfully taken and for compensation for loss. Replevin was particularly valuable in cases where a landlord seized property in excess of the value of unpaid rents. A successful action meant the return of the confiscated goods. Replevin is distinguished from **trover**, a similar common law action, in that it required the return of the property rather than the compensatory market value of the goods.

Reportorium Viride. Compiled in 1532–3 by John Alen, archbishop of Dublin (1528–34), *Reportorium Viride* comprises an annotated schedule of the churches of the dioceses of Dublin and Glendalough. It should be examined in conjunction with *Alen's Register*, a contemporaneous compilation of documents relating to the see. (White, 'The Reportorium', pp. 173–222.)

Representative Church Body. A corporation authorised by government to hold and manage the property of the Church of Ireland after it was disestablished in 1869. Although the church was largely disendowed the clergy were guaranteed a life income in the form of annuities payable by the state. To shed the administrative responsibility of paying the annuities Gladstone offered a bonus of 12% if the majority of the clergy in each diocese agreed to commute their annuities to a lump sum and vest it in a new paymaster, the Representative Church Body. A majority accepted the proposal and a sum in excess of £8 million was paid. Skilful management of the fund, augmented by a lay annual subscription known as the parochial assessment, secured the financial future of the church. *See* Irish Church Act, sustenation fund. (Acheson, *A history*, pp. 205–7.)

reprisals. Compensatory grants of land which were to be offered to Cromwellian settlers to persuade them to yield their holdings to Catholics restored by the **Acts of Settlement** and **Explanation**.

reredos. A decorative screen on the wall behind an altar.

rescript. A written reply from the pope to a petition or legal inquiry. This could be in the nature of an edict or decree.

reserved pleas. The four pleas which the crown reserved to itself when granting liberty or manorial status. These were arson, rape, **forestalling** and **treasure trove**.

resiant. Resident.

respit. In the legal sense, to postpone, defer or delay or to grant the same, particularly in relation to a sentence, duty or punishment.

Resumption, Act of (1700). The Act of Resumption (11 & 12 Will. III, c. 2) was introduced and carried by the opposition in the British house of commons to revoke William III's grants of forfeited estates in Ireland and to sell the resumed estates to defray army arrears and allied military expenses incurred during the Williamite war. William had granted a vast amount of forfeited land to his mistress, Elizabeth Villiers, to military commanders such as Ginkel and to favourites and advisers. Opposition fury at such profligacy during a period of strained national finances was the visible evidence of a deeper struggle for primacy between parliament and monarch, a struggle which resulted in humiliation and defeat for the king when, after a successful passage through parliament, the resumption act cancelled the royal grants and the forfeited estates were canted (auctioned) or sold at 13 times the annual rent to those who had purchased from the king's grantees. *See* Trustees Sale.

retting. The first stage in the process of preparing flax for linen-making. It involved weighting and submerging the flax stalks in water to rot the woody outer fibres and so prepare them for **scutching**.

revenue police. Public disorder and a significant loss of state revenue associated with the illicit distillation of alcohol prompted the establishment of the revenue police in 1800. Supported successively by the military, the peace preservation force and armed bands of enlisted men, this undisciplined, poorly-trained body made little headway until 1836 when a drastic overhaul was undertaken by its new chief, Col William Brereton. Brereton divided the country into four divisions and placed each under the supervision of a revenue lieutenant. To energise the force he sacked two-thirds of the men and re-cruited young, literate men of good character in their place. He ac-quired a steamer to harass distillers on the western islands. The force's success in curtailing the activities of poteen-makers led to its demise in 1858 when responsibility for illicit distillation was transferred to the Irish Constabulary. (Dawson, 'Illicit', pp. 283–94; Herlihy, *The Royal*, pp. 33–7; McDowell, *The Irish administration*, pp. 137–9; O'Sullivan, *The Irish constabularies*, pp. 18–19.)

reversion. 1: In conveyancing, refers to the granting of a lesser estate than that held by the grantor. The effect of such a grant is that at some future time the estate reverts to the grantor. If Smith holding the **fee simple** (freehold) to Ballyduff conveys a life estate to O'Brien, then upon O'Brien's demise the estate will revert to Smith 2: A grant of pro-perty by lease to commence after the termination of an earlier lease or under certain specified conditions 3: The return of property to the grantor or his heirs.

rerebrace. Arm greaves or armour for the upper arm.

revision. In 1878 the General Synod of the Church of Ireland authorised a revision of the *Book of Common Prayer* to eradicate anything that might be associated with Roman Catholic practice or theology. The names of all but a few specifically exempted saints were removed from the church calendar, a plain dress code was introduced for ministers at divine service, bowing to the altar was forbidden as was the ringing of bells during service, the use of incense, lighted lamps and candles, crosses on the communion table, the elevation of the chalice, proces-sions and the carrying of icons such as crosses, banners and pictures during service. (Daly, 'Church', pp. 29–37.)

rhymer. *See reacaire.*

Ribbonism. 1: A term used to describe the activities of a number of secret Catholic agrarian societies in the early nineteenth century 2: Rib-bonism, a continuation of the earlier **Defender** network, developed rapidly in Ulster (most notably in Armagh) in the early years of the eighteenth century. After 1815 the movement extended southwards and a new and rival centre emerged in Dublin. Exclusively Catholic, Ribbonism prospered in the northern half of the country where sectarian tensions were greatest but made little headway in Munster, possibly because of a continuing rift between labourers and farmers in the southern province. *See* Caravats and Shanavests. Ribbonmen, themselves, did not use the term Ribbonism; it was a term used by out-siders because ribbons were worn as a means of identification at a street-battle in Swatragh in 1810. The Ulster society was called The Society of Saint Patrick, that of Dublin, The Irish Sons of Freedom. Ribbon-ism was, essentially, a response to the rise of Orangeism and mimicked the masonic-style oaths, banners, sashes, parades and passwords of the

Orange lodges. Despite vigorous opposition and threats of excommunication from the Catholic church, Ribbon numbers grew, helped by the claims of senior Ribbonmen that the threats were a blind to conceal a secret alliance of church and Ribbonmen. Local societies or 'bodies' were led by a 'body master' and the cohort of masters in a parish constituted a jury or council which exercised discipline over the members and directed threats or acts of violence against anyone taking the land of an evicted tenant. Although the society attracted members from all classes, leadership was largely in the hands of shopkeepers, publicans and farmers. Ribbon demands included the concession of fixity of tenure (**tenant-right**), disestablishment of the Anglican church and civil rights for Catholics. (Garvin, *The evolution*, pp. 35– 45; Lee, 'The Ribbonmen', pp. 26–35; Ó Muireadhaigh, 'Na fir ribín', pp. 18– 32.)

right, writ of. Also known as a writ of *praecipe*, an instruction to the sheriff by the king ordering a wrongdoer to restore property of which another person was wrongfully disseised and to summon him before the justices if he failed to do so. It was an order to a man to do what he should have done already. Cases of right were originally resolved by **battle** in which champions for the parties fought a duel. By the time of Henry II, however, trial by battle could be replaced by jury verdict where the defendant so desired. Where an individual was wrongfully disseised of land, seisin was recoverable by ***novel disseisin***.

Rightboys (1785–8). An oath-bound secret society which agitated against church rates, priests' **dues** and the level at which **tithe** was fixed. Supporters of the Rightboy movement came from a broad spectrum of society across southern Ireland. Named after their fictitious leader, Captain Right, Rightboy activities included the posting of warning notices, grave-digging, the erection of gallows, the seizure of guns, the tendering of oaths and the sending of emissaries into neighbouring parishes to extend the campaign. The protest was accompanied by a relatively low level of violence – far less than was to be experienced during the later campaigns of the **Defenders**, the **Caravats**, the **Rockites** and the **Terry Alts** – and it was curbed by the use of troops, a magistracy act (27 Geo. III, c. 40, 1787) and a riot act (27 Geo. III, c. 15, 1787). (Donnelly, 'The Rightboy movement', pp. 120–202.)

Rights, Declaration of. A declaration accepted by William III and his wife, Mary II, in February 1689 which outlines the principles of the British constitution, notably the requirement of parliamentary consent for the levying of taxes, the annual convening of parliament, the right of MPs to freedom of speech, free elections and the right to trial by jury. The crown was not to keep a standing army during peacetime and its power to suspend laws was abolished. *See* mutiny act. In addition to taking the oath against transubstantiation, a requirement which barred Catholics from the throne, the monarch must not marry a Catholic.

ringfort. *See* rath.

rising out. Military service owed to a Gaelic overlord by an *urrí* or vassal, usually requiring the mustering of a specified number of horse and **kerne**.

roads, rodes. Punitive incursions by the English administration into the territories of the native Irish. *See* hostings, journeys, posse comitatus.

robinet. A light sixteenth-century field gun.

rochet. A surplice-like linen vestment worn by senior clergy.

Rockite. An agrarian protest group prominent in the early 1820s which sought regulation of rents, wages and **tithe**, protection of tenants threatened with eviction and wider access to land for tillage. The movement took its name from Captain Rock, the signature often appended to threatening letters. Heavily influenced by **Pastorini millenarianism**, Rockite agitation declined with the emergence in 1823 of the more respectable **Catholic Association**.

rococo. A decorative style dating from the eighteenth century which is characterised by the use of shell motifs.

Rocque, John. Influential and renowned Anglo-French cartographer who visited Ireland between 1754 and 1760 and produced his *Exact survey of the city and suburbs of Dublin*, a magnificent plan of the capital in 1756. He followed that with a county map, *An actual survey of the county of Dublin* in 1760. In both, Rocque's preference for depicting landscape and graphics is clear. His oyster-beds are, literally, stocked with oysters. Rocque was indifferent to administrative boundaries and eschewed writing where possible except in relation to toponym. Streams and lesser roads are less well drawn than rivers and main roads. Field boundaries, unlike parks and gardens, are representational rather than authentic. Rocque's vivid Kildare estate maps influenced a move away from the spartan **Down Survey** style of surveying towards the production of more elaborate estate and urban maps. (Andrews, 'The French school', pp. 275–92.)

rod. A perch or five and a half yards (5.029m). The rod was derived from the length of an ox-goad.

Rogation days. The Monday, Tuesday and Wednesday before Ascension Thursday. Rogation is the equivalent of 'litany' and on the three rogation days the litany of the saints was chanted by the clergy and people in public procession.

rolls. Government records composed of parchment documents stitched together to form continuous rolls. *See* close, memoranda rolls, patent, pipe rolls, plea rolls.

rolls, master of the. Keeper of government records (the rolls), formerly a senior judiciary figure in chancery and deputy to the lord chancellor.

rood. 1: One-quarter of an acre or 1,210 square yards 2: A cross or crucifix.

rood-loft. A loft above the chancel arch or screen in medieval parish churches where the rood or image of Christ crucified was placed on view. Where there was no rood-loft, the rood was supported by a rood-beam.

rood-tower. A tower built above the intersection of a cruciform church.

round tower. (Ir., *cloigtheach*, a bell house) Round towers appeared in Ireland around the tenth century. They were usually constructed to the west of a monastery with the doors of tower and church facing each other. (Barrow, *The round towers*.)

rotten borough. A borough where the franchise was vested in a few persons. The term is usually considered to refer to a decayed **borough** which contained few if any residents yet which retained the right to return two members to parliament, an entitlement which was exercised by the borough owner. Harristown, Co. Kildare, for example, had no houses yet returned two MPs. In reality, however, size was irrelevant. Any constituency, irrespective of population, where the franchise was vested solely in a corporation of 12 or 13 burgesses was rotten. In all, 86 members of the eighteenth-century Irish parliament were returned by rotten boroughs. Taken together with the nominees of the patrons of pocket boroughs, about two-thirds of the seats in parliament in 1790 were, effectively, private property.

royal. A gold coin valued by the 1477 parliament at 13s. 4d. Thus it was equivalent in value to a **mark**.

royal commission of inquiry. A royal commission of inquiry was one of the means by which parliament acquired knowledge about matters on which it proposed to legislate. Unlike the **select committee**, which comprised parliamentarians, commissioners of inquiry were often outsiders nominated for their expertise in the relevant field. That is not to say that the commissioners were wholly impartial. Royal commissions were often headed by and composed of members who were considered to be 'safe hands', men who could be relied on to present recommendations that would not offend government sensitivities. The report of the **Poor Inquiry** constitutes an instance where the procedure went awry. A commission of inquiry was not limited, as the select committee was, to the duration of a parliamentary session and the presentation of its report could take anything up to five years. Its value to the local historian lies in the voluminous detail that can be found in the minutes of evidence taken by the commissioners as they travelled through the countryside. Again some caution needs to be exercised when dealing with the minutes of evidence for the social composition of the witnesses must be carefully weighed against what they have to say about other sections of society. Important nineteenth-century royal commissions include the **Devon Commission** (occupation of land), the Poor Inquiry (condition of the poorer classes), and the **Bessborough Commission** (the working of Gladstone's **Landlord and Tenant Act**, 1870).

Royal Dublin Society. Founded in Dublin in 1731 as the Dublin Society by Thomas Prior and Samuel Madden to improve agricultural techniques, manufacturing industry and other useful arts. The society published a weekly account of its proceedings, collected statistics, popularised innovations and encouraged agricultural improvement by offering premiums. A model farm and model factories were set up to diffuse agricultural and industrial knowledge. It was supported initially by voluntary contributions but from 1746 was grant-aided annually with the sum of £500 from the civil list. In 1750 it received a royal charter and subsequently received funding from the Irish parliament. An annual spring show was held from 1815 at the society's headquarters in Leinster House and from the 1880s on its lands at Ballsbridge. In 1924 Leinster House was acquired by the Free State to house Dáil Éireann. (Bright, 'Reflections on the RDS', pp. 18–30.

Royal Irish Academy. The Irish Academy of Science, Polite Literature and Antiquities was founded in April 1785 by the first earl of Charlemont. Granted a royal charter in 1786, the academy developed into one of the foremost scholarly associations in Ireland, encouraging the publication of works of scholarship in a wide range of disciplines in its journals – *Transactions* (1787–1907) and *Proceedings* (1836–). Section C of the *Proceedings* covers history and archaeology. The academy is divided into two divisions, one for the sciences and one for humane studies. From its inauguration it has been renowned for its interest in Irish antiquities and history. Its collection of antiquities formed the core of the antiquities of the national museum when it was founded in 1877. Following the acquisition of the books of *Ballymote*, *Lecan*, *Leabhar na hUidhre* (*Book of the Dun Cow*) and an autograph manuscript of the *Annals of the Four Masters* in the late eighteenth century, the academy proceeded to assemble the single largest collection of Gaelic manuscripts in the world which are catalogued in 28 **fascicles** and two index volumes. It also holds the papers of a number of antiquarians, manuscripts of the **Ordnance Survey**, a pamphlet collection dating from the sixteenth century and transcripts of original archival material that was destroyed in 1922. The ambitious ten-volume series *A new history of Ireland* and the ongoing Irish historic towns atlas project were both inaugurated under the auspices of the academy.

royal service. *See* scutage.

royal schools. Under the scheme of plantation for Ulster a free grammar school was to be founded in each of the planted counties with additional land reserved for its maintenance. There were four operating by 1621 and five by 1625. Charles I made re-grants of the land given for educational purposes by James I and provided for additional royal schools in King's County and Co. Wicklow (Carysfort). There were 343 students (including 70 free scholars) enrolled in royal schools in 1831. Five of the original royal schools still exist at Armagh, Cavan, Dungannon, Enniskillen and Raphoe. (*First report of the commissioners of the Board of Education in Ireland*, HC 1809 (142) VII. 463: Akenson, *The Irish educational experiment*, pp. 27–29.)

Royal Society of Antiquaries of Ireland. Founded in 1849 as the Kilkenny Archaeological Society, the society assumed its present title in 1890 after two further name changes. It moved from Kilkenny to Dublin in 1868 where its extensive library is housed at 63 Merrion Square. It publishes an annual journal.

Rump. The Long Parliament in England after the exclusion in December 1648 of 100 members who favoured compromise with Charles I. It was dissolved in April 1653.

rundale. A collectively-farmed field system which comprised a '**clachan**' village, small gardens, permanently cultivated infield and occasionally-tilled, pastoral outfield zones, common meadow and summer transhumance (booleying) on the mountains. The infield was cultivated in individual strips which were re-allocated at intervals. Each tenant farmed strips dispersed across large tracts of arable land and shared access to the commonage for grazing. It has been claimed, on the basis of evidence from earlier field systems, that rundale was a pre-Norman survival but while continuous occupation has been proven at several sites no conclusive evidence has been advanced in support of the claim. Clachans and rundale occurred usually on reclaimed land and date from the late eighteenth century. Successive sub-division, the rapid increase in population and an over-reliance on the potato led to the virtual disappearance of rundale when famine struck in the 1840s. Known as runrig in Scotland. *See* ladder farm, striping. (Evans, *The personality*, pp. 58 ff.)

rusg. *See* raskins.

Rye House Plot. A plan devised by extremist Whigs to assassinate Charles II on his way from Newmarket to London.

S

s. (L., *solidus*, pl, *solisi*) The abbreviation used to denote a shilling.

sac and soc. (OE., *sac*, litigation and *soc*, suit.) Jurisdiction, the right of grantees to an estate (such as a manor) to hold court, to deal with offences and disputes and to enjoy the profits thereof. This franchise was granted by the crown and exercised by the lord in the manorial **courts leet** and **baron**. *See* toll and team.

sacramental test. *See* Test Act.

sacrist. An officer in some Irish medieval cathedral chapters, probably equivalent to – or deputy for – the treasurer. He was responsible for the cathedral plate, sacred vessels, relics and vestments.

sacristan. A sexton. He was a church official responsible for the upkeep of church property and for carrying out such duties as bell-ringing.

Saint Sepulchre, Liberty of. One of the four medieval Dublin liberties (the others were the liberty of St Patrick's, the liberty of Christ-Church and the earl of Meath's liberty), the archbishop of Dublin's liberty of St Sepulchre was organised on a manorial basis. It was administered by a **seneschal** and other officers including a marshall, **coroner**, weighmaster and clerk of the market. It had its **own grand** jury and three courts including a court of record for personal pleas, a court of criminal jurisdiction, a **court leet** where constables and the grand jury were sworn and a prison. In 1856 the jurisdiction of the archbishop of Dublin over the liberty of St Sepulchre was abrogated. *See* liberty. (Mills, 'Notices', pp. 31–41, 119–26; Wood, *Court book.*)

saker. 1: A siege cannon weighing about 1,500 pounds which fired shot of 5.5 pounds 2: An early modern, light artillery piece used on ships.

salient. In heraldry, a creature in the act of springing with the hind legs on the ground.

salfás money. Imported English **groat** or half-groat coins which bore the profile or half-face of Henry VII and Henry VIII.

sally. (L., *salix*) A willow tree, the rods of which were used for basket-making and, when twisted into **scollops**, to secure thatch to a roof.

sallyport. An opening in a castle wall to enable soldiers to sally forth against an enemy.

saltire. In heraldry, an ordinary comprising the crossing of a bend and a bend sinister, a device identical to St Andrew's cross.

saltpetre. Potassium nitrate, the chief constituent of gunpowder. Saltpetre commonly was used as a preservative.

Sandelians. A **mesolithic** hunter-gatherer people, claimed to be the first inhabitants of Ireland, so called after Mount Sandel on the River Bann where discoveries of microliths (used for harpoon barbs) and small axes possibly up to 9,000 years old were made. Unlike **Neolithic** peoples the Sandelians did not have the implements to clear forests for agricultural purposes and were restricted to hunting and fishing along the shores of rivers, lakes and the sea and the collection of nuts. Pottery and art were apparently unknown to them. (Woodman, *Excavations*; *Idem*, 'A mesolithic', pp. 92–100.)

savings clause. A clause appended to letters **patent** obtained under the Restoration **Act of Settlement** which reserved to named persons or their heirs certain rights such as **jointure**, **annuities** and even eventual restoration. The intention was to protect the entitlements of innocent relatives of landowners who forfeited their estates during the 1641 rebellion. It is not certain to what extent, if any, claimants were able to enforce savings clauses when they fell due.

say. A light, delicate woollen or serge cloth. Also known as 'bluesay'.

scavenger. A person hired by a civil parish to clear the streets of filth.

scollop. (Ir., *scolb*, a thin or split rod) A rod twisted at the middle, bent double like a staple and used to pin thatch to a roof.

scraws. (Ir., *scraith*, a sod) Sods used in roof construction. They were laid, vegetation upwards, on the timber framework as an underthatch and sometimes as the sole roof covering.

scriptorium. (L.) A building attached to a monastery where manuscripts were copied.

scutching. A stage in the process of preparing flax for linen-making. Following a period of submersion in water (**retting**) and drying, the flax stalks are beaten or scraped to rid them of woody fibre.

scutage. A payment, also known as royal service, exacted in lieu of **knight-service** (military service) and owed by all tenants-in-chief. In the fifteenth century scutages were levied with the consent of parliament or the **privy council** to finance a general **hosting** or raise additional troops. (Otway-Ruthven, 'Royal service', pp. 37–46.)

seal. Seals were used to authenticate documents and, in the case of royal seals, to signify the monarch's consent. They played a crucial role in the functioning of the administration. The principal seal was the great seal, the deputed authority of the crown, which was kept by the lord chancellor. Depicted on the great seal or seal of majesty are royal insignia and the image of the monarch seated. As the **chief governor** was constantly moving and the chancellor could not always be in attendance, the chief governor's private seal was used to activate the great seal and pass letters patent in the case of royal grants of lands or commissions. From 1560 a second royal seal, the signet or privy seal, was introduced and assigned to the keeping of the **secretary of state** to the **privy council** who accompanied the chief governor on his travels. All letters containing the chief governor's warrant were sealed by the secretary of state or keeper of the privy seal and then carried to **chancery** where they passed the great seal. The chancellor was forbidden to issue letters patent without having first received the governor's sealed **fiant**. (Jenkinson, 'The great seal', pp. 293–340.)

seam, seme. A horse-load or eight bushels.

seanchas. (Ir.) History or lore.

seanchaí. (Ir.) A storyteller, historian or genealogist.

searcher. A customer or exciseman who boarded and inspected a vessel to uncover dutiable goods. *See* gauger.

Seceders. A group of conservative Scottish Presbyterians who broke away from the Presbyterian Church of Scotland in 1733 when the loss of their right to choose ministers resulted in an increasingly liberal church. Seceders believed that ministers and ordinands should subscribe to the **Confession of Westminster** and when they appeared in Ireland in the 1740s they provided an alternative to the non-subscribing **Synod of Ulster**. They had their own synod, the Secession Synod, and remained a distinct group until 1840 when, with the re-imposition of compulsory subscription by the Synod of Ulster, both synods merged to form the **General Assembly of the Presbyterian Church in Ireland**. (Stewart, *The seceders*.)

secondary schooling. In nineteenth-century Ireland there was no state system of secondary education and what was available was provided by a small number of voluntary schools. When the national system of education was introduced in 1831 many schools which had been providing intermediate education ceased to do so because the new Board of Education would only support primary education. In 1837 the Wyse Committee recommended the provision of a centrally-funded non-denominational system of intermediate education but until the passage of the 1878 Intermediate Education Act (41 & 42 Vict., c. 66), second-level education was available only in the Protestant **diocesan, royal** (1608) and **Erasmus Smith** (1669) schools, Kilkenny College (1685), academy schools such as Belfast Academical Institution (1810) and a small number of Catholic secondary schools run by religious orders such as the **Christian Brothers**, the Jesuits, the Sisters of Mercy and the Loreto Sisters. The 1878 act created an unpaid board of commissioners to promote intermediate education. It was funded by the interest on the surplus revenue of the disestablished **Church of Ireland**, by a grant from the customs and excise and additional aid was provided from 1914 under the Intermediate Education Act (4 & 5 Geo V, c. 41). To avoid criticism that it was bolstering denominational education, the government proposed to indirectly aid schools by conducting annual examinations, rewarding successful candidates with scholarships and certificates and by paying results-based fees to school managers. Examinations were held at three levels: junior, middle and senior (and at preparatory level from 1890). Prize-giving led to an enlargement of the range of subjects on offer within the schools and helped establish uniformity but, as with the primary system, **payment-by-results** led to a mechanistic approach to teaching. In 1899 the **Palles Commission** criticised the narrow examination programme on offer and acknowledged the heavy burden placed on schools by the payment-by-results system. Palles, nevertheless, recommended a modified payments-by-results system. Public examinations would be retained but grants would be paid in block rather than on the basis of individual examination results. In the following year the commissioners opted instead to fund schools by means of capitation grants and made provision for the appointment of school inspectors. Between 1881 and 1911 the number of intermediate schools rose only slightly from 488 to 489 but the number of pupils doubled from 20,000 to 40,000, figures which represented but a tiny fraction of the school-age population. (Coolahan, *Irish education*, pp. 52–82.)

Second Reformation. A Protestant missionary attempt at the mass conversion of Catholics in the early decades of the nineteenth century. Many societies, including the aggressively proselytising **London Hibernian Society** (1806), the Hibernian Bible Society (1806), the Sunday School Society (1809), the Religious Tract and Book Society (1810) and the **Irish Society for Promoting the Education of the Native Irish through the Medium of their own Language** (1818) emerged during this period. Some, like the Religious Book and Tract Society – which distributed over four million tracts in ten years – attempted conversion through the printed word. Others, including the London Hibernian Society, established schools to provide a free elementary and religiously partisan education. Others again dispatched itinerant preachers, including Irish speakers, to convert the Irish from superstition and ignorance. The drive to convert Catholics was fuelled by the belief that, properly communicated, God's word would triumph over the ignorance and superstition of Catholicism. Second reformers claimed spiritual authority from scripture, apostolic descent from St Patrick and a civilising mission authorised by the state. The mission to rescue the Irish from the errors of popery sparked a pamphlet war. As the second reformation gained momentum missions were conducted and Catholic priests were publicly confronted, souring relationships already strained by the struggle for **Catholic emancipation**, **tithe** grievances and the debate over an appropriate educational system for the nation. In terms of numbers, the gains were short-term and largely erased by a vigorous pastoral response from the Catholic church. (Bowen, *The Protestant crusade*.)

secretary hand. A distinctive hand-writing style employed in drawing up legal and official documents between the fifteenth and seventeenth centuries. Secretary hand is characterised by considerable variation in letter form, the frequent use of abbreviations (which often appear as dashes or squiggles), erratic spelling and the absence of punctuation. Considerable practice is required before documents in secretary hand can be read fluently but several useful guides have been published to assist the reader. Gooder and Alcock are particularly useful in explaining form and content. (Gooder, *Latin*; Alcock, *Old title deeds*.)

secretary of state. In 1560 Elizabeth I ordered the appointment of a secretary of state to the **privy council** to act as custodian of the privy **seal** or signet, the instrument that authenticated the chief governor's warrants and activated the great seal of Ireland. The secretary of state was required to correspond with the privy council in England about developments in Ireland. In addition to overseeing the work of the clerks of the council he had the power to commit for treason or sedition and, later, to order the postmaster-general to open letters. By the eighteenth century the post had become a sinecure – the only remaining duty being to affix the signet to **fiants** – and the office was abolished in 1802. (Wood, 'The offices'.)

sectary. A member of a heretical group, the term was commonly applied to Protestant dissenters such as puritans during the seventeenth century.

secular. Unlike the **regulars** who are based in monasteries, secular clergymen perform their religious duties within the communities to which they are appointed.

sedilia. A stone seat, usually on the south side of the altar, used by the clergyman at moments of reflection or rest during mass.

seigniory. Lordship.

seisin, seizin. The possession of a **freehold** estate. Seisin did not necessarily imply occupation as the land could be leased.

seisin, livery of. In land conveyancing livery of seisin, effectively the legal delivery of freehold property into the possession of another person, refers to the physical entry onto the land by the purchaser and the symbolic handing over of a piece of turf or keys. Purchasers often appointed attorneys to perform this act. *See* feoffment and livery, to sue out.

seisin, primer. The crown entitlement to take, hold and enjoy the profits of an estate during the interval between the demise of a chief tenant and the suing out of livery, the payment of **relief** and the rendering of **homage** by his heir. *See* livery, to sue out.

sejant. In heraldry, a creature seated on its haunches.

select committee. During the nineteenth century parliament became increasingly concerned with all aspects of daily life and to fulfil its legislative function it needed to become knowledgeable about the matters on which it was to legislate. An investigation by a select committee was one of the means employed to acquire this knowledge. Membership was cross-party and representatives from both houses of parliament were eligible to participate although the majority of members and the chairman were drawn from the government party. Select committees had no executive powers but they were able to send for persons, papers and records pertinent to their investigations and any subject of the United Kingdom could be summoned to Westminster Palace to give evidence. Committee reports contain the actual report, the proceedings and (if taken) minutes of evidence heard by the committee. The minutes of evidence often provide detailed information on conditions in the localities. In the late nineteenth century the select committee ceased to be the main investigative tool as major inquiries were delegated increasingly to the **royal commission** or departmental inquiry.

selion. A strip of ridges in the open field system of agriculture.

seneschal. 1: A mayor, **portreeve** or **sovereign** 2: A steward, the most senior manorial official.

serjeant-at-law. A law officer who spoke on behalf of his client at litigation hearings. He made the formal complaint or claim on behalf of the plaintiff or responded for the defendant. Serjeants (*narratores*) were engaged and briefed by attorneys who performed all the preparatory legal work in the case, including the selection of appropriate writs to move the case forward to the next stage and ensuring their clients were present in court. In Ireland judges were chosen from the body of serjeants although English serjeants were also eligible and some judges had never served as serjeants – they were simply appointed serjeants on the day of their elevation. Serjeants were later nominated to replace judges of **assize** by the Dublin administration. In Ireland the last serjeant was appointed in 1919. *See* prime serjeant. (Brand, 'The early history', pp. 15–50.)

services. With the exception of the king or queen who were at the apex of the feudal pyramid, all tenants owed services to their immediate superiors. These included personal attendance, provision of knights or soldiers, farm produce, labour service and rent. *See* feudal incidents.

servitor. A royal official, usually a military officer, who was rewarded for service in the Nine Years War with a grant of confiscated land in Ulster. Unlike undertakers, servitors were permitted, at a surcharge of 50%, to take Irish tenants. They were required to reside on their estates for five years, to introduce a quota of able-bodied English or lowland Scottish colonists, to construct a **bawn** and to maintain a supply of arms for defensive purposes. *See* Pynnar's Survey.

sesona. (L.) A large field planted with only one crop at a time in the medieval three-field system of agriculture. (Simms and Fagan, 'Villages', p. 93.)

sessiagh. (Ir.) A Gaelic unit of spatial measurement which was equivalent to 20 acres in Tyrone and from 8–20 acres in Donegal. *See* acre, gnieve.

session, kirk session. Comprising ministers and elders, the session is the governing board of a **Presbyterian** congregation. It oversees religious and church matters, supervises the election of ministers, advises on the reception of new members and exercises church discipline. Each congregational session sends representative elders to the **presbytery**, the district church council.

Settling of Ireland, Act for the (1652). The Cromwellian act by which the claims of adventurers and arrears of pay due to soldiers were to be met by the confiscation and re-distribution of vast tracts of Irish land. Under the act the lives and estates of 105 named rebels were excepted from pardon as were the estates of persons who had not demonstrated 'constant good affection' to parliament, clauses which were sufficiently all-embracing as to ensure that almost every Catholic estate was liable to sequestration and their owners liable for transplantation.

settle bed. A settle, saddle or press bed was an item of furniture that served as a seat during the day and was opened at night to form a bed. (O'Neill, *Life*, p. 20.)

Settlement, Act of (1662). The Restoration act (14 & 15 Chas. II, c. 2) which attempted to resolve the conflicting claims of Catholics who sought restoration to their former estates and Protestants who wanted to freeze the Cromwellian land settlement and retain the lands they had acquired during the *interregnum*. The hopes of both were doomed as there was not sufficient land in Ireland to meet all claims. The act established a **court of claims** to process claims of **innocence** of rebellion (and hence entitlement to restoration) but within months it closed amidst fears that too many Catholics were being restored and before even a fraction of the scheduled cases had been heard. In the end Catholics succeeded in modifying rather than over-turning the settlement and success or failure in regaining former estates was determined by service to or influence within the royal court, legal acumen and economic factors rather than on questions of innocence or complicity in the war. (Arnold, *The restoration*.)

severalty, holding in. A holding in a person's own right without being joined in interest by another.

several fishery. A fishery in which the rights are vested wholly in the owner and in which the public or riparian (riverside) landlords have no rights.

sexton. A sacristan.

shambles. A meat and fish market.

Shanavests. *See* Caravats.

share, ploughshare. The sharp, pointed wooden or metal blade of a plough that opens the ground. *See* coulter, mouldboard plough, ard plough. (Mitchell, *The Shell guide*, pp. 143–4.)

sharecropper. A tenant farmer who receives seed, tools and land in credit and who works the land in return for an agreed share of the produce. *See* metayage.

sheela-na-gig. (Ir., possibly *síle na gcíoch*, hag of the breasts) A medieval carved representation of a grotesque naked female in a provocative pose often found in the exterior walls of a church. Sheela-na-gigs may have served the didactic purpose of alerting the faithful to the consequences of licentiousness. (Kelly, *Sheela-na gigs*.)

sheriff. (OE, shire-reeve) The senior law officer of a county, the sheriff was responsible for carrying out the directions of central administration. He received and implemented royal **writs**, collected and accounted for crown revenue at the **exchequer** and presided over the **assizes**. Most of the work was actually done by a sub-sheriff. The sheriff's duties included the selection of the **grand jury**, the supervision of parliamentary elections (as he does to this day) and the election of the **coroner**.

sheriff's peer. In Dublin, a freeman who had served as sheriff. A vacancy among the aldermen was filled from a list of four sheriff's peers supplied by the aldermen and elected by the commons.

shieling. A bothy, booley-hut or cabin of stone or turf erected for summer pasturing in the mountains.

shire. (AS, *scir*) A county. Shiring was the means by which royal writ was extended throughout the realm. In England it was the administrative unit above the 'hundred', in Ireland above the barony. *See* county. (Otway-Ruthven, 'Anglo-Irish', pp. 1–28.)

shovelboard. A game of push penny.

shrive. Anciently, to confess one's sins

Sick and Indigent Roomkeepers Benevolent Society. Founded in Dublin in 1790 by a group of small businessmen living in the area of Charles St West behind Ormond Quay, the Roomkeepers Society was (and remains) a non-denominational, non-political charitable body for the relief of the distressed during periods of crisis. Originally members subscribed 2*d*. per week or 8*s*. 8*d*. yearly which entitled them to recommend deserving persons for relief. Deserving persons were those of good character who had never begged but who, through unforeseen circumstances, had been reduced to poverty. Relief was given in the form of food or money. The society divided the city into four districts, each with a president and – from 1799 – a committee of trustees composed of residents of that district. The committees examined recommendations for relief submitted by members and organised visits to verify the claims therein. Subsequently a report was issued to the petitioning member detailing what action (if any) had been taken on foot of the recommendation. The society's headquarters was at Palace

Street near Dublin Castle for over 200 years. Currently it operates from 34 Lr Leeson Street, Dublin. (Lindsay, *Dublin's oldest charity*.)

sidesman. A man who took the collection at divine service.

sign manual. An autograph signature, especially that of the monarch, which authenticates a document. The royal sign manual was written in the upper left-hand corner of a document.

sinecure. An office with no duties for which one was paid. *See* non-cure.

sinister. In heraldry refers to the left side of a shield from the point of view of the person bearing it.

Sites and Monuments Record (SMR). The official record of an identified archaeological site or monument. SMRs are the records of Dúchas in the Republic of Ireland and the Environment and Heritage Service in Northern Ireland. Each site has a unique identification number which is linked to site description files, excavation reports, archaeological finds, drawings, photographs and bibliographical references. SMRs for sites in Northern Ireland can be accessed through the Monuments and Buildings Record facility in the Environment and Heritage Service building, 5–33 Hill Street, Belfast, during office hours on weekdays. A more limited service is provided in the Republic in the form of appointment-only visits to the former Dúchas headquarters in St Stephens Green, Dublin. (Brannon, 'The built heritage', pp. 116–127.)

sittings. The legal year has been divided into four terms or sittings since Anglo-Saxon times. Hilary term began in early January and ended before Easter. Easter began eight days after Easter Sunday and ended on the eve of Ascension day. Trinity began eight days after Whit Sunday and ended in early July. Michaelmas began on the Tuesday after the feast and ended at Advent. By the nineteenth century the terms were dictated by statute (Hilary, 11–31 January, Easter, 15 April – 8 May, Trinity, 22 May–12 June and Michaelmas, 2–25 November) but as the statutory terms were too short to process all the cases coming before the courts a system of out of term sittings or 'after sittings' was introduced in 1856. 'After sittings' enabled cases of *nisi prius* which had been heard at the **assize courts** out of term to be tried before the central courts. The terms were re-styled 'sittings' under the Judicature (Ireland) Act, 1877, and after independence the duration of sittings was extended. Hilary now lasted from 12 January to 31 March, Easter from 15 April to 18 May, Trinity from 1 June to 31 July and Michaelmas from 12 October to 21 December. Vacations, the intervals between sittings, are called Easter, Long (Summer) and Christmas.

Six Clerks. Officials in **chancery** who acted as agents for solicitors practicing in that court. They gained a monopoly of the right to act as attorneys in chancery and solicitors were obliged to employ them to appear on court records as representing their clients. Their income, which was derived from fees paid by solicitors for copies of documents filed in the court, helped make the cost of litigation in chancery prohibitive and led ultimately to their (amply compensated) demise in 1836 (Wm. IV, c. 74).

six-day labour. In 1613 an act for repairing highways and cashes (11–13 James I, c. 7) placed responsibility for road maintenance on the civil parish. The legislation required all landowners, tenants, cottiers and labourers to give six days free labour annually for road-building, using equipment supplied by the parish. In 1710 (9 Anne, c. 9) parliament tightened the earlier legislation to prevent evasion, enlarged the geographical area within which free labour was to be provided and lengthened the annual labour season. Henceforth labour duty could be exacted within a two-mile radius of the parish boundaries and the labour season, originally from Easter to 24 June, was extended to 1 August. Equipping the workers remained a function of the parish **vestry** which was entitled to levy the parish for the purpose. Six-day labour was unpopular and was discontinued after 1760 (33 Geo., II, c. 8) when grand juries assumed responsibility for funding road maintenance through the **county cess**.

skein. (Ir., *scian*) A dagger or knife.

skillet. A large cooking pot.

sláinte. (Ir.) Protection extended by a Gaelic lord to a lesser lord or client on payment of a fee or tribute. *Slánuigheacht* was the protection itself.

slean. (Ir., *sleaghán*) A narrow spade with a wing-bladed shaft for cutting turf.

slide car. A wheelless cart used for farmwork.

slipe. A sled.

sliocht. (Ir.) Sept or branch of a clan.

Smith, Erasmus. A London **adventurer** who received large estates in Ireland following the 1641 rebellion, Erasmus Smith vested some of his land in trust for the establishment of a number of grammar schools in Ireland. Following the Restoration the trust was granted a royal charter to construct grammar schools at Drogheda, Tipperary and Galway. As the income from the vested land exceeded the sum required to fund the grammar schools, the trustees secured an act of parliament in 1723 which enabled them to grant-aid the establishment of 'English' or primary schools wherever a landowner so wished and by 1824 there were over 100 such schools in existence. (*Ninth report of the commissioners of the Board of Education*, appendix, HC 1810 (194 X. 315; Ronan, *Erasmus Smith*.)

snaphance. An early spring-operated flintlock.

socage (common or free socage). A form of land tenure which required the payment of rent but did not comprehend the feudal incidents (obligations) of **wardship, marriage, relief, escheat** or licence to alienate.

The **Tenures Abolition Act** of 1662 abolished all forms of feudal tenure leaving just one, common socage (later known as **freehold**). *See* alienation.

Society for Promoting the Education of the poor in Ireland. *See* Kildare Place Society.

Society of United Irishmen. *See* United Irishmen.

sock, toll and theam. *See* sac and soc, toll and theam.

sodalities. *See* guilds, religious.

Solemn League and Covenant. An agreement reached between the Scots and Charles I's parliamentarian opponents in September 1643 to advance the Reformation and uphold the rights of parliament. Under the terms of the treaty the Scots were to dispatch a 20,000 strong army to England to be paid for by a parliamentary levy. In return, the Long Parliament (the **Rump**) promised to abolish the episcopacy of the church in England and to debate the future of Protestantism at Westminster. Both parties interpreted the covenant differently. The Scots, leaning heavily on the religious terms, foresaw the establishment of Presbyterianism and the abolition of episcopacy. The English, however, interpreted it as a civil arrangement, a move to secure the rights of parliament.

sole right. The claim in 1692 by the opposition in the Irish house of commons that parliament had the 'sole right' to originate financial legislation. Constitutional as well as venal motives lay behind the revolt which eventually frightened the **lord lieutenant** into proroguing the house. A concern for greater parliamentary control over taxation, administrative corruption, the belief that Catholics were being treated too leniently and a sense of grievance among some MPs that they had been bypassed in the distribution of patronage all played a part in the controversy. The sting was drawn, however, in 1695 with better management of the house, the co-option of leading agitators into high office, the introduction of new anti-Catholic legislation and a government compromise on the right to initiate money bills. *See* Poynings' Law. (Connolly, *Religion*, pp. 75–6; McGuire, 'The parliament of 1692', pp. 137–49.)

soum. A unit of grazing of mountain commonage. The term is synonymous with **collop** or cow's grass.

souperism. The practice during the Great Famine among some Protestant zealots of offering material benefits in return for religious conversion. Acceptance of such benefits was known disparagingly as 'taking the soup' because Catholics were required to attend Protestant service or bible class to be fed. Souperism was not practised widely and conversions were short-lived. Temporary converts were known as 'soupers' or 'jumpers'. (Bowen, *Souperism*.)

souterrain. An underground passage and chamber or a series of passages and chambers constructed usually (though not exclusively) within an enclosure (**rath**) and which may have served as a place of refuge during an assault or as a storage chamber for food. (Clinton, *The souterrains*.)

Southern Association. The non-subscribing southern wing of the **Presbyterian** church formed when the congregations of Cork, Wexford, Limerick, Bandon, Clonmel, Waterford, Sligo and Tipperary joined with the Dublin congregations in 1696. From 1708 Queen Anne granted £800 per annum (the 'English Bounty') to the southern congregations. Unlike their northern brethren – whose origins were Presbyterian and Scottish, the background to the Southern Association was Independent and English, circumstances which led to theological and structural differences between the two wings. The Southern Association was less hierarchical than the **Synod of Ulster**, did not claim binding authority over its members, adopted a congregational form of organisation and regarded synods as consultative rather than prescriptive assemblies. Northern Presbyterians also believed the southern congregations to be tainted by **Arianism**. In 1809 the Southern Association was re-styled the Synod of Munster when the non-subscribing Presbytery of Munster united with the Southern Presbytery of Dublin. In 1854 the southern body joined the **General Assembly of the Presbyterian Church in Ireland** which had been formed earlier by the merger of the Synod of Ulster and the **Seceders**.

sovereign. The senior official in a municipal corporation. Also known as the mayor, **portreeve** or **seneschal**.

spaldrick. A thatcher's rake-like comb.

spalpeen. A seasonal migratory labourer.

spandrel. The triangular space between the curves of two arches and the moulding or framework enclosing it.

sparre. A heavily-armoured Scottish mercenary soldier, so-called after the long-handled battle sparre (axe) he bore. A sparre was accompanied by a man acting as his harness bearer and a boy to carry his provisions. *See* gallowglass, redshank.

sparver. A canopy or wooden frame over a bed from which a curtain hung.

speaker. The officer and spokesperson for the house of commons whose functions include the controlling of debates and the arrangements of the house. The speaker is elected by the house and has no vote in a division except in cases of a tie where he/she has a casting vote. *See* undertaker (2).

spurtle, aspurticle. A long, two-pronged fork used to press thatching material into the roof.

squaring. *See* striping.

squire. Originally a young man of good birth who attended upon a knight. Under the feudal system he ranked below the knight.

stallage. 1: The liberty to erect stalls in a market 2: The fee payable for so doing.

stang. 1: A rood, rod or perch associated with open field strips. It was equivalent to to a quarter acre or 40 square perches 2: A linear rood was five and a half yards or 5.029m.

Stanihurst, Richard (1547–1618). Born in Dublin, Stanihurst was educated at University College, Oxford where he was a student of **Edmund Campion** and subsequently became tutor to Garret FitzGerald (son of the eleventh earl of Kildare). His *Description of Ireland* and account of Ireland during Henry VIII's reign form a considerable portion of the history of Ireland in **Holinshed's *Chronicles*** (1577). Stanihurst's favourable treatment of the Kildare rebellion landed him in trouble with the English privy council and he was compelled to revise the text. His treatment of the native Irish was not objective – though it mellowed in his later years – and he repeats some of the fabulous tales of Giraldus Cambrensis. He was heavily criticised by both Geoffrey Keating and Sir James Ware. In the second edition of the *Chronicles* (1587), John Hooker supplemented Stanihurst's history with material he compiled from contemporary Irish administrative records. Stanihurst translated Virgil's *Aeneid* into English but thereafter wrote only in Latin. His pseudo-historical *De rebus Hibernia gestis* was published in 1584, followed by *De vita S. Patricii Hiberniae apostoli* three years later. (Lennon, *Richard Stanihurst.*)

Stanley's 'instructions'. *See* Education, National System of.

Staple, Ordinance of the. *See* Statute Staple.

star chamber. *See* castle chamber, court of.

statant. In heraldry, an animal in profile with all four legs on the ground, the forepaws placed together.

State Paper Office. Senior government officials regarded their papers as private property and usually transported them back to England when their term in Ireland ended. The State Paper Office was established in 1702 for the purpose of making copies of the records of the **chief governor**, including books of entries, warrants, petitions and orders, so that incoming officials would have some idea of what their predecessors had been up to. The extensive collection of papers of the chief secretary (dating from 1790) escaped the destruction of state records in the Four Courts in 1922 as they were stored in the State Paper Office in the Birmingham Tower in Dublin Castle. The National Archives was established with the merger of the Public Record Office and the State Paper Office in 1986.

stations. The custom of saying mass in private houses that was common in the seventeenth and eighteenth centuries and which survives today.

statistical surveys. A series of county surveys prepared by landowners and Protestant clergymen under the supervision of the **Royal Dublin Society**. They contain valuable social and economic information about Ireland in the early nineteenth century. Surveys were not compiled for counties Fermanagh, Kerry, Laois, Louth, Limerick, Longford, Waterford and Westmeath and the survey of Tipperary remains in manuscript form in the National Library of Ireland. The list of counties surveyed (together with authors' names and compilation dates) includes:

Antrim	Dubourdieu	1812	Queen's Co.	Coote	1801
Kilkenny	Tighe	1802	Donegal	McParlan	1802
Armagh	–	1804	Roscommon	Weld	1832
King's Co.	Coote	1801	Down	Dubourdieu	1802
Cavan	–	1802	Sligo	McParlan	1802
Leitrim	Coote	1802	Dublin	Archer	1801
Clare	Dutton	1808	Tyrone	McEvoy	1802
Mayo	McParlan	1802	Galway	Dutton	1824
Cork	Townsend	1810	Wexford	Fraser	1807
Monaghan	–	1801	Kildare	Rawson	1807
Derry	–	1802	Wicklow	Fraser	1801

statute. An act of parliament. **Poyning's Law** (1494) severely circumscribed parliament in its legislative function. No parliament could be held in Ireland without licence from the monarch. The **chief governor** was required to certify under the great **seal** of Ireland the causes and considerations for holding the parliament and, once approved, parliament was unable to propose legislation or consider any matters other than those that had received the monarch's consent. Since parliament could not originate bills until it met and since it could not do so while in session, its sole function lay in accepting or rejecting bills which originated in the **privy council** or in Westminster. By 3 & 4 Philip and Mary, c. 4 (1556) permission was given to the lord lieutenant to certify cause to the king while parliament was in session but it was not until the late seventeenth century that original legislation in the form of 'heads of bills' began to issue from both houses. Heads of bills were propositions similar to acts of parliament with the single difference of commencing with 'We pray that it may be enacted' in place of 'Be it enacted'. Having passed either house, heads of bills were sent to the lord lieutenant and the Irish privy council and, if acceptable, were transmitted from there to the English (British from 1704) privy council, the English attorney-general and solicitor-general for their perusal. The heads were returned to the originating house via the Irish privy council having passed the great seal of England. After three readings in both houses they were finally dispatched to the lord lieutenant who gave the royal assent. At any stage once the bills left parliament they could be altered, amended or rejected but when returned with the English seal affixed the Irish parliament was unable to make any alterations. It must either accept or reject the bill *in toto*. In 1782 **Yelverton's Act** modified Poynings' Law to the extent that bills originating in either house were deposited in the lords' office and a copy attested by the Irish great seal was forwarded to England to receive the royal assent. The power of the lord lieutenant and the privy councils of Ireland and Britain to alter or originate bills for Ireland was removed. If approved by the king the copy was returned to Ireland with the English great seal affixed on the right side together with a commission to the lord lieutenant to give the royal assent. All bills except money bills were returned to the lords' office to await the royal assent. The monarch retained the veto over bills, a prerogative never subsequently exercised. Statutes are numbered by **regnal year** and chapter which serve as the call number in the National Library of Ireland. The 1878 Intermediate Education Act is numbered 41 & 42 Vict., c. 66 which means the sixtieth chapter of the statutes enacted in the forty-first and forty-second regnal years of Queen Victoria. (*Irish statutes*; Hayden, 'The origin', pp. 112–25; Johnston-Liik, *History of the Irish parliament*; Kelly, 'Monitoring', pp. 87–106)

Statute of Uses. *See* use.

statute rolls. The statute rolls which began as a series in 1427 comprised both the public and private statutes passed in the Irish parliament from Henry VI to James I. In 1861 there were 45 rolls. The original rolls were destroyed in 1922 except for the year 1594 – which Charles McNeill was reading when the anti-Treatyites burst into the Four Courts. However, the rolls for the years 1427–72 had already been published in two volumes by the Public Record Office and a volume for the years 1473–81 appeared in 1939 based on surviving **Irish Record Commission** transcripts. Both are printed in the original Norman French, the legal and general language of the court, with parallel English translations. The Record Commission's transcripts of the parliamentary rolls for 1484, 1485 and 1493 are to be published by the National Archives. (Berry, *Statutes*; *Idem*, *Statute rolls*; *Idem*, *Statute rolls of the parliament of Ireland, first to the twelfth years of the reign of King Edward the fourth* ; *Irish statutes: revised edition*; Morrissey, *Statute rolls*.)

Statute Staple. The Irish staple emerged in the thirteenth century as a regulatory body to govern the trade in basic or staple goods such as wool and hides. Dublin, Cork, Waterford and Drogheda were designated staple towns and it was only in these towns that such goods could be sold to foreign merchants. Later other towns, such as Carrickfergus, Belfast, Derry, Galway, Kilkenny, Limerick, New Ross, Sligo,

Wexford and Youghal were also so designated. By the seventeenth century the staple's significance as a trade regulatory body had declined and it became a means by which loans could be raised and spare capital ventured in relative security. The staple officers, comprising a mayor who was elected annually by the merchants of the staple and two constables, supervised the financial transactions and enforced repayment. The borrower entered into a bond of recognisance, known as a statute staple, to pay the creditor a fixed amount on a specified date plus interest at 10%. This fixed sum was usually twice the amount borrowed and represented security for repayment of the loan. Failure to repay could lead to imprisonment or the seizure of property. The records of the Dublin Staple are held in the city archives and have recently been issued on CD-ROM by Dublin City Archives. (O'Brien, 'The Irish staple', pp. 42–56; Ohlmeyer and Ó Ciardha, *The Irish statute staple books*.)

Steelboys, Hearts of Steel. In the late 1760s the absentee earl of Donegall attempted to raise a substantial sum of money to complete his mansion at Fisherwick Park in Staffordshire by imposing heavy fines upon his Antrim tenants as a consideration for renewing their leases. Inevitably, intermediate landlords sought to recoup their investments by canting farms at higher rates. Styling themselves Steelboys or Hearts of Steel, the under-tenants resisted and engaged in a campaign of intimidation, house-burning and cattle-houghing to deter others from settling on new terms or from taking up the farms of ousted tenants. Evictions, excessive rent demands, increased competition for land, unrest over **county cess** and a fodder famine encouraged the spread of discontent into counties Derry, Tyrone, Down and Armagh. In retaliation large numbers of troops were dispatched to the disturbed areas and several Steelboys were brought to trial at Carrickfergus but were acquitted by partisan juries. When the trials were brought to Dublin the defendants were again acquitted. After some fierce confrontations and executions the outrages dissipated about 1773, assisted by largescale emigration. (Donnelly, 'Hearts of Oak', pp. 7–73; Maguire, 'Lord Donegall', pp. 351–76.)

stinting. The regulation of cattle grazing on common land. When common land was stinted graziers with liberty of pasture on the commons were restricted to a specific number of cattle. *See* collop, soum, cow's grass.

stipend. Salary, payment.

Stopford rule. In 1844 Archdeacon Stopford of Meath began a campaign to change the national school regulation that required managers of **vested schools** to exclude all children from religious instruction unless their parents asked that they be present. The regulation was introduced as a safeguard against proselytism but to Stopford it hindered

Anglican ministers in their duty to convert Catholics. In 1847 the commissioners of education yielded and re-interpreted the rule to mean that school managers could not compel children of one denomination to be present at the religious instruction of another. By abolishing the safeguard the commissioners encouraged the drift towards denominational schooling for parents were unlikely to permit their children to attend schools where they would be targets for proselytisation. In non-vested schools the commissioners of education had already yielded on this issue to Presbyterians in order to secure their connection with the national system. From 1866, however, the attendance of children of one faith during the religious instruction of another faith was forbidden. (Akenson, *The Irish education experiment*, pp. 200–1 *passim*.)

stoup. A basin for holy water set into the wall at the entrance of a church.

Stowe Manuscript. Dating from c. 800 AD, the Stowe manuscript comprises extracts from the gospel of St John and liturgies of the eucharist, baptism and prayers for the sick. Stowe is so-called because it was found in the Duke of Buckingham's library at Stowe House. Possibly written in Tallaght, Co. Dublin, the manuscript contains 67 leaves of minuscule, angular script. It is preserved in the **Royal Irish Academy.**

Strafford Inquisition (1635–37). A series of inquisitions into landownership in Connacht conducted by the lord deputy, Thomas Wentworth (later earl of Strafford) as part of a wide-ranging programme to boost royal revenue. Wentworth arrived in Connacht with a commission to find the king's title to Connacht (with the exception of Leitrim) by instructing juries of the largest landowners in each county to find for the king or suffer the loss of their estates. All proved amenable with the exception of the Galway jury which relented only when the jurors were hauled before the court of **castle chamber** and heavily fined. Apart from some dispersed fragments only the records for Co. Mayo survive. They provide, barony by barony, a list of proprietors, the extent and location of their holdings together with notices of church lands, abbey lands, land held by **dower**, incidences of **wardship**, **reversions**, mills and fisheries. The existence of so recent an inquisition obviated the need for the the commissioners of the **Civil Survey** (1654–56) to survey Connacht. (O'Sullivan, *The Strafford inquisition*.)

strays. Wandering domestic animals which were impounded and, if left unclaimed, forfeited to the manorial lord. Owners of strays were liable to fines in the manorial courts. *See* waif, poundage.

string course. A moulded horizontal band around a building which projects out from the wall.

striping. An early nineteenth-century innovation associated with the **rundale** system of commonfield agriculture, striping was the process by which inter-mixed holdings within a single arable field were consolidated. Striping gave each farmer a consolidated share of the various qualities of land which he had previously held as a cluster of scattered plots. It was achieved by creating new straight boundaries at right angles to the contours and across the different soils while at the same time equalising access to water, roads and pasture. When mapped, evidence of striping can be seen in 'ladder farms', a series of parallel, long, narrow fields. A less common alternative was the practice of squaring which involved throwing the land into squares as opposed to stripes.

subsidy. A parliamentary grant to the crown. Subsidies were levied on property owners and were overseen by county commissions appointed to assess the levy and compile lists of taxpayers. The lists were conveyed to the **sheriff** who collected the levy. The names and payments of taxpayers were entered on the subsidy rolls which are records of the court of the **exchequer.** Twenty-four subsidies were voted between 1662 and 1668 and a further 24 from 1672, each subsidy being to the value of £15,000 and levied at the rate of 2s. 8d. in the pound on all owners of property of the value of £1 yearly or possessed of goods valued at £3 or more. The original subsidy rolls perished in 1922 but transcripts survive for the period 1634–69 in the Public Record Office of Northern Ireland and the National Archives. (*PRI rep. DK,* 33, pp. 44–47; Walton, 'The subsidy roll', pp. 47–96.)

suffragan. Subordinate, the relationship of a bishop to his archbishop.

sugán. (Ir.) A versatile straw rope used for tethering animals, making harnesses, tying thatch, mat-and basket-making, seating, mattresses and hen roosts. Straw rope also served as an improvised belt.

suit of court. The obligation to attend and participate in the manorial courts.

summonister (*summonitor*). An Irish **exchequer** official engaged in the collection of the royal revenue who cited defaulters and made out the first process. The office of summonister was abolished in 1835–6 by 5 & 6 Will. IV, c. 55.

super modo et causa, **writ of.** A writ requiring a statement of cause as to why an official carried out a particular action.

supersedeas, **writ of.** (L., you shall desist)A writ ordering a stay on legal proceedings.

supporters. In heraldry, figures of living creatures placed at the side of a shield and appearing to support it.

Supremacy, Act of. The supremacy act established the key tenet of the Reformation that the king rather than the pope was the supreme head of the church in England and Ireland. It was enacted by statute in England in 1534 and in Ireland in 1537 (28 Hen. VIII, c. 131). Queen Mary repealed the act in 1557 but it was re-enacted under

Elizabeth in 1560 (2 Elizabeth I, c. 1). The Irish parliament also prescribed the taking of the oath of supremacy for all office-holders and clergymen. In the short-term the act had little effect in Ireland because it carried no major theological implications for believers and no great effort was made to enforce it. Later it became the means by which Catholics were progressively excluded from office.

surcoat. A coat worn over a suit of armour. The term 'coat of armour' derives from the surcoat which bore a duplicate of the design on the noble's shield.

Surnames, Index of. An index to names recorded in the **tithe applotment** books and **Griffith's Valuation**, also known as the Householder Index. Surnames are conveniently listed in alphabetical order by barony and civil parish. Names which can be found in Griffith's Valuation are indicated by the letter 'G' together with a number indicating the frequency of that surname. The letter 'T' denotes an entry in the tithe applotment books. It is important to remember that Griffith's Valuation and the tithe applotment books are not censuses. Griffith's overlooked some families living in very poor houses or families sharing tenements in urban areas. The tithe applotment books are land surveys and so labourers and tradesmen and landless families are omitted. The index can be consulted at major repositories such as the National Archives, National Library and the Public Record Office of Northern Ireland.

surplice. A white broad-sleeved outer gown worn by priests and choristers.

surrender and regrant. From the mid-sixteenth century, the crown policy of accepting the surrender of land by native Irish lords and re-granting it under letters **patent** to be held with titles valid under English law. This process invalidated **tanistry** and **gavelkind** (the native Irish system of succession and inheritance) by introducing the feudal principle of **primogeniture**. The difficulty was that the native lords didn't actually own the freehold on the land they were surrendering – it belonged to the sept – and succession by primogeniture added a new layer of divisiveness to a system of succession that was, in any case, often a source of division in itself.

Survey and Distribution, Books of. The manuscript *Books of Survey and Distribution* contain, townland by townland, records of the transfer or recovery of land forfeited during the 1641 rebellion. They contain the names of the original landowners, the extent of their estates, the grantees under the Restoration land settlement and the **Commission of Grace**, purchasers under the **Trustees Sale** and the official instrument by which transfer or recovery was effected. There are two sets in the National Archives (Quit Rent and Headfort sets), a third in the Royal Irish Academy (Taylor set) and a fourth in the Public Record Office of Northern Ireland (the Annesley set). Some county books of survey and distribution have been printed by the Irish Manuscripts Commission. (Simington, *Books of survey*, I, II; MacGiolla Coille, *Books of survey*, III; MacGiolla Coille and Simington, *Books of survey*, IV.)

survey, manorial. A detailed and lengthy description of all aspects of a manor undertaken to discover areas of potential revenue within the manor as well as areas where revenue might be increased. It was often initiated upon the accession of a new lord and was conducted at a meeting of the manor known as a court of survey. A manorial survey comprises three parts: an outline of the manor boundaries, a jury presentment of the customs and appurtenances of the manor and finally a **rent roll** or **rental** of all the tenants, their names, details of their holdings and the rents they paid.

surveyor-general. Established in the sixteenth century, the office of surveyor-general was attached to the court of **exchequer**. The full title of office was 'surveyor, appraiser, valuer or esteemer and extensor general of all and singular the king's honours, manors, lordships, messuages, lands, tenements, woods, possessions, revenues and hereditaments in Ireland'. The surveyor-general performed an important function in the issuing of royal grants of land. Such grants were issued in terms of a specific monetary value and it was the surveyor-general's function to locate a suitable piece of land in crown hands and conduct a local inquisition to determine whether it was equivalent in value to the sum stated in the king's letter of grant. This function became redundant after the seventeenth century since no land remained in the sovereign's gift. In the eighteenth century the surveyors-general were responsible for civil buildings such as Dublin Castle and military fortifications. They controlled the money granted for barrack construction and were involved in their design and erection. Scandals associated with barrack contracts and sub-standard construction led to the circumscription of the powers of the surveyor-general and in 1762 the post was suppressed. Henceforth responsibility for barracks and fortifications was transferred to the Ordnance and the surveyor's residual responsibility for civil buildings devolved to the Barrack Board and **Board of Works**, the forerunner to the Office of Public Works. *See* patent. (McParland, 'The office', pp. 91–101; *Idem, Public architecture*, pp. 127–130, 135–8.)

survey, parliamentary. A parliamentary survey was equivalent to a **manorial survey** writ large to embrace a wide area. It resembles a manorial survey in structure, detailing the boundaries of each holding, the owner's name, the amount of land held and the nature of tenure. It also includes an estimated annual rental value, details of the number of houses on the land together with a description of appurtenances such as mills or kilns and the disposition of the tithe. The parliamentary survey known as the **Civil Survey** was conducted in Ireland between 1654–56 to ascertain the amount of land available to the **Commonwealth** to satisfy army arrears of pay and to recompense **adventurers** for money they had contributed towards quelling the 1641 rebellion. This was an unmapped survey and all acreages were estimated. A subsequent survey, the **Down Survey**, had a narrower focus but was more accurate. Each forfeited holding was physically measured and then mapped. The Down Survey eschewed the detail of the Civil Survey in all but the owner's name in 1641 and the amount of land he held. *See* Gross Survey.

sustenation fund. The perilous state of **Church of Ireland** finances after disestablishment led to the inauguration of the sustenation fund in 1870 which was used to support the Irish clergy. Church of Ireland parishioners were invited to contribute to the fund an average of 2% of their annual income or property values for 15 years and to subscribe a penny per week. Parishes also paid assessments into the fund. This prudent initiative and the generous response of the Anglican community ensured the financial stability of the church. *See* Representative Church Body.

sweat house. A small corbelled chamber used to treat rheumatic pains.

synod. 1: The governing or advisory assembly of a church 2: The annual assembly of **Presbyterian** presbyteries which meets to co-ordinate the work of the church and elect a moderator. *See* General Assembly of the Presbyterian Church in Ireland, presbytery, session.

T

tabard. A loose, sleeveless surcoat worn by peasants, monks and infantry. Emblazoned with the sovereign's arms it was the official dress of a **herald** or **pursuivant**. Knights in armour also wore short-sleeved tabards opened at the sides and emblazoned front and back and on the sleeves.

tail ploughing. A method of ploughing by tying a wooden plough to an animal's tail. Much derided by the English as a cruel practice, tail-ploughing prevented damage to the plough because the animal stopped whenever it struck a rock. (McAuliffe, 'Ploughing', pp. 9–11.)

tale-money, money in tale. 1: Money of account, cash 2: Money reckoned by counting the nominal value of the coins and not by weight.

tallage. 1: A crown tax imposed on the king's estates and on boroughs from the twelfth century. The boroughs were later exempted when they began to send representatives to parliament since they were now liable for taxes levied by parliament 2: Any payment exacted arbitrarily by the lord without the consent of his tenants.

tallow. The solid white fat (lard) of cattle and sheep procured by boiling and skimming. It was used for candle-making, soap and lubrication.

tally. A wooden stick which recorded details of payments into the lower **exchequer** and served as a receipt to the sheriff or official making the payment. The tally was split down the middle and one-half was retained in the **exchequer** to be matched with the payees half when his accounts were audited. Written records of the tallies were kept on the receipt rolls. (Connolly, *Medieval record*, pp. 18–19.)

tanner. A tradesman who converted hide into leather by infusing it in a liquid containing tannic acid which was extracted from the crushed bark of oak and other trees.

tánaiste. (Ir., second) The successor designate of a Gaelic lord, elected by the *derbfine* or kin group. In English this system of succession is known as **tanistry**.

tanistry. The practice of replacing a dead Gaelic lord by his *tánaiste*, or deputy who was elected during the lord's lifetime by the *derbfine* and who usually acquired his position by demonstrating that he possessed the martial skills and intelligence required for the job. Tanistry was designed to secure the survival of the sept by ensuring that the fittest were advanced to the lordship but it also encouraged division and uncertainty as the various aspirants jockeyed for power. The crown policy of receiving the surrender of Gaelic lands and re-granting the surrendered lands with title valid under common law and succession by **primogeniture** was designed to eliminate tanistry and create a feudal relationship between lord and crown.

tate, tathe. A Gaelic spatial measure equivalent to 60 acres in Fermanagh and Monaghan. It was known as a **balliboe** in Tyrone. In the sixteenth and seventeenth centuries Monaghan and Fermanagh were subdivided into a number of **ballybetaghs**, each of which was divided into **quarters**, each quarter containing four tates of 60 Irish acres. Hence, a rough table of equivalence reads:

      60a. Irish = 1 tate/balliboe
      4 tates = 1 quarter (240a. Irish)
      4 quarters = 1 ballybetagh (c. 1000a. Irish)

In Monaghan the tate corresponds with townland boundaries and civil parish boundaries almost always correspond with ballybetaghs. *See* acre.

team. *See* toll and team.

teasel. A prickly herb whose flower contained hooked bracts that were used in the woollen industry to raise a nap (a downy or hairy surface) on woollen fabric.

temperance society. Concern over the excessive consumption of alcohol and its effects on family and society prompted the emergence of temperance and total abstinence societies in nineteenth-century Ireland. The campaign to suppress intemperance was characterised by conflicting approaches towards resolving the problem. Temperance, meaning moderation, did not imply teetotalism and throughout the century a verbal war was conducted between the advocates of moderation, which included the bulk of the Catholic hierarchy, and those (such as Fr Theobald Mathew) who saw total abstinence as the only way forward in the battle against insobriety. Initially the impetus for moderation derived from Protestants in the 1820s who opposed spirit consumption, believing that spirits – rather than wine or beer – were the primary cause of drunkenness. Increasingly, however, total abstainers, who claimed that short-term pledges of abstinence were useless, came to occupy centre stage in the campaign to suppress intemperance. Fr Mathew, a Capuchin, embarked on a total abstinence crusade which peaked in the early 1840s and resulted in over half of the population of Ireland committing themselves to teetotalism. However, the movement was heavily tied to the cult of Mathew's personality and after the Great Famine teetotalism declined. From the 1860s, with some Catholic support, Protestant-dominated temperance societies focused on securing legislative action to restrict opening hours. The most successful and enduring legacy of the struggle against intemperance was the founding in 1889 by the Jesuit, Fr James Cullen, of the Total Abstinence League of the Sacred Heart, a body which later metamorphosed into the Pioneer Total Abstinence Association of the Sacred Heart or the Pioneer League. Eschewing populism, Cullen created an elite association of committed total abstainers who would act as pioneers for the slow, steady conversion of insobriety in the country. (Malcolm, *'Ireland Sober'*; Townend, *Father Mathew.*)

templars. *See* knights templar.

temporalities. The benefices, possessions and resources of a church.

tenant-in-chief. *See capite, in.*

Tenant League (1850–1859). The Tenant Protection Society, an agrarian combination, was founded in Callan, Co. Kilkenny, in 1849 to seek parliamentary support for changes in land law. It aimed to secure the fixing of rents by independent evaluation and agreements between tenants that they would not acquire the holding of an evicted tenant who had been prepared to pay the independently-fixed rent. In 1850 representatives of various **tenant-right** societies met in Dublin and founded the Tenant League. The league sought to achieve fixity of tenure, lower rents and legal protection for Ulster custom (tenant-right) through political means and formed itself into a political party. The two leading figures in the League were the former Young Irelander, Charles Gavan Duffy, and Frederick Lucas, an English convert to Catholicism. To achieve critical mass the Tenant

League joined with the **Catholic Defence Association** (a group of Irish Liberal MPs who were campaigning for the repeal of the **Ecclesiastical Titles Bill**), simply adding their goal of lower rents and protection of tenant-right to those of its ally. The alliance pursued an independent policy in parliament and opposed all governments that would not meet its demands. With clerical support the 1852 election returned 48 members of the alliance to Westminster but it was immediately riven by the acceptance of posts in the new administration by two of its leading members, William Keogh and John Sadleir. The alliance was reduced to 26 members in 1853 and to 12 two years later. It finally collapsed over an 1859 **Tory** parliamentary reform bill and the Tenant League went out of existence in its aftermath having made no progress on its aims. (Comerford, 'Churchmen', p. 400 *passim*; Whyte, *The Tenant League*.)

Tenant Protection Society. *See* Tenant League

tenant-right (Ulster custom). The custom of having the option of renewal upon the termination of a lease. Originating in the seventeenth century as a lure to attract tenants, it represented an acknowledgement of the tenant's right to remain in possession as long as he paid rent and fulfilled his obligations, to sell his interest without reference to the landlord and to receive compensation for improvements in the event of eviction. Under tenant-right an outgoing tenant could sell his interest in a holding – even a yearly one – although no valuable improvement had been made and despite the fact that the his interest had no legal standing. There were also restrictions on the amount a tenant's rent could be increased because of improvements effected on his holding. Ulster custom was a custom and not a right and was always liable to the caprice of the landlord. Fixity of tenure and free sale were attractive to tenants who did not possess tenant-right but they came at a price. Tenant-right might cost up to 40 times the annual rent to the incoming tenant. It was legalised by statute in those areas where it existed by Gladstone's **Landlord and Tenant Act** (1870). Following on the heels of the recommendations of the **Bessborough Commission** (1880), the **Land Law Act** (1881) gave statutory recognition to the claim for fair rent, free sale and fixity of tenure.

tenement. 1: Latterly and colloquially, a term used to denote a dilapidated urban building let by room or rooms 2: In the **Civil Survey** (1654–6) it is used to describe a small land-holding (including house and garden) let to a tenant 3: In the Tenement Valuation or Primary Valuation of Tenements (1846–52) the term refers to any land, house, mill, bog or fishery. *See* Griffith's Valuation.

ten pound castle. A tower house constructed with the aid of a subsidy of £10 which was offered in the four counties of the **Pale** between

1429 and 1447.

tenure. (L., *tenere*, to hold) The manner and conditions by which land is held or occupied. Tenure answers the question 'how is the land held?' *See* copyholder, customary tenure, entail, fee simple, fee tail, freehold, frankalmoigh, grand sergeanty, knight-service, lease, lease for lives, lease for three lives renewable forever, petty sergeanty, seisin, socage.

Tenures Abolition Act (1662). The legislative instrument (14 & 15 Chas II, c. 19) that abolished almost all forms of feudal tenure and most of the incidents including **aids**, **wardship**, **marriage**, and alienation fines. Existing tenures were converted into free or common **socage** (freehold) and all future tenures must be in common socage. **Heriots** and rents were preserved as were tenure by **copyhold** – which may not have existed in Ireland – and frankalmoign which did. The crown was recompensed for the loss of associated income by the imposition of a hearth tax.

termon land. An endowment of land granted to a monastery or parish church by a Gaelic lord in return for prayers and masses, the income from which was to be used to maintain the church. Typically the land was leased to a local sept or septs in return for dues or rents and the lessees were also required to provide **refection** to the bishop on his **visitation**. *See* coarb, erenagh.

ternybeg. (Ir., *tiarna beag*, a little lord) In the eighteenth century, a **middleman**.

Terry Alts. A nineteenth-century secret combination which agitated against the payment of **tithe**. Operating in counties Westmeath, Limerick, Galway and Clare, the Terry Alts offered largely non-violent resistance to the assessment and collection of tithe.

terrier. A written commentary containing details supplementary to a map. The terriers which accompany the maps of the seventeenth-century **Down Survey**, for example, bear a description of each barony and parish together with the names of the occupiers and the extent and the quality of each numbered plot. A **glebe** terrier was a written description of the church and accompanying glebe land together with a map or maps which were kept to show the bishop on his **visitation**.

Test Act. Anglican concern at the growth of Presbyterianism led to the appending by the English **privy council** of a test clause to the repressive anti-Catholic legislation of 1704 (2 Anne, c. 6, s. 17). It required all office-holders to receive communion according to the Anglican rite within three months of taking office and to acquire a certificate vouching for this. By this means Presbyterians were expelled from all civil and military offices under the crown and lost control of the northern boroughs, notably their strongholds of Belfast and Derry. Between 1704 and 1780 Protestant dissenters, although disbarred from municipal corporations, remained eligible to vote in the county constituencies and to sit in parliament. Eased somewhat by a series of indemnity acts (*See* Toleration Act), they became eligible again for public office when the test clause was repealed in 1780 (19 & 20 Geo. III, c. 6). The repeal of the Test Act, however, did not guarantee that they would actually be appointed. Presbyterians, unlike Roman Catholics, were now permitted to bear arms and participate in civil life. *See* Penal Laws, Presbyterian. (Beckett, *Protestant*, pp. 40–52, 83–105.)

tester (testoon). A shilling of debased issue which entered circulation c. 1542–3 during the reign of Henry VII. Although nominally of the value of 12 pence, its value sank as low as sixpence and it was later taken out of circulation.

tester bed. A bed with an overhead canopy.

testes adfuerunt. In Catholic marriage registers, the names of the witnesses present at a marriage.

thallage, thawlogue, thawluck. A half-loft located on either side of a chimney canopy.

theodolite. A surveying instrument used for measuring horizontal and vertical angles. Modern theodolites have been greatly elaborated to incorporate a telescope instead of sights, a level, a compass, a vernier scale (for measuring very small fractions of degrees), a micrometer and a vertical circle for measuring altitudes of elevations and depressions.

thingmote. In Norse Dublin, a mound near Suffolk Street where arbitrations were conducted.

Third Order Regular. *See* Franciscan Third Order Regular.

Thirty-Nine Articles. A statement of the doctrines of the Church of England adopted by the English bishops and clergy in convocation in 1562 and incorporated almost in their entirety in the Irish **Articles of Religion** in 1615. The articles affirm predestination and royal supremacy and endorse clerical marriage. Papal supremacy, Catholic ceremonies and traditions and the **Anabaptist** doctrine of the community of property are repudiated.

tholsel. Town hall.

'thorough'. A term used to describe Lord-Deputy Wentworth's policy of maximising crown income by increasing the efficiency of the machinery of state, notably the courts of **castle chamber**, **wards and liveries** and **high commission** together with the **commission for defective titles**. In purely financial terms Wentworth succeeded but his despotism, together with the replacement of senior officials by trusted nominees, unleashed an antagonism which rebounded on him when the Irish house of commons provided the evidence which sent him to his death in 1640. (Kearney, *Strafford*, pp. 69–84.)

'Three F's'. The three f's of fixity of tenure, fair rent and freedom of sale, collectively known as **tenant-right**, constituted the campaigning goal of agrarian agitators after the Great Famine. Tenant-right was legalised by statute in those areas where it existed by Gladstone's **Landlord and Tenant Act** (1870) and was given statutory recognition just over ten years later in his **Land Law Act** (1881).

Threshers. A non-political protest group, reminiscent of the Whiteboys of the late eighteenth century, which emerged in Connacht in 1806–7 agitating on the issue of **tithe**, priests' fees, wages and land prices.

Thurles, Synod of (1850). The first major gathering of the Catholic episcopacy for centuries, the Thurles synod was convened by the newly-appointed archbishop of Armagh, Paul Cullen, to deal with the controversial **Queen's Colleges** issue and to establish uniformity of discipline and devotional practice within the church. Although a majority of the bishops present voted a policy of total non-co-operation with the new university colleges, some favoured a more moderate line. Measures to counter the activities of Protestant missionaries were agreed. In pastoral matters the synod required that children of mixed marriages be raised as Catholics and directed that baptisms and marriages be conducted only in church. See Ecclesiastical Titles Act. (Larkin, *The making*, pp. 27–57.)

tidemill. A mill operated by harnessing the power of tide. Tidemills were constructed on narrow inlets and comprised a retaining wall and gate through which the rising tide flowed. At high tide the gate was closed. The retained sea-water was released through a millrace at low tide, powering the millwheel as it escaped.

tide-waiter. A customs and excise official who met ships arriving on the tide, boarded and searched them, searched all passengers and seamen embarking and disembarking and checked all goods being loaded or unloaded. (Ní Mhurchadha, *The customs*, p. 34.)

tie-beam. See cruck.

tiercel. A male of any kind of hawk, particularly a peregrine falcon or goshawk.

tipstaff. A court attendant or crier.

tithe. Payment owed to the church, nominally equivalent to one-tenth of earnings although in Ireland that proportion was rarely exacted. It was paid in kind until the seventeenth and eighteenth centuries when cash payments were substituted. Originally tithe was not absolute property but assigned in trust for the discharge of certain religious duties. After the Reformation it was unpopular in Ireland because the burden fell on the majority Catholic peasantry who benefited little from the recipients, the clergymen of the minority Church of Ireland. William Blackstone's neat eighteenth-century definition of tithe as 'the tenth part of the increase arising yearly from the profits of the land, the stock upon lands, and the personal industry of the inhabitants' identifies the three categories under which tithe was exacted. The profits of the land accrued from crops such as cereals, vegetables and fruit was known as **predial** (praedial) tithe. Lambs, colts and calves together with the products of animals such as milk, cheese, butter and eggs were deemed mixed tithe and the fruits of labour and industry were known as personal tithe. Tithe was levied on the potato crop only in Munster and parts of south Leinster where it was considered a staple like wheat or barley. Grasslands were exempt from 1736 until the Tithe Composition Act of 1823, thereby ensuring that the grazier and landlord interest, the richer section of the community, was heavily advantaged.

Tithe was also divided into two classes, great and small. This division derived from the medieval monastic practice of assigning the small tithe (the personal and mixed tithe and minor crops such as fruit or vegetables) to a **vicar** in return for the performance of religious duties. The great tithe of wheat, barley, oats and hay was paid to the monastic **rector**. After the **dissolution** the great tithe devolved to the crown and was granted or sold to laymen or bishops or cathedral chapters. Consequently tithe was not necessarily paid to the clergyman of a particular parish. He may not have been entitled to receive all or even any of the tithe. *See* perpetual curacy. Lay impropriation resulted in a significant loss of income to the Church of Ireland. As late as 1832 over one-seventh of parochial income was impropriate.

Tithe was collected not by a clergyman but by a **tithe-farmer** or tithe-proctor acting on his behalf. The clergyman received a fixed sum and the excess was retained by the proctor who was thereby motivated to exact every last penny. Inevitably the proctor was unpopular in local communities and particularly when he arrived to conduct the contentious annual valuation. Tithe was a recurring grievance throughout the eighteenth century yet anti-tithe agrarian societies often appeared more exercised about regulating the rate at which it was exacted than with the principle of tithe *per se*. *See* Whiteboys. The Tithe Composition Act of July 1823 (4 Geo. IV, c. 99) was introduced to remove some of the objectionable features by providing for the voluntary commutation of tithe to a fixed charge on the land. Commissioners appointed by the incumbent were to meet with parishioners to agree on a fixed sum to be paid by the parish. Parochial assessments were then conducted and the charge apportioned among tithe-payers relative to the amount and quality of land each held. This new charge did not fluctuate annually as it had done when the proctor valued the land and was to remain operative for 21 years. Pasturage was also brought within the compass of tithe. The Tithe Composition Act was not a success and contributed to the tithe war which began in November 1830 at Graiguenamanagh, Co. Kilkenny. Again the issue was the level at which tithe was exacted. The 1823 act had linked tithe with the average price of corn during the previous seven years, a period of high prices. When grain prices collapsed tithe-payers considered the fixed rate excessive. The situation was further aggravated in the 1820s by the campaign for **Catholic emancipation**. After the granting of emancipation in 1829 a vacuum was created which was filled by anti-tithe agitation. Finally, there was a sectarian overlay to the conflict. Catholics were growing ever more reluctant to contribute to an institution that reviled their beliefs and offered nothing in return.

In the early 1830s leadership on the issue was provided by the Catholic clergy, urban and middle-class repealers, Daniel O'Connell and wealthy Catholic graziers who had been caught for the first time by the extension of tithe to pasturage. In 1832 less than half the tithe was collected. In June of that year the Attorney-General's Act (2 & 3 Will. IV, c. 41) empowered the attorney-general to pay some of the 1831 arrears and to collect the rest by force. Stanley's composition act (2 William IV, c. 119) later in the year attempted to mitigate the worst aspects of tithe by making the assessment an official rather than a private arrangement, by slightly reducing the level of tithe, by exempting the poorest tenants from direct liability and by allowing a 15% rebate to landlords and better-off tenants who took responsibility for collecting it. However, less than one-third of tithe due between 1831 and 1833 was paid and government expeditions to collect the arrears cost more than was recovered. The violence continued. Under the **Church Million Act** (3 & 4 Will. IV, c. 100, 1833), the government assumed responsibility for the payment of all arrears for the years 1831–3 – subject to a scaling down of the amount owed – and no further attempt was made to pursue defaulters. By this time the Catholic church had begun to disassociate itself from tithe agitation and violence declined from 1835. In that year the **Lichfield House Compact** shifted the focus away from tithe to the principle of applying the supposed surplus to be generated by a new tithe reform act to extra-ecclesiastical purposes such as the education of the poor. O'Connell undertook not to press for the disestablishment of the Church of Ireland, the repeal of the union or parliamentary reform in return for a reduction in tithe, municipal reform and the appointment of Catholics and liberal Protestants to public office and the judiciary in Ireland. In 1838 (1 & 2 Vict., c. 109) tithe and tithe composition was abolished and replaced with a rentcharge set at 75% of the nominal value of the tithe. Tithe was subsumed into rents and collected by landlords who received a bonus of up to 25% for assuming that responsibility. Thus the tithe war ended in a reduction in the level of tithe, the exemption of poorer tenants, the assumption by the treasury of responsibility for the payment of the bulk of arrears accumulated over eight years and with landlords replacing the proctors as collectors of tithe. Tithe was not abolished when the Church of Ireland was disestablished in 1869 – it remained payable to the state although later legislation permitted owners and occupiers of tithable land to compound for it. *See* tithe agistment, tithe applotment, tithe-farmer, tithe fish. (O'Donoghue, 'Causes'; *Idem*, 'Opposition'.)

tithe agistment. The tithe on pasturage for dry and barren cattle was regularly collected in Ulster but not in the rest of the country. With the increase in pasturage in the eighteenth century this tithe became a potentially valuable source of income to the Church of Ireland. A test case before **king's bench** in 1707 resulted in an adjudication in favour of the clergy, a judgement that was upheld in 1722 by the **exchequer**. Inevitably this aroused the ire of landlords. In 1736 parliament rejected the claims of the clergy and threatened a committee of inquiry into the pastoral duties of bishops and clergymen. Fearful of what such a committee might uncover the clergy backed down thereby liberating the rich graziers while the poorer classes continued to bear a disproportionate burden. Tithe agistment was abolished by 40 Geo. III c. 23 (1800) and land set to pasture eventually came within the compass of tithe after the passage of the Tithe Composition Act of 1823 (4 Geo. IV, c. 99). *See* tithe.

tithe applotment. Tithe applotment was the process by which the value of **tithe** was calculated. The Tithe Composition Act (1823) allowed for the payment of tithe in cash rather than in kind and a nationwide valuation was conducted to calculate how much was due from each landholder. The valuation was carried out between 1823 and 1838 when tithe was replaced by a rentcharge. The original records of the early nineteenth-century tithe aplotments are available for inspection in the National Archives and the Public Record Office of Northern Ireland. Sadly, the applotment books were not compiled to a uniform schedule. Some record townland names, occupiers' names, the amount of land held and the amount payable. Others also include the landlord's name and an assessment of the productive capacity of the land. Thus regional comparisons are not easy. In the absence of contemporaneous **census** returns the applotment books provide compensatory genealogical data and when used in conjunction with the post-Famine **Griffith's Valuation** reveal much about changing landholding patterns. (Simington, 'The tithe', pp. 295–98.)

tithe farmer, tithe proctor. The assessor and collector of tithe who paid the beneficial clergyman or tithe-owner a fixed sum and made a profit by maximising the amount collected. The tithe-farmer appeared in early summer to view the crops and estimate the likely yield. Just before harvest he returned to bargain with the grower. The practice of valuing crops by quantity in good years and by price in scarce years was particularly resented. Long-term failure to pay, and payment often lagged over a year behind, could result in a summons to appear before two magistrates who issued decrees in relation to the debt. For sums above £10 debtors could be summoned before the bishop's court. Disputes between tithe-farmers and tithe-payers were referred to the owner of the tithe for his adjudication. The Tithe Composition Act (1823) legislated for the extinction of the tithe-farmer by allowing for the voluntary commutation of tithe to a fixed charge on the land.

tithe fish. It was customary for tithe on fish to be paid one-half in the parish of origin of the fishermen and one-half where the fish were landed.

tithing. In feudal times, a form of social control that made groups of 10–12 villagers responsible for the good behaviour of each other. The tithing was the unit of collective responsibility associated with the **View of Frankpledge**.

titulado. Person of distinction or title, nobleman, gentleman. The term is used in the 1660 **poll tax** records to denote the leading proprietor(s) in a parish. The precise rank of each *titulado* is noted because the poll tax was levied according to a graduated scale. *See Census of Ireland circa 1659.*

toft. A holding comprising a dwelling (plus outbuildings) and land. A **tenement**.

togher. 1: A spatial unit of land measurement in Antrim, consisting of between two and three hundred acres 2: A wooden causeway.

tolboll. The payment of a certain volume of beer to the lord by the brewer when brewing. In the course of a lawsuit in the sixteenth century St Thomas' Abbey, Dublin, claimed to have received a grant from King John of the tolboll of a gallon and a half of the best and as much of the second brew of the taverns of Dublin. Henry II continued the grant provided the abbey maintained 60 paupers and scholars in food, drink and clothing. (Berry, 'Proceedings', pp. 169– 73.) *See* ale silver.

Toleration Act (1719). The act (6 Geo. I, c. 9) which granted freedom of worship to dissenters. They retained their entitlement to vote and sit in parliament but were denied admission to local government and the magistracy. The act failed to satisfy **Presbyterians** because it did not revoke the sacramental test which barred them from taking office. *See* Test Act.

toll (tholl) and team (theam). Rights associated with the soc or jurisdiction of a manor. Toll was the right to exact a toll, tribute or custom on the sale of goods or cattle on a manorial estate and the right to take profits. Team was a grant to a manorial lord which entitled him to have, restrain and judge **bondsmen** or **villeins** and to adjudicate the rightful possession of cattle. *See* sac and soc.

toll thorough. A toll exacted by a corporate town in consideration of services performed in the maintenance of streets (*pavage*), bridges (*pontage*) and walls (*murage*).

toll-road. Toll-roads were created on major arterial routes to ensure that the burden of road maintenance was not borne by those inhabitants living in the baronies through which they passed. *See* six-day labour. Parliament legislated for the first Irish turnpike or toll-road, the Dublin to Kilcullen route, in 1729 and continued to legislate for new and existing toll-roads into the nineteenth century. The roads were supervised by a turnpike trust and financed by private capital in the expectation that tolls would meet maintenance costs and return a profit on the venture. Initial capital was raised by the issuing of debentures which yielded between 5% and 6% per annum. The Irish toll-road system failed to generate sufficient income to fund proper maintenance, interest payments were frequently in arrears and local inhabitants resented the double-taxation of tolls and county cess. The nineteenth-century railway boom hastened its demise. Following a commission of inquiry the turnpike trusts were wound up in 1855 and 1856. The term 'turnpike' may derive from the barrier across the road which was turned or opened to allow passage to carts. (Broderick, *An early toll-road*.)

tonnage (tunnage). A customs duty of so much per ton or (in the case of wine) per tun.

top-entry house. A nineteenth-century single-storey, over-basement, suburban house.

Topographia Hiberniae. *The Topography of Ireland* was written by Giraldus de Barri or Giraldus Cambrensis (Cambria) between 1185 and 1188 and contains an account of Ireland in the early years of the Norman invasion. The work is the result of a number of visits he made to the east and south-east of the country. Written in three parts, the book treats of topography and fauna, wonders and miracles, the history of Ireland and the nature of its inhabitants. It has been severely criticised for its inaccuracies, tall tales and credulity but it also provides a rare insight into twelfth century Ireland without which our understanding of the period would be greatly impoverished. *See Expugnatio Hibernica.* (Cambrensis, *Topographia*; Martin, 'Gerald of Wales', pp. 279–292.)

Topographical Dictionary of Ireland, A. Samuel Lewis' two-volume gazetteer of Ireland with accompanying atlas appeared in 1837. The aim of the dictionary was 'to give, in a condensed form, a faithful and impartial description of each place'. Lewis compiled the material for his dictionary by drawing on official sources (census returns, parliamentary reports and inquiries, reports of the Board of Education and Ordnance Survey data) and by corresponding with ministers or resident gentleman in the localities. Correspondents also vouched for the proofs before the work was committed to print. Arranged by county, city, town and parish, entries typically include statistical data, brief histories, notes on topography, geology and flora, aspects of civil and ecclesiastical administration, details of economic activity and the names and residences of gentry. (Lewis, A *topographical dictionary*.)

toponym. A descriptive placename derived from some topographical feature in the landscape, e.g. Tulach mór, a great mound.

tort. A breach of legal duty for which a civil action may be taken. Thus reckless behaviour which imperils life or health or which provokes mental stress, defamation and the violation of privacy or property rights are all actionable under the law of torts. Negligence, the failure to perform a duty of care, is a central concept in torts. It is imperative, however, to establish that a duty of care was owed to the injured party and that an injury was indeed inflicted.

tory. 1: In Ireland, a **rapparee** or rural bandit 2: The term was first used in political circles in 1679 by **Whigs** to disparage those who supported the accession to the throne of James, duke of York. Many Tories reluctantly accepted the new order which followed the '**glorious revolution** of 1688' but remained essentially conservative. They opposed the Whig philosophy of a contract between the ruler and the ruled and, as staunch Anglicans in England and Ireland, resisted attempts to introduce measures of toleration for dissenters. Although they enjoyed a brief period in office in 1710–14, their unease about the revolution during the reigns of George I and George II led to their complete exclusion from power between 1714 and 1760. When William Pitt the younger was elected prime minister in 1783 the Tories became the party of government until the 1830s after which they began to style themselves Conservatives. In the early eighteenth century Irish Toryism was strongest among Anglican churchmen but it declined because of its association with Jacobitism and because the dominant Whigs proved to have little sympathy for **Presbyterians**.

towerhouse. Medieval in origin, the towerhouse consisted of a small stone keep of three or four storeys. The living quarters were in the upper storeys. Towerhouses originally had a courtyard or **barmkin** attached. Some had a thatched hall adjoining the tower which served as the living quarters.

Town Improvement Acts (1849, 1854). The 1849 act (12 & 13 Vict., c. 85) removed the few governmental functions such as lighting and firefighting that had been retained by the general **vestry** and vested them in Dublin corporation.. That of 1854 (17 & 18 Vict., c. 103) provided for the erection of town commissioners in towns with populations of 1,500 or more. By 1871 almost 80 towns had achieved a local administration under this act, bringing the number of municipal authorities in Ireland to over 110. *See* Municipal Corporations Reform Act.

townland. The smallest and most enduring land division of the county (which it preceded), possibly deriving from **quarters** of the ancient **ballybetaghs** (or **tates** in the case of Monaghan). Larger townlands often comprise areas of poorer land and so the area of townlands may have been determined by its productive capacity. There are over 60,000 townlands in Ireland, ranging in size from Millbank in Co. Dublin at three roods one perch to Sheskin in Co. Mayo at 7,012 acres. Townland names are overwhelmingly of Gaelic origin but many, including those suffixed with 'town', are Anglo-Norman and a few are the eighteenth and nineteenth creations of local landlords. Some townland names disappeared due to amalgamation or division by the nineteenth-century **Ordnance Survey** which also created new townlands, straightened boundaries and transferred portions of one townland to another. Mapped for the first edition of the Ordnance Survey, the townland became the basic unit for the taking of the **census** (although townland populations have not been published since 1911) and for **Griffith's Valuation**. (Crawford, 'The study', pp. 97–115; Ó Dálaigh, Cronin and Connell, *Irish townlands*, pp. 9–13.)

Townland Index. The *General alphabetical index to the townlands and towns, parishes and baronies of Ireland*, or *Townland Index*, was published in three editions (1851, 1871, 1901) as a townland location finder. Entries provide the relevant Ordnance Survey map reference, the name of the civil parish, barony, county and poor law union (from 1901 the district electoral division and number) for each townland.

towne. A Gaelic unit of spatial measurement employed in Offaly, Carlow and Antrim, equivalent to 20 **great acres**.

townreed. A township.

tracery. Embroidered architectural work in Gothic windows.

transept. The 'arms' of a cruciform church.

transplantation. Following the suppression of the Confederate Rebellion in 1652, Catholic landowners were ordered into Connacht to make way for **adventurers** who had contributed financially to the quelling of the revolt and for soldiers who had served in the war, all of whom were to be recompensed with grants of forfeited land. In addition to those transplanted from the other provinces, landowners in Connacht suffered transplantation to locations elsewhere in the province to accommodate the newcomers. (Simington, *The transplantation.*)

traverse. In a legal action, to deny the plaintiff's claim.

treasurer. 1: The senior official in the court of exchequer 2: A member of a cathedral **chapter** and fourth in rank behind the **dean, precentor** and **chancellor**, the treasurer was responsible for the cathedral plate and valuables. He performed parish duties as well.

treasure trove. It was the prerogative entitlement of the crown to receive treasure that had been deliberately concealed, the owner of which was unknown. The rule of 'finders keepers' applied if the treasure had been casually lost or deliberately parted with for the crown entitlement lay in the concealment and not the abandonment thereof. It was the function of the **coroner** to determine the fate of treasure trove which he performed by conducting an inquest.

trencher. A flat piece of wood or metal or a slice of bread that was used as a plate.

trews (trowes, trouse). Tight-fitting, ankle to hip hose worn by the native Irish.

tricha-cét. (Ir., three thousand) Originally an ancient Gaelic spatial unit with military associations, roughly an area of 3,000 fighting men that was further subdivided into units of 100. Later, in theory at least, it came to refer to a land division of 30 **ballybetagh**s, each ballybetagh comprising 12 ploughlands of 120 arable acres each. (Hogan, 'The tricha-cét', pp. 148–235).

triforium. In a church, the wall above the aisle arches but below the **clerestory**.

Trinity. A court session beginning in June and lasting until 31 July. *See* sittings.

tripartite deed. An **indenture** drawn up between three parties, each of whom receives a copy of the deed.

trivet. A triangular frame on which an oven-pot rested.

troper. A book of tropes (phrases, sentences, verse and cadences) which were introduced as embellishments before or after the *Introit* and hymns during the celebration of the mass.

trover. An action at common law invoked for the recovery of the market value of property wrongfully taken plus compensation for the loss of use, interest and legal expenses. *See* replevin.

truck. The payment of wages in kind or the part-payment of wages in cash plus kind. Although forbidden by statute from as early as 1715 the truck system persisted into the nineteenth century. The Truck Acts of 1831 and 1887 forbade the payment of wages, either wholly or in part, by goods rather than money.

truss. A timber blade used in couples to support a roof. *See* cruck truss.

Trustees Sale. Under the English **Act of Resumption** (11 & 12 Will. III, c. 2, 1700) parliament disallowed the bulk of William III's grants of forfeited Jacobite estates and vested them in trustees who were to sell them and apply the proceeds to meet officers' arrears, transport, clothing and other miscellaneous debts arising from the Williamite War. The trustees met with little success when they tried to obtain additional convictions for outlawry against unconvicted Jacobites and the amount of available forfeited land shrank when Protestants who had purchased from grantees such as Albemarle, Athlone and Romney were allowed retain their lands on favourable terms. They established a **court of claims** to hear the claims of any person with an interest in an estate forfeited before 13 February 1689 (the accession date of William and Mary). The auctioning of vested land began in October 1702 but an economic downturn due to restrictions on the export of wool, fears that excessive **quit-rents** might apply to purchased lots, disinterest on the part of English buyers and anxieties about a Stuart restoration conspired to deter buyers and more than half the land remained unsold. The trustees were eventually compelled to sell on favourable terms to the Hollow Blades company which failed to prosper and the company later divested itself of its property portfolio to (largely) Irish purchasers. The trustees sale failed to realise even half of the £1.5million which had been dangled before the English house of commons as a lure to agree to the resumption. (Simms, *The Williamite confiscation*, pp. 121–157.)

tuath. Minor Irish lordship thought to be roughly co-terminous with a **barony**. *Tuatha*, however, are not identical to baronies for in the eleventh century there were 90 *tuatha* and we have 273 baronies today.

tuck mill. A mill used to shrink cloth.

tun. 1: A large cask 2: Of wine, contained 252 wine-gallons. It was equivalent to two pipes or four hogsheads.

tunnage. A variable impost on wine and oils introduced in 1569, levied at so much per **tun**.

turbario. An Irish swordsman or pikeman.

turbary. A bog.

turbary rights. The right to cut turf on a bog.

turnpike. *See* toll-road.

twentieth parts. A crown tax of twelve pence in the pound levied on all benefices as they were valued at the time of the Reformation. In 1711 the crown forgave the twentieth parts. *See* Board of First Fruits, *valor ecclesiasticus*.

U

Ulster, Annals of. A fifteenth- and sixteenth-century compilation also known as the *Annals of Senait MacManus* after its original compiler, Cathal MacGuire of the MacMaghnusa sept, who lived on Senait Island (Ballymacmanus Island or Belle Isle) in Lough Erne. The *Annals* commence with brief notices of matters of an ecclesiastical nature in 444 and become more elaborate from the sixth century with the inclusion of substantial entries for Armagh and (later) Derry until 1220. Entries continue until 1498, the year of MacGuire's death, after which they are extended to 1541 by Ruaidhridhe Ó Caisidé and to 1604 by Rory Ó Luinín. *The Annals of Ulster* are written partly in Latin and partly in Irish, sometimes both appearing within the same sentence. (Hennessy and MacCarthy, *Annála*; MacAirt and Mac Niocaill, *The Annals*.)

Ulster custom. *See* tenant-right.

Ulster Cycle. An early prose saga which deals with Conor MacNessa, the king of Ulster, and his warriors, the Red Branch Knights. It includes such tales as the Cattle-Raid of Cooley (*Táin Bó Cuailnge*), the deeds of Cuchulainn and the tragedy of Deirdre and Naoise. (Dillon, *Early Irish literature*, pp. 1–31.)

Ulster king of arms. The chief Irish **herald**. It is not clear how the king of arms in Ireland became known as Ulster. It may derive from the fact that there had been an Ireland king of arms at an earlier date though the bearer appears to have had little connection with this country and thus the monarch's second Irish title, earl of Ulster, was chosen. Ulster was created by letters **patent** in 1552 as the sole authority for the issuing of patents of arms and recording pedigrees. He also performed ceremonial duties, regulated protocol and precedence at state ceremonies and assisted in the introduction of new peers to the house of lords. Broadly speaking, his duties revolved around arms, pedigrees and ceremonies and it is from these that the records of his office largely derive. In 1943 the office was renamed the Genealogical Office and Ulster was replaced by the chief herald. (Barry, 'Guide', pp. 1–43.)

Ulster Revival. *See* evangelical revival.

Ulster, Synod of. The Synod of Ulster was the supreme governing body of northern Presbyterians until July 1840 when it merged with the **Seceders** to form the **General Assembly of the Presbyterian Church in Ireland**. *See* Arianism, New Light, Presbyterian, *regium donum*, Remonstrant Synod, Southern Association and Westminster, Confession of.

ult. (L.) An abbreviation of *ultimo* meaning last as in of the last month.

Thus 23 *ult.* means the twenty-third day of the month previous to the current month.

ultra vires. The term which describes when an official embarks on a particular course of action that is beyond his legal authority.

ultramontanism. (L., *ultramontanus*, beyond the mountains) A view of church-state relations which favoured papal over state control and church centralisation. Although initially wary of encouraging such thinking for fear of arousing the ire of national governments, the papacy gradually endorsed ultramontanist principles, most notably in the Syllabus of Errors (1864) and the declaration of the dogma of papal infallibility (1870). The archbishop of Dublin, Paul Cullen, who was educated in Rome, was the most important ultramontanist prelate in Ireland in the nineteenth century. *See* gallicanism. (Bowen, *Paul Cardinal Cullen*, pp. 15–20.)

undertaker. 1: The scheme for the plantation of Ulster presented in 1609 foresaw the colonisation of the escheated counties by two distinct groups of planters: undertakers and **servitors**. An undertaker undertook to implement plantation in a specified area at his own expense and agreed to fulfil certain conditions imposed by government. It was stipulated that undertakers must reside on their holdings for five years, import English or Scottish tenants, construct a fortified bawn and keep a supply of arms. Unlike the servitors, they were prohibited from taking native Irish tenants. *See* Irish Society, Pynnar's Survey 2: In Ireland in the eighteenth century, an influential and important parliamentary figure who undertook to carry the king's business through parliament in return for a share in the disposal of patronage, sinecures and pensions. As the lord lieutenant was absent from Ireland for long periods when parliament was in recess, the business of government was left in the hands of undertakers such as William Connolly and Henry Boyle. All the leading undertakers were speakers of the house of commons and held other important posts. (Hayton, 'The beginning', pp. 32–54; McCracken, 'The conflict', pp. 159–79.)

Uniformity, Act of. Two acts requiring religious uniformity were passed by the Irish parliament, the first of which, together with the **Act of Supremacy**, constituted the key statutory provisions for the establishment of Protestantism in these islands. The 1560 Act for the Uniformity of Common Prayer and Service in the Church (2 Eliz. I c. 2) was designed to bring **dissenters** into the fold of the **Church of Ireland**. The second, enacted a century later, was intended to keep them out. The Elizabethan act insisted on the use of the English *Prayer Book* by all clergy on pain of imprisonment and legislated for the imposition of recusancy fines on anyone refusing to attend divine service on Sunday. The latter imposition fell into disuse by the close of the seventeenth century but it was not removed from the statute books until 1793. The second act (7 & 8 Chas. II, c. 6, 1666) attempted to establish uniformity within the Church of Ireland by excluding **Presbyterians** and those with Presbyterian sympathies. It did so by requiring episcopal ordination of clergy and an undertaking from ministers not merely to use the revised *Book of Common Prayer* but also to give public assent to it. As an additional safeguard, schoolmasters were prohibited from teaching school without licence from a bishop of the Church of Ireland.

Union, Act of (1800). The act (40 Geo. III, c. 38) which terminated the Irish parliament and transferred its legislative functions to the imperial parliament at Westminster. Ireland was to be represented in the house of commons by 100 members (a number negatively disproportionate to its population) and in the house of lords by 32 peers (including four bishops). The Irish executive, headed by a figurehead **lord lieutenant** and the effective governor, the **chief secretary**, remained, sharing the responsibility for Irish affairs with the secretary of state for home affairs. Although in theory, then, direct rule from Westminster came into force on 1 January 1801, in reality the executive in Dublin Castle continued to exercise considerable control over the administration of Ireland, notably in the areas of education, health and the economy. Many Catholics favoured the union because they were led to believe that the act would be accompanied by an emancipation act, a belief that was quickly shattered by George III's antipathy to enlarging the Catholic franchise. Some Protestants saw legislative union as a means of transforming their minority status in Ireland into a majority within the union, others feared it for the very reason that many Catholics favoured it – that Catholic emancipation would be included in the union package. (Bolton, *The passing of the Irish act.*)

Unionist Party. An almost exclusively Protestant political party founded in 1885–6 to fight government proposals for Irish home rule. From 1921 it was the governing party in Northern Ireland until the northern parliament was prorogued in 1972. (Jackson, *The Ulster party*; Savage, 'The origins', pp. 185–208.)

Unitarianism. A Protestant non-conformist religious movement which denies the divinity of Christ and the doctrine of the Trinity, believing that God exists only in the one person. Unitarianism also stresses the free use of reason in religion. In Ireland the Unitarian church is known as the Non-Subscribing Presbyterian church which originated in the early decades of the eighteenth century with the refusal of a number of Presbyterian congregations to subscribe to the **Westminster Confession of Faith** and their secession to form the Presbytery of Antrim. Although they remained associated with the **Synod**

of Ulster they severed that connection in the 1820s when subscription was made compulsory and they withdrew to form the Remonstrant Synod.

United Irishmen. The Society of United Irishmen was founded in Belfast in October 1791 by a Protestant middle-class group dedicated to radical parliamentary reform and a truly representative, non-sectarian national parliament. Its leading members included Theobald Wolfe Tone, Napper Tandy, Archibald Rowan Hamilton, Lord Edward FitzGerald and Samuel Neilson. Government moves against the society together with the failure of FitzWilliam's Catholic emancipation bill in 1795 convinced many United Irishmen of the futility of seeking a constitutional resolution to the reform issue and encouraged them to plan for an armed insurrection. When fighting broke out in May 1798 the movement had already been hamstrung by the arrest of many of its leaders. Despite some successes, lack of military discipline and a shortage of arms told against the rebels and by mid-July the revolt was over. The society, too, almost disappeared but for a brief resurgence in Robert Emmett's abortive coup in 1803. (Curtin, *The United Irishmen*; Dickson, Keogh and Whelan, *The United Irishmen*; Jacob, *The rise*.)

universities. *See* Queen's Colleges.

Unlawful Societies Bill (1825). *See* Goulborn's Act.

urrí. (Ir., sub-king, pl, *urrithe*) Sub-king or lesser chieftain, the client of a senior Gaelic lord. Written in English as urraught or urriagh.

use, feoffment to. Until the abolition of feudal tenures in the mid-seventeenth century the feoffment or trust to use was a popular conveyance employed by chief tenants to avoid a number of crown taxes (specifically the **feudal incidents** of **wardship**, **relief**, **escheat** and **marriage**) and to circumvent certain statutory measures concerning family settlements, wills and **mortmain**. The feoffment to use achieved its end by exploiting the distinction between the common law interpretation of land law and that of equity, the view of **chancery**. Under common law a chief tenant's heir was obliged to pay **relief** to pass livery and assume ownership. Where the heir was a minor, wardship and marriage also applied. In a feeoffment to use **seisin** of the property was conveyed to a group of family intimates (feoffees) to the use (benefit) of the chief tenant and his heirs. According to common law, legal title to the land now lay with the feoffees or trustees and since the landowner was no longer seised of the land neither he nor his heirs were liable for the incidents. Security for the landowner lay in the certainty that the equitable side of chancery would uphold his beneficial interest. It is important to remember that feeoffees were not required to perform any duties in the management of the estate; their role was purely a nominal one. The use was also employed to circumvent common law prohibitions on family settlements, the bequeathing of land by **will** and, in earlier times, the conveyance of land to corporate bodies such as religious foundations. The Statute of Uses was introduced in England in 1534 and in Ireland 100 years later to close these loopholes and increase royal revenue by declaring seisin to lie with the beneficiary of any trust to use. Feoffments to use were rendered unnecessary by the 1634 Statute of Wills –(which permitted testators to bequeath land by will) and the 1662 Tenures Abolition Act (which abolished feudal tenures and most of the feudal incidents). (Wylie, *Irish land law*, pp. 78 ff.)

utfangeneth. *See* outfangtheof.

utrum, juris utrum. A writ which lies for the minister of a church whose predecessor has wrongfully alienated the lands and tenements thereof.

V

vade mecum. (L., go with me) A ready reference manual, companion, handbook or guidebook that can be carried about.

vail. A gratuity or tip given to servants by departing guests.

valor ecclesiasticus. Following the Reformation the **first fruits** of all ecclesiastical benefices were impropriated by the crown and an additional tax, the **twentieth parts**, was imposed on all ecclesiastical incomes. In order to levy the tax a *valor* or valuation was conducted on benefices. Religious houses were not included in the valor for they were to be dissolved. In terms of detail the Irish valor is inferior to the extensively detailed English equivalent, entries simply recording the living and its monetary valuation. (*Valor*; Ellis, 'Economic problems', pp. 239–265.)

valuation. The value of a property were it to be rented for a full year. Thus a manorial valuation refers to its annual rental value and not the value were it to be sold. The Primary Valuation (1848–65), or **Griffith's Valuation** as it is more commonly known, was intended to establish the valuation of each house and holding in the country for the purposes of local taxation. The valuation books contain the names of occupiers of land and buildings, the names of lessors, the extent and valuation of the property together with a very brief description of the tenement.

verge. A rod placed in the hand of a tenant by the lord to represent the **fief** into which he was being invested. *See* fealty, homage, investiture.

verger. An usher or sacristan.

verso. Abbreviated *v.* in references, *verso* refers to the side of a manuscript page that is to be read second, in other words, the back or left-hand side. *Recto* (r.) is the front of the page or right-hand side, the side to be read first. *See* folio.

vested schools. The commissioners of national education required schools built with its support to adhere to its rules and be vested in local trustees. Non-vested schools received only annual grants for books and salaries and were subject to the commissioners' rules only for as long as they were in receipt of aid. The rules for both were the same. In 1840, in order to secure the connection of **Presbyterian** schools to the national system, the commissioners reinterpreted the status of non-vested schools and developed a number of unwritten rules to satisfy the demands of the **Synod of Ulster** which refused to countenance the presence of Catholic clergymen in Presbyterian schools. The commissioners now declared that clergymen of a persuasion different to that of the school manager were not entitled to provide religious instruction in the school – it must be provided elsewhere. They were permitted to visit the schools but only as members of the public. Non-vested schools were no longer required to allocate a separate day for religious instruction and children of a minority faith need no longer be excluded from the religious instruction classes of the majority. They might leave class if they wished but neither teachers nor managers bore any responsibility in the matter. These alterations effectively undercut the supposedly non-denominational status of the national system. *See* Education, National System of, Stopford rule.

vestry. 1: An early form of local government, the parish or general vestry was an institution of the Established church which supervised the maintenance of roads and bridges and took responsibility for abandoned children, fed and maintained the poor and buried the destitute. *See* six-day labour. These civic services were financed by a local tax, the parish **cess**. After the abolition of the **penal laws** the vestry included all ratepayers irrespective of religious affiliation although the officers must be Anglicans. The ability of civil parishes to fulfil their civic functions varied significantly from place to place and, in general, Irish parishes failed to match the elaborate English parish system. In parishes where the Anglican congregation was small a comprehensive system was clearly impracticable but where strong concentrations of Anglicans existed – as in Dublin city – a sophisticated operation including fire-fighting, a parish watch, constables, street-cleaning (scavenging) and lighting was maintained. The 1833 **Church Temporalities Act** disestablished the parish by abolishing parish cess. Subsequently its local government and health functions devolved to the **grand jury**, later to the **poor law union** and later again to the county and rural district councils under the 1908 **Local Government Act** 2: A church sacristy. (Refaussé, *A handbook*.)

vestry, select. Unlike the general vestry, the select vestry comprised only ratepaying Anglicans. It was responsible for the physical maintenance of the church building and for payment of the minor church officers such as the **sexton**. From this body were elected annually the two **church-wardens** who administered the parish. They were assisted by volunteers and occasionally other appointees such as **overseers** who collected the parish **cess** and distributed money and assistance to those on the poor list.

veto controversy (1808–1821) The veto controversy occupied centre stage in the debate on **Catholic emancipation** in the early decades of the nineteenth century. Some pro-emancipationists believed that a crown veto over Catholic episcopal appointments would reassure Protestants and smooth the path towards emancipation. Indeed, the pope agreed to such a limited veto in 1815 as a *quid pro quo* for legislative action on the issue. Others, including Daniel O'Connell, sought unqualified emancipation and opposed the veto. The controversy ended in 1821 with the rejection by the house of lords of William Conyngham Plunket's emancipation bill (which included the veto). From that date the veto ceased to be an issue as campaigners agitated for full emancipation. After Plunket's bill fell O'Connell wrote: 'Even the Vetoists must admit that securities do no good because we are kicked out as unceremoniously with them as without them'. This did not prevent him from agreeing to other securities, the **'wings'**, to facilitate the passage of the (unsuccessful) 1825 emancipation bill. (O'Ferrall, *Catholic emancipation*, pp. 3–9.)

vicar. Whether the senior Anglican clergyman in a parish was a **rector** or a vicar depended on the disposition of the **tithe**. Where the great tithe was appropriated to a cathedral chapter or dignity or impropriated to a layman the incumbent was a vicar and he was entitled to the small tithe only. He was a vicar because he performed the ecclesiastic duties vicariously for the cathedral chapter, monastic institution or lay impropriator. An incumbent in full possession of the parish tithe was a rector. *See* appropriate, impropriate.

vicars choral. Minor canons, skilled in singing, who deputised for the prebendaries (canons) for choral purposes in the cathedral and kept records of choir attendance. Not all vicars choral performed such duties. Often they simply collected the money associated with the post. In many cathedrals the vicars choral were endowed separately from the dean and chapter and they usually held a parish as well.

viceroy. The lord lieutenant.

Victorine Canons. An order of canons devoted to mystical theology which was founded by Richard of Saint-Victor, Paris. The Rule of St-Victor, a strict **Augustinian** rule, was introduced to the canons of the priory of St Thomas the Martyr in Thomascourt, Dublin, sometime after 1192 by John Comyn, archbishop of Dublin. Since it was customary for Victorine houses to enjoy abbatial dignity, the priory was thereafter referred to as Thomas' Abbey and the prior was elevated to the status of an abbot. Comyn's desire to introduce the Victorine rule appears to have derived from his earlier association with the English Victorine houses at Bristol and Keynsham in Somerset, formed when he served as **archdeacon** of Bath. (Gilbert, *Register of the abbey*; Gwynn, 'The early history', pp. 1–35.)

villate. A land measure equivalent to 100–120 acres, also known as a **carucate** or **ploughland**.

villein. A serf or unfree peasant bound to a lord or estate. The Gaelic equivalent was known as a **betagh**, or in Latin as *hibernicus, nativius* or *betagius*.

Vincent de Paul, Society of St. A voluntary, charitable society founded in Paris in 1833 by Antoine-Frederic Ozanam to provide short-term relief to the poor in times of distress. The provision of financial and other assistance through a system of home and institutional visitation has been a consistent feature of the society's work since its establishment in Ireland in 1844. Latterly, the SVP has adopted a more proactive approach to the issue of poverty. Counselling and budgeting services, resource centres, hostels for the homeless and drugs projects are the visible evidence of a policy which aims to promote self-sufficiency and personal initiative.

virgate. An early English land measure, usually equivalent to about 30 acres but which varied regionally between 20 and 40 acres.

visitation, episcopal. It was the duty of every Church of Ireland bishop to visit the parishes in his diocese yearly to oversee the activities of his ministers, examine the condition of church buildings and receive a briefing on lay adherence and devotion. The records of these visitations, which were performed more frequently and more conscientiously in some dioceses than others, are contained in visitation books which list the benefices, the clergy, the patron and parish officials, outline the physical condition of the church and church buildings and note the extent of the **glebe**. The vicar-general sometimes deputised for the bishop at visitations and in the nineteenth century visitations were replaced in some areas by annual convocations or synods of the diocesan clergy. The records of Anglican visitations are held in the Representative Church Body Library. Throughout the eighteenth century and long after the penal religious laws had fallen into disuse, Catholic bishops remained cautious about keeping records. Nevertheless, the evidence contained in Archbishop Butler's visitation book suggests that by the middle of the century they were conducting parochial visitations to inquire into the state of church buildings and furnishings, clerical discipline, education and religious life in the localities. Where visitation records survive they should be found in the relevant diocesan archives. *See* visitation return. (Ronan, 'Archbishop Bulkeley', pp. 56–98; Dwyer, 'Archbishop Butler'.)

visitation, heraldic. *See* herald.

visitation, metropolitan. The triennial supervisory visitation of the **metropolitan** or archbishop of all the **suffragan** sees in his province. Until the visitation was completed to the satisfaction of the archbishop all the ecclesiastical powers of the suffragan (excepting ordinations and confirmations) were suspended.

visitation, regal. Regal or royal visitations were conducted by commissioners appointed to investigate the state of the Anglican church in the dioceses. Under Elizabeth I they were used to inquire into the property of the various episcopal sees. Commissions were also issued in 1607, 1615, 1622 and 1633–4 and the reports of the commissioners provide valuable information on Church of Ireland clergy and help to explain why the task of enforcing religious uniformity proved unattainable. Four volumes of manuscript transcripts of regal visitations (1615–1634) are preserved in the National Archives and some printed versions can be found in the journal *Archivium Hibernicum*. (Phair, 'Seventeenth-century regal visitations', pp. 79–102.)

visitation return. A report made by parish clergy prior to a visitation by the local Catholic bishop. It was a formal account of the state of the church and religious practice in the parish with additional information on social and economic conditions. From the middle of the nineteenth century the return was made on printed forms. Where they have survived visitation returns should be found in diocesan archives.

Volunteers. Founded in Ulster in the late 1770s to oppose a French invasion, the Volunteer organisation was a largely Protestant body of gentry, farmers and businessmen. Against a background of war with the American colonies, France, Spain and Holland, the government acquiesced in its formation and supplied it with arms. The movement grew rapidly, principally because it enabled its members to parade in public in colourful uniforms and perform useful policing duties. Later it became a vehicle for articulating concerns about the national interest and its strength ensured that its views could not be ignored. The combination of foreign wars and the parading of the Dublin corps of the Volunteers outside parliament in 1779 enabled Grattan to extract legislation for free trade from the government. The Volunteers continued to hold reviews but largely avoided political intervention during the next few years, a moderation which provoked a radical minority to secede to form an independent corps under Napper Tandy. In February 1782 a Volunteer convention at Dungannon denounced the British claim to legislate for Ireland. This demonstration of popular opinion, coupled with the shock defeat at Yorktown some months previously, contributed towards the successful parliamentary agitation for the repeal of the **Declaratory Act** and the amendment of **Poynings' Law**. *See* Yelverton's Act. After 1782, as Volunteer demands became more radical, the aristocrats were frightened away and its influence declined. The movement enjoyed a resurgence following the French Revolution but government action to suppress the Ulster Volunteers together with the Gunpowder and Convention acts of 1793 and the raising of the **militia** led to its virtual disappearance. *See* Convention Act. (Smyth, 'The Volunteers', pp. 113–36; Ó Snódaigh, *The Irish Volunteers*.)

voyder. An early rubbish bin.

W

waif. 1: Something loose and straying 2: The right of the manorial lord to any items of property (including animals, stolen goods and **jetsam**) which were found apparently ownerless and which remained unclaimed after due notice was given. *See* stray.

waiter, tide waiter. A customs official who met and examined ships arriving on the tide.

wake. The practice of laying a corpse out at home whereupon friends and neighbours spend the night mourning and consoling relatives.

ward. *See* watch and ward.

wardship. A feudal incident. The sovereign was entitled to the guardianship and custody of chief tenants who succeeded to their inheritance in minority. This involved the administration of the estate and the right to arrange marriage. Usually the crown sold the wardship to the highest bidder and the purchaser was entitled to receive the profits from the estate and a marriage fee. After the Reformation guardians were also required to raise wards in English habit and religion and have them educated in Trinity College, Dublin. Chief tenants could avoid this eventuality by vesting their estates in family intimates using a conveyance known as a trust or feoffment to **use**. The **Tenures Abolition Act** (1662) extinguished the **feudal incidents** and the necessity for such conveyances. *See* livery, to sue out and **ousterlemain**.

Wards and Liveries, Court of. A financial court which derived from Henry VIII's desire to increase crown revenue from the **feudal incidents** of **wardship**, **marriage** and **relief**. Established statutorily in 1540–2 (32 Henry VIII, c. 46 and 33 Henry VIII, c. 22), the court of wards emerged because of the growing practice among chief tenants of making feoffments to **use** to avoid the incidents. The granting of monastic lands to laymen following the **dissolution** increased the number of chief tenants and therefore the possibility of increasing crown revenue. On reaching full age a ward was not to pass livery without reference to the court of wards. As a result, liveries were united with wardships in the court and the office of master of liveries merged with it. In Ireland a regular court of wards and liveries was formalised in 1622. It was concerned with revenue arising out of wardship and livery, matters touching the levy or discharge of debts due to the crown, concealments of tenure, refusal of marriage and the levy of consequential fines, inquisitions *post-mortem*, interpretation of uses and wills and problems of land law whether in the interests of the crown, wards or tenants. Writs of **inquisition *post-mortem*** were issued to determine whether the incoming heir to a tenancy-in-chief was a minor. The court was abolished by the **Tenures Abolition Act** of 1662. (Treadmill, 'The Irish court', pp. 1–27; Kearney, 'The court of wards', pp. 29–63.)

warden. *See* church-warden.

warren, connywarren. A rabbit colony. Rabbits were introduced into Ireland by the Anglo-Normans who constructed warrens and farmed the rabbits as a source of food and clothing.

wash mill. 1: A mill race where sheep are washed 2: A mill where lime was applied to leather after it was shorn of hair and washed 3: A machine where limestone and clay were mixed in the process of brickmaking.

waste. *See* year day and waste

watch and ward. The system of night and day security which operated from medieval times. Statute required every collection of three or more English houses to appoint a constable to keep watch during the winter nights. The watch operated during night-time and the ward was responsible for daytime security. Originally all adult males between the ages of 15 and 60 were expected to serve in rotation without payment but from 1750 some watchmen demanded and received recompense for their services. From 1719 grand juries and justices of the peace were required to erect watch houses and equip watchmen with watch-bills, halberts or staves. An annual levy of 3*d.* on all householders was exacted to pay for the equipment (6*d.* from 1723). At sunset watchmen were stationed at town gates and at key locations in the town where they observed the streets and called the time on the hour. They were empowered to stop and examine suspects, detain any who failed to give a good account of themselves and present them before a magistrate the next day. Catholics were not excluded from the watch although there was provision to mount a purely Protestant watch during periods of unrest. Each of Dublin's 21 civil parishes had its own poorly-funded and notoriously inefficient watch. Unchecked public disorder led to the creation of a centralised permanent **police** force in 1786 which, after several attempts at reformation, metamorphosed into the **Dublin Metropolitan Police** in 1838. (Herlihy, *The Royal Irish Constabulary*, pp. 21–23.)

wattle. A frame of upright stakes intertwined with twigs used to make fences, walls or roofs.

way, waia, wey, weigh. A measure of dry goods that varied regionally and according to the type and quality of the goods being weighed. In England a sack of wool weighed 364 pounds and two ways of wool were equal to a sack, making a way of wool equal to 182 pounds. A way of cheese, however, weighed anything from 224 to 330 pounds. A way of salt was equivalent to 25 **quarters**.

wedge tomb. Dating from the Bronze Age, the east-west aligned wedge tomb comprises a long, main burial chamber, higher and wider at one end and covered by a sloping, flat-slab roof. Wedge tombs often contain an ante-chamber or portico which is separated from the main chamber by a large slab. Although usually single-chambered, some wedge tombs have a second, smaller chamber at the eastern end. (Ó Ríordáin, *Antiquities*, pp. 62–66.)

weights and measures, keeper of. A government official whose duty it was to enforce weights and measures regulations.

Westminster, Confession of. The **Presbyterian** confession of faith. Modelled on the **Irish Articles of Religion**, it was drawn up by the Westminster Assembly which met in Westminster Abbey between 1643 and 1649. The confession declared scripture the sole doctrinal authority and affirmed predestination (the belief that 'some men and angels are predestinated unto everlasting life, and others foredained to everlasting death'). It contains reformed views of the sacraments and the ministry. The issue of subscription to the Westminster confession divided Presbyterians over the next two centuries. A requirement that ministers and ordinands to the ministry subscribe to the confession created dissension within the **Synod of Ulster** for some Presbyterians disapproved of its theology and others rejected human formularies as a test of faith. A minority who favoured compulsory subscription seceded from the synod in the eighteenth century. In the nineteenth century, however, the position was reversed. Subscription was made compulsory and the liberal **New Light** group which opposed subscription withdrew to form the **Remonstrant Synod**.

wether. A castrated ram.

Whately Commission. *See* Poor inquiry.

wherry. A fishing vessel, a yawl.

Whig. A term derived from the Scots Gaelic for a horse thief and applied disparagingly to those in the seventeenth century who opposed royal absolutism. Whigs favoured a more limited constitutional monarchy, upheld the principles of the 'glorious revolution' and, in Ireland, pressed for stiff measures against Catholics and Jacobites. Comprised largely of aristocrats and wealthy middle-class individuals, Whiggism began to crystallise into a political party from about 1784 under Charles James Fox because of the American War of Independence and the emergence of William Pitt the Younger's **Tory** party. By this time the Whigs had begun to develop reforming social and political policies and had come to articulate the views of religious dissenters and industrialists. In the nineteenth century the term 'Whig' began to fall into disuse and was replaced by 'Liberal'. *See* regency crisis, whig club.

whig club. Following the **regency crisis**, whig clubs were formed in Ireland to press for the continued independence of the Irish parliament, the eradication of corruption in the administration and modest parliamentary reforms. The involvement of 'patriots' such as Henry Grattan and Lord Charlemont together with up to 90 Irish MPs gave the movement considerable weight but by contemporary European standards theirs was a conservative liberalism.

Whiteboys (1761–5). An eighteenth-century secret agrarian society, so called because they wore white shirts over their clothes and white cockades. Whiteboys agitated against the spread of pasture, **tithe** and the price of **conacre** land. The movement first emerged in the early years of George III's reign with the spread of pasturage. A hike in cattle prices following an extended outbreak of cattle murrain in Europe accelerated the process. From 1758 – when free importation of cattle into Britain was granted for five years – huge areas of land were turned over to pasture, commons were enclosed and peasants evicted. Whiteboys reacted forcefully to the enclosure of commons. They destroyed fences, dug up ground, houghed (hamstrung) cattle and sent threatening letters. Whiteboys also opposed the rate at which tithe was exacted. The iniquity of the tithe system under which Catholic peasants were compelled to support a body of (frequently non-resident and hostile) Anglican clergymen was compounded in 1736 when the Irish house of commons condemned **tithe agistment** on pasturage for dry and barren cattle and effectively exempted rich graziers from tithe, thereby throwing an increased burden on the poor. Whiteboys waged war against the **tithe-farmer**, struck their own tithe rates and warned tithe-payers against exceeding those rates. They also seized arms to furnish their escapades. As a result tithe was not paid over large areas and landlords feared to distrain for unpaid rent and avoided impounding trespassing cattle. In 1765 parliament declared all Whiteboy activities to be capital offences and grand juries were empowered to levy compensation on disturbed baronies. Magistrates were empowered to search for arms and compel witnesses and suspects to answer on oath on pain of imprisonment but many cases collapsed in court through intimidation or bribery. Whiteboyism, which was strongest among the Catholic peasantry, the landless and the poor of Munster and parts of Leinster, declined for a number of reasons. Repression and the enrolment of large numbers of volunteers under the direction of magistrates checked the movement and the struggle for survival after the drought and harvest failure of 1765 together with a smallpox epidemic in 1766 sapped its energy. (Donnelly, 'The Whiteboy movement', pp. 20–54.)

Wide Streets Commission. Founded in 1758 (31 Geo. III, c. 3), the Wide Street Commission was a statutory planning body which radically altered the streetscape in several parts of the city of Dublin. It began in 1758 by clearing away a confused streetline and warren of houses between the Royal Exchange (now City Hall) and the furthest downstream bridge, Essex Bridge, to create Parliament Street. Later came the planning of the Sackville Street – Carlisle Bridge – Westmoreland Street line which, by way of a reconstructed Dame Street, connected with the first project in Parliament Street. The commission laid out a pattern of broad straight thoroughfares and transformed the Tudor and Stuart city into Georgian Dublin. It was abolished in 1849 (12 & 13 Vict., c. 97) and its powers were vested in Dublin Corporation which retains the commission's records in its archives. (McCullough, *A vision*.)

widow's dower. Also known as **jointure**, it was the entitlement of the widow of a chief tenant to one-third of the estate of her deceased spouse during her lifetime. In the eighteenth century it was usually an annual allowance equivalent to one-tenth of her dowry.

Williamite Confiscation (1690–1703). The confiscations which followed the defeat of the Jacobites in the war of 1689–91 led to a decline of one-third in the proportion of land held by Catholics in Ireland from 22% in 1688 to 14% by 1703. This was a relatively mild decline when compared with a proportional Catholic loss of two-thirds after the earlier Cromwellian and Restoration settlements and was largely attributable to the fact that William was anxious to transfer his forces to the continent. To do so, however, he was forced to treat generously with Jacobites who were still in arms at Limerick and Galway. All who were admitted to the benefit of the articles of Limerick and Galway secured their estates (almost one-half of the land in Catholic hands in 1703 was held by **articlemen**). Others were pardoned and, with the war concluded, the government had no appetite to prosecute Jacobites who had not yet been outlawed. Less fortunate were those who were in France when the siege of Limerick ended, those who had been killed or taken prisoner in battle and the many Catholics who had submitted after the defeat at the Boyne. These, together with those who opted to leave and fight in France, suffered forfeiture of their estates. *See* Limerick, Treaty of. (Simms,

The Williamite.)

wills. Until the seventeenth century the feudal rule of succession by **primogeniture** made it legally impossible under common law to devise freehold land by will. Nevertheless a landowner could achieve precisely the same effect by conveying his property in trust to family intimates to dispose of upon his death according to the uses declared in his will. *See* use. In 1634 the Irish Statute of Wills (10 Chas. I, sess. 2, c. 2) permitted for the first time the transmission of freehold land by will provided the testament was in writing. No signature or witnesses were required until the **Statute of Frauds** (1695) enacted that all wills involving real estate be signed by the testator in the presence of three witnesses who must also append their signatures in the testator's presence. It was always legal to bequeath personalty (moveable goods or chattels) and oral bequests were regarded as valid until the 1837 Wills Act (7 Will. IV & 1 Vic., c. 26) which required all wills of realty and personalty to be signed and witnessed by two people in each other's presence. Until 1858 testamentary jurisdiction lay with the **ecclesiastical courts**. Thereafter responsibility for proving wills was transferred to a civil court of probate, the Principal Registry in Dublin, whose records (but not the indexes) were consumed by the fire in the Four Courts in 1922. This was a great loss for wills and inventories offer rich pickings to historians re-constructing the social and economic world of earlier societies. The loss was partly mitigated by the acquisition of testamentary extracts compiled from probate records in the nineteenth century by **Sir William Betham** and others and an extensive collection of wills has been assembled by the National Archives courtesy of solicitors' offices throughout the state. *See* probate, use. (Berry, *Register*; ffolliott and O'Byrne, 'Wills', pp. 157–80; Phair, 'Sir William Betham', pp. 1–99.)

Windsor, Treaty of (1172). A concord between Henry II and Rory O'Connor wherein O'Connor acknowledged Henry as his overlord and agreed not to upset the status quo by disturbing those areas, including Leinster and that part of Munster from Dungarvan to Waterford, where the Norman conquest was most complete. O'Connor was to make a tribute of one hide from every ten animals slaughtered. For his part, Henry recognised O'Connor as king of Connacht and empowered him to judge or remove any of that province's lords who rebelled against either man or who refused to pay tribute. When necessary he could call on the assistance of the constable. Henry also announced his intention to make his son, John, king of Ireland. The treaty was broken by Henry in 1177 when he took counties Cork and Limerick into his own hands and granted away Desmond and Thomond.

'wings'. Sops to Protestant sensitivities contained in the unsuccessful 1825 Catholic emancipation bill, so called because they were intended to help the bill fly through parliament. They proposed the payment of Catholic clergy from state funds (thereby increasing government leverage over the church) and the disfranchisement of the forty-shilling freeholders. Daniel O'Connell agreed to the 'wings' to facilitate the bill's passage through parliament. He was criticised for sacrificing the franchise and the issue split the Catholic movement but he recovered. In an open letter the English reformer William Cobbett denounced O'Connell and asked the Irish freeholders: 'Did you ... ever dream that Emancipation could possibly mean disfranchisement?' *See* veto controversy.

winnow. To remove the chaff from the grain by fanning.

withernam, capias in. A writ for reprisals or compensation. In an action of **replevin** where goods were unlawfully seized and removed from the jurisdiction of the sheriff so that he was unable to return them to the plaintiff, a writ of *capias in withernam* was issued directing him to seize goods in lieu of those taken and deliver them up to the aggrieved party.

woad. A herb of the mustard family, the leaves of which were used to make a blue dye.

Wood's halfpence. In 1722 a controversy arose over the granting of a **patent** to the English iron merchant William Wood to mint an Irish halfpenny. Fearing a debased coinage with the profits going to English speculators and resenting the absence of an Irish mint, the Irish ascendancy raised hell over the issue and the patent was withdrawn. Jonathan Swift helped frustrate the proposal by penning the critical *Drapier's Letters*.

wool-fells. Unsheared sheepskins.

workhouse. Workhouses were constructed under the Poor Law Act (1838) for the relief of the poor. They were located centrally in each **poor law union** and 163 were built in the nineteenth century. *See* poor law.

workhouse test. A principle adopted to ensure that only the genuinely distressed would apply to the workhouse for relief. Conditions within the workhouse were designed to be less attractive and therefore 'less eligible' than conditions outside. The dietary regime was monotonous and inferior and daily life was characterised by regimentation, discipline and hard labour.

worsted. A fabric made from closely twisted yarn that was spun from long staple wool to produce a smooth compact finish. It was used for carpet-making, knitting and embroidery.

wreck of the sea. Goods or cargo cast ashore by the sea from a stricken vessel which were properly crown property but frequently granted to subjects and monastic institutions as a franchise.

writ. 1: The written command of a law court (judicial writ) or sovereign. Writs were used by the crown to convey grants of lands, to grant commissions or to convey instructions in the form of **charters**, letters **patent** and letters **close**. All writs had to be accounted for. Local officials such as the sheriff must return the writ endorsed with details of action taken in the case 2: A summons used to commence an action (original writ). Until the nineteenth century no action could commence in the common law courts without the issuing of a writ from **chancery**. Specific writs applied in each legal action and failure to select the appropriate writ, however conclusive the evidence, was a guarantee that the suit would fail. Writs were also prohibitively expensive. *See certiorari*, civil bill, error, *forma pauperis, habeas corpus, mandamus, withernam.*

Wyndham Act (1903). Sponsored by George Wyndham, secretary of state for Ireland, the Irish Land Act (3 Edw. VII, c. 37, 1903) remedied a major deficiency in the earlier **Purchase of Land (Ireland) Act** (1891) which had tied landlord income from the sale of their holdings to government stock. In the intervening years the value of such stock had decreased by a fifth and landlords were disinclined to sell in such circumstances. Wyndham's act replaced the stock with cash payments and, as an added incentive, a 12% bonus on the purchase price was offered. The act abolished the guaranteed deposit stipulation that had been introduced by the 1885 **Purchase of Land (Ireland) Act** and which had also proved unattractive to landlords. Henceforth, the land commissioners, through their agents, the estates commissioners, were empowered to purchase whole estates rather than individual holdings. Once agreement was reached between a landlord and his tenants on the terms of the sale and the necessary paperwork completed, all documentation was submitted to the commissioners for consideration. If satisfied, the commissioners advanced the entire purchase price in cash and vested the holdings in the tenants in **fee simple** subject to repayment at the rate of $3^{1}/_{4}$% over $68^{1}/_{2}$ years. £150 million was allocated by the government to fund the scheme and about 220,000 holdings were purchased. Two succeeding acts improved the plight of poorer tenants. Under the Evicted Tenants (Ireland) Act (7 Edw. VII, c. 56, 1907) the estates commissioners were given the power of compulsory purchase to acquire the holdings of evicted tenants and reinstate them. Birrell's **Irish Land Act** (1909), which authorised the compulsory purchase of land in congested districts, resulted in the acquisition of 600,000 acres and the sale of 50,000 holdings.

Y

yawl. A fishing vessel, a wherry.

year day and waste (Fr., *ann jour et wast*). A **feudal incident** and a form of **escheat**. The crown was entitled to receive and hold the land of an attainted felon for a year and a day and to profit (waste) its natural resources, in other words, to exact as much profit from the estate for the duration of a year and a day.

Year of Grace. *See* evangelical revival.

Yelverton's Act. The 1782 act (21 & 22 Geo. III, c. 47) which, following the repeal of the **Declaratory Act** by the British parliament a month earlier, amended Poyning's Law (1495) and established the legislative independence of the Irish parliament. Henceforth the power of the **lord lieutenant** and the privy councils of Ireland and Britain to alter or originate bills for Ireland was removed. The king retained the power to suppress legislation but neither he nor the parliament at Westminster could alter bills approved by both houses of parliament. A year later the Renunciation Act (23 Geo. III, c. 28) confirmed the right of the Irish parliament to legislate exclusively for Ireland. Yelverton's Act was named for Barry Yelverton, MP for Carrickfergus, who first moved the bill. *See* 'patriot' party.

yeoman. 1: A prosperous tenant 2: A prosperous tenant who held land in freehold.

Yeomanry Corps. An almost exclusively Protestant military force of voluntary part-timers established in 1796 (37 Geo. III, c. 2) by the **lord lieutenant**, Earl Camden, to shore up the inadequacies of the politically and religiously unreliable **militia** and to replace the regulars who had been drafted abroad to meet the French threat. Heavily infiltrated by Orangemen, the yeomanry corps had a propensity to engage in sectarian outrages and earned a reputation for brutality and indiscipline during the 1798 rebellion. In 1830, after a ten-year lapse, the yeomanry corps was revived to meet the challenges of the **tithe** war but its re-emergence inflamed rather than eased tensions and it was disbanded in 1834. (Blackstock, *An ascendancy army*; Morton, 'The rise', pp. 58–64.)

yoke. A short cross-beam upon which a **purlin** rests. It was fixed to the roof trusses just below the apex. *See* cruck.

Young, Arthur (1741–1820). An influential English agriculturalist and writer, Young's own excursions into farming and estate management proved, paradoxically, unprofitable. He toured Ireland in 1776 and from 1777 was employed as agent to Lord Kingsborough in Co. Cork for two years. His *A tour in Ireland*, a two-volume travel book containing a wide-ranging commentary on contemporary Irish agriculture, was published in 1780. Young used official sources as well as personal observations and records compiled as he progressed through 29 counties of Ireland. In some instances his vision of Ireland is fanciful but he was scathing of the evils of landlordism and advocated the creation of new employment opportunities to counter the losses which attended the spread of pasture. (Young, *A tour in Ireland*.)

Young Ireland (1842–48). Founded in the early 1840s by Thomas Davis, John Blake Dillon and Charles Gavan Duffy, Young Ireland was a mainly middle-class, non-sectarian, repeal movement which proposed a nationality embracing all creeds, classes and races within Ireland. Young Irelanders aimed to create internal union and external independence. The chief vehicle for the dissemination of Young Ireland ideals was the *Nation* newspaper. Initially the Young Irelanders were members of the **National Repeal Association** but they became disenchanted with Daniel O'Connell's attitude to federalism (a local legislature dealing with domestic affairs but subordinate to Westminster), his stance on the **Queen's Colleges** bill and his renunciation of the use of force. They seceded in 1846 to establish the Irish Confederation when O'Connell required members of the Repeal Association to eschew the use of physical force. Sparked by news of the French revolution in February 1848 the Young Irelanders launched into the single engagement 'battle of Ballingary' ('the battle of Widow McCormack's cabbage patch') in July, a fiasco that resulted in the transportation or flight abroad of the movement's leaders. Although the movement had little popular or clerical support, was poorly structured and fizzled out miserably, Young Ireland bequeathed a legacy of romantic nationalism to later generations. (Davis, *The Young Ireland*.)

Young Ulster. A secret organisation, founded by Frederick Crawford in 1892 to oppose home rule for Ireland, which enjoyed a brief existence before being swallowed up by larger anti-home rule bodies. Membership was open only to those who possessed a gun and 100 rounds of ammunition. In 1913 Crawford became a founder member of the Ulster Volunteer Force.

Z

Zoilomastix. (1625–6) An attack by layman and soldier Philip O'Sullivan Beare on the writings of **Giraldus Cambrensis** and **Richard Stanihurst** on Ireland, Zoilomastix also contains important biographical detail of an ecclesiastical nature. The original is preserved in the University Library, Upsala, Sweden. (O'Donnell, *Selections*.)

Bibliography

Aalen, F. H., Whelan, Kevin and Stout, Matthew (eds), *An atlas of the Irish rural landscape* (Cork, 1997).

'Abstracts of decrees of the court of claims for the trial of innocents' in *PRI rep. DK*, 19, appendix v (1887).

Acheson, Alan, *A history of the Church of Ireland, 1691–1996* (Dublin, 1997).

Adams, I. H., *Agrarian landscape terms: a glossary for historical geography* (London, 1976).

Akenson, Donald H., 'Pre-university education, 1870–1921' in Vaughan, W. E. (ed.), *A new history of Ireland*, vi (Oxford, 1996).

— *The Irish education experiment* (Dublin, 1970).

— *The Church of Ireland: ecclesiastical reform and revolution, 1800–1885* (New Haven and London, 1971).

Alcock, N. W., *Old title deeds* (Sussex, 1986).

Almqvist, Bo, 'The Irish Folklore Commission: achievement and legacy' in *Béaloideas*, 45–7 (1977–9).

Ancient Irish histories: the works of Spencer, Campion, Hanmer and Marlborough, i (repr., 2 vols, New York, 1970).

Andrews, J. H., *Plantation acres: an historical study of the Irish land surveyor and his maps* (Omagh, 1985).

— 'The French school of Dublin land surveyors' in *Ir. Geography*, v (1967).

— *History in the ordnance map: an introduction for Irish readers* (Dublin, 1974).

— *A paper landscape: the ordnance survey in nineteenth-century Ireland* (Oxford, 1975).

— *Shapes of Ireland: maps and their makers, 1564–* (Dublin, 1997).

Appleby, John C. and O'Dowd, Mary, 'The Irish admiralty: its organisation and development c.1570–1640' in *IHS*, xxiv, no. 95 (1985), pp. 299–320.

Armagh Register. Chart, D. A. (ed.), *The register of John Swayne … 1418–1439* (Belfast, 1935); Lawlor, H. J. (ed.), 'A calendar of Archbishop Fleming' in *RIA Proc.*, xxx, C, no. 5 (Dublin, 1912), pp. 94–190; Murray, L. P. (continued by Aubrey Gwynn), 'Archbishop Cromer's register' in *Louth Arch. Soc. Jn.*, vi–x (1926–44); Quigley, W. G. H. and Roberts, E. F. D. (eds), *Registrum Iohannis Mey, the register of John Mey, archbishop of Armagh 1443–1456* (Belfast, 1977); Smith, Brendan (ed.), *The register of Milo Sweetman … 1361–1380* (IMC, Dublin, 1996); Sughi Mario Alberto (ed.), *Registrum Octaviani alias Liber Niger; the register of Octavian de Palation, archbishop of Armagh, 1478–1513* (IMC, Dublin, 2000).

Arnold, L. J., *The Restoration land settlement in county Dublin, 1660–1688* (Dublin, 1993).

— 'The Irish court of claims of 1663' in *IHS*, xxiv, no. 96 (1984–5).

Asplin, P. W. A., *Medieval Ireland, c. 1170–1495* (Dublin, 1971).

Atkinson, Robert (ed.), *The book of Ballymote* (Dublin, 1887).

— (ed.), *The Yellow Book of Lecan* (Dublin, 1896).

Barnes, Jane, *Irish industrial schools 1868–1908: origin and development* (Dublin, 1989).

Barrow, L., *The round towers of Ireland* (Dublin, 1979).

Barry, John, 'Guide to the records of the Genealogical Office, Dublin, with a commentary on heraldry in Ireland and on the history of the office' in *Anal. Hib.*, 26 (1970).

— 'The appointment of coarb and erenagh' in *IER*, 5th. ser., xciii (1960).

Bartlett, Thomas, 'Defenders and Defenderism in 1795' in *IHS*, xxiv, no. 94 (May 1985).

— *The fall and rise of the Irish nation: the Catholic question, 1690–1830* (Dublin, 1992).

Bartlett, Thomas and Jeffrey, Keith (eds), *A military history of Ireland* (Cambridge, 1996).

Beames, Michael, 'Cottiers and conacre in pre-famine Ireland' in *Journal of Peasant Studies*, ii (1975).

— *Peasants and power: the Whiteboy movement and their control in pre-famine Ireland* (Brighton, 1983).

Beckett, J. C., *Protestant dissent in Ireland, 1687–1780* (London, 1946).

Begley, Donal F. (ed.), *Irish genealogy: a record finder* (Dublin, 1981).

Belmore. *Commission on manual and practical instruction in primary schools under the Board of National Education in Ireland: Final report of the commissioners*, HC 1898 [C.8923] XLIV.

Bergin, Osborn, 'Pairlement Chloinne Tomáis' in *Gadelica*, i (1912–13).

Berry, H. F., 'Proceedings in the matter of the custom called tolboll, 1308 and 1385; 'St Thomas' abbey v. some early Dublin brewers, &c.' in *RIA Proc.*, xxviii, C, no. 10 (1910).

— (ed.), *Register of wills and inventories of the diocese of Dublin 1457–1483* (Dublin, 1896–7).

— (ed.), *Statutes and ordinances and acts of the parliament of Ireland, King John to Henry V* (Dublin, 1907).

— (ed.), *Statute rolls of the parliament of Ireland, first to the twelfth years of the reign of King Edward the fourth* (Dublin, 1914).

— (ed.), *Statute rolls of the parliament of Ireland, reign of Henry the sixth* (Dublin, 1910).

Bessborough. *Report of Her Majesty's commission of inquiry into the working of the Landlord and Tenant (Ireland) Act, 1870, and the acts amending the same*, HC 1881 [C2779] XVIII. I; *Minutes of evidence*, pt I, HC 1881 [C2779] XVIII. 73; *Minutes of evidence*, pt II, HC 1881 [C2779] XIX. I; *Index to minutes of evidence and appendices*, HC 1881 [C2779] XIX. 825.

Best, R. I., Bergin, Osborn and O'Brien, M. A. (eds), *The Book of Leinster, formerly Lebar na Nua chongbala* (5 vols, Dublin, 1954–67).

Best, R. I. and McNeill, E. (eds), *The annals of Innisfallen* (Dublin, 1933).

Bew, Paul, *Land and the national question 1858–82* (Dublin, 1978).

Binchy, D. A. (ed.), *Críth Gablach* (Dublin, 1941).

Blackstock, Alan, *An ascendancy army: the Irish yeomanry, 1796–1834* (Dublin, 1998).

Bolster, E., 'A landgable roll of Cork city' in *Collect. Hib.*, xiii (1970).

Bolton, G. C., *The passing of the Irish act of union: a study in parliamentary politics* (Oxford, 1966).

Bottigheimer, Karl S., *English money and Irish land: the 'adventurers' in the Cromwellian settlement* (London, 1975).

Bourke, P. M. Austin, 'Notes on some agricultural units of measurement in use in pre-famine Ireland' in *IHS*, xiv, no. 55 (1964–5).

Bowen, Desmond, *Souperism: myth or reality* (Cork, 1970).

— *Paul Cardinal Cullen and the shaping of modern Irish Catholicism* (Dublin, 1983).

— *The Protestant crusade in Ireland, 1800–1870* (Dublin, 1978).

Boyle, K., 'Police in Ireland before the Union' in *Ir. Jurist*, viii (1973).

Bradshaw, Brendan, *The dissolution of the religious orders in Ireland under Henry VIII* (Cambridge, 1974).

Brand, Paul, 'The early history of the legal profession of the lordship of Ireland, 1250–1350' in Hogan, V. and Osborough, W. N. (eds), *Brehons, serjeants and attorneys: studies in the history of the legal profession* (Dublin, 1990).

Brannon, Nick, 'The built heritage and the local historian' in Gillespie, Raymond and Hill, Myrtle (eds), *Doing local history: pursuit and practice* (Belfast, 1998).

Brewer, John D., *The Royal Irish Constabulary: an oral history* (Belfast, 1990).

Bright, Kevin, 'Reflections on the RDS, 1731–2001' in *DHR*, lvi, no. 1 (Spring, 2003).

Broderick, David, *An early toll-road – the Dublin–Dunleer turnpike, 1731–1855* (Dublin, 1996).

Brook, E. St John (ed.), *Register of the hospital of St John the Baptist without the New Gate, Dublin* (Dublin, 1936).
— (ed.), *The Irish cartularies of Llanthony Prima and Llanthony Secunda* (Dublin, 1955).
Buckley, Anthony B. and Anderson, T. Kenneth, *Brotherhoods in Ireland* (Cultra, 1988).
Buckley, K. L., 'The Irish Land Commission as a source of historical evidence' in *IHS*, viii, no. 29 (1952).
Burke, Peter, *The French historical revolution: the Annales school, 1929–89* (Cambridge, 1990).
Caldicott, C. E. J., Gough, H. and Pittion, J–P. (eds), *The Huguenots and Ireland: anatomy of an emigration* (Dublin, 1987).
Calendar of state papers preserved in the Public Record Office, domestic series, 1547–1695 (81 vols, London, 1856–1972).
Calendar of state papers relating to Ireland, 1509–1670 (24 vols, London, 1860–1912).
Calendar of the Carew manuscripts preserved in the archiepiscopal library at Lambeth, 1515–1624 (6 vols, London, 1867–73).
Cambrensis, Giraldus, *Expugnatio Hibernica, the conquest of Ireland* (edited by Scott, A. B. and Martin, F. X., Dublin, 1978).
— *Topographia Hiberniae* (translated by John J. O'Meara (Mounrath, 1982).
Canny, Nicholas, 'The flight of the earls, 1607' in *IHS*, xvii, no. 67 (1970–1).
— *The formation of the Old English elite in Ireland* (Dublin, 1975).
Carleton, S. T., *Heads and hearths: the hearth money rolls and poll tax returns for county Antrim 1660–69* (Belfast, 1991).
Casey, Michael, 'The most illustrious order of St Patrick' in *DHR*, xliv, no. 2 (Autumn, 1991).
Chandler, Edward, *Photography in Ireland* (Dublin, 2001).
Clark, Mary and Refaussé, Raymond (eds), *Directory of historic Dublin guilds* (Dublin, 1993).
Clarke, Aidan, 'The history of Poyning's law, Pt 2: 1615–1641' in *IHS*, xviii, no. 70 (Sept. 1972).
— *Prelude to restoration in Ireland; the end of the commonwealth, 1659–1660* (Cambridge, 1999).
— *The graces, 1625–41* (Dundalk, 1968).
Clear, Caitríona, *Nuns in nineteenth-century Ireland* (Dublin, 1987).
Clinton, M., *The souterrains of Ireland* (Dublin, 2002).
Clune, George, *The medieval gild system* (Dublin, 1943).
Comerford, R. V., 'Gladstone's first Irish enterprise, 1864–70' in Vaughan, W. E. (ed.), *NHI*, v, pt 1 (Oxford, 1989).
— 'Churchmen, tenants and independent opposition, 1850–56' in *NHI*, iv (Oxford, 1989).
Connell, J., *Finances of the Church of Ireland* (Dublin, n.d.).
Connolly, Philomena, *Medieval record sources* (Dublin, 2002).
Connolly, S. J., *Religion, law and power: the making of Protestant Ireland 1660–1760* (Oxford, 1992).
— *The Oxford companion to Irish history* (Oxford, 1998).
— 'Law, order and popular protest in early eighteenth-century Ireland: the case of the houghers' in Corish, P. J. (ed.), *Radicals, rebels and establishments* (Belfast, 1985).
— 'The houghers: agrarian protest in early eighteenth-century Connacht' in Philpin, C. H. E. (ed.), *Nationalism and popular protest in Ireland* (Cambridge, 1987).
Connor, R. D., *The weights and measures of England* (London, 1987).
Conway, Colmcille, 'Sources for the history of the Irish Cistercians, 1142–1540' in *Ir. Cath. Hist. Comm. Proc.* (1958).
Cooke, Jim, 'The Dublin Mechanics' Institute 1824–1919' in *DHR*, lii, no.1 (1999).
Coolahan, John, *Irish education: its history and structure* (Dublin, 1981).

Cooney, Dudley Levistone, *The Methodists in Ireland, a short history* (Dublin, 2001).

Corcoran, Rev. T. (ed.), *State policy in Irish education, AD 1536 to 1816* (Dublin, 1819).

Corish, Patrick J., 'Cardinal Cullen and the National Association of Ireland' in *Repertorium Novum*, iii (Dublin, 1961).

— *Maynooth College, 1795–1995* (Dublin, 1995).

Corish, Patrick J. and Sheehy, David C., *Records of the Irish Catholic Church* (Dublin, 2001).

Cosgrave, Liam, 'The King's Inns' in *DHR*, xxi, no. 2 (March, 1967).

Cosgrove, Art, 'England and Ireland, 1399–1447' in *NHI*, ii (Oxford, 1987).

Cowper. *Report of the royal commission on the Land Law (Ireland) Act 1881 and the Purchase of Land (Ireland) Act 1885*, HC 1887 [C4969] XXVI. 1; *Minutes of evidence and appendices*, HC 1887 [C4969] XXVI. 25; *Index to evidence and appendices*, HC 1887 [C4969] XXVI. 1109.

Crawford, E. Margaret, *Counting the people: a survey of Irish censuses, 1813–1911* (Dublin, 2003).

Crawford, Jon G., 'The origins of the court of castle chamber; a star chamber jurisdiction in Ireland' in *American Journal of Legal History*, xxiv (1980).

Crawford, W. H., 'The evolution of the linen trade in Ulster before industrialisation' in *Ir. Econ. & Soc. Hist.*, 15 (1988).

— 'The study of townlands in Ulster' in Gillespie, Raymond and Hill, Myrtle (eds), *Doing Irish local history* (Belfast, 1998).

Cregan, Donal F., 'The Confederate Catholics: the personnel of the Confederation, 1642–9' in *IHS*, xxxix, no. 116 (November, 1995).

Cronin, Denis, Connell, Paul and Ó Dálaigh, Brian (eds), *Irish townlands: studies in local history* (Dublin, 1998).

Crossle, Philip, *Irish masonic records* (n.p., 1973).

Crossman, Virginia, *Local government in nineteenth-century Ireland* (Belfast, 1994).

Crosthwaite, J. C. and Todd, J. H. (eds), *The book of obits and martyrology of the cathedral Church of the Holy Trinity commonly called Christ Church, Dublin* (Dublin, 1844).

Cullen, L. M., 'Population trends in the seventeenth century' in *Economic and Social Review*, vi, no. 2 (1975).

— 'Catholics under the penal laws' in *Eighteenth-century Ireland*, i (1986).

Culliton, James A., 'The Four Courts, Dublin' in *DHR*, xxi (1966–67).

Cunningham, Bernadette, 'The composition of Connacht in the lordships of Clanricard and Thomond, 1577–1641' in *IHS*, xxiv, no. 93 (1984).

— *The world of Geoffrey Keating: history, myth and religion in seventeenth-century Ireland* (Dublin, 2000).

Curtin, Nancy, *The United Irishmen: popular politics in Ulster and Dublin, 1791–98* (Oxford, 1994).

Daly, Gabriel, 'Church renewal 1869–1877' in Hurley, Michael (ed.), *Irish Anglicanism, 1869–1969* (Dublin, 1970).

Danaher, Kevin (Caoimhín Ó Danachair), 'Hearth and chimney in the Irish house' in *Béaloideas*, xvi (1946).

Davies, Oliver and Quinn, David B. (eds), 'The Irish pipe roll of 14 John, 1211–1212' in *UJA*, 3rd ser., no. 4 (1941).

Davis, Richard, *The Young Ireland movement* (Dublin, 1987).

Dawson, N. M., 'Illicit distillation and the revenue police in Ireland in the eighteenth and nineteenth centuries' in *Ir. Jurist*, xii (1977).

de Blácam, Aodh, *Gaelic literature surveyed* (Dublin, 1929).

de Blaghd, Earnán, 'The DMP' in *DHR*, xx, no. 1 (1964).

de Breffny, Brian (ed.), *Ireland: a cultural encyclopaedia* (London, 1983).

de Vere White, Terence, 'The Freemasons' in Williams, T. Desmond (ed.), *Secret societies in Ireland* (Dublin, 1973).

Devon. *Report from Her Majesty's commissioners of inquiry into the state of the law and practice in respect to the occupation of land in Ireland*, HC 1845 [605] XIX. I; *Minutes of evidence*, pt i, HC 1845 [606] XIX. 57; *Minutes of evidence*, pt ii, HC 1845 [616] XX; *Minutes of evidence*, pt iii, HC 1845 [657] XXI; *Appendix to minutes of evidence*, pt iv, HC 1845 [672] XXII; *Index to minutes of evidence*, pt v, HC 1845 [673] XXII. 225.

Dickson, David, 'Middlemen' in Bartlett, Thomas and Hayton, D. W. (eds), *Penal era and golden age: essays in Irish history, 1690–1800* (Belfast, 1979).

Dickson, David, Keogh, Daire and Whelan, Kevin (eds), *The United Irishmen: republicanism, radicalism and rebellion* (Dublin, 1993).

Dillon, Myles (ed.), *Lebor na cert: the book of rights* (London, 1962).

— *Early Irish literature* (Chicago, 1948).

Diocesan Schools. *Fourth report of the Board of Education in Ireland*, HC 1810 (174) X. 209; *Fifth report of the commissioners of Irish education inquiry*, HC 1826–7 (441) XIII. 359.

Dolley, Michael, 'The Irish coinage, 1534–1691' in Moody, T. W., Martin, F. X. and Byrne, F. J. (eds), *NHI*, iii (Oxford, 1976).

Donnelly, J. S. Jr, 'The Rightboy movement 1785–8' in *Studia Hibernica* 17/18 (1977–8).

— 'The Whiteboy movement 1761–5' in *IHS*, xxi, no. 81 (1978).

— 'Hearts of Oak, Hearts of Steel' in *Studia Hibernica* 21(1981).

— 'Pastorini and Captain Rock: millenarianism and sectarianism in the Rockite movement of 1821–4' in Clark, S. and Donnelly, J. S. (eds), *Irish peasants: violence and political unrest, 1780–1914* (Wisconsin and Manchester, 1983).

Dooley, Terence, *Sources for the history of landed estates in Ireland* (Dublin, 2000).

Duffy, Patrick J., 'Social and spatial order in the MacMahon lordship of Airghialla in the late sixteenth century' in Duffy, Patrick J., Edwards, David and FitzPatrick Elizabeth (eds), *Gaelic Ireland c. 1250–1650: land lordship and settlement* (Dublin, 2001).

Duffy, Seán (ed.), *Atlas of Irish history* (Dublin, 1997).

Duhigg, Bartholomew, *History of the King's Inns, or an account of the legal body in Ireland* (Dublin, 1806).

Dunning, P. J., 'The Arroasian order in medieval Ireland' in *IHS*, iv, no. 16 (September 1945).

Dwyer, Charles (ed.), 'Archbishop Butler's visitation book' in *Archiv. Hib.*, xxxiii (1975), pp. 1–90 and *Archiv. Hib.*, xxxiv (1976–7), pp. 1–49.

Education Inquiry. *First report of the commissioners of Irish education inquiry*, HC 1825 (400) XII; *Second report of the commissioners of Irish education inquiry*, HC 1826–7 (12) XII; *Ninth report of the commissioners of Irish education inquiry*, HC 1826–7 (516) XIII; *Report from the select committee to whom the reports of education in Ireland were referred*, HC 1828 (341) IV.

Edwards, R. Dudley, 'The beginning of municipal government in Dublin' in *DHR*, i, no. 1 (March, 1938), pp. 2–10.

— (ed.), 'The minute book of the Catholic Committee, 1773–92' in *Archiv. Hib.*, ix (1942).

Edwards, Robin Dudley and Moody, T. W., 'The history of Poynings' law, Pt 1: 1494–1615' in *IHS*, ii, no. 8 (Sept. 1941).

Ellis, S. G., 'Economic problems of the Church: why the Reformation failed in Ireland' in *Jn. Ecc. Hist.* 41, 2 (1990).

— *Reform and revival: English government in Ireland 1470–1534* (Woodbridge, 1986).

— *Ireland in the age of the Tudors 1447–1603* (London, 1998).

Emerson, N. D., *The Church of Ireland and the 1859 revival* (Belfast, 1959).

Erck, John Caillard (ed.), *A repertory of the inrolments of the patent rolls of chancery in Ireland, James I* (2 vols, 2 parts, 1846–1852).

Evangeliorum quattuor Codex Durmachensis (2 vols, 1960).

Evans, E. Estyn, 'The flachter' in *UJA*, 3rd ser., iv (1941).

— *Irish heritage: the landscape, the people and their work* (Dundalk, 1942).

— *The personality of Ireland* (revised edition, Belfast, 1981).

Fagan, Patrick, *Divided loyalties: the question of an oath for Irish Catholics in the eighteenth century* (Dublin, 1997).

Falkiner, C. Litton, 'The Hospital of St John of Jerusalem in Ireland' in *RIA Proc.*, xxvi, C (1906–07).

— *Illustrations of Irish history and topography, mainly of the seventeenth century* (London, 1904).

Farrell, Brian 'The patriot parliament of 1689' in Farrell, Brian (ed.), *The Irish parliamentary tradition* (Dublin, 1973).

Feenan, Dermot and Kennedy, Liam, 'Weights and measures of the major food commodities in early-nineteenth century Ireland: a regional perspective' in *RIA Proc.*, C, cii (2002).

Ferguson, James F., 'The "mere English" and the "mere Irish"' in *Transactions of the Kilkenny Archaeological Society*, i (1849–51).

ffolliott, Rosemary and Begley, Donal F., 'Guide to Irish directories' in Begley, Donal F. (ed.), *Irish genealogy: a record finder* (Dublin, 1981).

ffolliott, Rosemary and O'Byrne, Eileen, 'Wills and administrations: a prime source for family research' in Begley, Donal F. (ed.), *Irish genealogy: a record finder* (Dublin, 1981).

Finnegan, Ruth and Drake, Michael (eds), *Sources and methods for family and community historians: a handbook* (Cambridge, 1994).

FitzPatrick, William J., *History of the Dublin Catholic cemeteries* (Dublin, 1900).

Fitzsimons, Fiona 'Fosterage and gossipred in late medieval Ireland: some new evidence' in Duffy, Patrick, Edwards, David and FitzPatrick, Elizabeth (eds), *Gaelic Ireland c. 1250–1650: Land, lordship and settlement* (Dublin, 2001).

Flanagan, Kieran, 'The chief secretary's office, 1853–1914: a bureaucratic enigma' in *IHS*, xxiv. no. 94 (1984–5).

Flood, W. H. G., 'The Premonstratensians in Ireland' in *IER*, 5th ser., ii (1913).

Ford, P. and G., *A guide to parliamentary papers: what they are, how to find them, how to use them* (Oxford 1955).

— *Select list of British parliamentary papers, 1833–1899* (Oxford, 1953).

Foundling Hospital. *Journal of the house of commons of the kingdom of Ireland*, vi, xcvi–xcvii; *Eighth report from the commissioners of the Board of Education in Ireland*, HC 1810 (193) X; *Third report of the commissioners of Irish education inquiry*, HC 1826-27 (13) XIII; *Report of George Nicholls on institutions receiving grants from public funds in 1842*, HC 1842 (389) XXXVIII.

Frame, Robin, 'Commissions of the peace in Ireland' in *Anal. Hib.*, 35 (1992).

— 'The judicial powers of the medieval Irish keeper of the peace' in *Ir. Jurist, new ser.*, ii (1967).

Freeman, A. Martin (ed.), *Annála Connacht AD 1224–1544* (Dublin, 1985).

— (ed.), *The compossicion booke of Conought* (Dublin, 1936).

Galloway, Peter, *The order of St Patrick and its knights* (Phillamore, 1999).

Garvin, Tom, *The evolution of Irish nationalist politics* (Dublin, 1981).

Geoghegan, Patrick M., *The Irish act of union: a study in high politics, 1798–1801* (Dublin, 1999).

Gilbert, J. T. (ed.), *Register of the abbey of St Thomas the martyr, Dublin* (London, 1889).

— (ed.), *Crede mihi; the most ancient register book of the archbishops of Dublin before the reformation* (Dublin, 1897).

— *History of the Irish Confederation and the war in Ireland, 1641–43* (7 vols, Dublin, 1882–91).

Gillespie, Raymond, 'A manor court in seventeenth-century Ireland' in *Ir. Econ. Soc. & Hist.*, xxv (1998).

Gillespie, Raymond and Kennedy, Brian P. (eds), *Ireland: art into history* (Dublin, 1994).

Goodbody, Olive C., *Guide to Irish Quaker records 1654–1860* (Dublin, 1967).

Gooder, Eileen A., *Latin for local history* (London, 1961).

Graham, A. H., 'Lichfield House compact, 1835' in *IHS*, xii, no. 45 (1960).

Gray, Tony, *The Orange Order* (London, 1972).

Greaves, Richard L., *God's other children: Protestant nonconformists and emergence of denominational churches in Ireland, 1660–1700* (Stanford, 1997).

Greer, D. S., 'The development of civil bill procedure in Ireland' in McEldowney, John and O'Higgins, Paul (eds), *The common law tradition* (Dublin, 1990).

Grenham, John, *Tracing your Irish ancestors: the complete guide* (Dublin, 1992).

Gribbon, H. D., 'Irish Baptist Church records' in Ryan, James G. (ed.), *Irish Church records* (Dublin, 1992).

Griffin, Brian, *The bulkies: police and crime in Belfast, 1800–1865* (Dublin, 1998).

Griffith, A. R. G., *The Irish board of works, 1831–1878* (New York & London, 1987).

Griffith, Margaret C. (ed.), *Calendar of inquisitions formerly in the office of the chief remembrancer of the exchequer prepared from the mss of the Irish record commission* (Dublin, 1991).

— 'A short guide to the Public Record Office of Ireland' in *IHS*, viii, no. 29 (1952–3).

— 'The Irish Record Commission' in *IHS*, vii, no. 25 (1950).

Grubb, Isabel, *Quakers in Ireland 1654–1900* (London, 1927).

Guide to the Genealogical Office, Dublin (Dublin, 1998).

Gurrin, Brian, *Pre-census sources for Irish demography* (Dublin, 2002).

Gwynn, Aubrey, 'The early history of St Thomas Abbey' in *RSAI Jn.*, lxxxiv (1954).

Gwynn, Aubrey and Hadcock, R. Neville, *Medieval religious houses, Ireland* (Dublin, 1970).

Gwynn, Edward (ed.), *The rule of Tallaght: teaching of Mael Ruain* (Dublin, 1927).

Haddick-Flynn, Kevin, *Orangeism: the making of a tradition* (Dublin, 1999).

Hall, Dianne, *Women and the church in medieval Ireland* (Dublin, 2003).

Hamilton, Gustavus Everard, *An account of the Honourable Society of King's Inns, Dublin, from its foundation until the beginning of the nineteenth century* (Dublin, 1901).

Hand, G. J., 'Medieval cathedral chapters' in *Ir. Cath. Hist. Comm. Proc.* (1956).

— *English law in Ireland, 1290–1324* (Cambridge, 1967).

Harbison, Peter, *The high crosses of Ireland* (3 vols, Bonn, 1992).

Harbison, Peter, Potterton, Homan and Sheehy, Jeanne (eds), *Irish art and architecture from prehistory to the present* (London, 1970).

Hart, A. R., *A history of the king's serjeant at law in Ireland* (Dublin, 2000).

Hatchell, G. (ed.), *Abstract of grants of land and other hereditaments under the Commission of Grace 36–37 Charles II and 1–4 James II, 1684–1688* (Dublin, 1839).

Hayden, Mary, 'The origin and development of heads of bills in the Irish parliament' in *RSAI Jn*, lv (1925).

Hayes, R. J., (ed.), *The manuscript sources for the history of Irish civilisation* (11 vols, Boston, 1965); *First supplement, 1965–75* (3 vols, Boston, 1979).

Hayes McCoy, G. A., 'The hobelar: an Irish contribution to medieval warfare' in *Irish Sword*, ii (1954–6).

Hayton, David, 'The beginning of the "undertaker system"' in Bartlett, T. and Hayton, D. W. (eds), *Penal era and golden age: Essays in Irish history, 1680–1800* (Belfast, 1979).

Helferty, Seamus and Refaussé, Raymond, *Directory of Irish archives* (3rd. ed., Dublin, 1999).

Hennessy, W. M. (ed.), *The annals of Loch Cé: a chronicle of Irish affairs, 1014–1590* (2 vols, London, 1871).

Hennessy, W. M. and MacCarthy, B. (eds), *Annála Ulaidh: Annals of Ulster* (Dublin, 1887–91).

Henry, Francoise (ed.), *The Book of Kells* (London, 1974).

— *Irish high crosses* (Dublin, 1964).

Herity, Michael, *Irish passage graves: neolithic tomb-builders in Ireland and Britain, 2500 BC* (Dublin, 1974).

Herlihy, Jim, *The Royal Irish Constabulary* (Dublin, 1997).

Hick, Vivian, 'The Palatine settlement in Ireland: the early years' in *Eighteenth-century Ireland*, iv (Dublin, 1989).

Hill, George, *An historical account of the plantation in Ulster at the commencement of the seventeenth century 1608–1620* (1st ed., Belfast, 1877, repr., Shannon, 1970).

Hill, Myrtle and Gillespie, Raymond (eds), *Doing Irish local history* (Belfast, 1998).

Hogan, Edmund, *Onomasticon Goidelicum locorum et tribuum Hiberniae et Scotiae* (Dublin, 1910).

Hogan, James, 'The tricha-cét and related land measures' in *RIA Proc.*, xxxviii, C, no. 7 (1928–9).

Holdsworth, William, *A history of English law*, i (London, 1903).

Hoppen, K. Theodore 'The papers of the Dublin Philosophical Society 1683– 1708: introduction and index' in *Anal. Hib.*, 30 (1982).

— 'The Dublin Philosophical Society and the New Learning in Ireland' in *IHS*, xiv, no. 54 (1964).

— *Elections, politics and society in Ireland 1832–1885* (Oxford, 1984).

Hughes, J. L. J., 'The chief secretary in Ireland, 1566–1921' in *IHS*, viii, no. 29 (March, 1952).

— 'The Dublin court of conscience' in *DHR*, xv, no. 2 (1959).

Hughes, T. J., 'Town and baile in Irish placenames' in Stephens, Nicholas and Glasscock, R. E. (eds), *Irish geographical studies in honour of E. Estyn Evans* (Belfast, 1970).

Iggers, George G., *Historiography in the twentieth century* (Hanover and London, 1997).

Inquisitionum in officio rotulorum cancellariae Hiberniae asservatorum repertorium, (2 vols, Dublin, 1829).

Irish fiants of the Tudor sovereigns during the reigns of Henry VIII, Edward VI, Philip & Mary and Elizabeth I (3 vols, Dublin, 1994).

Irish statutes: revised edition, 3rd Edwd II to the Union, AD 1310–1800 (London, 1885).

Jackson, Alvin, *The Ulster party: Irish unionism in the house of commons, 1884–1911* (Oxford, 1989).

Jacob, Rosamond, *The rise of the United Irishmen, 1791–94* (London, 1937).

James, F. G., *Lords of the ascendancy: the Irish house of lords and its members, 1600–1800* (Dublin, 1995).

Jefferies, Henry A., 'Erenaghs in pre-plantation Ulster: an early seventeenth-century account' in *Archiv. Hib.*, liii (1999).

Jeffery, F., *Irish Methodism: An historical account of its traditions, theology and influence* (n.p., 1964).

Jenkinson, Sir Hilary 'The great seal of England: deputed or departmental seal' in *Archaeologia*, lxxxv (1936).

Johnston-Liik, Edith Mary (ed.), *History of the Irish parliament 1692–1800: commons, constituencies and statutes* (6 vols, Belfast, 2002).

Journals of the house of commons of the kingdom of Ireland (19 vols, Dublin, 1796–1800).

Journals of the house of lords of the kingdom of Ireland 1634–1800 (8 vols, Dublin, 1783–1800).

Kaestle, Carl F., *Joseph Lancaster and the monitorial school movement; a documentary history* (New York and London, 1973).

Keane, E. and Eustace, P. B., (eds), *The King's Inns admission papers, 1607–1867* (Dublin 1982).

Kearney, H. F., 'The court of wards and liveries in Ireland 1622–41' in *RIA Proc.*, lvii, C, no. 2 (1955).

— *Strafford in Ireland 1633–41: A study in absolutism* (Cambridge, 1959).

Keating, Geoffrey, *Foras feasa ar Éirinn: the history of Ireland* (edited and translated by Comyn, David and Dinneen, P. S., 4 vols, London, 1902–14).

Kelly, Eamonn P., *Sheela-na gigs* (Dublin, 1996).

Kelly, Fergus, *A guide to early Irish law* (Dublin, 1988).

Kelly, James, 'Monitoring the constitution: the operation of Poynings' Law in the 1760s' in Hayton, D. W. (ed.), *The Irish parliament in the eighteenth century* (Edinburgh, 2001).

— *Prelude to Union; Anglo-Irish politics in the 1780s* (Cork, 1992).

Kelly, Rev. Mathew, *Calendar of Irish saints, the martyrology of Tallagh; With notes of the patron saints of Ireland* (Dublin, 1857).

Kenny, Colum, *King's Inns and the kingdom of Ireland: the Irish inns of court, 1541–1800* (Dublin, 1992).

Keogh, Daire, *Edmund Rice, 1762–1844* (Dublin, 1996).

Kerr, Donal A., *'A nation of beggars'? Priests, people and politics in famine Ireland, 1846–52* (Oxford, 1994).

Kilroy, Phil, *Protestant dissent and controversy in Ireland, 1660–1714* (Cork, 1994).

Kinealy, Christine, *This great calamity: the Irish famine 1845–52* (Dublin, 1994).

— *Tracing your Irish roots* (Belfast, 1991).

King, Carla, *Michael Davitt* (Dundalk, 1999).

Kolbert, C. F. and O'Brien, T., *Land reform in Ireland* (University of Cambridge, 1975).

Larcom, T. A. (ed.), *The history of the survey of Ireland commonly called the Down Survey, by Doctor William Petty, AD 1655–6* (Dublin, 1851).

Larkin, Emmet, *The making of the Roman Catholic Church in Ireland, 1850–60* (North Carolina, 1980).

— *Alexis de Tocqueville's journey in Ireland July–August 1835* (Dublin, 1990).

— *The Roman Catholic Church and the plan of campaign, 1868–88* (Cork, 1978).

Lascelles, R., *Liber munerum publicorum Hiberniae* (2 vols, London, 1852).

Lawlor, H. J., 'A calendar of Archbishop Fleming' in *RIA Proc.*, xxx, C, no. 5 (Dublin, 1912).

— 'A calendar of the Liber Niger and Liber Albus of Christ Church, Dublin' in *RIA Proc.*, xxvii, C, no. 1 (1908).

— 'Calendar of the Liber Ruber of the diocese of Ossory' in *RIA Proc.*, xxvii, C, no. 5 (1908).

Leadham, I. S., *Coercive measures for Ireland 1830–1880* (Dublin, 1880).

Lee, Joseph, 'The Ribbonmen' in Williams, T. Desmond (ed.), *Secret societies in Ireland* (Dublin, 1973).

Lennon, Colm, *Richard Stanihurst the Dubliner 1547–1618* (Dublin, 1981).

Lennox Barrow, G., 'The knights hospitallers of St John of Jerusalem at Kilmainham' in *DHR*, xxxviii, no. 3 (1984–5).

Lewis, Samuel, *A topographical dictionary of Ireland* (2 vols with atlas, London, 1837).

Lindsay, Deirdre, *Dublin's oldest charity: the Sick and Indigent Roomkeepers Society, 1790–1990* (Dublin, 1990).

Lohan, Rena, *Guide to the archives of the Office of Public Works* (Dublin, 1994).

Lucas, A. T., 'Contributions to the history of the Irish house: a possible ancestry of the bed outshot' in *Folk Life*, 8 (1970).

— *Furze: a survey and history of its uses in Ireland* (Dublin, 1960).

Lydon, J. F., 'A survey of the memoranda rolls of the Irish exchequer, 1294–1509' in *Anal. Hib.*, 23 (1966).

— 'The middle nation' in Lydon, James (ed.), *The English in medieval Ireland* (Dublin, 1984).

Lyne, Gerard J., 'Three certified Gross Survey transcripts for county Galway' in *Anal. Hib.*, 35 (1992).

Lyons, F. S. L., *Charles Stewart Parnell* (London, 1977).
— *The Irish parliamentary party, 1890–1910* (London,1951).
Lyons, Mary Cecilia, *Illustrated incumbered estates, Ireland, 1850–1905* (Clare, 1993).
Mac Airt, Seán (ed.), *Leabhar Branach* (Dublin, 1944).
— (ed.), *The annals of Innisfallen* (Dublin, 1951).
Mac Airt, Seán and Mac Niocaill, Gearóid (eds), *The Annals of Ulster to* AD *113*, part 1 (Dublin, 1983).
Macalister, R. A. S. (ed.), *Lebor Gabála Érenn: The book of the taking of Ireland*, parts i–v (Dublin and London, 1938–56).
— (ed.), *The book of Mac Carthaigh Riabhach; otherwise the book of Lismore* (Dublin, 1950).
McAnally, Sir Henry, *The Irish militia, 1793–1816: a social and military study* (Dublin and London, 1949).
McAuliffe, J. J., 'Ploughing by horses' tails' in *Irish Book Lover*, xxix (1943–5).
McCaffrey, James (ed.), *The black book of Limerick* (Dublin, 1907).
McCavitt, John, 'The flight of the earls, 1607' in *IHS*, xxix, no. 114 (1994).
McClelland, Aiken, 'The later Orange Order' in Williams, T. Desmond (ed.), *Secret societies in Ireland* (Dublin, 1973).
McCracken, J. L., 'The conflict between the Irish administration and parliament' in *IHS*, iii, no. 10 (1942).
— 'The political structure, 1714–60' in Moody, T. W. and Vaughan, W. E. (eds), *A new history of Ireland*, iv (Oxford, 1986).
McCullough, Niall (ed.), *A vision of the city: Dublin and the Wide Street Commissioners* (Dublin, 1991).
McDowell, R. B., *The Irish administration, 1801–1914* (London, 1964).
McErlean, Thomas, 'The Irish townland system of landscape organisation' in Reeves-Smyth, T. and Hammond, F. (eds), *Landscape archaeology of Ireland* (Oxford, 1983).
MacGiolla Coille, B. and Simington, R. C. (eds), *Books of survey and distribution*, IV, Co. Clare (Dublin, 1967)
MacGiolla Coille, B. (ed.), *Books of survey and distribution*, III, Co. Galway (Dublin, 1962).
McGrath, C. I., 'Securing the Protestant interest: the origins and purpose of the penal laws of 1695' in *IHS*, xxx, no. 117 (1996–7).
McGuire, J. I., 'The Dublin convention, the Protestant community and the emergence of an ecclesiastical settlement in 1660' in Cosgrove, Art and McGuire, J. I. (eds), *Parliament and community* (Dublin, 1983).
— 'The parliament of 1692' in Bartlett, T. and Hayton, D. W. (eds), *Penal era and golden age: essays in Irish history, 1690–1800* (Belfast, 1979).
McNeill, Charles (ed.), *Calendar of Archbishop Alen's register, c. 1172–1534* (Dublin, 1949).
— (ed.), *Registrum de Kilmainham, 1326–1350* (Dublin, 1932).
MacNeill, Niall, *The Ordnance Survey of Ireland* (Dublin, 1966)
Mac Niocaill, Gearóid (ed.), *Crown survey of lands 1540–41* (Dublin, 1992)
— 'The origins of the betagh' in *Ir. Jurist*, new ser., i (1966).
McParland, Edward, 'The office of the surveyor-general in Ireland in the eighteenth century' in *Architectural History*, xxxviii (1995).
— *Public architecture in Ireland, 1680–1760* (New Haven and London, 2001).
McVeagh, John, *Richard Pococke's Irish tours* (Dublin, 1995).
Madden, P. G., 'The Ordnance Survey of Ireland' in *Ir. Sword*, v (1961–2).
Magray, M. P., *The transforming power of the nuns: women, religion and cultural change in Ireland, 1750–1900* (New York, 1998).
Maguire, W. A., 'Lord Donegall and the Hearts of Steel' in *IHS*, xxi, no. 84 (September, 1979).

Malcolm, E. L., 'Ireland Sober, Ireland Free': Drink and temperance in nineteenth-century Ireland (Dublin, 1986).

Malcomson, A. P. W., 'Absenteeism in eighteenth century Ireland' in Ir. Econ. & Soc. Hist., i (1974).

Maltby, A. and J., Ireland in the nineteenth century: a breviate of official publications (Oxford, 1979).

Marshall, J. D., The tyranny of the discrete: a discussion of the problems of local history in England (Aldershot, 1997).

Martin, F. X., 'Gerald of Wales: Norman reporter in Ireland' in Studies, lviii, no. 231 (1969).

Mason, William Shaw, A statistical account, or parochial survey of Ireland, drawn up from the communications of the clergy (3 vols, Dublin, 1814–1819).

Maxwell, Constantia, Irish history from contemporary sources, 1509–1610 (London, 1923).

Megarry, R. E., A manual of the law of real property (London, 1947).

Micks, W. L., An account of the constitution, administration and dissolution of the Congested Districts Board for Ireland from 1891 to 1923 (Dublin, 1925).

Miller, D. W., 'The Armagh troubles, 1785–95' in Clarke, S. and Donnelly, J. S. (eds), Irish peasants: violence and political unrest, 1780–1914 (Manchester, 1983).

Miller, Liam and Power, Eileen (eds), Holinshed's Irish Chronicle 1577 (Dublin, 1979)

Millett, Benignus, The Irish Franciscans, 1651–1665 (Rome, 1964).

Mills, James (ed.), 'Notices of the manor of St Sepulchre, Dublin, in the fourteenth century', in RSAI Jn., xix (1889).

— Calendar of the justiciary rolls, 23–31 Edw 1, 33–35 Edw I (2 vols, Dublin, 1907–1914).

Milne, Kenneth, The Church of Ireland – a history (3rd. ed., Dublin, 1994).

— The Irish charter schools, 1730–1830 (Dublin, 1997).

Mitchell, Frank, The Shell guide to reading the Irish landscape (Dublin, 1986).

Moody, T. W., The Londonderry plantation, 1609–41 (Belfast, 1939),

Morrin, James (ed.), The patent rolls of Henry VIII, Edward VI, Philip & Mary, Elizabeth I and Charles I (3 vols, Dublin, 1861–1863).

Morrissey, J. F. (ed.), Statute rolls of the parliament of Ireland, twelfth and thirteenth to the twenty-first and twenty-second years of the reign of king Edward the fourth (Dublin, 1939).

Morton, R. G., 'Mechanics institutes and the attempted diffusion of useful knowledge in Ireland, 1827–79' in Irish Booklore, ii (1972).

— 'The rise of the Irish yeomanry' in Ir. Sword, viii (1967–8).

Moryson, Fynes, An itinerary of his travels (4 vols, Glasgow, 1907).

Mulchrone, Kathleen (ed.), The Book of Lecan – Leabhar Mór Mhic Fhir Bhisigh Leacain (Dublin, 1937).

Murnaghan, J. A., 'The lordship of Ireland and the counties palatine' in Studies, ii, no. 5 (March, 1913).

Murphy, Rev. Denis (ed.), The annals of Clonmacnoise being annals of Ireland from the earliest period to AD 1408 (Dublin, 1896).

Newark, F. H., Notes on Irish legal history (Belfast, 1960).

Nicholls, K. W., 'Medieval Irish chapters' in Archiv. Hib., xxxi (1973).

Ní Mhurchadha, Maighréad, The customs and excise service in Fingal, 1684–1765 (Dublin, 1999).

Nolan, William, Tracing the past: sources for local studies in the Republic of Ireland (Dublin, 1982).

Nolan, William and Simms, Anngret (eds), Irish towns: a guide to sources (Dublin, 1998).

Norgate, Kate, 'The bull Laudabiliter' in EHR, vii (1893).

Nowlan, Kevin B., 'Disestablishment 1800–1869' in Hurley, Michael, SJ (ed.), Irish

Anglicanism 1869–1969 (Dublin, 1970).

O'Brien, George, 'The Irish staple organisation in the reign of James I' in *Econ. Hist.*, 1 (1926).

O'Brien, Gerard, 'The establishment of poor-law unions in Ireland 1838–43' in *IHS*, xxiii, no. 90 (1982).

O'Brien, Gerard and Dunne, Tom (eds), *Catholic Ireland in the eighteenth century: collected essays of Maureen Wall* (Dublin, 1989).

O'Brien, R. Barry, *The Irish land question and English public opinion with a supplement on Griffith's Valuation* (London, 1881).

O'Broin, Leon, 'The Invincibles' in Williams, T. Desmond (ed.), *Secret societies in Ireland* (Dublin, 1973).

O'Byrne, Eileen (ed.), *The convert rolls* (Dublin, 1981).

O'Clery, Michael, *The martyrology of Donegal: A calendar of the saints of Ireland* (edited with the Irish text by James Todd and William Reeves, Dublin, 1864).

O'Connell, Daniel and O'Ferrall, Barnabas (eds), *Commentarius Rinuccinianus* (6 vols, Dublin, 1932–49).

O'Curry, Eugene, *Lectures on the manuscript materials of ancient Irish history. Delivered at the Catholic University of Ireland during the sessions of 1855 and 1856* (Dublin, 1861, repr., 1964).

Ó Dálaigh, Brian, Cronin, Denis A. and Connell, Paul (eds), *Irish townlands: studies in local history* (Dublin, 1998).

Ó Domhnaill, Seán, 'The maps of the Down Survey' in *IHS*, iii, no. 12 (1942–3).

Ó Donnchadha, Tadhg (ed.), *Leabhar Cloinne Aodha Buidhe* (Dublin, 1937).

O'Donnell, Thomas J., *Selections from the Zoilomastix of Philip O'Beare Sullivan* (Dublin, 1960).

O'Donoghue, Patrick, 'Causes of opposition of tithes 1830–1838' in *Studia Hibernica* 5 (1965).

— 'Opposition to tithe payments in 1830–31' in *Studia Hibernica* 6 (1966).

O'Donovan, John (ed.), *Annals of the kingdom of Ireland by the Four Masters* (7 vols, Dublin, 1851).

O'Dowd, Mary, '"Irish concealed lands" in the Hastings manuscripts in the Huntingdon Library, San Marino, California' in *Anal. Hib.*, 31 (Dublin, 1984).

O'Dowd, M. and Edwards, R. D., *Sources for early modern Irish history, 1534–1641* (Cambridge, 1988).

O'Dwyer, Peter, *Célí Dé: spiritual reform in Ireland, 750–900* (Dublin, 1981).

O'Farrell, Patrick, 'Millenialism, messianism and utopianism in Irish history' in *Anglo-Irish Studies*, ii (1976).

O'Ferrall, Fergus, *Catholic emancipation: Daniel O'Connell and the birth of Irish democracy* (Dublin, 1985).

O'Flaherty, Eamon, 'The Catholic Convention and Anglo-Irish politics, 1791–3' in *Archiv. Hib.*, xl (1985).

Ó Gráda, Cormac, *Malthus and the pre-famine economy* (Dublin, 1982).

O'Hagan, Rev. Fergus, 'Catholic Association papers in the Dublin diocesan archives' in *Archiv. Hib.*, xxxix (1984).

Ohlmeyer, Jane (ed.), *Ireland from independence to occupation, 1641–60* (Cambridge, 1993).

Ohlmeyer, Jane and Ó Ciardha, Eamonn (eds), *The Irish statute staple books, 1596–1687* (Dublin, 1998).

Ó Muireadhaigh, Sailbheastair, 'Na Carabhait is na Seanbheisteanna' in *Galvia*, viii (1961).

— 'Na fir ribín' in *Galvia*, x (1964–5).

O'Neill, Marie, 'The Ladies Land League' in *DHR*, xxxv (Dec 1981–Sept 1982).

O'Neill, Timothy P., *Life and tradition in rural Ireland* (London, 1977).

O'Neill, Thomas P., *Sources of Irish local history* (Dublin, 1958).

Ó Ríordáin, Seán P., *Antiquities of the Irish countryside* (4th ed., London, 1965).

Osbrough, W. N., *Studies in Irish legal history* (Dublin, 1999).

Ó Siochrú, Micheál, *Confederate Ireland, 1642–49: a constitutional and political analysis* (Dublin, 1999).

Ó Snódaigh, Padraig, *The Irish Volunteers 1715–1793: a list of units* (Dublin, 1995).

Ó Súilleabháin, Seán, *A handbook of Irish folklore* (Dublin, 1942, Detroit, 1970).

O'Sullivan, David J., *The Irish constabularies 1822–1922* (Kerry, 1999).

O'Sullivan, William (ed.), *The Strafford inquisition of county Mayo* (Dublin, 1958).

O'Toole, James (ed.), *Newsplan: report of the Newsplan project in Ireland* (London and Dublin, 1992).

Otway-Ruthven, A. J., *A history of medieval Ireland* (London, 1968).

— 'Anglo-Irish shire government in the thirteenth century' in *IHS*, v, no. 17 (Mar. 1946).

— 'The chief governors of medieval Ireland' in *RSAI Jn.*, xcv (1965), pp. 227-36.

— 'Enclosures in the medieval period' in *Ir. Geography*, v, no. 2 (1965).

— 'Knight-service in Ireland' in *RSAI Jn.*, lxxxix (1959).

— 'Royal service in Ireland' in *RSAI Jn.*, xcviii (1968).

Palles. *First report of the commissioners on intermediate education (Ireland) with appendix*, HC 1899 [C9116, C9117] XXII; *Final report*, HC 1899 [C9511] XXII; *Minutes of evidence*, HC 1899 [C9512] XXIII.

Palmer, Norman Dunbar, *The Irish Land League crisis* (New York, 1978).

— 'The chief governors of medieval Ireland' in *RSAI Jn.*, xcv (1965).

Palmer, S. H., *Police and protest in Ireland and England, 1780–1850* (Cambridge, 1988).

Parkes, Susan M., *Irish education in the British parliamentary papers in the nineteenth century and after, 1801–1920* (Cork, 1978).

— *Kildare Place: the history of the Church of Ireland Training College, 1811–1969* (c. 1984).

Parliamentary Gazetteer of Ireland (3 vols, Dublin, London and Edinburgh, 1845– 6, new ed., 6 vols, Bristol, 1998).

Parliamentary register of Ireland or history of the proceedings and debates of the house of commons of Ireland (17 vols, Dublin, 1784–1801, repr., Bristol, 1999).

Pender, Seamus (ed.), *A census of Ireland, circa 1659* (Dublin, 1939).

Phair, P. B., 'Seventeenth-century regal visitations' in *Anal. Hib.*, 28 (1978).

— 'Sir William Betham's manuscripts' in *Anal. Hib.*, 27 (1972).

— 'Guide to the Registry of Deeds' in *Anal. Hib.*, 23 (1966).

Phythian-Adams, Charles, *Re-thinking English local history* (Leicester, 1987).

Pike, Clement E., 'The origin of the regium donum' in *R. Hist. Soc. Trans*, 3rd series, iii (1909).

Pollard, H. B. C., *The Ancient Order of Hibernians and the revival of the IRB* (London, 1922).

Pomfret, John E., *The struggle for land in Ireland* (New York, 1930).

Poor Inquiry. *First report of His Majesty's commissioners for inquiring into the condition of the poorer classes in Ireland, with appendix and supplement*, HC 1835 [369] XXXII; *Second report of His Majesty's commissioners for inquiring into the condition of the poorer classes in Ireland, with appendix and supplement*, HC 1837 [68] XXI; *Third report of His Majesty's commissioners for inquiring into the condition of the poorer classes in Ireland, with appendix and supplement*, HC 1836 [43] XXX.

Power, T. P., (ed.), 'A minister's money account for Clonmel 1703' in *Anal. Hib.*, 34 (1987).

Powis. *Report of the commissioners appointed to inquire into the nature and extent of instruction afforded by the several institutions in Ireland for the purpose of elementary or primary education; also into the practical working of the system of national education in*

Ireland, HC 1870 [C6] XXVIII.

Prendergast, J. P., 'The Ulster creaght' in *RSAI Jn.*, iii (1855).

Prochaska, Alice, *Irish history from 1700: a guide to sources in the Public Record Office* (London, 1985).

PRI rep. DK, 33 (Dublin, 1901).

PRI reps DK, 35–54 (1903–1927).

PRI, rep. DK, Appendices to 7–9, 11–13, 15–18, 21. (Calendar of fiants, Henry VII–Elizabeth, 1521–1603).

PRONI, *Guide to church records* (Belfast, 1994).

PRONI, *Guide to the records of the Irish Society and the London companies* (Belfast, 1994).

Proudfoot, V. B., 'Clachans in Ireland' in *Gwerin*, ii (1958–9).

Prunty, Jacinta, *Maps and mapmaking in local history* (Dublin, 2004).

Public Instruction. *First report of the commissioners of public instruction (Ireland)* HC 1835 (45) (46) XXXIII; *Second report of the commissioners of public instruction (Ireland)* HC 1835 (47) XXXIV.

Quinn, David B., 'Anglo-Irish local government, 1485–1534' in *IHS*, i, no. 4 (1939).

Quinn, Michael, 'The diocesan schools, 1570–1820' in *JCHAS*, 2nd ser., lxvi (1961).

Raftery, Barry, *La Tène in Ireland: problems of origin and chronology* (Marburg, 1984).

Refaussé, Raymond, *A handbook of Church of Ireland vestry minute books in the Representative Church Body library* (Dublin, 1994).

— *Church of Ireland records* (Dublin, 2000).

Reilly, James R., 'Richard Griffith and his valuation of Ireland' in *The Irish at home and abroad*, iv, no. 3 (1997).

Report on the manuscripts of the earl of Egmont, vol. i, pt i (HMC, London, 1905).

Return of owners of land of one acre and upwards in the several counties, counties of cities and counties of towns in Ireland (Repr., Baltimore, 1988).

Richardson, D. S., *Gothic revival architecture in Ireland* (2 vols, New York, 1968, reprint, 1983).

Richardson, H. G. and Sayles, G. O., *The Irish parliament in the middle ages* (new ed., Philadelphia, 1964).

Roberts, Paul, 'Caravats and Shanavests: whiteboyism and faction-fighting in east Munster, 1802–11' in Clark, Samuel and Donnelly, J. S. (eds), *Irish peasants: violence and political unrest, 1780–1914* (Manchester, 1983).

Roebuck, Peter, 'The Irish registry of deeds' in *IHS*, xviii, no. 69 (1972–3).

Ronan, M. V., 'Archbishop Bulkeley's visitation of Dublin, 1630' in *Archiv. Hib.*, viii (1941).

— *Erasmus Smith: a romance of confiscation* (Dublin, 1937).

— 'Religious customs of Dublin medieval gilds' in *IER*, 5th ser., xxvi (1925).

Rusling, G. W., 'The schools of the Baptist Irish society' in *Baptist Quarterly*, xxii, 8 (1968).

Ryan, James G. (ed.), *Irish church records: their history, availability and use in family and local history research* (Dublin, 1992).

— *Irish records: sources for family and local history* (Dublin, 1988).

Savage, D. C., 'The origins of the Ulster unionist party, 1885–6' in *IHS*, xii, no. 47 (1961).

Senior, Hereward, 'The early Orange Order, 1795–1870' in Williams, T. Desmond (ed.), *Secret societies in Ireland* (Dublin, 1973).

Shaw-Smith, David, *Ireland's traditional crafts* (London, 1984).

Shearman, H., 'The citation of British and Irish parliamentary papers' in *IHS*, iv (March 1944).

Sheehy, M. P., 'The bull Laudabiliter; a problem in medieval diplomatique and history' in *Galway Archaeological Society Journal*, xxix (1960–1).

Simington, R. C. (ed.), *Books of survey and distribution*, I, Co. Roscommon (Dublin, 1949).

— (ed.), *Books of survey and distribution*, II, Co. Mayo (Dublin, 1956).

— 'The tithe composition applotment books' in *Anal. Hib.*, 10 (1941).

— *The transplantation to Connacht, 1654–58* (Dublin, 1970).

— (ed.), *The Civil Survey AD 1654–1656*, vii (Dublin, 1945).

Simms, Anngret and Fagan, Patricia, 'Villages in county Dublin: their origins and inheritance' in Aalen, F. H. A. and Whelan, Kevin (eds), *Dublin city and county: from prehistory to present* (Dublin, 1992).

Simms, J. G., 'The Civil Survey' in *IHS*, ix, no. 35 (1954–5).

— 'The original draft of the civil articles of Limerick, 1691' in *IHS*,viii, no. 29 (March, 1952).

— *The treaty of Limerick* (Irish History Series no. 2, Dublin, 1961).

— *The Williamite confiscation in Ireland 1690–1703* (London, 1956).

— *William Molyneaux of Dublin, 1656–1698* (Dublin, 1982).

Simms, Katherine, 'Guesting and feasting in Gaelic Ireland' in *RSAI Jn.*, cviii (1978).

Smyth, P. D. H., 'The Volunteers and parliament, 1779–84' in Bartlett, Thomas and Hayton, D. W. (eds), *Penal era and golden age: essays in Irish history, 1690–1800* (Belfast, 1979).

Stalley, Roger, 'Irish gothic and English fashion' in Lydon, James (ed.), *The English in medieval Ireland* (Dublin, 1984).

Stewart, David, *The seceders in Ireland with annals of their congregations* (Belfast, 1950).

Stokes, W., *The life and labours in art and archaeology of George Petrie* (London, 1868).

Stokes, Whitley (ed.), *Céli Dé: The martyrology of Oengus the Culdee* (London, 1907).

— (ed.), *Félire Húi Gormáin: The martyrology of Gorman* (London, 1895).

Stout, Matthew, *The Irish ringfort* (Dublin, 2000).

Strain, R. W. M., *Belfast and its charitable society: a study of urban social development* (Oxford, 1961).

Swift, Jonathan, *The Drapier's letters* (edited by Herbert Davis, Oxford, 1935).

Thompson, Paul, 'The voice of the past' in Perks, Robert and Thomson, Alistair (eds), *The oral history reader* (London, 1998).

Thornley, D., *Isaac Butt* (London, 1964).

Todd, J. H. (ed.), *Cogadh Gaedhel re Gallaibh: the war of the Gaedhil with the Gaill* (London, 1867).

Townend, Paul A., *Father Mathew, temperance and Irish identity* (Dublin, 2002).

Treadmill, Victor, 'The Irish court of wards under James 1' in *IHS*, xii, no. 45 (1961).

Trevelyan, Charles, *The Irish crisis* (London, 1848).

Valor beneficiorum ecclesiasticorum in Hibernia (Dublin, 1741).

Vaughan, W. E., 'Richard Griffith and the tenement valuation' in Davies, G. L. H. and Mollan, R. C. (eds), *Richard Griffith, 1784–1847* (Dublin, 1980).

Wakefield, Edward, *An account of Ireland, statistical and political* (2 vols, London, 1812).

Wall, Maureen (McGeehin), 'The Catholics in the towns and the quarterage dispute in eighteenth-century Ireland' in O'Brien, Gerard and Dunne, Tom (eds), *Catholic Ireland in the eighteenth century: collected essays of Maureen Wall* (Dublin, 1989).

— *The penal laws, 1691–1760* (Dundalk, 1960).

Walton, Julian C., 'The subsidy roll of county Waterford, 1662' in *Anal. Hib.*, 30 (1982).

Watt, J. A., 'Laudabiliter in medieval diplomacy and propaganda', in *IER*, 5th ser., lxxxvii (1957).

— 'Ecclesia inter Anglicos et inter Hibernicos: confrontation and co-existence in the medieval diocese and province of Armagh' in Lydon, James (ed.), *The English in Ireland* (Dublin, 1984).

Webb, John J., *The guilds of Dublin* (Dublin, 1929).

— *Municipal government in Ireland: medieval and modern* (Dublin, 1918).

West, Trevor, *Horace Plunkett: co-operation and politics* (Bucks, 1986).

White, N. B., 'The Reportorium Viride of John Alen, Archbishop of Dublin, 1553' in

Anal. Hib., 10 (1941).

— *Extents of Irish monastic possessions 1540–1* (Dublin, 1943).

— *The 'Dignitas Decani' of St Patrick's Cathedral, Dublin* (Dublin, 1957).

Whyte, J. H., *The Tenant League and Irish politics in the eighteen-fifties* (Irish History Series no. 4, Dublin, 1963).

Widdess, J. D. H., *The Richmond, Whitworth and Hardwicke Hospitals. St Lawrence's Dublin. 1772–1972* (Dublin, 1972).

Wigham, Maurice J., *The Irish Quakers: a short history of the Religious Society of Friends* (Dublin, 1992).

Williams, T. Desmond, 'The Irish Republican Brotherhood' in Williams, T. Desmond (ed.), *Secret societies in Ireland* (Dublin, 1973).

Wood, Herbert, 'The offices of secretary of state for Ireland and keeper of the signet' in *RIA Proc.*, xxxviii, C, no.4 (1928).

— (ed.), *The chronicles of Ireland, 1584–1608* (Dublin, 1933).

— (ed.), *A guide to the public records deposited in the Public Record Office of Ireland* (Dublin, 1919).

— (ed.), *Court book of the liberty of St Sepulchre* (Dublin, 1930).

— 'The court of castle chamber or star chamber in Ireland' in *RIA Proc.*, xxxii, C (1914).

— 'The office of chief governor of Ireland 1172–1509' in *RIA Proc.*, xxxvi, C, no. 12 (1921–4).

— 'The public records of Ireland before and after 1922' in *R. Hist. Soc. Trans.*, 4th ser., xiii (1930).

— 'The Templars in Ireland' in *RIA Proc.*, xxvi, C, no. 14 (1906–07).

Wood, Herbert, Langman, Albert and Griffith, Margaret (eds), *Calendar of the justiciary rolls in Ireland, 1–7 Edw II* (Dublin, 1956).

Woodman, P. C., 'A mesolithic camp in Ireland' in *Scientific American* 245, no. 2 (August, 1981).

— *Excavations at Mount Sandel 1973–77* (Belfast, 1985).

Wylie, J. C. W., *Irish land law* (2nd ed., Oxford, 1986).

Young, Arthur, *A tour in Ireland; with general observations on the present state of the kingdom: made in the years 1776, 1777, and 1778, and brought down to the end of 1779* (2 vols, London, 1780).

Useful Reference and Research Guides

Aalen, F. H., Whelan, Kevin and Stout, Matthew (eds), *An atlas of the Irish rural landscape* (Cork, 1997).

Asplin, P. W. A., *Medieval Ireland, c. 1170–1495* (Dublin, 1971).

Begley, Donal F. (ed.), *Irish genealogy: a record finder* (Dublin, 1981).

Cheney, C. R., and Jones, Michael, *A handbook of dates for students of British history* (Cambridge, 2000).

Connolly, Philomena, *Medieval record sources* (Dublin, 2002).

Connolly, S. J., (ed.), *The Oxford companion to Irish history* (Oxford, 1998).

Corish, Patrick J. and Sheehy, David C., *Records of the Irish Catholic Church* (Dublin, 2001).

Crawford, E. Margaret, *Counting the people: a survey of Irish censuses, 1813–1911* (Dublin, 2003).

Cronin, Denis, Connell, Paul and Ó Dálaigh, Brian (eds), *Irish townlands: studies in local history* (Dublin, 1998).

de Breffny, Brian (ed.), *Ireland: a cultural encyclopaedia* (London, 1983).

Dooley, Terence, *Sources for the history of landed estates in Ireland* (Dublin, 2000).

Evans, E. Estyn, *Irish heritage: the landscape, the people and their work* (Dundalk, 1942).

— *The personality of Ireland* (revised edition, Belfast, 1981).

Ford, P. and G., *A guide to parliamentary papers: what they are, how to find them, how to use them* (Oxford, 1955).

— *Select list of British parliamentary papers 1833–1899* (Oxford, 1953, reprinted Shannon, 1969).

Gillespie, Raymond and Kennedy, Brian P., (eds), *Ireland: art into history* (Dublin, 1994).

Grenham, John, *Tracing your Irish ancestors: the complete guide* (Dublin, 1992).

Guide to the Genealogical Office, Dublin (IMC., Dublin, 1998).

Gurrin, Brian, *Pre-census sources for Irish demography* (Dublin, 2002).

Gwynn, A. and Hadcock, R. N., *Medieval religious houses: Ireland* (London, 1970).

Harbison, Peter, Potterton, Homan and Sheehy, Jeanne (eds), *Irish art and architecture from prehistory to the present* (London, 1970).

Helferty, Seamus and Refaussé, Raymond, *Directory of Irish archives* (3rd. ed., Dublin, 1999).

Hill, Myrtle and Gillespie, Raymond (eds), *Doing Irish local history* (Belfast, 1998).

Johnston-Liik, Edith, *History of the Irish parliament 1692–1800: commons, constituencies and statutes* (4 vols., Belfast, 2002).

Lalor, Brian (ed.), *The encyclopaedia of Ireland* (Dublin, 2003).

McDowell, R. B., *The Irish administration, 1801–1914* (London, 1964).

Maltby, A. and J., *Ireland in the nineteenth century: a breviate of official publications* (Oxford, 1979).

Nolan, William, *Tracing the past: sources for local studies in the Republic of Ireland* (Dublin, 1982).

Nolan, William and Simms, Anngret (eds), *Irish towns: a guide to sources* (Dublin, 1998).

O'Dowd, M. and Edwards, R. D., *Sources for early modern Irish history, 1534–1641* (Cambridge, 1988).

Ó Súilleabháin, Seán, *A handbook of Irish folklore* (Dublin, 1942, Detroit, 1970).

O'Neill, Thomas P., *Sources of Irish local history* (Dublin, 1958).

O'Toole, James, *Newsplan: report of the newsplan project in Ireland* (Dublin, 1992).

Parkes, Susan M., *Irish education in the British parliamentary papers in the nineteenth century and after, 1801–1920* (Cork, 1978.)

Prochaska, Alice, *Irish history from 1700: a guide to sources in the public record office* (London, 1985).

Prunty, Jacinta, *Maps and mapmaking in local history* (Dublin, 2004).

Refaussé, Raymond, *Church of Ireland records* (Dublin, 2000).

Ryan, J. G., *Irish church records: their history, availability and use in family and local history research* (Dublin, 1992).

— *Irish records: sources for family and local history* (Dublin, 1988).

Wylie, J. C. W., *Irish land law* (2nd. ed., Oxford, 1986).

See also A *new history of Ireland* (Oxford, 1976–) a vast ten-volume project on Irish history (of which nine volumes have been published) together with some ancillary works.

Web Sources for Local Historians

ARCHON (*Historical Manuscripts Commission Archives Register*)	www.hmc. gov.uk/
A2A (Access to archives)	www.a2a.org.uk/
Bodleian Library, Oxford	www.bodley.ac. uk/
British Museum	www.british-museum.ac. uk
Church of Jesus Christ of Latter-Day Saints	www.familysearch.org/
Cork Archives Institute	www.corkcorp.ie/faciliies/facilities_archives.html
Dublin City Archives	www.iol.ie/resource/dublincitylibrary/archives.htm
Garda Archives	www.esatclear.ie/~garda/
Genealogical Office	www.nli.ie/
General Register Office (Belfast)	www.groni.gov.uk
General Register Office (Dublin)	www.groireland.ie/
Irish Archirectural Archive	www.iarc. ie/
Irish Folklore, Dept. of (UCD)	www.ucd.ie/archives
Kildare Archaeological Society	http://kildare.ie/archaeology/
King's Inns, Society of	www.kingsinn.ie/html/home.html
Law Society of Ireland, The	www.lawsociety.ie/
Linen Hall Library	www.linenhall.com/
Marsh's Library	www.marshlibrary.ie/
Military Archives	www.military.ie/military_archives
National Archives	www.nationalarchives.ie/
National Gallery of Ireland	www.nationalgallery.ie/
National Library of Ireland	www.nli.ie/
National Print Museum	http://ireland.iol.ie/~npmuseum/
NUI Cork	www.booleweb.ucc. ie/
NUI Galway	www. nuigalway.ie/
NUI Maynooth (links)	www.may.ie/local history
Ordnance Survey	www. osi.ie/
Public Record Office (N.Ire)	http://proni.nics.gov.uk/
Public Record Office (Kew)	www.pro.gov.uk
Queen's University	www.qub.ie
Registry of Deeds	www.landregistry.ie
Representative Church Body Library	www.citc.ie/library.htm
Royal Irish Academy	www.ria.ie/
Trinity College, Dublin	www.tcd.ie/Library
UCD Archives	www.ucd.ie/archives
Valuation Office	www.valoff.ie/

More books from Mercier Press

An Introduction to
Irish High Crosses

Hilary Richardson and John Scarry

The Irish high crosses are the most original and interesting of all the monuments which stud the Irish landscape. They are of international importance in early medieval art. For their period there is little to equal them in the sculpture of Western Europe as a whole.

This book gives basic information about the crosses. A general survey is followed by an inventory to accompany the large collection of photographs which illustrate their variety and richness. In this way readers will readily have at their diposal an extensive range of the images created in stone by sculptors working in Ireland over a thousand years ago.

The Sheela-na-gigs of Ireland and Britain
The Divine Hag of the Christian Celts

Joanne McMahon & Jack Roberts

Sheela-na-gigs are carvings of female images depicted as naked and posing in a provocative manner which accentuate the most powerfully evocative symbol of the vulva. They were erected on many churches of the medieval period and were almost invariably placed in a very prominent position such as over the main entrance door or over a window.

This book is written from a non-academic perspective and the illustrated catalogue section is a very comprehensive, alphabetically listed reference to all known sheela-na-gigs in Ireland and Britain.

Mapping Ireland
From Kingdoms to Counties

Seán Connors

A unique and attractive book of early Irish maps, county by county, beautifully reproduced in colour with an accompanying history.

A SHORT HISTORY OF ORANGEISM

Kevin Haddick-Flynn

Tracing the development of the Orange tradition from its beginnings during the Williamite War (1688–91) to the present day this book comprehensively covers all the main events and personalities. It provides information on such little known organisations as the Royal Black Preceptory and the Royal Arch Purple Order, as well as institutions like the Apprentice Boys of Derry.

Military campaigns and rebellions are set against a background of intrigue and infighting, and anti-Catholic rhetoric is matched with anti-Orange polemic. This compelling book narrates the history of a quasi-Masonic organisation and looks at its rituals and traditions.

SARSFIELD AND THE JACOBITES

Kevin Haddick-Flynn

This books examines Sarsfield's military career in detail, with special focus on his role as the most outstanding Irish soldier of the Williamite War. Special attention is given to his presence at the Boyne, Athlone and Augrim; his heroic defence of Limerick and his part in negotiating the famous Treaty. Episodes like his celebrated raid on the Williamite siege train at Ballyneety are thoroughly covered as are his final days with the 'Wild Geese' in Flanders.

THE LEGACY OF HISTORY
for making peace in Ireland

Martin Mansergh

The value of looking back is to understand where we are and why; to honour that which was noble; to acknowledge and try to correct what went wrong. This book helps to flesh out and to put into perspective the background to the problems with which we have had to deal, as well as highlighting what remains to be done.